Contents

Part Three. Social administration: the organisation and delivery of welfare

SOCIAL POLICY

Themes and approaches

Revised Second Edition

Paul Spicker

First published in Great Britain in 2008 by

The Policy Press
University of Bristol
Fourth Floor
Beacon House
Queen's Road
Bristol BS8 1QU
UK

Tel +44 (0)117 331 4054
Fax +44 (0)117 331 4093
e-mail tpp-info@bristol.ac.uk
www.policypress.org.uk

© Paul Spicker 2008

British Library Cataloguing in Publication Data
A catalogue record for this book is available from the British Library.

Library of Congress Cataloging-in-Publication Data
A catalog record for this book has been requested.

ISBN 978 1 84742 062 6 paperback
ISBN 978 1 84742 063 3 hardcover

The right of Paul Spicker to be identified as author of this work has been asserted by him
in accordance with the 1988 Copyright, Designs and Patents Act.

The statements and opinions contained within this publication are solely those of the
author and not of the University of Bristol or The Policy Press. The University of Bristol
and The Policy Press disclaim responsibility for any injury to persons or property resulting
from any material published in this publication.

The Policy Press works to counter discrimination on grounds of gender, race, disability,
age and sexuality.

Cover design by Qube Design Associates, Bristol.
Front cover: Image kindly supplied by Getty Images
Printed and bound in Great Britain by Hobbs the Printers, Southampton.

Prefaces

From the preface to the first edition: the study of social policy

This book has three main aims. The first is that it should serve as a text for students taking undergraduate and professional courses in social policy. Social policy calls for both a theoretical and an empirical understanding of the world. It is almost impossible to make sense of much of the theory without having some idea of what goes on in practice. All too frequently, students learn theoretical models uncritically, without knowing why they matter (if they do) or how to judge them. On the other hand, empirical material can drive out the theory which is necessary for understanding, and an emphasis on factual material often gives the impression that studying social policy consists of a long list of Things to Know. A text has to make sense to students, while also laying the foundations for future work.

As a teacher of social policy, I have tried many ways of introducing students to the subject, beginning for example with services, with clients, with theories, with dominant themes, with history and with politics. Every approach has its own disadvantages. An introduction to services – the 'Cook's tour' – lays a good foundation, but is difficult to make sense of, and it risks becoming a jumble of facts. Client-based approaches are stimulating for many students, but the material is often disconnected, and the literature has never supported it adequately. Ideologies are not difficult to learn, but students lack the material to examine the precepts critically, and all too often they lead to a view of the world divided between Angels and Devils, where nothing the Devils say makes any sense at all. Building a course around dominant themes, like 'welfare and inequality' or 'producers and consumers' (both themes I refer to later in this book) suffers from the problem that students lack the material to unpick the framework offered by the lecturer, either by using alternative examples or by bringing different theoretical perspectives to bear. The historical approach offers an immediate way of organising material, but it traps many students on the tramlines; once they have started in a chronological sequence, they cannot see how to get out of it. Political approaches, which begin with descriptions of ideology, institutions and processes, help to offer a framework with case studies, but there are risks – one is that description will dwarf the theoretical material, the other that the lure of current political issues will drive out deeper analysis.

The main conclusion to draw from this is that students need to establish some kind of explanatory framework, which they can relate to material from a range of sources. A textbook cannot cover all the ground; there are some things which are done effectively in books, and some which are not. It is particularly difficult to give a useful account of 'the facts'. There are too many facts to absorb; social policy is a wide-ranging subject. Specific facts are not always appropriate for courses in different countries. Even when these problems are overcome, another remains: the material dates very quickly. Books take a long time from conception to delivery, perhaps two years and often much more; the facts which can be included are usually older still.

By contrast, textbooks can cover theoretical issues fairly well. The teacher can supplement the text with case examples, contradictory material, or alternative patterns of explanation. Several texts in social policy approach the subject from a theoretical viewpoint, but there are recurring problems: the presentations are often narrowly focused, case illustrations date, and the structure of many books is pulled out of shape by a strongly held value system.

This book tries to offer a theoretical basis for the discussion of social policy. I have tried to stand back from specific detail and take a wide view. Many issues are dealt with very briefly; there are whole books, and even whole shelves of books, written on some subjects I have referred to in a paragraph. The point of doing this is that I am trying to offer students, at the outset, a map of the terrain. Maps are used for many different purposes; there are street maps, maps of regions, maps of countries and maps of the world; and we do not expect to find the same kind of detail on a continental map that we do on a road map of our own country. The main reason for having continental maps is to give people some idea of the spatial relationships between smaller units – an indication, in other words, of where things stand in relation to each other, and where to look in more detail later.

This means, of course, that the book does not offer a full course in social policy, because some vital elements are missing. What it is trying to do is rather more general: it attempts to explain the nature of social policy, to put it into a social and political context, to examine the kinds of option open to social policy makers in general terms, and then to follow through the process by which welfare is organised and delivered. The framework which the book offers has to be supplemented both by other reading and by the kinds of perspective and case studies which can be made available in a taught course. On that basis, the book should be useful to students working at a range of levels, as a complement to their other studies.

I referred at the outset to three aims, and so far I have only considered one; but the other two have been no less important. The second aim, which the book shares with my other work, is to try to make out the case for theoretical examination in social policy. Social policy has often been criticised for its lack of theoretical input, because of the emphasis in so much of the literature on empirical developments and a short-term concern with policy. The literature on the theory of the subject has grown in the last 15 years. However, the increasing emphasis on theoretical content has not really been matched by an increase in awareness about theoretical methods. There is a limit to what I can do in a book of this kind, but I have included a discussion of the range of methods and some applications.

The third aim has been to make a contribution to the study of social policy in its own right. There has not been very much written about the scope and methods of social policy; the focus of subject has shifted in recent years, but there has been very little discussion about the nature of the change. The main sources are now between 20 and 40 years old, but the subject has been changing; it is not only that the policy agenda is different, but so are the areas which people think of as important, and the ways in which the subject is studied. In the absence of clear conventions and shared understandings, much of the work done for the book has to be original. Many of the issues which are discussed in the book may seem basic, and their relevance should be obvious to those who begin with a working knowledge of the subject; but I had no template to work on for a third of the chapters here, because the linkages had not been made elsewhere, and at least a third more of the text relies on a new synthesis of material from disparate sources. The book is concerned, then, with the conceptual development of the subject.

The chapters are not completely self-contained. This is not like many introductory texts in sociology or psychology, which deal with a set of topics independently; nor, for that matter, is it like most other texts in social policy. It was conceived and planned as a whole. Themes, approaches and a specialised vocabulary are introduced and discussed in context, and later material builds on the foundations of what has been discussed earlier. Issues and terms which are introduced in earlier parts of the book are not explained again when they recur at later stages, but there is a glossary to help with some of the more recondite terms.

The second edition

The central purpose of this book was to establish a theoretical basis for understanding social policy. Much of the work in the first edition had to be constructed from first principles; the material on the focus of policy, welfare strategies, law and social policy, the organisation of social services or service delivery was not available in the same form anywhere else, and is still not. It was also, I think, the first textbook in social policy to include a discussion of research methods as part of the practical focus of the subject; that, at least, has been fairly widely established since. In the second edition, I have taken the development of the field forward, particularly in the treatment of the methods of social policy.

The framework of *Social policy* combines theoretical, methodological and institutional issues. In theoretical terms, the main developments have been the movement into the mainstream of concepts, like solidarity and social inclusion; an exploration of postmodern ideas; and a 'cultural turn', focusing social policy on cultural aspects of social relationships. In methodological terms, there has been nothing to compare with the explosion of research methods experienced in the 1980s, but there have been significant developments, particularly through the focus on evidence-based policy. The main developments in the institutional literature have been concerned with governance, both national and international. The process by which conceptual developments get translated into practice is characteristically slow. Ideas like deliberative democracy, path dependency or policy streams all date from at least the early 1990s, and it may be some time yet before they get fed into the policy process. By contrast, it is striking how the obscure academic ideas of 30 or 40 years ago have moved to the mainstream of policy. Rational planning, partnership, empowerment and voice have become established norms.

The first edition had a long shelf-life. Because the book was written for an international audience, I had avoided the kind of information which is specific to a particular location or pattern of services. That also meant that the book did not have many of the sort of references or examples which would date it. The second edition has been updated in some respects – more than a third of the references were published after the first edition – but theory develops slowly, and the most recently published material is not necessarily the best, or the best way to explain a point. The material has been selected, like examples in the rest of the book, to be of interest to an international audience; I have tried to avoid ephemeral issues, or topics that are only of interest in one country. There are some fairly visible changes. I have added a 'box' to each chapter, considering issues and controversies; there are figures and tables to aid understanding; and each chapter finishes with issues for discussion. Social policy is often the subject of animated, deeply felt disputes. I hope that reflecting some of the areas of difference will help to bring the subject to life for the book's readers.

The most significant changes, however, may be more difficult to spot. The structure of several chapters has changed; there are new treatments of some significant issues, such as needs and social services; several sections have been rewritten or reordered. Where new material has been included, it has been dovetailed into the shape of the text; some material has been dropped. Many of the new inclusions are relatively brief, as the material in the first edition was brief; the aim is to map the terrain, not to discuss issues in greater depth. Refining and improving the coverage has been a difficult process, but it is central to the book's aims.

The book is now laid out in four parts. The introduction explains what social policy is, and discusses its relationship with the social sciences. Part One is concerned with welfare and society; it looks mainly at the 'social' elements in social policy. It considers social policy in a social context, the relationship between problems and responses, and the nature of social need. Part Two focuses on the 'policy' in social policy. It looks at the nature of policy, political ideas and values, the social services and the welfare state. Part Three is concerned mainly with social administration. It looks at the structure of social services and the process of implementation at different levels, considered service delivery and the impact of services on the people who use them. Part Four is concerned with the methods and approaches of social policy, considering evaluation, research and policy analysis.

Paul Spicker
The Robert Gordon University

About the author

Paul Spicker holds the Grampian Chair of Public Policy at The Robert Gordon University, Aberdeen, and is Director of the Centre for Public Policy and Management. His research includes studies of poverty, need, disadvantage and service delivery; he has worked as a consultant for a range of agencies in social welfare provision.

His books include:

Stigma and social welfare (Croom Helm, 1984)

Principles of social welfare (Routledge, 1988)

Social housing and the social services (Longmans, 1989)

Poverty and social security: Concepts and principles (Routledge, 1993)

Planning for the needs of people with dementia (with D S Gordon, Avebury, 1997)

Social protection: A bilingual glossary (co-editor with J-P Révauger, Mission-Recherche, 1998)

Social policy in a changing society (with Maurice Mullard, Routledge, 1998)

The international glossary on poverty (co-editor with D Gordon, Zed, 1999)

The welfare state: A general theory (Sage, 2000)

Policy analysis for practice: Applying social policy (The Policy Press, 2006)

Liberty, equality and fraternity (The Policy Press, 2006)

The idea of poverty (The Policy Press, 2007)

ONE

Introduction: the nature of social policy

The nature of social policy
What is social policy?
What does social policy study?
Why does social policy matter?
Social policy and the academic disciplines
Studying social policy

The nature of social policy

What is social policy?

Social policy is concerned with the study of the social services and the welfare state. The subject developed from 'social administration', which was devoted to preparing people for work in the social services in practice. One of the best-known descriptions of the field comes from David Donnison:

> The teaching of Social Administration began in Britain before the First World War ... 'for those who wish to prepare themselves to engage in the many forms of social and charitable effort'. ... The social services are still the main things they (students) study. That means they are also interested in people's living conditions, the processes which lead to the recognition of human needs and problems, the development of organised means for meeting needs and resolving problems, and the impact which social services and social policies have on living conditions and on society in general.[1]

The social services are where social policy began, and they are still central to understanding what the subject is about. The main social services can be taken to include social security, housing, health, social work and education – the 'big five' – along with others which raise similar issues, such as employment, prisons, legal services and drains. Drains – not to be confused with sewers – are worth a moment of our attention. The draining of surface water is important to control flooding, to limit problems from insects and to prevent the spread of disease.[2] If one is concerned not just with topics that are dramatic and emotionally exciting, but with the kind of things that are important to people, which are intended to make people's lives better, which might be taken for granted when they are there and make life intolerable when they are not, then drains are a fairly good example.

Social administration was always intended to be study for a purpose, for administrators and practitioners to learn about the problems and processes they would be dealing with. However, the field has never been confined solely to practical administration. Donnison wrote, nearly 50 years ago:

> Narrowly defined, social administration is the study of the development, structure and practices of the social services. Broadly defined, it is an attempt to apply the social sciences ... to the analysis and solution of a changing range of social problems. It must be taught in both these senses if it is to be of any value.[2]

The watershed in the development of social policy was an essay by Richard Titmuss, written in 1955, on the 'Social division of welfare'. Titmuss argued that it was impossible to understand the effects of welfare policies in isolation from the rest of society; there were many other channels through which 'welfare' was delivered.[4] The theme was picked up, for example, by Hilary Rose in an essay on the 'Sexual division of welfare', in which she argued that it was not possible to understand the impact of policy on women without putting this into its social context.[5] The present-day focus on social policy rather than on social administration reflects a general trend for people working in the field to be less interested in the details of how services are run, and more in the broader sweep of policy and politics.

What does social policy study?

'Social Policy and Administration' is about problems as well as policy; about ends as well as means. Titmuss suggested that the major fields of research and teaching were:

1. The analysis and description of policy formulation and its consequences, intended and unintended.
2. The study of structure, function, organisation, planning and administrative processes of institutions and agencies, historical and comparative.
3. The study of social needs and of problems, of access to, utilisation and patterns of outcome of services, transactions and transfers.
4. The analysis of the nature, attributes and distribution of social costs and diswelfares.
5. The analysis of distributive and allocative patterns in command-over-resources-through-time and the particular impact of social services.

6. The study of the roles and functions of elected representatives, professional workers, administrators and interest groups in the operation and performance of social welfare institutions.
7. The study of the social rights of the citizen as contributor, participant and user of social services.
8. The study and role of government (local and central) as an allocator of values and of rights to social property as expressed through social and administrative law and other rule-making channels.[6]

Titmuss's vision of the subject represented, at the time it was formulated, a distinctive and expansionist view of the subject. Issues of needs, rights and distribution are central, but the underlying rationale for the selection of issues is not clear. Describing the subject in more general academic terms tends to redefine the focus. One attempt to identify the broad area was made by Lafitte:

> If economic policy is concerned with maximising wealth and with the citizen-producer, one might say that social policy looks to the distribution of economic enjoyments and to the citizen-consumer.[7]

Fiona Williams is not explicit about the scope of social policy, but she does describe the field as studying 'the relationship between welfare and society, and different views on the best means of maximising welfare in society'.[8] These approaches, representing strongly contrasting views of the subject, do not refer directly to policy or services at all; social policy is primarily seen as a study of welfare.

These definitions are in an important sense prescriptive rather than descriptive; they are concerned with what social policy should be, not what it is. The approach to 'welfare' in social policy has been much narrower than this suggests; its focus mainly falls, not on the nature of welfare in general, but on people who lack welfare. Although Titmuss's arguments invited consideration of the wider distributive implications of social welfare policy, they did so mainly as a counterpoint to his central interests in needs, problems and diswelfare. Many people would argue, after Tawney, that the problem of poverty is also the problem of wealth: Orton and Rowlingson, for example, argue that 'it is high time social policy analysts put riches on the agenda'.[9] The simple truth, however, is that the study of social policy hasn't been genuinely concerned with wealth, and the kind of material which is studied in courses in social policy departments and published in social policy journals does not normally include studies of the position of the relatively advantaged, unless it is done by way of contrast. There is a good reason for this: social policy is still, at root, a practical subject, and studying the lifestyles of the rich tells us little or nothing that we need to know about the application of social policy to practice. Social policy has been concerned with disadvantage and deprivation, and with issues relating to social protection, because those are the issues that its practitioners have to work with.

The central focus of social policy is the study of social welfare and the social services. The main areas which social policy studies are:

- policy and administrative practice in health administration, social security, education, employment services, social care and housing management;
- the circumstances in which people's welfare is likely to be impaired, including disability, unemployment, mental illness, intellectual disability and old age;
- social problems, like crime, addiction and family breakdown;
- issues relating to social disadvantage, including race, gender and poverty; and
- the range of collective social responses to these circumstances. This is often interpreted in terms of responses by the 'welfare state', but in other countries it may equally be understood as extending to mutual aid, voluntary effort or industrial organisation.

Several generalisations might be made about this field of study.

1. *Social policy is about welfare.* The idea of welfare is used in a number of different ways. In its widest sense, welfare can mean 'well-being', and in that sense it is taken to mean the benefit of individuals or groups, which is the sense in which it is used in economics; people have increased 'welfare' when their material goods increase and lead to increased satisfaction. However, the idea also refers, more narrowly, to certain sorts of collective provision which attempt to protect people's welfare. 'Social welfare' commonly refers to the range of services provided by the state. (It should be noted that 'welfare' is also sometimes used, particularly in the literature of the US, to refer to certain types of benefit, especially means-tested social security, which are aimed at people who are poor.) There is no 'correct' usage, and there is considerable scope for confusion, because people writing about welfare may want to refer to any of the different uses.

   Social policy can be represented as being concerned with 'well-being' in general, but if that were true the subject might be more concerned with leisure activities or consumer affairs than it tends to be; those who argue for this kind of approach, after Cahill[10], are really interested in a different subject area. It is probably truer to say that social policy is concerned with people who lack well-being – people with particular problems or needs – and the services which provide for them. The kinds of issue which social policy tends to be concerned with, then, include problems like poverty, poor housing, mental illness and disability. The boundaries are indistinct, because often people's needs have to be understood in terms of the facilities available to others; our idea of good housing, an adequate income or good health affects our view of what people need or what is a problem.

2. *Social policy is about policy.* Social policy is not primarily a way of looking at social, economic or political relationships, problems or institutions, although it overlaps with all of those and more; it is interested in issues like this because they are important for understanding policy and practice. Social policy does not study food in itself, but it does affect the regulation and distribution of food; it is not concerned directly with child development, but it is with education and services to help children; it is not concerned with physical health, but it is very much concerned with policies to promote health and the provision of medical care. The distinctions between the areas of interest are hazy, and there are many issues which lie in disputed territory. The core elements of a policy are its origins, its goals, the process of implementation and the results. If we are to accept that social policy should be studied in its own right, rather than through specific issues like food or health, we ought to show that there is some value in considering the elements in policy and administration which are common to different issues. This is something which this book has to do.

3. *Social policy is concerned with issues that are social.* This can be taken, again, in a broad sense, but it also implies that there is some kind of collective social response made to perceived problems. There are issues which are important to welfare which are not social, in the sense either that they are personal (like child development, love and friendship) or that they go beyond the social (like the national economy, or international relations). They may touch on areas of social policy at times, but they are not the main focus of the subject.

4. *Social policy is an applied subject.* Saying that the subject is applied is not the same as saying that it studies issues that matter; it is applied because it is also saying what should be done about them. Social policy has three characteristic modes of operation. The first is that it is concerned with prescriptions as well as analysis, and outcomes as well as processes. If knowledge is not geared to practical effects, it is not much use. The second issue is that it generally starts with problems and issues, and finds methods and approaches which fit the problem, rather than the other way around. The third point, which follows from the other two, is that the study of social policy is multidisciplinary. Dealing with a wide range of situations, and beginning with problems rather than methods, means that there can be many different ways to tackle the issues. Although some methods will be more appropriate than others, the selection of methods has to depend on context; there is no single route to truth.

The scope of the subject extends across a broad spectrum, because social policy usually seeks to understand social responses by trying to put material into some kind of context. This context may be of many kinds – historical, social, economic and psychological among them. But the study of the context is not social policy itself, even if it is of interest to students of social policy. That is important, if only because it distinguishes social policy from the other subjects, and helps to explain what the limits of the subject are. Social policy is not a subject that studies topics in social science as items of interest in their own right. The study of subjects like culture, gender, the body or globalisation may be helpful for understanding policies and responses to issues, but they are not an adequate substitute for the study of social policy in themselves.

Why does social policy matter?

Why does social policy continue to focus on social services in particular, and what is the justification for concentrating on its main area of study? The main reason is probably the most practical one: people who have an interest in the social services, and who want to pursue careers in related fields, want to know more about them. But there are other reasons besides – not least that social policy offers a way of studying the kinds of issue which matter to people in real life. Social policies are important; they affect the way that people live. If social policy is exciting as a study, it is because it engages with serious social problems, looks at how those problems can be dealt with, and examines strategies for putting responses into practice. Social policy has often drawn in people who are concerned about social wrongs, and who want to put them right.

This kind of aim sits very uncomfortably with the role of social policy as an academic subject. David Donnison was one of the leading academics in the subject for many years; but he also involved himself in policy, at one stage running the commission responsible for social assistance in Britain.[11] He once wrote a blistering attack on a book on the subject which he felt was rather too academic.

> The academics who dominated this field in the sixties entered it from other disciplines. ... They wanted to change the world and thought the academy offered a base for learning and teaching of the sort that might ultimately influence events. ... [The approach of this writer] is interesting because he represents the new generation of academics. ... Every assertion is pinned to an author and a date – rather as a timorous climber moves, unable to take a step unless securely roped to someone else ... that convention is tolerable if the view from the top of the mountain is sufficiently arresting. [But this] ... is a demonstration of credentials which we are being offered, not an opportunity to learn new things .... I hope [the writer] may yet join the company of those who believe ... that their job is not merely to understand the world but to change it.[12]

There is a place for books which describe, analyse and help people to understand; the book you are reading now has more to do with developing understanding of the field than it does with changing the world. But it is easy to share Donnison's anger; there would be something distasteful about rummaging through the chronicles of human misery without trying to produce any positive effect.

It is difficult to prove that any academic study 'matters'. The things it studies may be important, but that does not mean that studying it makes any direct contribution. Poverty, suicide, disability or child abuse are not (or should not be) subjects for entertainment or prurient interest. Understanding more about them is often important in the personal development of students, but it is not always clear whether the study does anything for people who are poor, emotionally distressed, disabled or victimised. There are three main arguments for studying the problems:

1. Social policy is an important part of professional preparation. The people who are studying it are often going to work in fields – like social work, health visiting, housing or education – where they will come into contact with people in these kinds of situation, and they will understand the situations a little better.

2. People who have studied social policy have made a considerable contribution to policy making. It has always been true that careful, considered research tends to have less effect on policy than a sharp blow below the belt, a point which I shall return to in due course, but there are many cases in which research into social problems has had a major effect on provision: examples in Britain are Booth and Rowntree on poverty,[13] Bayley on mental handicap and community care,[14] or Rowe and Lambert on residential child care.[15]

3. The study of social policy can help to change the way that people think about the issues. This is the main defence of any academic subject. The people who are most likely to be affected are its students; social policy stresses, not only a certain set of intellectual disciplines, but the importance of particular types of social experience. Through those people, it affects a wider society; this kind of study does help to change social behaviour and attitudes. Like many academics, I still have a naive faith in the value of study, and the effect it is likely to have on the way that people think. The better people understand a social issue, the more complicated it seems to become. As part of the process, simplistic solutions and ideological dogmas have to be rejected; so, people try to come to terms with different views about an issue before selecting whatever seems best. Part of the purpose of a book like this is to challenge some of the comfortable certainties we all have.

Social policy and the academic disciplines

The problem-oriented character of social policy means that methods and approaches have to be selected to fit the issues, rather than the other way round. To deal with problems in practice, social policy needs to draw on the insights of a wide range of academic subjects. Social policy, Donnison argues, 'is not a discipline; it is a field in which many disciplines must be brought to bear'.[16] A reader in the subject in the 1970s described social policy as a form of 'applied social science', seeking to identify its relationship to a range of disciplines.[17] That still seems appropriate today, although some writers, including Fiona Williams and Pete Alcock, have chosen to describe social policy as a discipline in its own right.

   The boundaries between social policy and other subjects are often indistinct. It is commonly taught along with sociology, social work or politics, where it is identified with 'public policy'.

Sociology. Kay Jones once referred to social policy as starting at the 'problem end of sociology',[18] and many people in the field would still see social policy as dependent on sociological method. Peter Townsend has identified the areas in which interest has expanded as including 'the distribution of income, wealth and public expenditure; the changing patterns of industrial and social structure; the impact of changes on workers and families'.[19] That seems to extend social policy into the area of sociology; Townsend argues, not just that social policy has a close relationship with sociology, but that an understanding of social policy is fundamental to broader sociological analysis.

   Sociology, equally, has been changing. The emphasis on non-normative social analysis has given way in many places to a committed and critical stance, focusing mainly on patterned social inequality. There are many institutions where the teaching of social policy has become a microcosm of sociology, concerned with social issues like race, gender, sexuality and culture, but not considering issues of policy development, social administration or service delivery. Where this happens, it leaves out large parts of the agenda of social policy, and fails to equip students for practice.

Social work. Social policy developed as an academic complement to social work, and the subjects have traditionally been close. As time has gone on, the interchange between the subject areas has fallen away: Michael Hill writes that

> the linking of social policy and social work tends to confine the former to a narrow range of concerns, with a strong emphasis on social pathology and on policies directly oriented to the social welfare of the deprived. What has been characteristic of the development of

social policy teaching in the UK in recent years has been a desire to move away from its close identification with social work ...[20]

In intellectual terms, ironically, the subjects have grown closer in the course of the last 30 or so years. Social work is much less focused on social pathology than it used to be, and the practice of social work has also changed, moving away from an individualised model of professional social work to an emphasis on care management. With that change, there is a greater emphasis on both the management of social services, an issue once considered to fall squarely in the area of social policy and administration, and the social context in which policy decisions are made. Social work's practical emphasis on skills and methods of intervention still offers a useful complement to the skills and insights developed in social policy.

Public policy. The boundaries and approaches of social and public policy can be defined in very similar terms. Minogue describes public policy as follows:

> The search for a general explanatory theory of public policy necessarily implies a synthesis of social, political and economic theories ... Public policies do things to economies and societies, so that ultimately any satisfactory explanatory theory of public policy must also explain the interrelations between the state, politics, economics and society. This is also why people from so many 'disciplines' – economics, politics, sociology, anthropology, geography, planning, management and even applied sciences – share an interest in and make contributions to the study of public policy.[21]

There are, however, important differences in the areas of interest, and the subject matter is not alike. Public policy is centrally concerned with the study of the policy process. Social policy is not centrally concerned with the process, but with the content of policy. Public policy may be concerned with content in so far as it offers an insight into process; social policy is concerned with process in so far as it offers an insight into content. Public policy is of interest to people from different disciplines because they need to know about the policy process; social policy uses material from different disciplines because this is how the problems of social policy have to be addressed. This has implications for the agenda; public policy is interested in issues like pensions, defence or energy policy, because they are examples of the kind of process the subject is concerned with, but it is not interested in substantive issues like poverty or need in their own right.

There are many other subjects which make a contribution – among them economics, history, epidemiology, geography, management, psychology, philosophy and law. Social policy has a chameleon-like quality; whatever it is taught with, it tends to adopt something of the character of that subject. There are, however, areas which social policy does not really touch on, and it may be helpful to review some of the areas which social policy does relate to, contrasted with some others which it does not have much to do with. Some indications are given in Table 1.1. The material in this table is subject to the reservation made earlier – there are very few issues which social policy might not have something to do with – and there are always exceptions.

TABLE 1.1: SOCIAL POLICY AND THE SOCIAL SCIENCES				
	Relationships	**Processes**	**Problem areas**	**Institutions**
Sociology				
Shared interests	Gender	Socialisation	Deviance	Family
Distinct interests	Personal encounters	Structure and agency	Military power	Religious worship
Economics				
Shared interests	Labour market	Recession	Economic inequality	Public spending
Distinct interests	Money market	Trade	The firm	Banks and finance houses
Politics				
Shared interests	Power	Legislation	Race relations	Government
Distinct interests	Political change	Voting	International relations	Party structures
Psychology				
Shared interests	Pro-social behaviour	Child development	Attitude change	Psychiatry
Distinct interests	Crowd behaviour	Mentation	Perception	–
Social work				
Shared interests	Worker–client relations	Community care	Child abuse	Personal social services
Distinct interests	Family functioning	Counselling	Group interaction	–

The effect of using different kinds of approach is that social policy sometimes comes up with ideas which are distinctive to the subject, because they do not properly 'belong' anywhere else. Ideas like altruism, stigma, welfare rights and poverty are used in other subjects besides social policy, but they are not always used in the same way. There is a characteristic literature in social policy, and a particular way of understanding the concepts.

Box 1: Social science and social policy

Social policy has been identified with 'applied social science', because it uses the methods of social science to describe, analyse and evaluate policy. However, social policy does not finish with social science. Social policy is about developing policy – identifying what policies are doing, examining the effects, and offering prescriptions for practice.

One of the justifications given for many academic studies in social science is that understanding an issue should suggest a way to solve it. Pawson and Tilley suggest that what analysts do is to look for a 'generative mechanism' (that is, a set of causal relationships) which can explain what is happening, and go from that to identify appropriate responses.[22] Anthony Giddens, similarly, once wrote: 'The more we understand about why poverty remains widespread, the more likely it is that successful policies can be implemented to counter it'.[23]

There are three key problems with this approach. The first is that social phenomena are complex. 'Poverty' is not one issue, but many. The same is true for many other difficult issues – crime, unemployment, addiction, mental illness and so on. Arguably that is precisely why they are difficult. But it follows that if there is not a single issue to deal with, the idea that it is possible to identify a central 'cause' is questionable. The first task of social science is to identify what the issues are; explanation comes only later, if it comes at all.

The second problem is that even where there is a clear, identifiable issue, there may be several generative mechanisms to consider, not one. Take, for example, the case where a local firm closes down, making people unemployed. Understanding the issue might typically require understanding of the productive sector the firm is in, the local labour market, the system of social protection, the national economy and international trade. A relatively simple problem starts to look very complex when all the generative mechanisms are considered. If it is possible to identify causes in social science, their identification usually takes the form of a range of contributory factors, rather than direct mechanisms.

The third, critical flaw in the argument is that even once these issues are resolved, it does not follow that there will be a practical solution. The way into a problem is not the way out of it. If you fall down a well, what you know about the principles of gravity will be next to useless, and reviewing the process of falling in will probably not help much either. In the same way, understanding issues like poverty, unemployment or inequality does not necessarily mean that a solution presents itself. There are measures that do seem to have worked – economic growth as a response to poverty,[24] public works as a response to unemployment[25] or redistribution in response to inequality[26] – have little to do with explanations about cause, and everything to do with outcomes.

Social science provides prescriptions for policy in a different way. The process of understanding, analysing and explaining issues is essential for marshalling and selecting evidence. Descriptive statements rarely mean much in their own right; if facts are important, it is because they relate to some kind of context. Social policy depends on social science to do that. The methods and approaches used in the social sciences can be invaluable; but even a good explanation is uncertain to provide a secure basis for policy. There comes a point, then, where social policy parts company with the other social sciences.

Studying social policy

Social policy is concerned with practical problems, and that leads to a particular emphasis on methods and approaches. Although much has been written about the methods and rationale of judgments about policy, surprisingly little has been done to examine the analysis of social policy in its own right. This is partly because people working in social policy have been more concerned with outcomes than with methods; more importantly, it reflects the way in which social policy has tended to draw on insights from social science disciplines, rather than attempting to establish agendas and approaches which might be distinctive to the subject.

The central purpose of this book is to establish a theoretical base for understanding social policy. It is not a comprehensive introduction to social policy; it needs to be read together with the kind of introduction which describes services, agencies and issues in the context of a particular country. It is unusual for books in this area to discuss the methods and approaches of social policy systematically, partly because that is thought of as the province of the academic disciplines, and partly because it is not always consistent with the focus on current policy. It is more typical for work in social policy to tackle a part of an issue at a time; studies appear which collate empirical evidence, while others offer a critical appraisal, reassessment of existing evidence and the development of arguments about policy.

I return to the issue of methods and techniques of social policy in the final part of the book. In the interim, students who are new to the subject should be looking at different kinds of research to give them a taste of what social policy is like. Studies on poverty have developed considerably in the last 20 years, shifting the field from a narrow focus on economics and household incomes to a broader, richer understanding. Drèze and Sen's *Hunger and public action* is a provocative, unsettling book, using arguments from economics, politics and history.[27] Drèze and Sen argue that people do not starve because there is not enough food where they live, but because they have no right to the food which is already there. Governments, political rights and democratic structures can change things. The *Millennium Survey* in the UK applies a particular kind of survey method for identifying and understanding the way people in a society understand poverty; it asks people what they think is essential, and then tries to identify who is not able to afford those things.[28] The World Bank's *Voices of the poor* brings together research from developing countries where poor people are asked about their experience, and what matters to them.[29] The result is one of the best books ever written about poverty.

These are all examples of conventional books and reports. In recent years, however, there has been a significant shift away from the use of academic literature in the conventional sense. It has always been true of social policy that much of it lived in a 'grey' literature, contained in short pamphlets and reports rather than books and academic journals. The arrival of the Internet has opened up this kind of material to the world: the rules of public services, local authority reports, the records of organisations, are easily and directly available. Much of this work is ephemeral, because the issues which it deals with are likely to be concerned with the policy of the moment. It is worthwhile to browse through this kind of material at the outset, because it helps to explain what kind of enterprise people working in social policy are engaged in.

ISSUE FOR DISCUSSION

Can the agenda of social policy envisaged by Titmuss be addressed without a knowledge of economics or law?

Part One
Social policy and society

TWO

Welfare in society

The social context of welfare

Welfare has to be understood in a social context. That statement is axiomatic for most writing on social policy, but it verges on the trivial; it says very little about what kinds of life people lead or what will make their lives better. Its importance rests not so much in what it says, as on what it denies. Much writing about politics and economics relies on individualistic premises. Bentham wrote, for example, that

> The community is a fictitious body, composed of the individual persons who are considered as constituting as it were its members. The interest of the community is, then, what? – the sum of the interests of the several members who compose it.[30]

If we accept that this is true, it should be the individual, not society, on whom we would have to concentrate. Economic analysis does not begin with a review of perspectives on society, and it could be argued that analysis for social policy does not need to either. But it can be misleading to concentrate on the actions of individuals to the exclusion of others. There are social actions, and relationships. Relationships are not only developed between people; there can be relationships between or within organisations, like government and industry, or administration and professions, which are not reducible to the interactions of the people who are involved.

Welfare is generally understood as a social concept. It is easier to see that assumptions are being made if we try to put another word in this section's opening sentence in the place of 'welfare': 'X has to be understood in a social context'. The phrase makes sense if we use words like 'housing', 'health care' or 'education'. It makes very little sense, however, if we substitute relatively specific phrases like 'central heating', 'pharmaceuticals' or 'nature rambles' instead. The point is that the first group of words assumes a social content; the second class of words does not. Welfare is taken in a social sense; it is assumed to have a social content; and it is evaluated normatively on that basis. Understanding the social context is part, then, of the process of understanding social policy.

The social context, and the range of relationships people have in society, is complex. It is difficult to identify all of the relevant relationships in a book of this kind, but fortunately it is not absolutely necessary to do so – this is not an introduction to sociology. A book like this does need, however, to map out the general terrain, to introduce the concepts which are most directly relevant to social policy, and to show how they relate.

This is a difficult, and disputable, process. One of the central things to bear in mind is that virtually all the concepts in the study of society are *contested*: there is not one meaning of words like 'the individual', 'the family' or 'the community', but many. This makes it difficult to talk sensibly about a policy 'for families or communities': the question it immediately prompts is, 'what does it mean'? As knowledge of the area of discourse develops, the issues become progressively more confused, not less; there is not much room for certainty.

The person in society

Human beings. The first, and most obvious, thing to say about people is that they are human beings; they have bodies, they have biological needs, for things like food, water and shelter, and they have human needs, for things like contact with other people. There have been attempts to interpret 'welfare' in a restricted, 'biological' sense apparently divorced from social circumstances: people need so many calories a day, so many vitamins, so much water and so on, and their welfare can be said to be protected when they have these things available. This is usually referred to in terms of 'subsistence' or 'basic needs'.[31] Peter Townsend has been very critical of this kind of argument, which is often used to justify a minimalist, mean approach to welfare: for the poor, Townsend writes, the argument 'carries the dangerous implication that meagre benefits for the poor in industrial societies are more than enough to meet their needs'.[32] The idea of subsistence should not be dismissed out of hand, if only because issues like nutrition and water supplies are so important for welfare: Lipton has argued for a 'biological' approach to poverty not least because so many people in developing countries have their basic needs unmet.[33] But the biological approach can never really be sufficient, either; people's food intake is not simply a question of nutritional constituents, but what is socially acceptable as food (insects, dogs and rats have a nutritional value), available and edible.

The biological character of human beings is taken for granted most of the time – until the moment when issues about our physical humanity surfaces into political argument, when arguments about biology become very contentious indeed. The body is important for welfare, and there is a growing literature in social policy about it.[34] For people in extreme poverty, the body is the most important asset a person has; the ability to sell labour, to move about, or to associate with other people, often depend on a person's physical attributes, like beauty or physical strength.[35] In developed economies, the issues which focus around the body may be less stark, but they are still crucial; they include disability, body image, health and sexuality. At the same time, these arguments are not genuinely, or even principally, biological; they have to be seen through the lens of a social context. It is questionable, then, whether a focus on 'the body' serves as more than a shorthand for a range of disparate issues concerned with our physical natures.

Individuals. The idea that we are 'individuals' is widely held, although it is not always clear what it is supposed to mean. We do not live in isolation from other people; we grow up in families, and the way we develop and the way we live is constantly conditioned by other people. Individualism is a way of thinking about the world. In the past, it was a radical doctrine, used to challenge the established order of society; putting the stress on each person separately makes it difficult to justify social structures which oppress people and deny them the opportunity for self-expression or personal development. In modern society, by contrast, much of this radical purpose has been undermined. Individualists argue that since what we have is the product of individual action, we have to leave the results alone.[36] Individualism has become a conservative doctrine – a justification for the maintenance of existing social structures – rather than a means of criticising them.

Individualism is still important, however, as a way of thinking about society. There are still many established social structures which oppress particular groups; liberal thinking has played an important role in opposition to sexism and racism. The classic complaint about sexism is that gender is taken to obliterate women's individual characteristics, so that women are assumed to slot into certain social roles. 'Liberal feminism' – the argument that women should have equal opportunities to men – is an important branch of feminist thought.[37]

Individualism also plays an important role as an analytical approach. 'Methodological individualism' is at the root of much thinking about economics, and particularly of micro-economic theory – that is, theory about the way in which parts of society or industry behave. The assumption is made that if a number of people all make individual decisions, then the extremes are likely to be cancelled out; it is possible to think about the 'average' individual, and to make predictions about collective social behaviour by examining the behaviour of this person.[38] This has been a very effective mode of argument, but there are dangers: the average man, 'homo economicus', should not be confused with real people. It is probably true, for example, that the demand for health care falls when the cost increases, or that landlords overall respond to financial incentives; but it does not follow that we know how all patients or landlords are going to behave, and in social policy the behaviour of minorities is very important. Methodological individualism becomes dangerous, politically, when economists assume that everyone is going to behave in the same 'rational' economic fashion. When some do not, the assumption that a measure will increase welfare may well be wrong.

The person. A 'person' is not quite the same thing as a human being. Some organisations are treated as 'persons' in law; they are given rights, like the ability to make contracts or to take legal action, while some human beings can be denied the same status. In sociology, persons are defined mainly in terms of their social relationships – the roles they have, and the connections they have with others.[39] People who are cut off from social relationships, like people institutionalised with dementia, can become non-persons.[40] The heading of this section – the person in society – is tautologous. If there is no society, there is no person.

Human beings are social animals, and there are social aspects to our needs. Social contact (or 'affiliation'), affection, reproduction and living with others are also basic to the human condition. By asserting that people are social, we move towards an important insight: that their welfare is defined in terms of the society of which they are a part. If we are trying to improve people's welfare, it is helpful to try to understand something about the way that people are, and how welfare policies will change their conditions.

Social networks

The family. The family is probably the most important social unit in modern society, if only because it is the base for a great part of social interaction; but the generalisation disguises a number of different functions which conventionally are packaged together. The idea of the family is also used, however loosely, to refer to many kinds of household where people who are related by birth or marriage live together. The household is also an important unit; most people live with other people, sharing or dividing up income and expenses to some degree. The family is important for the development of a whole set of relationships – including partner, parent, friendship and affiliation; and it is important to recognise that the relations between adult members of a family – like the relationship between adult children and their ageing parents[41] – can be crucially important for policy. And, perhaps most significant of all, the family is basic to socialisation, or preparing people for society, which implies a major focus on the experience on families with children.

The very generality of the idea of 'the family' makes it difficult to make much sense of the term in relation to policy; 'family policy' can be taken as narrowly or as widely as one wishes. Where there are formal 'family policies', they tend to be policies specifically geared to families with children. Family policy in France is a notable example; support for families and the promotion of the birthrate has long been accepted, by both left and right, as a central part of state activity.[42] But writing about 'family policy' usually means something less specific, and in many ways more deep-rooted, than any formal policy. The role of the family in society is taken to define the limits of social policy – the point at which the social becomes the private. The United Nations (UN) Convention on the Rights of the Child declares a conviction that the family is 'the fundamental group of society and the natural environment for the growth and well-being of all its members and particularly children' and continues:

> States Parties shall respect the responsibilities, rights and duties of parents or, where applicable, the members of the extended family or community as provided for by local custom, legal guardians or other persons legally responsible for the child, to provide, in a manner consistent with the evolving capacities of the child, appropriate direction and guidance ...[43]

There is arguably a presumption here that the state and collective services will not normally intervene. The formal rules which govern intervention in cases of domestic violence, child abuse or sexual abuse are written in the shadow of a substantial unwritten code, which presumes that families should be shielded from intervention unless there are very strong reasons to the contrary. The provision of domiciliary support by the state is generally built around the pattern of care which a relative delivers – and has to recognise that that care is often greater than anything the public services can deliver.[44] Despite its vagueness, and considerable ambivalence, the idea of 'the family' exerts a considerable influence on social policy.

The community. There are significant ambiguities in the concept of community: Hillery, in a well-known article, identified 94 different definitions. The only thing they had in common was that they all dealt with people,[45] although even that may not be true – I have come across some approaches to community regeneration which seem to be about buildings instead. For simplicity, communities might be defined in at least four different ways:

1. We sometimes identify people as being part of a community when they live in the same area, although this is debatable – it is not difficult for people to live near each other with very little social contact. One of the complaints made about clearance policies was that they broke up communities; moving people out of their areas disrupts patterns of contact.

2. A community might be seen as a social network which comes about through a set of interactions between people; this does not have to be geographical – we also talk about the 'Jewish community' or the 'Bengali community', and part of the reason for doing so is that membership of such communities defines patterns of social contact as well as other kinds of experience. Welfare systems in Europe often depend heavily on this kind of community, or 'solidarity', which offers the opportunity to use existing social networks as a basis for developing mutually supportive arrangements.[46]

3. People might be thought of as a community if they have a culture in common. The term 'culture' is generally used to identify a set of behaviour patterns; it might refer to language and history, common experiences, norms and values, and lifestyle. This tends to be at its most important in discussions of nationality and race, but for practical purposes it may also be important to identify subculture within a dominant culture – structured variations from the norm. The idea that there might be a 'culture of poverty' was very influential in the US in the 1960s, when policies against poverty were often directed towards educating people out of the supposed 'culture'.[47]

4. People might be considered to form a 'community' when there are interests in common: the 'business community' might be an example. It is possible, however, to have interests in common without any social contact; this overlaps with the other main approach to defining social groups, which views groups in relation to the social structure.

Although the idea of community has never truly played a very large part in the politics of welfare, it has been a recurrent theme. Modernisation of housing rather than clearance is supposed to 'preserve communities'; 'community care' builds on the strength of community networks; 'community policing' uses local networks to build up trust and effective working relationships. But the term does not always have a specific content; communities are generally accepted as legitimate, and placing policies in relation to communities has been an important way of justifying the policies. Among the services which have been justified in terms of community there are 'community industry', 'community transport' and 'community arts'. This seems mainly to mean that these issues are socially oriented – indeed, the term 'social' could have been used as well as the term 'community'.

The workplace. The workplace is an important forum for social interaction, although it is more than that: work and work status are tied in with the economic structure of society, and so with class, status and power. In much of Europe, the workplace has been the central location from which organised social action has been developed; mutual insurance to deal with social contingencies and 'solidaristic' arrangements tends to depend on an association with a particular place of work or professional group. In several countries, including France and Australia, social policy is concerned as much with industrial relations as it is with the provision of welfare. In France, there are special insurance 'régimes' for people in different occupational groups – for example, for rail workers or power workers. In a number of other countries, the trades unions have been responsible for the administration of benefits and services, such as unemployment benefits in Denmark, or the former arrangements for health services in Israel. Equally, employers may take on the responsibility for 'occupational welfare', the provision of services to their workers: the best-known model is Japan, where firms – acting as a larger 'family' – can take responsibility for education, health and pensions.[48]

If the importance of the workplace in social policy seems to have been diminished in recent years, it is for two main reasons. One is that the state has been increasingly seen as the main route through which welfare can be provided; where the state fails to provide, responsibility has been undertaken primarily by women and the family. The second is that people can only participate in such a system if they have work; the attention of many writers in social policy has shifted away from people in work, which was the traditional concern of 19th-century collectivists, towards those who are excluded from the labour market, or marginal to it.

The nation. Nationhood might be held to consist of a common history, culture or language; it is sometimes associated, like community, with geographical location; it might be seen, like citizenship, as membership of a political community. These disparate meanings are often used simultaneously, which makes nationhood rather an odd concept;[49] it is difficult to know whether it can sensibly be included in a consideration of the social context of policy, or whether it should be treated instead as a political ideal. Miller argues (to my mind unpersuasively) that the nation is the only meaningful 'community' to which individuals can relate, and so the only sensible base for policy decisions.[50] The argument is important because it identifies a set of moral sentiments which can have a powerful influence on policy. In Belgium, nationalism has led to pressure for decentralised policy, running against the grain of established institutional structures. However, Béland and Lecours argue that this cannot be seen as a reflection of social structures; the social arrangements reflect more complex, diffuse and overlapping networks of solidarity with different sorts of boundary from the supposed 'national' identities.[51]

This influence of 'the nation' on social policy is in most cases a negative one; like the idea of the 'family', nationhood is used more as a restraint on policy than a means of developing or encouraging it. Nationhood seems to define, for some, the limits of moral responsibility; it is common for different rules to apply to nationals and non-nationals, or for immigrants to be denied benefits and services which are available to others[52] (see Box 2). There is a moral argument for this kind of discrimination, which is referred to as 'particularism'; because social responsibilities are developed within the framework of a particular society, they are only meaningful within the context of that society, and the same standards cannot legitimately be applied elsewhere.[53] The standard case against this argument is universalist, implying that moral standards should be applied to everyone.

Box 2: Support for migrants

The UN estimates that there are 191 million migrants worldwide – at 3% of the world's population, a surprisingly modest figure.[54] Some 30 to 40 million of these are 'unauthorised' or illegal migrants. Immigration is mainly into the richer countries of the northern hemisphere; three quarters of all migrants are in 12% of countries.[55]

One of the dilemmas that confronts many welfare states is the issue of support for migrants. If welfare is based in solidarity, or networks of social relationships, then people coming from beyond those networks do not have the same entitlements as those who are within them. If it is based in rights of citizenship, it is not clear that migrants are part of the political community who are entitled to those rights. The exclusion of migrants is, in the view of some, justifiable exclusion. Unsurprisingly, then, different kinds of welfare system offer different levels of support to migrants.[56] In some, they are able to establish earned rights through contribution and work-record; in others, this is much more difficult. It remains true, however, that migrants are likely to work in lower-paid employment, and to have lower benefit entitlements, than the host populations.

The argument for including migrants is threefold. The first is the universalist argument: that migrants, like other people, have human rights – rights which people have as part of common humanity. The problem with this argument is that if it applies to people who have entered a country, it applies equally to people who have not entered the country. It is not clear that the obligation to a person from Africa to Europe looking for work is any less than the obligations to someone who continues to live in Africa – indeed, if human rights are related to needs, there may be an argument that the claim of the person still in Africa is greater.

The second is an argument about the society which the migrant joins. The effect of not extending the same protection to migrants as to others is to create a two-tier society – a society in which some are included and some are not. This is tolerated in some societies, but many others would find it unacceptable. (The argument is often described as one about 'racism', but it is more general than that: it extends to all forms of exclusion within a society.)

Third, there is a view that society incurs a special obligation to its migrants, in return for their contribution to the economy, culture and social life of a community. This view is not universally shared, because some people view the change associated with migration with horror; but many of the world's most successful, vigorous societies are migrant cultures.

The universalist values held by many writers on social policy have favoured an internationalist perspective. Titmuss, for example, expressed reservations about the idea of the 'welfare state' because it seemed to him to assume that welfare fell mainly within the area of one state, rather than being the responsibility of everyone.[57] Beveridge described his report as being a contribution to the 'common cause' of the allies.[58] These issues have been of great importance in the past, and with the resurgence of nationalism in Europe, and the challenges posed by European Union, they seem set to grow in importance now. The European Union has been developing a policy based on the progressive extension of 'solidarity'; the kinds of solidarity which are being developed are likely to cut across national boundaries. However, solidarity, like nationhood, has the potential to exclude people as well as to include them; both concepts can be taken to define the limits of social responsibility, and so to define not only who should be protected, but also who will be left out.[59] Banting suggests that where there is ethnic diversity, there is a potential tension with solidaristic systems, and diverse societies tend also to set limits on welfare systems.[60]

Inclusion and exclusion

The growth of individualism in the post-war period has made some people working in the English-speaking tradition reluctant to accept that a 'society' means anything. The philosopher Michael Oakeshott criticised the idea as implying an association without saying anything about what the connection really is,[61] and Margaret Thatcher famously commented that 'there is no such thing as society'. 'Society' is often taken in the English-speaking literature to be a single, monolithic structure. The approach to the subject in Europe, and particularly in France, has led to a different understanding of the basic idea. In Catholic social teaching, people are represented as part of a set of social networks. The networks are held together by mutual support and obligation – the principle of solidarity.[62] From birth onwards, everyone finds themselves part of social roles, and networks of obligation – the obligations of family, community and social contact. The representation of society as a series of concentric circles, represented in Figure 2.1, is a useful shorthand, but the connections between and across the circles are just as important; because of solidarity, the networks overlap and intertwine. A society is a network of such networks.[63]

There are people, however, who are not fully integrated into social networks. Some people are 'marginal', in the sense that they stand on the periphery of such a society. Some are excluded altogether.[64] The idea of 'social exclusion' has been mauled and twisted by people who were not familiar with the conceptual base, but it was developed, initially, to refer to people who were not part of the networks of solidarity that others experienced – people who were left out of the systems of support developed in welfare states.[65] This idea was soon enough extended to refer to people who were not part of any networks – people who were left out, shut out or pushed out. People are left out when the support that is available does not extend to them – for example, unemployed school leavers

FIGURE 2.1: PEOPLE IN SOCIETY

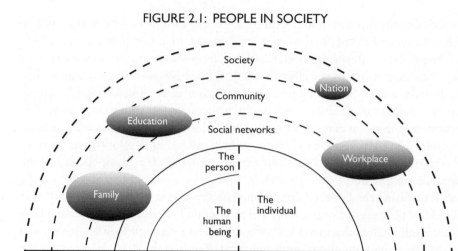

or long-term unemployed people who have been able to contribute to social insurance schemes. They are shut out when they are barred from participating in society – like asylum seekers who are denied the ability to work or to contribute. They are pushed out when they are deliberately rejected. For much of the last century, people with intellectual disabilities were institutionalised, moved to 'colonies' and denied the chance to have children, so that their 'degeneracy' would not spread to the rest of the population.[66]

Social inclusion, conversely, is the process of combatting exclusion – seeking to ensure that people become part of the networks of solidarity and support which apply to others. In France, benefits for '*insertion*' combined financial support with a set of agreements intended to bind people to social networks. The *Revenu Minimum d'Insertion* is based on two contracts; one between the individual and the local authority (the *commission locale d'insertion*), the other between the authority and service providers. The kinds of contract made may be about employment, but they can also be concerned with education, health, housing or whatever the excluded person needs to be integrated with society. This model has been widely imitated – there are similar policies in Belgium, Portugal, Spain and Italy – and the idea of inclusion has extended from France to the policy of the European Union.[67]

Stigma

The problem of 'stigma' refers to the experience of social rejection and loss of status which people suffer when they receive services. There are physical stigmas: people can be socially rejected if they have some kind of attribute or characteristic which sets them apart, like a physical disability or a disease. Mental stigmas are associated with problems like mental illness and addiction. There are moral stigmas, when people are rejected because of something they have done or are thought to have done, like single parents and offenders – and even, in the case of abused children, what people imagine they may be going to do in the future.[68] There are stigmas related to dependency and the receipt of social services. And there are, besides, people whose status is already low – like people on low incomes, or people living in poor areas. These different types of stigma overlap: people who are disabled, single parents or mentally ill are also likely to be poor, while people who are poor or mentally ill are often morally condemned.[69]

The problems of stigma apply to many of the people who social services are intended to deal with, often long before they come into contact with the services. Jeremy Bentham argued, long ago, that there was nothing particularly humiliating about forcing poor people to wear a badge to show that they were dependent on the parish for relief; after all, aristocrats sported coats of arms, and war veterans wore medals. The problem that the paupers were experiencing was not the badge in itself, but the social rejection of their condition.[70] There are arguments to support the position: means-testing in the tax system may not be liked, but it is not usually described as stigmatising. It may be possible, on this argument, for social services to be organised so as to disguise the condition. For example, psychiatric wards situated in general hospitals are less likely than psychiatric hospitals to identify to the world that a patient is receiving psychiatric care; and attention to children in schools does not seem to attract the same concern as attention through social work.

At the same time, it is important to recognise that social services also carry a stigma in their own right. Part of this is the association with other people who are stigmatised. Receipt of care in a psychiatric hospital carries a stigma, and there is some reason to think that having been in a hospital is more likely to lead to social rejection than the symptoms of the illness itself.[71] A standard complaint about basic social assistance is that 'it lumps the unemployed, sick, widowed, aged and others into one undifferentiated and inevitably stigmatised category'.[72] One of the central arguments for universal services has been that the inclusion of everyone in the target group makes it possible to protect the vulnerable without stigmatisation.

Stigma has been an important element in the development of social policy; even as the deliberate imposition of stigma was part of the punitive policies of the Poor Law, its removal became one of the symbols of the 'welfare state'. It has been accused of being a 'myth'. Klein refers to the effects it is supposed to have on the take-up of benefits as 'the phlogiston of social theory: a label attached to an imperfectly understood phenomenon'.[73] But myths have an important role. What people believe in a society, Thomas and Znaniecki famously argued, is likely to be true in its consequences; Sorel points to the political power of 'myths' in changing the way that people behave.[74] Whether or not 'stigma' refers to a real set of problems (as I believe it does), concerns about stigma have had a major effect on policy. Titmuss, for whom stigma was one of the central concepts in the study of social welfare, argued:

> there should be no sense of inferiority, pauperism, shame or stigma in the use of a publicly provided service: no attribution that one was being or becoming a 'public burden'. Hence the emphasis on the social rights of all citizens to use or not to use as responsible people the services made available by the community.[75]

Social structure and social divisions

The image of society which tends to emerge from an emphasis on individuals and different kinds of social group is complex and diverse, and there are those who believe that society is so complex that it is difficult to offer sensible generalisations about it. This belief has been expressed through three main schools of thought. Individualists, like Jeremy Bentham, argue that society consists of nothing but the sum of the individuals who make it up; there is no such thing, then, as a 'structure' of society. Pluralists, like Robert Dahl,[76] accept that there are many different kinds of group, but that their interactions are complex and do not always conform to definite patterns. Organic conservatives, following Edmund Burke,[77] think that there is a 'social order', but that the balance established between different factors is so intricate and involved that it is not possible to know how it all works or what the effects of trying to change society might be. (The same point is made by liberals like Spencer[78] and Hayek[79].)

There are many writers, however, who believe that it is possible to identify patterns and structures in social relationships. Relationships within the family, for example, are not worked out independently by each family in turn; domestic relationships are largely configured by expectations relating to gender. Relationships at school and work tend to be patterned by people's social class. For the most part the way that people live is cast in conventional social terms. The most important patterns of this kind concern class, status and power; they are manifested in inequalities in economic capacity, race or ethnicity, and gender. Views about the relative importance of each of these factors vary: socialists have mainly concerned themselves with economic and status differences, Marxists have emphasised the importance of employment and power, and feminists have focused on gender. These views tend to overlap, and a school of 'critical social policy' has emerged, which emphasises the importance of all these forms of structured inequality, and seeks to interpret problems and policy primarily in terms of patterned relationships of social division. Critical social policy lies at the opposite extreme, then, to individualist and pluralist interpretations of society.

Inequality

The problem of inequality has been one of the main issues to which social policy has been addressed in the past. Inequality refers not to the fact that people are different, but that people are advantaged or disadvantaged in social terms.[80] This kind of advantage and disadvantage leads to differential access to opportunities and rewards in society. The kinds of area in which people are disadvantaged are the distribution of resources, gender and race.

Resources. It is not surprising to discover that income and wealth are unevenly distributed; this is a pattern which obtains across many societies. The possession of resources is often a key to access to the structure of social advantage; conversely, lack of resources implies cumulative disadvantages in material circumstances, lifestyle and opportunities. Extreme disadvantage in resources is generally referred to in terms of 'poverty', although it can be misleading to identify poverty too closely with inequality – in so far as poverty refers to the lack of resources, people can lack resources when others are in similar conditions, and measures which reduce inequality do not necessarily alleviate poverty.

Gender. Gender is a major factor in social divisions. Although there is a biological difference between the sexes, the social construction of gender bears only a limited relationship to such differences; with gender identification comes a set of social roles, or particular expectations, which subsequently determine the range of opportunities available to women and men. The understanding of gender divisions has become increasingly important for the analysis of social policy, not simply because issues affecting women are part of the agenda which social policy must tackle, but also because a number of the traditional concerns of social welfare – like poverty, health and old age – have important gender-related dimensions.[81] There is a strong argument, for example, that poverty is being 'feminised', because women are considerably more vulnerable to the conditions of poverty. (The main reservation to make about this position is that it seems to assume that something has changed; it is quite possible that poverty has always reflected gender divisions.[82])

Race. 'Race', like gender, is a socially constructed concept; unlike gender, the term covers a wide range of different types of characteristics, and it is used variously to indicate physical differences, cultural issues and historical antecedents. This very diversity makes it difficult to offer sensible generalisations about the circumstances of 'races', and the political abuse of the concept prompts some need for caution. At the same time, different racial groups are subject to important disadvantages in racially differentiated societies. Racial discrimination refers to the deliberate use of adverse selection as a means of putting people from particular racial groups in an inferior position, but deliberate discrimination is not necessary to explain much racial disadvantage; the cumulative effect of denial of access to the resources, opportunities and conditions of life available to others is a deepening and extension of the experience of disadvantage.

One of the words I have used in describing this kind of relationship is that relationships are 'patterned'; they are similar to other relationships. The view that social relationships are 'structured' puts the point rather more strongly; it means that people's social position is determined by the position of other people. The position of women cannot be understood without reference to the position of men. People in minority ethnic groups are defined by their differences from the ethnic majority. People are poor, not simply because they do not have enough, but because others have the things that they do not: Tawney argued, famously, that 'What thoughtful rich people call the problem of poverty, thoughtful poor people call with equal justice a problem of riches'.[83]

Although there has been growing emphasis on different forms of inequality, it is probably still true to say that the main concepts used to identify the pattern of relationships are class, status and power. Class, broadly speaking, refers to economic position; status, to a set of social roles; and power, to the ability to affect the behaviour of others. As is often the case in social science, however, the terms are ambiguous, and used differently by different people.

Class

The idea of 'class' is commonly understood in three main ways.

Productive relations. In Marx's thought, class is defined by people's relationship to the system of production in society. Marx believed that there were two main classes in 'capitalist' societies: the bourgeoisie, or capitalists, who owned and controlled the means of production, and the proletariat, who sold their labour power. These were not the only classes, however, although Marx believed that the others would fade in importance; there was also the rump of the old feudal aristocracy who owned land, an intermediate group of entrepreneurs who owned their own production, and a 'lumpenproletariat' of poor non-workers who Marx dismissed as social parasites. The Marxist use of class is not very important for policy purposes, although it still shapes the way in which many people think about class relations.

Economic position. Max Weber argued that a class consisted of a common set of economic circumstances.[84] By this criterion, there are a large number of classes in society: we might distinguish many groups, including owners, managers and workers; salaried and waged employees; professional, bureaucratic and manual workers; or workers and non-workers. Weberian analyses have been used, for example, to distinguish different 'housing classes' according to what kind of tenure a household occupies,[85] or to distinguish the characteristics of an 'underclass' who are marginal to the labour market and dependent on welfare benefits.[86] This kind of argument has been important for welfare because it defines the groups to which a response is necessary. Peter Townsend's argument that disabled people should be seen as a class[87] is based on the hope that a general social response – a universal benefit for all disabled people – can be arranged in response. In the 'underclass' debate, the idea has been used to identify a group of people who are at the bottom of the heap – a point which can be interpreted to support or to criticise people in that position. There are strong objections to the term from some who see the argument as a way of lumping together people in very different circumstances and blaming them for their circumstances.[88]

Class as occupational status. Class can also be seen as a set of relationships between economic circumstances and social status. This is the conventional classification used in much social science research, which ranges from social class I to V or VI, or by advertisers who classify people as A, B, C and so forth. Economic factors alone are not enough to determine class; occupation, and to some extent the educational qualifications required for different kinds of occupation, is taken as a major indicator of status. This has probably been the most influential of the various concepts of class, because it lends itself to empirical analysis – indeed, one could argue that it is principally an operational definition of class rather than a theoretically based set of distinctions. If we wish to study the effect of inequality in relation to resources, health, education or housing, classification by socioeconomic status has proved to be one of the most robust and most effective ways of doing it.

Status

The concept of status itself has a range of different uses. Status can be seen as a form of structured social identity, defining the way that people see themselves and that others see them. To say that people have a certain status means that they will have certain opportunities, or life chances, and will be able to live to certain material and social standards; Weber comments that status 'is in the main conditioned as well as expressed through a specific style of life'.[89] The pursuit of equality in education has often been concerned with access to the structure of opportunities determined by educational and occupational status; this is true both of the concern to offer opportunities to working-class children for higher education,[90] and in the US the use of 'affirmative action' to enhance the prospects of African-Americans to become doctors and lawyers.[91]

Status can also be seen in terms of social roles. People have various roles in society; a status consists of a set of roles, which conditions expectations about the way people are to behave and how others are to behave towards them.[92] This view has been particularly important in understanding the position of people on benefits, who have notably low status; the effect of failing to contribute to society is to be in breach of social norms, with the consequence that people are stigmatised and socially rejected when they are out of work for an extended period.[93]

Overlapping with this, status can be seen as a quality of social esteem; people have 'high status' when they are treated with honour, and 'low status' when they are stigmatised. Part of the aim of 'welfare states' has been to invest citizens equally with a status entitling them to draw on the resources of the society: Titmuss argued that universality – the establishment of rights for all citizens – was intended to remove degrading differences in their status.

> One fundamental historical reason for the adoption of this principle was the aim of making services available and accessible to the whole population in such ways as would not involve users in any humiliating loss of status, dignity or self-respect. ... If these services were not provided by everybody for everybody they would either not be available at all, or only for those who could afford them, and for others on such terms as would involve the infliction of a sense of inferiority and stigma.[94]

Power

The concept of power is particularly complex; power is understood in different ways, and different sorts of power are exercised in various ways by different groups.[95] Power is defined by Russell as the 'production of intended effects'.[96] Lukes points out, however, that power is not only to do with what is intended. If someone is powerful, or in a dominant position, other people will often act in the way they think appropriate; this implies that a number of effects might not be intended at all.[97] Saying that people have power can mean that they have the capacity to do things, that they change the way that other people behave, or that they are in relationships of dominance.

The structure of power in society is sometimes referred to as a way to explain why decisions, actions, accepted values and even failures to act work in the interests of some people rather than others. For example, a forceful argument about the nature of power has been made by feminists who have argued that society is fundamentally patriarchal.[98] Patriarchy has a range of uses – like any other concept in social science – but in its simplest form, it can be taken to mean men have power over women. This power is expressed both in the sense of direct control and in the sense that women have to alter their patterns of behaviour to accommodate the demands of a male society; Marxist feminists have argued that it is reflected in the sexual division of labour and the way in which men are able to control resources both inside and outside the home.[99] Redressing the balance implies not simply 'equality', in the sense of the removal of disadvantage, but empowerment; unless women gain power equivalent to men's, the disadvantages will subsequently recur.

There are three major questions to answer in the discussion of power:

- *What kind of power is being considered?* Economic strength, social influence and political power are connected, but they are distinct; they may well be held by different people and expressed in different ways.
- *How far is power concentrated?* Elite theorists argue that power is exercised or held by relatively few people; this might take the form of a ruling élite, a small number of people able to make all the important decisions, but it might also be based on a restricted number of élites who exercise power in particular contexts.[100] Pluralists believe it is diffused across many different groups. No one group has the power consistently to sway decisions. Pluralism is often misrepresented by non-pluralists to mean the belief that power is equally and fairly distributed in society,[101] which is not needed for the idea; it means only that no one has enough power to be in control.
- *Who benefits?* This question represents an important challenge to many of the assumptions behind welfare policy: welfare policy is not necessarily intended to benefit the recipients. Some 'social control' is mainly directed for the benefit of others (like child protection, which involves substantial controls on parents, or slum clearance, which improves the material standards of the wider society), but there are other aspects, like penalties for refusing jobs which are offered, which can be argued to serve the interests of employers.

The examination of 'interests' can lead to a distorted perspective. Any coercive action can be seen as a defence of social order, and so of the status quo, but this is not just in the interests of those who are powerful – remember that the victims of crime are disproportionately poor people. It is easy to represent any inequality that arises after a policy has been put into practice as the result of deliberate intent; but in an unequal society, any policy which does not actually shift the balance is likely to have unequal effects, and no intention or relationship of dominance is required to explain the consequence. Power is important only if it has some identifiable effect. If unequal consequences reflect the structure of power in society, it is because there is something about the structure of power which directly or indirectly creates the conditions which produce those consequences.

The structure of disadvantage

The idea that social inequality is 'structured' can be interpreted in a number of different ways. Class, status and power define patterns of advantage and disadvantage; but what does the pattern look like? There are four main ways of describing it.

Hierarchical inequality. The first is that society contains complex levels of inequality; wherever in the structure one is located, there is generally speaking someone above and someone below. This is sometimes described as a 'hierarchical' structure, although strictly speaking any set of rankings, including a stratified structure, might also be seen as hierarchically ordered; the important point to note is that the distribution of status and resources is continuous rather than discontinuous. Income and wealth are not simply split between the 'rich' and the 'poor', with the result that any categorisation of the level of 'poverty' might be arbitrary; the claim that there are divisions or stratified levels is often a convenience, imposed as a means of interpreting the data.

Stratification. A stratified society is split into a range of levels. The class system is not, by most accounts, divided into 'upper' and 'lower' classes; rather, there is a series of different classes who occupy different social positions. Information about inequalities in health uses information about class because it works as a way of following through differential opportunities and prospects over time.

Social divisions. Society can be seen as divided – for example, between rich and poor, male and female, or 'black' and 'white'. This kind of distinction is better described as a social division rather than a form of 'stratification', for reasons which are most clear in the division of 'male' and 'female', where there are no intermediate stages. The idea of social division implies both that people can be distinguished from others by virtue of certain characteristics, and that their position can be identified with others. The point is not, then, just that poor people are not like the rich, or that women are not like men; it is that poor people have a social position also occupied by other poor people, and that women share a common social position. Gender acts as a primary dividing characteristic because the position of women is conditioned in terms of a set of roles and expectations associated with their gender. Race divides society because the combined effect of prejudice and racial differentiation is to limit the scope of people from different racial groups for social action. (Note that this is framed in different terms from the divisions of gender; these issues do not describe the same kinds of social relationship. The statement here about racial groups could also be applied to women and men; but the statement made about women could not be applied to racial groups.) An emphasis on social division implies a policy aimed at particular blocs, or broadly defined groups, in society, like women, racial minorities or the poor. Issues affecting these groups, and the general problems of bloc-regarding approaches to policy, will be discussed in more detail later.

Postmodern views. An alternative set of views which has gained increasing currency in the course of the last twenty years is a 'postmodern' critique of society. Postmodernism is difficult to pin down, but the core of the argument is that society is no longer understandable in terms of the patterns of thinking which characterised most of the 20th century. There is, instead, diversity – a rainbow effect of different identities, possibly individualised or atomised, often coupled with uncertainty about the nature of social relationships. According to Giddens, we have moved beyond tradition, and beyond scarcity.[102] For Giddens,

> The welfare state cannot survive in its existing form ... [welfare systems need] to escape from reliance on 'precautionary aftercare' as the main means of coping with risks; be integrated with a wider set of life concerns than those of productivism; develop a politics of second chances ... and focus on what I have called a generative conception of equality.[103]

Peter Taylor Gooby has been critical of postmodern approaches; he argues that they undermine the radical and critical impact of social policy as a subject.[104] The society Giddens is imagining here is one where poverty and need have ceased to be primary concerns. This is not a situation many people working in social policy in practice would recognise.

These views are often held simultaneously, even if there are tensions between them. But different understandings about social structure do lead to differences in approaches to policy. Stratification and hierarchy can be modified by giving people the opportunity to be socially mobile, and to cross boundaries; postmodern diversity can be manipulated, even if it is difficult to pin down; but the divisions of gender and race do not really allow people to cross. In a hierarchical society, measures which help some people necessarily change their position relative to others can mean that poor people gain at the expense of slightly less poor people, or even that richer people from one group like women might gain at the expense of poorer people in another. In a postmodern society, the effects of policy become unpredictable and uncertain. Where society is divided, by contrast, the gains to some people in a group might help to advance the whole group – which is one of the justifications for trying to ensure that women are appointed to boardrooms, or that African-Americans can become lawyers.

Society and social policy

In order to understand the impact of social policies, it is important to see those policies in the context in which they are being applied. This means that we have to know something about the society that policies are trying to affect. Welfare services have been criticised at times for problems, like the persistence of poverty, which have their origins in society rather than the services which respond to them. Problems of this sort have to be understood, in the first place, in social terms, because it is through the social structure that problems of poverty and inequality occur.

One view of 'social policy' has been that it consists of policy to change the nature of a society. Townsend, for example, suggests that social policy refers to 'the institutionalised control of agencies and organisations to maintain or change social structure and values'.[105] Ferge, by contrast, distinguishes social policy (as policy for welfare) from policies that are intended to change society, which she refers to as 'societal' or 'structural' policy.[106] There is an argument for seeing any social policy in structural terms, but in general, social policy does not have to set out to alter social relationships. It can happen, then, that social policy does not affect or address inequalities – or that, even if social policy makes a difference to inequality, it does not make very much. In these cases, the explanation lies in the study of social relationships, and not in the policy.

Taking social relationships as given means that, on occasions, academic writing about welfare in society tends to give the impression that welfare is a sort of optional add-on to the existing economic or social structure. This is a convenient way of describing the impact of policy, but it is not really the way the world is; work, income, wealth and material goods have developed in a context in which some welfare services were already available, and this affects issues like security, the value of work and the importance of social status. When we consider individual policies, however, it is helpful to begin from the proposition that there is a status quo which the policy will somehow affect. We can then try to work out what the effect of a policy is, by comparing it with what we believe would happen if nothing was done, or with the effect of other alternative policies.

ISSUE FOR DISCUSSION

If people's circumstances are improving, does it matter if they are disadvantaged?

THREE

Problems and responses

Social problems
The extent of a problem:
incidence, prevalence, distribution and intensity
Responding to social problems
The focus of policy
Individuals
Households and families
Communities
Blocs
Society

Social problems

Social policies are sometimes represented as responses to social problems. They are rather more than this, because there are policies which are not at all centred on 'problems'; any policy which is designed to change or maintain social structures or relationships could be described as a social policy, and it has been argued that the failure to make such policies can also be treated and analysed as a form of social policy.[107] But a focus on social problems is helpful in the first instance, because it helps to point our attention to some issues which affect all social policies.

Social issues become 'problems' because they need to be solved: some kind of response is called for. It is not always the case that people agree about what constitutes a problem. This might be because of lack of awareness. In Victorian times, for example, many people denied that there was a problem of poverty: Southwood Smith used to take selected dignitaries for a tour in London to persuade them.[108] More recently, doctors seemed unaware of the problem of physical child abuse, which was 'discovered' by radiologists;[109] child sexual abuse was hardly heard of until the 1980s, and there are still many who deny the existence of ritual abuse.[110] It might also, however, happen that people are aware of the conditions which others think of as a problem, and do not see a problem there. It seems fairly clear that many people do not think that hitting children is a problem unless it leads to serious physical injury. Many people, and many parents, think that this is not remotely problematic and should rather be seen as a desirable part of their social and moral education. The view that children should not have less protection than adults has gradually been taking hold, and several countries have now legislated to prevent parents hitting children.

The main issue which arises from this is that the definition of problems is different in different places. Definitions are not 'objective', then, if by this we mean that they are fixed on some standard which can be identified outside the context and society where they are applied. This does not mean that problems are 'subjective', however; they are not simply made up or arrived at by anyone who pleases. A better way to describe them is that they are 'inter-subjective', and the understanding of problems grows through a series of shared perceptions and beliefs.[111] Problem are 'socially constructed'; the pattern of relationships in society shapes the circumstances which lead to a problem, the way the problem is understood, and the extent to which it is perceived as a problem. Youth, old age, worklessness or educational attainment are not fixed, unchanging concepts; they mean different things in different places, and way they are understood and responded to is different.

The second major point about social problems is that they are social, which means that they occur in a social context and are recognised as such. Many problems are not social; problems in personal relationships, for example, are not usually treated as 'social' in their origins or their required responses. Grief is not usually thought of as a social problem; nor, for the most part, is pain. They become social at the point where they are constructed in social terms, or when a social response is called for. This requires some caution, because discussing whether or not issues are social can be taken in itself as an attempt to put them onto the social agenda. It could be argued, from what I stated earlier, that domestic violence is not a social problem; the trouble with this statement is that it is liable to be taken not as a description of how the problem is responded to (which would probably be accurate) but as a moral statement about what ought to be seen as a social problem (which would be highly disputable).

Understanding problems is important for social policy for a fairly obvious reason: it helps to understand the nature of a problem in order to respond to it. Part of the difficulty here is that people understand the issues differently. The problems of an abused child might be seen as a failure of family life; but they might also be seen as a reflection on the social acceptance of corporal punishment. Educational failure might be seen as the product of individual inadequacy, culture and upbringing or social deprivation. It often happens that the 'common-sense' assumptions made for policy rest on a series of complex, scarcely examined assumptions. It seems hard now to understand what policy makers were doing when they bracketed mental illness with intellectual disability,[112] or child abuse and neglect with juvenile crime;[113] the associations are based in assumptions about the relationships between problems which now look wholly unconvincing. But equally questionable assumptions are made when, for example, racial issues are identified with poverty, or mental illness is linked to dangerousness. When social problems are recognised, they are interpreted or 'constructed' in a particular way; they might have to be reinterpreted, or 'deconstructed', to make an effective response possible.

The extent of a problem: incidence, prevalence, distribution and intensity

The first question that needs to be asked about a problem is what kind of problem it is, which is why issues of definition and social construction are key concepts. The next step in policy discussions is usually to ask questions about its size and shape. This is usually done in terms of 'social indicators'. Social indicators are what most lay people think of as 'statistics', but the connection between indicators and the kind of 'statistic' which one learns about elsewhere in the social sciences is fairly tenuous, so it is helpful to have another word. They are referred to as 'indicators' because they show the direction in which changes take place, rather than being specific measures of social problems and responses.[114] At times people may give the impression that well-known indicators, like the European poverty threshold (60% of median income) or the unemployment rate, are 'measures' of a problem, or that performance targets like 'reducing by two thirds the mortality rate among children under 5' (one of the UN's Millennium Development Goals[115]) are precise assessments of what is to be achieved. They are not. Indicators give an insight into a problem; they are a way of capturing information, not of capturing the problem itself. What they do offer is a way of judging whether problems are getting better or worse, and whether policies are working.

There are four key dimensions to a problem. The first is the *prevalence*, or how frequently a problem is found. It is usually treated as a proportion (for example, 5% of a population) or a rate (3 people in 1,000), taken at a point in time – epidemiologists call this 'point prevalence' to distinguish it from prevalence over a period of time. The *incidence*, which is related to this, is how many new cases are happening. Increasing incidence usually implies increasing prevalence, but this is not necessarily the case – if more people exit from a problem group than come into it (for example by dying) the prevalence can fall when the incidence is rising.

The *distribution* of the problem is about the relative position of people with the problem compared with others. The importance of distribution is often exaggerated. It is often true, for example, that people in minority ethnic groups are more likely than others to be poor[116] – this is important as an issue in equity, and a mark of racial disadvantage. It is not the same, however, as saying that people in minority groups are likely to be poor – most are not. I argued in a critical pamphlet in the UK that

> Poverty is an important issue for those concerned with race and ethnicity. But it is not generally true that minority ethnic groups are

poor. It is not true that membership of a minority group is a passport to poverty, unemployment or overcrowding. And it is not true that poor people are likely to be from ethnic minorities.[117]

The assumption that people in racial minorities are poor is stereotypical – and, arguably, stigmatising of people in both categories.

The same fallacy is found, in a different way, in discussions of the influence of biological inheritance on social policy. Biology and inheritance are usually identified in terms of 'hereditability', which is supposed to refer to the variance that is explicable genetically, but which mainly refers in practice to variation between cases reflecting differences between families. (Advocates of genetic explanations usually depend on the further assumption that links between families are genetic, which is questionable.) For example, between 40% and 70% of the variation in obesity appears to be hereditable – obesity runs in families. However, hereditability is a distributional figure, not an indicator of prevalence. The gene pool changes very slowly. If the prevalence of problems changes markedly in less than a generation, inheritance cannot be the main cause for the fluctuation; the explanation has to lie elsewhere. The startling rise in obesity in developed countries is clearly the result of social factors, and particularly the nature of people's diets.[118] Distributional factors are used to identify causal relationships; they are also important for understanding issues like inequality and disadvantage. In the consideration of social problems, however, prevalence and incidence usually matter much more.

The fourth dimension which has to be considered is the *intensity* of a problem. Many of the indicators which are used are dichotomous: people are counted on the basis that either they have the problem or they do not. Many social issues, however, like poverty, disability or educational attainment, are not simple categories; they are complex, multifaceted issues. The issue of intensity relates to the relative severity and depth of a problem. It may be important to consider, not only the position of people with problems relative to those without, but also the relative position of people with problems compared to others whose problems are more or less severe.

Box 3: The misconstruction of problems

The history of social policy is festooned with examples of theoretical approaches which have gone sour – ideas which have misled practitioners, which have been misapplied, or which simply failed to deliver. Box 1 makes the case that trying to deal with the causes of problems is misconceived – not just because it is difficult to do, but because the way into a problem is not the way out of it. That is not all. People who think they know what the causes of a problem are often get it wrong. Sometimes this is positively dangerous.

A notorious example is the belief that social problems are inherited and biologically transmitted. This has been one of the most influential views in the history of social policy. In the late 19th century, the idea of 'degeneracy' was seen as the root of a range of interrelated problems – idiocy, insanity, crime, poverty, worklessness and prostitution.[119] Boies, writing in the US, proclaimed: We believe it is established beyond controversy that criminals and paupers both, are degenerate; the imperfect, knotty, knurly, worm-eaten, half-rotten fruit of the race'.[120] According to Cooley, the sociologist, 'such things as crime, pauperism, idiocy, insanity and drunkenness have, in great measure, a common causation, and so form, practically, parts of a whole'.[121]

The leading account of degeneracy at that time was a social study of a degenerate family, the Jukes. 'In the present investigation', Estabrook wrote,

> 2,820 people have been studied ... 2,094 were of Juke blood and 726 of 'X' blood who married into the Juke family; of these 366 were paupers, while 171 were criminals; and 10 lives have been sacrificed by murder. In school work 62 did well, 288 did fairly, while 458 were retarded two or more years. It is known that 166 never attended school; the school data for the rest of the family were unobtainable. There were 282 intemperate and 277 harlots. The total cost to the State has been estimated at $2,093,685.[122]

In fact, 'the Jukes' were not a single family at all – but it happened then, as it has happened in other cases, that the researchers were so certain they knew what the problems were that they didn't think that inconvenient details like that really mattered.[123]

The same confidence about identifying the cause was rapidly translated into policy. The initial response to degeneracy was to seek to separate degenerates from the community; it was an important motor force in the development of colonies for people with intellectual disabilities, and for the building of large institutions, confining them along with people who were mentally ill.[124] Subsequently, the emphasis shifted to eugenics, which sought to stop degenerates from breeding – preventing unfit people from having children. Indiana permitted involuntary sterilisations on eugenic principles in 1907, and Virginia passed a 'Eugenical Sterilization Act' in 1924, which was approved in the US Supreme Court. This was the model for the Nazis' eugenics law of 1933.[125] The Nazis began by preventing people from sexual relationships and isolating them from social contact, proceeding only later to kill them.[126] Although Nazism gave eugenics a (deservedly) bad name, people with intellectual disabilities were routinely sterilised, in several western countries, until at least the 1970s.[127]

Some reservations about the general proposition that problems are inherited have been considered in this chapter, but this is about more than bad science. It shows what can happen when people are convinced that complex problems have a single origin. It shows what can happen when people try to address the cause, when they have the wrong cause. And it shows, worst of all, what can happen when they are absolutely convinced they are right.

Responding to social problems

The way that a problem is responded to is shaped by the way the problem is defined and understood, but it is not determined by it. Some responses to problems are *direct*, in the sense that the response is intended to deal with the immediate problem as presented. If people do not have money, they can get money. If they do not have a job, they can get work. This is sometimes criticised as a way of dealing with symptoms, rather than with the underlying problems. But relieving symptoms is not necessarily such a bad idea; at least it hits the mark, and there are circumstances in which one cannot deal with the root of a problem unless some obstacles are removed first. It is not impossible to respond to people's health problems while they are sleeping rough, but it is markedly more difficult.[128]

The second kind of response is concerned with *causes* rather than effects. Addressing 'causes' is contentious, because it is difficult to find agreement about what the causes of social problems are (Box 1), and because sometimes the solutions are radically wrong (Box 3). In many ways strategies which address causes have been more influential in policy, because of the fear that if the causes are not addressed then the problems will simply recur.

A third approach is *key intervention*. This is based on an analysis of the relationships between different aspects of a situation. If the relationships between the parts are identified correctly, it may be possible within a complex set of issues to pick out the ones which will affect the others. A simple example is giving support to childcare in order to increase female participation in the labour market, or (more contentiously) offering support to landlords in an attempt to improve access to affordable housing. Other examples depend on a more elaborate set of assumptions about complex social relationships; for example, it has been argued that education is the key to equality,[129] or that democratic processes are key to the prevention of famines.[130]

Although it is possible to relate the response to problems to the patterns of social organisation considered in the previous chapter, there is no necessary link between them. Even if the problem is social, the response might be individual – or vice versa. Table 3.1 gives some illustrative examples.

TABLE 3.1: PROBLEMS AND RESPONSES

	Responses		
Problems	*Individual and family*	*Community-based*	*Social*
Individual and family	Social casework	Childcare	Health promotion
Community	Rehousing	Regeneration	Public order
Social	Employment	Local economic development	Public health

The way to reach lots of people individually might be to have a category-based policy (such as using nursery education to reach children in difficulties); conversely, there are many examples where collective problems like unemployment are responded to through individualised programmes for the unemployed person. These responses are not 'right' or 'wrong', but both are subject to objections on the grounds of the misdirection of resources. The first example might seem to be wasteful, if the level of provision is extensive and the true target limited in numbers; in the worst cases it may fail to meet the needs of the target group, either by omission or because there is no way of directing resources to them within the system. The second example suffers from the problem that it involves a huge amount of time and effort to deal with mass unemployment on an individualised basis; it may, beyond that, put an inappropriate responsibility on individuals for circumstances beyond their control.

Responses have to be translated into practical action. Policies are usually 'targeted', or aimed at somebody. The idea of targeting is misunderstood; the word has acquired some very negative connotations, because it is often identified with a particular kind of residual, individualistic policy. The World Bank website suggests: 'The main objective of targeting is to deliver more resources to the poorest groups of the population'.[131] But there is no intrinsic reason why the target should be the needs of poor individuals; it may be possible, for example, to aim policies at broader categories of people (like single parents or residents of particular neighbourhoods), and the World Bank has also argued for 'indicator targeting', picking on regions, age groups, gender or other kinds of common characteristic.[132] Targeting means only that policies have to be directed at someone or something.[133] The next section considers some of the alternative focuses that might be adopted.

The focus of policy

The 'focus' of policy refers to the people or social units who the policy directly affects. This is not quite the same as saying that the policy has to be intended to help particular people, because the people who are helped are not necessarily the people who the policy is focused on. One way of helping unemployed people, for example, is to expand the economy – the intention is to reduce unemployment, but the focus of policy is the economy. Similarly, one way of reducing racial disadvantage might be to offer specialised training and education to people from minority ethnic groups in deprived areas – a fairly narrowly targeted way of achieving a very general social objective.

Social policies have commonly focused on a range of different targets. They include policies aimed at individuals, families, households, communities, different kinds of social group, and the whole society. The question of which focus is most appropriate can be taken in two different ways: to what extent these groups can be seen as the source of the problems, and to what extent it is appropriate to focus on such groups as a means of responding to the problem. I plan to concentrate on the latter, but it is still important not to lose sight of the former, because ideas about causation play such a large part in the formation of policy.

Individuals

A focus on the 'individual' is usually read as a focus on the person who has needs or problems – though, as explained in Chapter Two, these ideas are not quite the same. Approaches to problems and policy which concentrate on dealing with people one at a time are usually described as 'individualised', although sometimes you will encounter the term 'pathological'. Pathological theories are those which see the cause of a problem in terms of the unit which has the problem; so, if individuals are poor, ill-educated or homeless, a pathological explanation is one which tries to find the reasons for their condition in terms of the characteristics or behaviour of those individuals. This is an important aspect of policies, but as ever it is necessary to make a distinction between what policies are intended to do and the methods which they use; individualistic policies do not have to be pathological.

The central argument for concentrating responses on individuals is that problems are always experienced at the individual level, even if they are also experienced at other levels. Any general policy which ignores their individual position runs the risk of not doing something for at least some individuals. Even in countries where there are general policies for the support of the population as a whole, there is usually some kind of 'safety net' to protect the position of people whose circumstances are different enough to mean they would not be protected otherwise. Closely related to this argument is an argument about effectiveness. If resources are going to be used to help people in need, it is important to ensure that people in need actually benefit, and the only way to be sure of this is to protect them at the individual level. Anything else risks people being left out. The point can be supplemented by an argument about the best use of resources; concentrating resources on the people who are most in need should give the maximum benefit with the minimum waste. This is also more directly redistributive; if money is taken from the best off and given to the worst off, society will be more equal.

For individualists, the individual is not only the basic unit in society, but also the unit which undertakes obligations, makes agreements, or tries to gain redress against injustice. Individual rights have proved in practice to be a very effective strategy for the delivery of welfare. If individuals gain entitlements, and are able to claim benefits and services themselves, and to have some kind of direct redress against the providers of services or the government, it introduces an important set of checks and balances, as well as making services much more responsive to the circumstances of the individual. The US Constitution was designed around this principle; individual actions are protected by the Constitution and the

Bill of Rights, and constitutional action has been used to protect such issues as voting rights, racial equality and the rights of prisoners. A striking example is *Wyatt v Stickney*, which established a 'constitutional' right for patients in mental institutions to have decent living conditions, including adequate meals, comfortable bedding and a television set in the day room.[134]

The arguments for an individual focus are strong ones; but there are also compelling arguments against the concentration of responses on individuals. It may be desirable to identify individuals in need, but it is not easy to do; it requires some kind of test. Tests of need are likely to be intrusive and administratively complex; one of the arguments for 'indicator targeting', going for the broad range of problems rather than the individual level, is that it is often the only practical way to arrange services. The practical experience of individual testing is that it often leads to inefficiencies; many people who are entitled to benefits do not receive them. Lastly, and perhaps most important, individual tests of need are believed to be socially divisive; the effect of concentrating on the individual is often to attach blame to people for their circumstances.

Households and families

The basic units of contemporary societies are not 'individuals', but households and families. A household is defined in terms of a group of people who live together, sharing resources and responsibilities. Families are a special kind of social unit, defined in terms of a particular network of personal and social relationships and responsibilities. The two categories overlap considerably, although they are not the same – family relationships apply to many people who do not live together, and many people who live together do not have the kinds of responsibility which are encountered in a family. In the case of the family, it should be noted that there are other reasons why it might be thought of as the focus of policy – implicit in the idea of 'family policy' referred to in the previous chapter. There are certain social issues, particularly childbirth and socialisation, which are primarily addressed socially in the context of the family. That being the case, it is difficult to avoid consideration of how policies work at the level of families when these issues are discussed.

The basic argument for concentrating responses on families and households is simple enough: it is how people actually live. People do have responsibilities to each other; they do share resources; they do share their liabilities. Measures which ignore the realities run the risk of becoming unfair, although the unfairness can work in different ways. Two people who share responsibilities with each other do not have the same resources and liabilities as two people who live separately. A single parent is particularly vulnerable, because of the combination of reduced resources and much higher needs than each partner in a couple. These circumstances can only be distinguished by a rule which defines couples differently from single parents, and from single people living with others. However, this kind of rule is the source of considerable potential conflict, and it often leads to intrusive and degrading enquiries. One of the problems associated with 'household means tests' (used in Britain before the Second World War) or the aggregation of resources in a family is that it calls for different responses according to the make-up of the household. This leads to differences and inequities in the treatment, for example, of same-sex couples, adults living with their elderly parents or people living with others who are not members of their family. This can lead to some perverse effects – for example, creating financial incentives for households to break up, requiring wives to give up work when their husband is unemployed, or encouraging children to leave home.[135]

There are other problems with this kind of focus:

- It is very easy to lose sight of individuals within a household or family. This has particularly worked against women; feminists have argued that women in a household or family which is well-resourced are not necessarily able to take advantage of the resources, and in some cases these women might be classified as 'poor' although the household cannot be.[136]
- There are problems and aspects of social disadvantage which derive from the structure of households and families, which have the effect of making many policies based on them inequitable. A woman is likely, because of conventional social structures, to interrupt employment in order to care for children or others. An arrangement which ignores this situation is inequitable. But taking the situation into account – offering, for example, support and extra resources – is likely to reinforce it, creating disincentives to alternative social arrangements.
- The objections which were raised against targeting individuals all remain; it is still difficult to identify needs, and inequities arise.

Communities

It can be difficult to say just what focusing on a 'community' involves, because the term is so ambiguous. For this purpose, however, I shall concentrate on two main kinds of approach: focusing on areas, and focusing on people with existing networks of responsibility, or 'solidarities'. The arguments for and against concentration on people with common characteristics, like racial or religious groups, are slightly different, and are considered in the next section.

The main reason for concentrating on geographical areas is that problems often present themselves on an area basis. There is a good argument for this, and a bad argument. The bad argument is that problem areas are a convenient way of identifying people with problems. Problems like poverty, crime and poor health tend to be found in the same places – the visible deprivation which results has fuelled criticisms of the 'underclass' which is supposed to inhabit these areas.[137] This can be misleading. Poverty in developed economies is still widespread. Poor areas have higher proportions of poor people, but that does not mean that only poor people live there, or that there are no poor people elsewhere. The same arguments are less likely to apply in poorer countries; it will still be true that poor people will be widespread, but where many people are poor, the proportion of people who are poor within poor areas will be higher, but that does not mean that most poor people will be in such areas, or that this is necessarily an effective way of getting resources to people who are disadvantaged. The consequence is that area-based policy has often led to a misplaced distribution. Individuals, families and social groups are not necessarily served by an area-based policy; the way in which an area is defined makes a great deal of difference to whether or not it is going to receive resources; very deprived areas may gain at the expense of other areas which are also poor but not quite so badly off.

The good argument is that some problems are area-based. Geographical areas do affect the people in them – those who are not poor, as well as those who are. Issues of social organisation, economic development and the physical environment demand an area-based response. Issues like renovation, housing design, communications and social relationships need to be thought about spatially.[138]

Communities are not simply geographical units. Social networks are important as a basis for social provision. The term 'social capital' is also used to describe the value of such networks, because they clearly add to people's capacity to do things.[139] The work of voluntary organisations, the informal care given to children or older people, the connections between people in social clubs, are all examples of social capital. (The idea has been enormously helpful in persuading economists in international organisations to take account of the value of otherwise intangible social activities. Svendsen and Sørensen describe it as a 'methodological revolution ... where ... non economic resources are being included on the same footing with more visible, economic assets' – while at the same time they find that the networks they are investigating have little direct economic impact.[140])

The idea of the 'welfare state' is too often based in an artificial model in which the state makes its contribution without reference to a social context; the role of informal carers is often much more important than anything the state can offer. However, relying on such networks tends to assume patterns of responsibility which in practice lead to a disproportionate burden being adopted by particular people. 'When the word "community" is used', Elizabeth Wilson writes, '... it should be read as "family". Furthermore, for "family" we should read "women"'.[141]

Blocs

Groups of people who share common characteristics might be referred to (after Rae) as 'blocs' in society.[142] Women, minority ethnic groups, old people and disabled people are defined not so much by what they have in common as by a set of social distinctions – between men and women, disabled and non-disabled, and so forth. These distinctions are important, not so much because of the common characteristics of the groups, but because they represent social divisions – the 'fault lines' of a society. Distinctions which are important in one country might seem unimportant in another. The distinction in Northern Ireland or the Netherlands between Catholic and Protestant scarcely seems to matter in writing on social policy in Britain or the US. In Italy, regional differences are important; in Belgium, linguistic differences; in much of Africa, the key differences are tribal.

Bloc-regarding policies are policies which are aimed at social groups like this. The basic arguments for aiming at blocs are these:

- They are the source of the kinds of social disadvantage which social policy is so often trying to address. If there are problems of disadvantage, oppression or exclusion, there is a case for seeking to change the social relationships which bring them about.

- They set the context in which social policies have to operate. A policy which ignores key social divisions can often have unintended effects, and might reinforce the divisions. For example, people in relatively advantaged groups are generally paid more than those who are disadvantaged; so a pensions scheme which is based on past earnings will give greater resources to people who are already better off. Access to social services can be prejudiced by direct discrimination, but services which rely on waiting lists or residence – like housing or some forms of schooling – may also work indirectly against outsiders or people who are in less stable circumstances. One of the most trenchant and persistent criticisms of the welfare state has been that it tends to favour the middle classes, those who are already best provided for but who are in a position to use the services provided.[143]

- The approach is simple. The argument for 'indicator targeting' is at its most powerful in developing countries, where deprivation is widespread and fine distinctions are difficult to administer, but it still has its place in developed societies.

However, there are also considerable problems in addressing blocs adequately:

- There is a problem of equity. Once groups are being dealt with, the position of individuals might be ignored. The position of a social group is rarely uniformly worse than that of another group. Giving preference to women may mean that a rich woman is given priority for service over a poor man. Creating opportunities for people in minority ethnic groups might create opportunities for middle-class people in minority ethnic groups above other people in the ethnic majority.

- The kinds of group considered here, like 'women' or 'minority ethnic groups', are very mixed, referring to large numbers of people in very diverse circumstances. The way in which the problem is constructed does not necessarily reflect all the divisions. The distribution of disadvantage in the UK, for example, may be better explained by religious group than by 'race',[144] but the main statistics are drawn from crude distinctions largely based on skin colour. There is a risk that blanket policies will favour some groups over others. This was one of the problems aired in the US courts about the policy of 'affirmative action'. In the Bakke case, a Jewish student sued a college (successfully) which excluded him from a medical course in favour of an African-American student with lower grades.[145]

Society

The idea of 'society' is often contentious, and it can be difficult to identify what focusing on a 'society' means if it is not focusing on the individuals, groups and communities who make it up. It seems clear that certain kinds of policy are intended to benefit a whole society, or a nation; it is much less clear that a society can offer a focus for policy. One of the best examples is macro-economic policy – that is, policy for the whole economy; the application of monetary policy or fiscal policy is not specific to particular individuals or groups, and the effects are experienced across the economy as a whole.

In a sense, such policies are 'unfocused', because the benefits are not necessarily attributable to any particular individual or group. A public park, for example, is a facility available to anyone who wants to use it. It is very difficult to attribute specific gains or benefits to any particular users, and even any set of users. But there is little doubt in most people's minds that parks are a good idea, and the world is better for having them than not. Economists refer to such provisions as 'public goods'.[146] Pure public goods are rare. Other examples might be public services like police, transport and communications networks, although these are more disputable. They are used for the good of a society rather than identifiable groups or individuals in that society. Public goods are characterised by the absence of rivalry for their use, and their lack of exclusiveness. Some commentators add further conditions: a possible criterion is that people are unable to opt out of the good (like defence – once it is provided, everyone has it). Another potentially important factor is joint supply, so that there is no extra cost involved in providing for a further person – but there may still be a problem of congestibility, which is that public use of goods like parks and roads can change the character of the good, diminishing its value to other people.[147]

The central argument for taking a generalised approach is that it increases the welfare of society as a whole; people are better off. This is difficult to prove, because the costs are clearly attributable and the benefits are not, but it is still persuasive, because the communal benefits from parks and roads are fairly evident. There are, however, some grounds for caution. In cases where it has been possible to attribute the benefits from such policies specifically, it often turns out that their effects are inegalitarian, favouring people who are already best provided for over those who are least well off. Parks are often located in places where they serve the middle classes; transport subsidies tend to favour people who can afford to travel most; sponsored cultural activities are favoured by the middle classes. This kind of policy has been objected to on the basis that the middle classes are liable to 'hijack' welfare services – although it can equally be argued that the services which are available to middle-class people tend to be better for everyone else as well.[148]

ISSUE FOR DISCUSSION

Who is targeted in policies intended to reduce unemployment, and who should be?

FOUR

Needs

Well-being

Although the main focus of this book is on 'welfare' in a different sense, welfare can mean 'well-being'. Well-being is understood by economists mainly in terms of what people choose. Choices are mainly determined according to the value that people attach to different options, and this is affected by norms, beliefs and emotions. The choices which people make can be understood in terms of their 'utility', or perceived value to the people making the choice. Figure 4.1 shows some conventional utility curves, also called indifference curves because each curve describes a set of choices which are of equal worth to people. Well-being is increased when utility is maximised – in the graph, when choices are made from a higher curve – and reduced if utility is reduced. Utility is not necessarily increased by having more of something; once they have their basic quota, most people do not want more families, more spouses, or more parents. When people are considered as a group, welfare is held to be increased if the utility of the group is increased.[149]

The economic analysis of welfare tends to emphasise what people choose, not what they need, what is in their interests or what they ought to have. There is a strong moral argument to say that people are the best judges of their own interests, but it is not the only view; it could equally be argued that there are 'objective' interests, things without which it is not possible for people to have welfare. They might include the necessities for physical survival, education and scope for autonomous action, and many other things.[150] In other words, welfare can be seen as depending on the satisfaction of 'needs', not just of choices.

Besides the view that choices are equivalent to well-being, there are some other contentious premises taken as read made in the economic approach. The second is that people's choices are rational – which may be true when differences

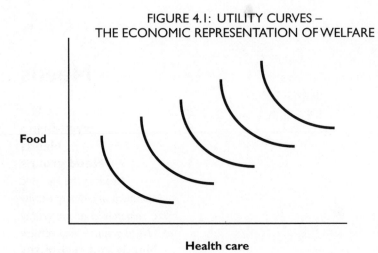

FIGURE 4.1: UTILITY CURVES –
THE ECONOMIC REPRESENTATION OF WELFARE

Food

Health care

are averaged out, but is often not true either for individuals or for a whole society. Third, people try to maximise their advantage; more is nearly always better. Figure 4.1 presents a choice between food and health care. This kind of analysis is often helpful, because people do have to make choices between different types of consumption, and this is a practical way of representing the choices; but the suggestion that people will generally prefer, given the opportunity, to have more food, or more medicine, and that this is the same thing as their welfare, is very questionable. Fourth, it is assumed that choices are expressed effectively through the combination of individual choices within a market system; it might with equal justice be argued that the market system, and the process of socialisation, conditions and constrains choices. Obesity is not rising in developed economies simply because individuals have made personal choices about food; it reflects the kind of food available, methods of preparation, methods of distribution and relative costs – not to mention all the other aspects of lifestyle which affect physical activity.[151] Fifth, analytical welfare economics generally takes it that a group is nothing more than the sum of the people who make it up: social groups, religious congregations, cities, cultural groups or nations have no specific interests that are not the interests of their individual members (although businesses, oddly enough, may have). Theoretical economists often trumpet the finding that social provision is inconsistent with the consequences of individual preferences as proof that it is incompatible with welfare.[152] All this shows is how limited the economic conception of well-being really is.[153]

Alternative views of 'well-being' are related to other kinds of value position. Well-being can be interpreted in terms of 'happiness', 'interests' or what is 'good' for people, and needs, understood as things without which they are liable to suffer.[154] One of the central problems in increasing 'well-being' is that it may not be understood in the same way by different people, and the enhancement of welfare from one perspective may be seen as its reduction from another. Bernard Shaw warns us not to do unto others as we would have them do unto us; their tastes may not be the same.

Needs

The idea of 'needs' is used to refer to things that people have to have – things which are, in some sense, 'essential'. Needs, Feinberg suggests, are 'welfare interests' – if people do not have them they will be harmed.[155] The sorts of interest that Feinberg thinks of as essential include:
* physical health and vigour;
* physical integrity and functioning;
* the absence of pain or disfigurement;
* a minimum degree of intellectual activity;
* emotional stability;
* the absence of groundless anxieties and resentments;
* engagement in a normal social life;
* a minimum amount of wealth, income and financial security;
* a tolerable social and physical environment; and
* some freedom from interference by others.[156]

This is a popular game among writers about need, who have often come up with lengthy lists of essential items. The idea of 'basic needs' used at times in the UN defines them as follows:

> Firstly, they include certain minimum requirements of a family for private consumption: adequate food, shelter and clothing, as well as certain household furniture and equipment. Second, they include essential services provided by and for the community at large, such as safe drinking water, sanitation, public transport and health, education and cultural facilities.[157]

Doyal and Gough have an even longer list, based on people's ability to participate in society.[158] Lists of this kind can never be final, because needs are socially defined and constructed. They are 'socially constructed' because they stem from a set of social relationships or they are the consequence of specific social arrangements. Children, for example, are dependent, not simply because they are weak or less competent than an adult, but because they are required to be dependent – they are not allowed to work and they have to attend school.

The 'social definition' of needs is a more complex idea. Social expectations and patterns of behaviour determine what is thought of as 'harm', as 'basic', or as 'essential'; the meaning of 'need' is necessarily defined in those terms. The issue of 'disability' offers an example. One of the key issues in understanding disability is the distinction between the idea of disability as a physical limitation – sometimes referred to as the 'medical' model – and the idea of disability as a social concept. Understood in physical terms, a disability is the functional restriction which results from some kind of limitation – the inability to perform certain tasks. The 'social model' of disability reinterprets disability in a social context, arguing that limitations are as likely to arise from social assumptions, the design of the environment and the effect that such assumptions have on opportunities and capacity. Short-sightedness or colour-blindness are not treated as disabilities; the loss of an eye or a kidney are sometimes treated as disabling conditions, but not necessarily. By contrast, amputation, disfigurement or previous experience of schizophrenia are often treated as disabilities. There may be a rationale behind this – the definition of 'disability' depends, at least in part, on the identification of conditions which are considered particularly problematic – but much of it is conventional.

The idea of needs is particularly important for social policy in practice. Needs are what many social policies, and social services, respond to. Some of the needs are 'human needs', needs which everyone shares as a human being – for example, needs for food, water, warmth and shelter. But many, and possibly most, human needs are met through mechanisms which have little to do with social policy; people are typically fed and housed through the operation of economic relationships, not by the development of collective social action or social services. The focus of social policy tends to fall, instead, on areas where needs are not met through this sort of mechanism. By contrast with a general focus on human need, social policy is concerned with circumstances where needs remain unmet, and some kind of response is required; and with people in circumstances where they are likely to experience needs which are in some way distinguishable from the general, universal needs that everyone has.

Need groups

Need groups, refer to people in similar circumstances which require some kind of collective response. They include:
- the times of the life cycle when needs are long term and predictable, like old age and childhood;
- the position of people who are restricted in their abilities to undertake ordinary activity, like people with physical disability, chronic mental illness or intellectual disabilities; and
- contingencies which people are vulnerable to at different points of their lives, like poverty, homelessness, sickness or unemployment.

Although each of these categories is narrower than a general concern with human needs might be, it is important to recognise that these circumstances affect a very wide range of people. Everyone is at some stage a child; most people will eventually be elderly. It has been argued that up to a third of the population will receive psychiatric treatment at some point in their lives, which indicates high levels of risk, while over a third of all elderly people are likely to be physically disabled at some stage. And, on the World Bank's very conservative estimate, nearly half the world's population is poor.[159]

Needs in the life cycle

Childhood. Children have, of course, the same needs as anyone else, such as needs for basic essentials or for emotional support. But they also have two distinguishable sets of needs. The first set of needs is developmental – the things a child needs to grow into an autonomous adult. Mia Kellmer Pringle identifies these as needs for love and security, new experiences, praise and recognition, and responsibility.[160] Most of these needs are not seen directly as the province of government, but one of the first provisions made for children in most countries is the provision of basic education; the Sachs report suggests that it is one of the most important initial measures to counter poverty.[161] The second set of needs is based on children's dependency; it has to be recognised that their capacity to meet their own needs is limited. The idea of childhood as a prolonged period of dependency and vulnerability is not new, but its length is; child labour laws generally date from the early 19th century, universal education in most countries is a relatively recent introduction – some developing countries are only in the process of introducing it – and the age of leaving school and entering the labour market has progressively been increased. The UN Convention on the Rights of the Child defines children's rights in terms which emphasise their dependency, and their place in the family:

> the child, for the full and harmonious development of his or her personality, should grow up in a family environment, in an atmosphere of happiness, love and understanding.[162]

It does happen, of course, that sometimes the needs of children reflect problems within the family: abuse and neglect are usually deficiencies in the family environment, for example. In those cases, it may happen that children need to be separated from the family – usually being placed with substitute family care. In most cases, however, responses to the needs of children tend to be understood in terms of the circumstances of the family. When a child is poor, it is because the family is poor – and the first step for getting support to a child, for example in engagement in education or obtaining health care, is to make arrangements to engage the family in the process. This has not always been true: compulsory education has been introduced despite the resistance of families, and schools have been used as the basis to provide children with nutrition and health care.

Parenthood. The dependent position of children largely explains the demands that the family puts on the position of parents, but it does not explain everything about it. Many assumptions are made about the position of parents: for example, that biological parents have a special bond towards children and responsibility to them, that the mother will be the primary carer, that motherhood is not compatible with a role in the labour market. These assumptions are deeply entrenched, but they are very questionable. The arguments about the position of women are probably most familiar, and they have been increasingly challenged in the course of the last 40 years or so, with the establishment of 'second-wave' feminism. The assumption of a biological link is no less capable of challenge. In France, parenthood is constructed legally as a social responsibility rather than a biological fact; parents are asked to accept children at birth, and if they do not do so, a child may be born with one parent, or no parents.

The effect of the assumptions is to condition a pattern of life where women are likely to interrupt their time in the labour market, and where family income falls at the point where a baby is born. There are different ways to respond to this. One has been to institute practices like maternity leave and maternity benefits; another has been to increase family allowances for very young children (because the point when a family is most vulnerable to a fall in income is when the child is too young to receive child care outside the family). These are further examples, then, of needs which are 'socially constructed' – needs which are made necessary by the social conditions which produce them.

Old age. Old age is another social construct, and because the conventions differ in different social services, the discussion of old people's needs does not always take place on the same basis. For the purposes of social security, 'old age' is generally equivalent to pension age; and provision for old age has been stretched to cover support for 'older people', including people who are fit, active, but have effectively withdrawn from the labour market. In the case of children, it is possible to argue that children have needs which others do not. In the case of older people, it is not really possible to do so. In so far as old people have common needs, it reflects retirement rather than old age – that is, the withdrawal or exclusion of people above a certain age from the labour market. The common needs of older people for income maintenance in retirement have been described as 'structural dependency'. Dependency reflects their economic position and relationship to society, not their capacity.[163]

When it comes to health and social care, the focus tends to shift to people who are much older – typically over 75. The condition of old people does reflect their capacities to some degree, but that degree is very limited; there is no intrinsic reason why a person who is 75 should be disabled or in ill-health. Although elderly people are much more likely than others to be in poor health, this is not a necessary aspect of old age; poor health arises not simply because of old age, but also because diet, housing, occupation and lifestyle in previous times have not been conducive to good health. Having said that, hopes for improvement in the physical capacity of elderly people over time have not been generally realised.[164] A significant minority of elderly people are physically disabled, and in Europe dementia affects about 7% of the elderly population.[165] The services which are provided for old people tend either to be dedicated to elderly people in poor health (such as residential nursing care) or based on the assumption that they are likely to be physically dependent (such as sheltered housing, which seeks to provide the reassurance to old people and their families by providing a backup or emergency service in the event of problems). In practice, large parts of general health services are necessarily used by older people, because they make up a large proportion of people in need of care.

Other common problems include poverty, reflecting an extended period on low incomes, and the low incomes of previous generations; isolation, as friends and families die or move away; bereavement, when spouses die; housing, because old people often live in older housing, which may be deteriorating or unsuitable for current needs; and the problems of carers. Many older people are looked after by their spouses, male or female, or by women in the next generation who are themselves ageing.

Limitations in ordinary activity

Physical disability. Physical disability is not one problem, but a term referring to a wide range of issues of different kinds. It includes people who have lost limbs, who are blind or deaf, who have difficulty moving or walking, who are unable to sustain physical effort for any length of time, and so on. It sometimes refers to people who are physically different even if they able to function as well as anyone else. The treatment of disability as if it was a single problem may mean that disabled people receive insufficient or inappropriate assistance. The problems that disabled people have in common are not so much their physical capacities, which are often very different, but limitations on their lifestyle. Income tends to be low, while disabled people may have special needs to be met. Socially, disabled people may become isolated, as health declines, they struggle to manage on the resources they have, and they may be socially excluded.

The World Health Organization (WHO) identifies three elements in disability: problems in bodily function or structure, which they used to call 'impairment'; problems relating to activities, or 'disability'; and problems related to social participation, which they called 'handicap'.[166] The term 'handicap' is now considered unacceptable by many people with disabilities, and the idea of a 'social model of disability' has been adopted in its place – but, as Edwards argues, 'both are couched in terms of disadvantage due to social factors'.[167] The accusation that WHO had ignored this aspect in its classification is not true.

The social model of disability understands disability in terms of the social norms and expectations which shape the experience of people with disabilities. The primary emphasis in services based on this model has been 'normalisation' (not 'independence', but the promotion of autonomy and 'social role valorisation') and 'empowerment'.

Mental illness. 'Mental illness' is a broad term covering a range of conditions. The most important are:

- *functional psychoses*, mainly schizophrenia and manic depression. Schizophrenia is itself a set of conditions rather than a single illness. It is characterised by a complex array of symptoms including, for example, a clouding of consciousness, disconnected speech and thought, variations of mood, feelings that one is being externally controlled, and hallucinations (which can be auditory, visual or tactile). Manic depression leads to severe and sometimes prolonged extremes of mood: in 'manic' phases, constantly active and extrovert; in a depressed state, withdrawn and negative. Drug therapy can be used against the cycle;
- *organic psychoses*, caused by infections, drugs, metabolic disturbances or brain traumas;
- *neuroses*, including anxiety states, phobias, obsessional states, hysteria and some depressions; and
- *'behavioural'* disorders. These are not true 'illnesses'; they are identified as disorders because people behave differently to others, not because anything is malfunctioning. Probably the most important is psychopathy (also known as 'sociopathy'), which is characterised mainly by a lack of social awareness, consideration or conscience towards others.

Mental illness is very common, but most of it is not treated by any specialist response, and in policy terms the forms of illness are less important than the experience of psychiatric care. For many years, mental illness led to prolonged hospitalisation, often in antiquated institutions intended to isolate 'mad' people from the community. The main reasons for the move away from this practice were the 'drug revolution' of the 1950s, which made treatment possible outside hospitals; disillusionment with the role played by large institutions; and substantial increases in the relative cost of institutional care. The needs of psychiatric patients have to be understood in terms of this major shift in policy and practice. The trend to 'community care' should mean, in principle, that people with mental illness are reintegrated into the community rather than isolated. Essential services include community psychiatric support, to enable continued health care and medication; social support, to counter the problems of social exclusion associated with mental illness; accommodation, including access to ordinary housing, and the provision of a range of supportive residential units, including half-way houses and staffed group homes; and access to income and employment opportunities. There has been a trend to favour shorter-term psychiatric care in general hospitals, and the use of the older hospitals has been changing, for example as a base for psychiatric services rather than a closed institution.

Intellectual disability. Intellectual disability refers to a state of slow or impaired mental development. (This is not universal usage: in the UK, the term 'learning disability' is used, but in US literature, 'learning disability' refers to special educational needs.) Although it is sometimes associated with other conditions – a high proportion of people with the most severe intellectual disabilities are also severely physically disabled – most has no physical or organic origin. (Down's syndrome, probably the best-known cause, accounts for only about a sixth of all cases.)

The effect of intellectual disability is not only a matter of 'learning', because development is important for a range of social activities, including physical competence and social functioning. The tasks which most children have to learn – like personal care, household tasks and basic education – become different for people who have to learn them at different stages of their life. The wide range of capacity consequently stretches from people with complex learning and physical disabilities, who may not be mobile or able to manage basic self-care like washing or eating, through people who have difficulties with shopping, cooking, reading, or using money, to some who can do any of these things.

Because many intellectual disabilities develop from birth or early childhood, the problems have tended to be constructed in terms of aid to families. In practice, the main support for most people with intellectual disabilities comes, not from the state or voluntary organisations, but from families. The main effect of services is to supplement the care given by these families.

Risk, vulnerability and insecurity

It has become fashionable in social policy to talk in terms of 'risk'.[168] This is a clumsy term, which lumps together issues that need to be understood distinctly. Risk can be interpreted in several ways:

- the probability that something will happen (like the risk of death or disability as a result of smoking), identified in terms of incidence over time (in epidemiological terms, 'cumulative incidence');
- a 'lack of basic security', a term which is closely identified with poverty;
- insecure circumstances, which imply that policy has to deal with unpredictable contingencies; and
- vulnerability, which is the possibility that when things happen, the vulnerable person might suffer harm.[169]

People can be vulnerable without being insecure (for example, low-paid public sector workers, who have secure employment but little capacity to deal with emergencies); they can be insecure, or 'at risk', without being particularly vulnerable (as many entrepreneurs are). It is vulnerability, rather than risk, which is the main focus of social protection policies.

Poverty. Poverty is a complex, often disputed concept. It can refer to material deprivation, economic circumstances and/or social relationships.[170] Poverty is understood as material deprivation because people who are poor are people who need something, like food, housing or clothing. The problem of 'fuel poverty', for example, happens because people are not able to heat their houses. But need is not always enough. Poverty can also be seen as multiple deprivation – not the lack of one thing, like fuel, but of several. People experience poverty, on this definition, from a constellation of different needs, which occur separately or together. More generally still, poverty can be seen as a very low standard of living – circumstances in which people are not able to access or use the goods, amenities or activities that other people can access.

Poverty refers to economic position when people lack resources, especially income. Someone who is in need but who has enough income would not be thought of as 'poor'. People can find themselves suddenly in great need – like the victims of flooding – but they do not necessarily become 'poor'. The identification of poverty with income is often interpreted in terms of economic inequality. People whose income is significantly below that of the people around them are said to be at an 'economic distance' which cuts them off from full participation in society. In Europe, for this reason, poverty is widely measured as 50% or 60% of the median income. (The median is the middle point of the income distribution.)

Poverty is also seen, however, as a matter of social relationships. The view of Amartya Sen, which has been particularly influential in international organisations, is that poverty has to be understood in terms of lack of rights and power: people experience poverty if they do not have the right to use the resources which are around them.[171] In the press and ordinary speech, people are often thought of as poor when they are receiving benefits; the problem of poverty is seen as a problem of 'dependency', and critics of the welfare system have argued that there is a 'dependency culture'. But probably the most persuasive example of this view of poverty is *Voices of the poor* [172] – the evidence that across the world, poor people describe their experiences and understanding of poverty in terms of their relationships to the society around them.

Homelessness. Homelessness occurs when people have nowhere to live. It is, like the other categories in this chapter, a socially constructed concept. That statement may sound strange, because the question of whether people have somewhere to live seems like a simple matter of fact. The problem rests in the question of where people can live. In many developing countries, people who have nowhere to live have the option of squatting – finding an occupied bit of land and putting up a shelter on it. But this is not an option everywhere. There are some countries, like India, where the system of landholding is highly developed, and the opportunities to squat are limited. The issue of homelessness is probably better understood, then, as an issue of rights – whether people have the right to occupy land, or to get access to the housing that exists, rather than a simple question of whether people have a shelter.

Homelessness is closely linked to poverty. This happens because housing and land tenure are generally distributed through markets, and in any market, the resources are most accessible to those with the capacity to command them – the money, the legal rights or the political power. (In parts of Africa, women are unable to hold rights in property, and poverty follows.[173])

If homelessness is about lack of access, and lack of entitlement, it is a broader issue than the question of whether someone has a shelter. People with limited command over resources have to occupy unfit, unsanitary and inadequate housing, because they have to take the best alternative they can. 'Homelessness' is sometimes taken to mean not just that a person has no accommodation, but also to indicate people who live in unsatisfactory and insecure accommodation.

Unemployment. Unemployment means something only where there is employment, in a formal economy. Some poorer societies lack the structures for exchange and employment; integration into a formal economy is essential for economic development and the avoidance of poverty. The process of forming such an economy often creates hardship, and vulnerability.

Employment depends on a labour market, where people are effectively able to sell their labour. People are underemployed if the pattern of employment is insufficient to meet their needs or their skills; they are unemployed if they are without work, and unable to sell their work. The patterns of labour markets are diverse. There is nothing in the structure of a modern economy that guarantees that work will be available for everyone who ought to work, and at times labour markets create only limited opportunities for employment. Casual work, for example, is work which is available only intermittently – some industries have developed offering work on a daily or weekly basis, and in some developing countries there are still patterns of work where people will sit at roadsides hoping to be picked up by an employer for a day's labour. Some work is seasonal, for example in agriculture and tourism or building, and employment will only be available at certain times of the year. Some unemployment is 'cyclical': there are times in different industries when demand is strong, and others where it is deficient. Some is 'structural' – based in circumstances where the skills and capacities of the workforce are not related to the demand for labour from employers. Arguably the decline of manufacturing industry in Western Europe has left a serious structural problem for the labour force; the European Union's 'structural funds' exist to realign the supply of labour in regional markets with demand. 'Voluntary' unemployment occurs when work is available but people choose not to work at the wage available – for example, parents and carers who withdraw from the labour market, people who are discouraged, or people who take early retirement instead.

Responses to unemployment are usually made in one of two ways: an attempt to increase the demand for jobs, by stimulating the economy, creating work or subsidising jobs, or an attempt to deal with individuals who do not work, by education and training, incentive or punishment. Employment is important for people, and it is especially important to avoid poverty, but it does not follow that everyone in a society needs to be employed. It may be possible to find ways to legitimate people's non-participation in the labour market, for example by reclassifying people who are unemployed as something else (single parents, disabled people or incapacitated people), or by removing people from the labour market through earlier retirement, military service or prolonging education.

Incapacity for work. Like unemployment, 'incapacity for work' is a term of art; it depends on the structure of an economy and the alternatives available. It can refer both to a person's individual inability to continue to do work for which the person is otherwise qualified – for example, as a result of the impact of vibration white finger on a machinery operator – or to a presumed inability to do any work in the society. Incapacity is often confused with disability, and in countries where no distinction is made between incapacity and disability, people with disabilities have to present themselves as 'incapacitated', while people who are unable to work because of a medical condition such as depression have to present themselves as 'disabled'. But people who are disabled may well be able to work, and people who are not disabled (for example, people with a specific condition that prevents them pursuing their occupation) may not be.

The reasons for responding to incapacity are distinct from the reasons for responding to disability. Services for people with disabilities are usually concerned with meeting needs, compensating for disadvantage, meeting extra costs, improving personal capacity and promoting employment, among several others. Services for people with incapacity are more likely to be concerned with social protection, income maintenance during interrupted employment and economic efficiency.

Need groups – an overview

This catalogue of needs is far from exhaustive, and the defining lines are very blurred. In the first place, the categories all cover a range of diverse conditions. 'Old people' have little in common beyond age and the expectation of retirement. The range of physical disabilities is vast. Particular issues within the broad categories, like the problems of AIDS or child neglect, convey such a complex constellation of problems that they could reasonably be classified as categories in their own right.

Second, people in each category are vulnerable to a range of other problems. People who are poor are not simply short of basic necessities, such as food, clothing, fuel and shelter; they lack security, health and the social position (like status and power) which might help them to improve their situation.[174] Homeless people tend to be poor – if they had command over resources, they could obtain housing; their conditions create problems with health;[175] often they are also marginalised in their community (because where there are social networks on which they can draw they do so).[176] Mental illness is commonly associated with problems in behaviour and communication, which have a profound effect on social relationships and the ability to function in a social context. People with mental illness are vulnerable to poverty, because they are unable to participate in the labour market, and to homelessness, because in addition to their poverty the networks of family and friends which others rely on are disrupted.[177]

Despite the limitations of such categorisations, there is a purpose in considering people in terms of such 'groups'. Even if the problems which people experience are complex and individuated, there are common patterns: the circumstances of people in the different groups reflect a common social experience. The exclusion of old people from the labour market has a profound effect on their circumstances, and common problems generally call for some kind of common pattern of response. In some cases it is the response itself, like the requirement that children should attend compulsory education, which defines people as constituting a group. People with mental illness have varied circumstances, but the most common response – the experience of psychiatric care – has itself created common patterns of need, notably issues related to institutional care and subsequent discharge. Service responses are commonly planned in terms of the client groups to whom they are directed.

Box 4: Underclass or moving target?

Focusing on the poor depends on identifying who the poor are. Much of the attention to the problem in poverty research since Victorian times has been concerned with identification of the poor as a static group; the implicit assumption has been that once poor people are identified, it is possible to respond to their conditions. Key concepts like the 'culture of poverty', the 'cycle of disadvantage', 'intergenerational poverty' and the 'underclass' depend on the idea that poverty is longstanding, continuous and difficult to escape from.[178] There is a widespread belief that poverty is passed from one generation to another: 'if we do nothing, these children will not only be born poor but they will live poor and die poor'.[179]

Since the 1970s, however, there has been increasing work done on the dynamics of poverty – the changes in people's lifestyles and prospects which happen over time. In most developed countries where work has been done, people are vulnerable to poverty for indeterminate periods, at different times and stages of their lives.[180] Some circumstances lead to people being poor for several years – examples are the poverty of old people, and the poverty of people with disabilities – but most people who are poor are poor for relatively short periods – perhaps three or four years, typically because of unemployment, limiting illness or relationship breakdown. Conversely, many people – and in the UK, most people – are likely to have been poor for an extended period (at least a year) at some stage in the relatively recent past.[181] Poverty leads to disadvantage – that is, to worse prospects than others have – but that is not the same as saying that people who are poor now will continue to be poor. Poor people are not, however, generally poor throughout their lives. The idea that poor people have poor children, who grow up to be poor adults, is an important myth – it has had major effects on policy – but it is misconceived.

The constantly changing pattern of poverty creates a problem in choosing a focus. If there is not a clearly definable population which is poor, it is difficult to work out a policy which can respond to the problems. Dealing with ephemeral issues like low income or access to housing does not prevent poverty. The people who appear to be poor at one point in time will shortly be replaced by others. Policy makers like to think that their responses are going to be effective; they may think that there is little to be gained politically in pursuing a policy where the waters close over any action that is taken. Common responses have been:

- to fix on targets which will not change so rapidly (for example replacing bad housing);
- to emphasise different aspects of policy (for example the European emphasis on 'social protection' in adverse circumstances, rather than the relief of poverty);
- to emphasise the underlying conditions of economic development, so that those who become poor will have improved circumstances and opportunities; or
- to focus resources on the most disadvantaged people within the ranks of the poor.

'Old' needs and 'new' needs. In recent years, a number of writers have suggested that the focus on certain need groups has been superseded by the need to respond to new patterns of social need, arising out of a changing economic and social environment. These patterns include, for example, single parenthood, long-term unemployment, the needs of young people, pressure to balance participation in the labour market with family care, and 'atypical employment biographies'.[182] These contingencies have contributed to a perception of 'new poverty', especially in Northern Europe.[183] However, there is nothing 'new' about most of these needs, or about policies to respond to them; the problems of single parents, long-term unemployed people and the working poor were central to the Poor Law Report of 1834,[184] while issues related to gender became a progressively greater part of the social policy agenda throughout the 20th century. What is relatively 'new' – although still not that new – is the recognition in various European régimes that welfare structures built around a regular employment record or stable domestic circumstances are unable to provide for many social contingencies. The Beveridge Report, in the UK, developed provision to include a casualised labour force, but failed to account for issues like divorce; the gaps in the system became a concern with the 'rediscovery of poverty' in the 1960s. In France, the watershed came in the 1970s, with the recognition that the generalisation of social security would not extend to people without work records; in Germany, it arguably happened only later, with the reunification of East and West.

The idea of 'new' needs may have some value, however, as a political critique. One of the besetting problems of the welfare states has been complacency – the assumption that provision is basically satisfactory, and that people who fall through the net must have misbehaved in some way. The argument runs that because society has changed, so must welfare provision. This serves both as a salutary reminder that there are problems to be dealt with and as a convenient political excuse to engage with long-neglected issues.

Needs and responses

'Needs' refer, in part, to problems which people experience: people who suffer from mental or physical impairments, for example, are deemed to have 'needs' on that basis. Many of the needs described in this chapter are clearly socially constructed. Because 'problems' are often social, needs are too.

Needs are not simply problems, however; they are also needs for something. We speak of needs for money, for domestic help or for residential care. Needs have to be understood, not only in terms of problems, but also in terms of responses. People are thought of as being in need not simply because they have a problem, but because they are lacking something which will remedy that problem.[185] There are circumstances in which people with a degree of impairment have no identifiable 'needs' as a consequence: for example, some people with mild dementia continue to function normally in their own home.[186] The response to a problem, like the problem itself, has to be seen in terms of the society in which it is happening. The definition of a need depends not just on the recognition of a problem – like disability, child abuse, old age and so forth – but an association of that problem with a particular kind of response. Items which might not have been thought of as 'needs' a hundred years ago – like inside toilets, washbasins or children's toys – have become recognised as needs because their absence presents problems and other more pressing problems no longer obscure their importance. Other items which scarcely existed a hundred years ago – like telephones, computers, cars and fridges – are becoming needs as they become the main route to provide socially necessary facilities (communications, transport or food storage). This also means that needs change over time.

There is no simple, fixed relationship between the kind of problems that people experience and the kinds of response which have to be made. Impairments are mainly responded to by trying to cure or repair the loss of ability; but impairments are only part of a general experience of disablement. Disability can be responded to by addressing an underlying medical condition, through treatment; it might be responded to by addressing the functional problems created by it – which implies either that a service is provided to help a person overcome functional limitations (for example occupational therapy) or that services themselves seek to overcome those limitations (for example the provision of meals and home helps). But it might also be responded to by seeking to change social relationships. This can be done through the development or maintenance of relationships (in theory, one of the purposes of day care); reducing social disadvantage (which can be achieved by providing services, and by offering special facilities like holidays); or compensating for that disadvantage by the development of alternative patterns of social life (for example through sheltered housing).

It is difficult, then, to establish precisely what services people 'need'. There is often not just one possible response, but a range of options. People who are socially isolated might have that isolation reduced in a number of ways: for example by introducing a number of people into their home, like voluntary visitors or even 'companions'; by bringing them into contact with people outside their home, through lunch clubs or day centres; and by changing the home, commonly via sheltered housing or residential care. People who need housework done might have it done through domestic assistance, but they might also have it done through substitute family care or residential care. Strictly speaking, there can be no such thing as a 'need' for a lunch club or a home help; rather, there are needs which services of this kind may be able to satisfy to a greater or lesser degree.

The position is also complicated because people may be able to deal with their problems in different ways. Many of the 'needs' attributed to elderly or disabled people, including cooking, cleaning and company, would not be experienced in the same way by a rich person; it is possible to buy the services of a cook, a housekeeper or a companion. Once the arrangement has been made the disabled person would not usually be thought of as still in need; and that implies that needs are, among other things, subject to the amount of money that a person has. This also means that, in discussions of social welfare policy, it is difficult to separate the discussion of needs from the question of responses. Arguments about need are as likely to be arguments about resources as they are about the extent of problems.

'Needs' are not neutral concepts. Like most ideas in social policy, they have a normative purpose – they are used to make an argument for provision. It is implicit in the idea of need that some kind of response is possible – and it generally follows that something must be done. I have argued, in previous work, that every statement of need is, explicitly or implicitly, a claim. Usually, in discussions of social policy, claims of need can be seen as a form of claim made against services.[187] The next part of the book moves on from consideration of problems and needs, to views of how responses can be made.

ISSUE FOR DISCUSSION

Are there needs which should not be met?

Part Two
Policy

FIVE

Public policy

The nature of policy
Formal processes: law and the state
Governance
Public policy
Comparing policies

The nature of policy

The idea of 'policy' is ambiguous, and often infuriatingly elusive. Politicians, when they use the word, generally seem to have in mind some sense of a deliberate set of approaches – the things they have chosen to do. When this is looked at in more detail, however, it fragments into a wide range of disparate issues. Hogwood and Gunn pick up a range of meanings of the term.[188] A policy might be, among other things,

- a label for a field of government activity and involvement – like 'family policy' or 'transport policy';
- an expression of a desired state of affairs or general purpose – 'our policy is to support the family';
- a set of specific proposals;
- the decisions made by government;
- a process of formal authorisation (like the policy of a local authority, as opposed to 'practice' or 'agency discretion');
- a strategy, programme or agenda for action – a defined sphere of activity involving particular, interrelated measures;
- a theory or model where actions are assumed to produce certain results. Townsend argues that social policy 'can be defined as the underlying as well as the professed rationale by which social institutions and groups are used or brought into being to ensure social preservation or development'.[189] Maintenance - keeping things as they are - is also a policy decision. Policy can be can be implicit, 'unspoken and even unrecognised'. On this view, it is possible to read back from the results to a set of intentions, and even to 'non-decisions' – points where policy fails to address issues because of its underlying assumptions;[190]
- the product of a process of decision making. This understanding of is mainly used in academic discussions of the subject: when people ask what a 'policy' is they are actually looking at what has come out of the policy

process. Stone, for example, describes policy formation as a process of negotiation or bargaining in the 'polis' or political community.[191] Policy is not rational; it is formed through bluff, bargaining, the use of influence, loyalty, horse trading and so on.

When welfare is considered in terms of 'policy', outcomes are often attributed, in some way, to design – that is, to the deliberate intentions of policy makers. The description of methods and outcomes is often used as a way of identifying such intentions. There are dangers in trying to read intentions from effects; there can be a world of difference between what policy makers intend and what actually happens. At the same time, understanding what policies are intended to do is an important part of understanding social policy in a more general sense.

Formal processes: law and the state

Many social policies are made and developed through the state. The limits of 'the state' are not always easy to define, because the term is used very loosely; depending on the context, it can be taken to mean several things. Berki defines the state as 'an institutional structure whose primary and distinctive function is the maintenance of authority in a given territorial unit'.[192] The narrow interpretation of this structure is that the state is concerned with the formal political institutions of a society. A wider view of the state would describe it as the means through which governmental power is exercised (which could include, for example, schools or hospitals) or the full range of government activity (which might include sponsorship of the arts). The formal political institutions of a society are conventionally classified in three categories: legislative (or law making), judicial, and executive (concerned with government and the civil service). The US has a strong division of labour between the different branches, referred to as the 'separation of powers', and this has been influential in the government of many other countries. Social policy in practice tends to focus on executive functions, but before moving too strongly in that direction, it is helpful to consider the legislative framework.

The making of law is central to the activities of government: law is an important part of how a modern state exercises power. Lay people often think of law in terms of 'criminal' law, which is mainly concerned with prohibition and punishment; it is through criminal law, for example, that people are sent to prison, that parents can be punished for neglecting or maltreating children, or that people are protected against fraud and corruption. But this is only a small part of the role of law in society. Law is, much more generally, a system of rules and procedures through which the actions of individuals and people collectively can be regulated and governed. Hart argues that laws can be classified as primary or secondary rules. Primary rules set the terms by which other laws can be determined. They include rules of recognition – systems for recognising formal authority, and the laws themselves; rules of change, which make alteration in the rules possible; and adjudication, which is necessary for application and enforcement of the rules. Secondary laws are the rest.[193]

Law making is important in social policy in four ways:

- *Constitutional law.* Laws form the framework through which policies are exercised. The powers of institutions have to be defined by law; they have to be given the competence to act. The institutions of the European Union have been working to establish competence in various areas related to welfare, including health, education, gender issues and social security; the European Commission is still in the process of attempting to identify a role in relation to older people, disabled people, racial minorities and people who are poor.[194]

- *Rule making.* Law is used to establish the rules by which a policy is pursued. Law has been described as a system of 'norms', that is, expectations which are coupled with sanctions in order to produce particular effects.[195] So, for example, a law which states that people must send their children to school is a positive norm (requiring people to do something); a law which states that people must not do something, such as renting out houses which are unfit for human habitation, is a negative norm. But legal principles are not confined to what people should and should not do. One of the implications of constitutional law is that different bodies require their roles to be defined, and there is an extensive use in many systems of 'permissive' law, which gives organisations the power to undertake actions at their discretion.

- *Administrative law.* Law is used to define executive processes – that is, the means by which services are to be delivered. Although social security systems have developed independently from the state in many countries, there has usually come a point when the state steps in. Legislation has been introduced to establish procedures by which the state could take on most of the responsibility for social protection. Similarly, and often by the same processes, laws are used to regulate the conduct of the administration.

- *Enforcement.* There is often a negative sanction attached to laws, so that people or organisations who disregard them are liable to suffer some kind of penalty. A penalty against an organisation is not necessarily a penalty against the people who work for it, and it is sometimes difficult to think of any penalty which can be effective against a governmental organisation determined to break the rules; 'respect for the rule of law' is often the main sanction available.

There is a considerable overlap between the establishment of norms and the provision of a means of enforcement. There are, however, many examples of laws which are not enforced, or enforceable. Some laws are exhortatory, encouraging people to act in a particular way. A Japanese law for the welfare of older people, for example, states:

> The aged shall be loved and respected as those who have for many years contributed toward the development of society, and a wholesome and peaceful life shall be guaranteed to them.[196]

> Other laws offer guidelines rather than firm norms. The European Union has developed a system of what is called 'soft law', consisting partly of recommendations and partly of generalised agreement about principles, which national governments are free to interpret.[197]

Social policy is not only made through the process of legislation. It can be made that way, in so far as laws are passed which set out the policy, but it is also possible for policies to be developed at other levels, by the executive arms of government. Delegation of authority to the executive is fairly common, because much of what happens in social policy takes place at a level which legislators are inclined to think is beneath their notice. These processes are not very different in principle, however, because in a properly constituted government the executive has to be empowered by the legislative authority before decisions can be taken.

Governance

There is a common misconception about governments, both in academic literature and in the popular mind, that their actions are dependent on force. The 'command theory of law' developed by Austin[198] supposes that government works by telling people what to do. Compulsion works by imposing sanctions (that is, negative consequences or punishments) on people. This is a characteristic part of criminal law. The ability to impose sanctions almost certainly has a wider effect on compliance with a government's wishes. Because governments can require people to do things, they often do not have to. For example, it is compulsory for parents to arrange education for their children: in most cases this means that they have to send their children to school. There are relatively few people who fail to do so, and that means that the direct use of coercion, even if it underlies many aspects of policy, is limited in practice. At the same time, some sanctions are widely disregarded: for example, laws about dog licensing in the UK fell into disuse before their abolition because of non-compliance.

   The central problem with the command theory is not that governments cannot compel people, even if there are limits; it is that it relies on a distortion of perspective. Governments do much more than this, and much of what they do has very little to do with compulsion. Probably the most important role of government, which is implied by the discussion of law, is the establishment of rules and procedures – a framework for social life. The rules established by governments shape people's personal lives – for example through marriage, family law and property ownership – as well as the structure of organisations, like education and employment. People's ability to function in society depends heavily on their entitlements – Sen argues that entitlements are fundamental to the issue of poverty[199] – and societies where people are excluded from such arrangements, like the societies where women cannot own property, have commensurate problems. Regulation is the process of establishing a framework of rules; it is fundamental to the process of government.

In the liberal democracies of the West, there is a presumption that any intervention that is made by government should be minimal. Rather than regulating or coercing people, then, most democratic governments will begin with persuasion. This takes the form of government-sponsored education, propaganda, advertising and other means of opinion-forming – although it can stretch, potentially, to lies, indoctrination, even state-sponsored religions. Beyond propaganda, governments can seek to encourage or discourage particular sorts of activity in other ways – typically through the use of selective rewards or penalities. Governments subsides activities they wish to encourage, and they may try to deter other action through taxation. In the context of social policy, this is often described (slightly misleadingly) in terms of 'incentives' and 'disincentives'.[200] An incentive offers a potential gain to people who change their behaviour in a particular way – like a prize for invention or a financial reward for desired behaviour, like marriage. Disincentives, conversely, imply potential penalties or costs. People do not respond proportionately to rewards or punishments,[201] or directly; the effectiveness of this kind of action depends strongly on context and culture.

Governments do not have to confine themselves to trying to influence the actions of other people. In some cases, where they consider that the issues are sufficiently important, they do the work themselves. They can buy things for the population, acting as a purchaser; they can run industries; they can provide services. They are major employers – sometimes they are the most significant employer in a national economy. Governments, in the modern world, are economic actors as much as they are political ones. Although some aspects of this kind of intervention have become unfashionable – it is less common than it was 40 years ago for governments to act as bankers for industrial start-ups, to manage agricultural production or to develop industrial sectors themselves – it is still fairly common for governments to take direct responsibility for defence, the economic infrastructure (like roads and rail) and of course the social services.

Figure 5.1 outlines some of the principal methods of governance. It is not a complete account of the way that governments operate – I have not even touched on the ways the public sector can shape people's lives – but it serves to illustrate two main points. The first is diversity. Governments have a huge range of different options open to them in pursuit of their political aims. The second is the limitations of government behaviour. The diversity of options reflects both a reluctance to use straightforward compulsion and at times the difficulty which governments have in achieving their ends by any of the means available to them.

FIGURE 5.1: METHODS OF GOVERNANCE

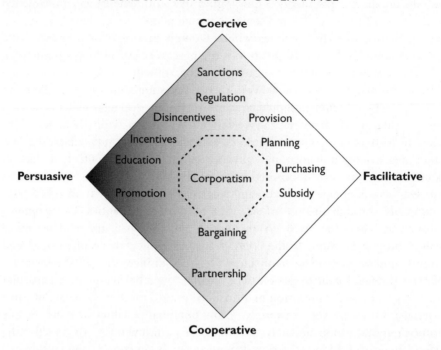

In recent years, the emphasis in government has consequently fallen on partnership, negotiation and collaboration, rather than direction and command structures. Governments are being encouraged to accept the limitations of what they can do. This is particularly true of governments in developing countries, and the 'encouragement' is being done by international organisations like the International Monetary Fund and the World Bank. In part, this reflects a change in political and economic thinking, which emphasises the importance of independent actors in economic development. It also reflects, however, a more realistic view about the capacity of governments; many governments in the poorest countries have limited capacities, and despite often worthy aspirations, their capacity to act, to establish frameworks and to regulate the environment is limited. Ideally, where a government has the capacity, the government will be able to plan services by encouraging and developing patterns of service; several European governments work on a 'corporatist' model, structuring the roles of a range of agencies within the framework of the government's priorities. In developing countries, the process of negotiation and bargaining is more likely to reflect the uneven balance of power between government, non-governmental organisations, international agencies and private enterprise; often governments in developing countries have less influence than other parties.

Box 5: Perverse incentives in family benefits

The accusation is frequently levelled against governments that their actions lead to unexpected, unanticipated effects. There are criticisms of 'perverse incentives' – measures which lead people to act in the opposite way from that intended. The main arguments are that:

- people have more children in response to economic incentives;
- young, poor mothers are particularly affected;
- there is an incentive to have an illegitimate child; and
- that by giving such incentives, benefits trap people in dependency.[202]

There is very little evidence to show that financial incentives do affect the decision to have children. The problem is that any data which might seem to show an effect are massively outweighed by the swell of data showing factors which have a greater influence – factors such as the impact of infant mortality, the changing role of women, increasing education, later marriage and the availability of contraception.[203] On UNICEF figures, the countries where fertility has increased over 30 years have been the poorest: in nearly every other case there has been a fall.[204]

The second part of the argument is that there is a differential impact of incentives on poor mothers than there is on others. This is possible. In developed economies, the numbers of young, poor mothers have generally fallen, in line with the general reduction in fertility. As the prospects of women have improved, the numbers of children born to all teenage mothers has fallen. Teenage motherhood mainly affects a residual group, for whom the same prospects are not available. For young women in that group, motherhood may be the best available option for personal development.[205] That is why teenage motherhood is more prevalent in richer countries among poorer women, those who have lower educational achievement and those who lack career prospects.

The concern with illegitimacy goes back to the arguments of the Victorian Poor Law, which was fuelled by a concern about 'bastardy'. Illegitimacy has been treated as a matter of concern both because children without fathers are more likely to be deprived,[206] and because mothers are likely to be dependent, although the same arguments would also apply to divorce. There are strong links between marital dissolution and unemployment, whether the unemployment precedes the marriage or happens during the marriage.[207] Illegitimacy is directly associated with poverty; women who are poor for a period prior to pregnancy are much more likely to have children when they not married.[208]

The reasons for the association are disputed. Murray suggests that higher benefits have had the effect of making women on benefits more desirable as partners.[209] Wilson argues by contrast that single parenthood stems from a shortage of 'marriageable' or economically stable males, and comments that 'the increasing inability of many black men to support a family is the driving force behind the rise of female-headed families'.[210]

The final issue to be considered is the question of whether benefits inculcate dependency. This is not consistent with the evidence,[211] for three reasons:

- Welfare does not appear substantially to affect unemployment.[212]
- The assumption that welfare leads to long-term dependency is largely untrue. The evidence on the dynamics of poverty in several developed countries is that many people pass through stages when they have low incomes, that dependency tends to be episodic, and that the composition of the dependent population fluctuates.[213] The countries where people are poor for very long periods of time tend to be those with less welfare provision.
- The problems are created by the systems that focus on the poor. In so far as there are inducements to dependency, they are produced by systems that require people to be poor as a condition of receiving benefit.

The discussion of 'perverse incentives' is partly concerned with effects, but it is also about morality. Murray asserts that 'people must be held responsible for their actions'.[214] This is not about incentives at all: it is about rewards and punishments. Illegitimacy and serial monogamy are often treated as 'immoral' behaviour, which means that circumstances associated with poverty are likely to attract moral condemnation. The language of incentives is used to justify giving rewards for good behaviour, or punishing people for bad behaviour, and it is used to convey a moral message, about behaviour which is approved or disapproved of. Like many debates in social policy, this one does not seem to be about the evidence; it has much more to do with moral judgements.

Public policy

Governments operate and manage a range of practical activities. The broad areas of policy are commonly divided into economic policy, foreign policy and 'domestic' policy; in those terms, social policy might be seen as a subcategory of domestic policy, along with law, and other issues like culture, environmental policy or the public services. This conventional distinction does not work particularly well, however; it seems clear that aspects of social policy cut across all these fields (including economic and foreign policy). It also seems to interpret 'policy' in a fairly general sense; public policy in this sense is whatever government happens to do, or not to do.

The area of activity which is run directly by government is referred to as the 'public sector'. This includes a wide range of activities, including for example direct economic engagement in publicly owned industries, the business of managing government, such as the civil service, and the provision of services to other agencies, like government laboratories or defence procurement.

Part of the role of government is to provide services. The public services are a broad class of services, generally within the public sector although some may be operated by autonomous or voluntary agencies. Public services have four key characteristics. First, public services are 'public', which is to say that they are developed for reasons of public policy. They are intended in principle to meet the objectives of governments, donors or governing bodies – rather than the aims of purchasers, clients or producers. (They are not necessarily public in the sense of being developed by governments. The provision of medical care in Europe has been heavily influenced by the position of mutual societies and occupational insurance.) Second, they are services, in the sense that they do things for members of the public. Third, they are redistributive: the people who pay for services are not the people who receive them. And fourth, public services are operated as a trust. The duties of a trustee are held towards the body that commissions the service, rather than the service's recipients. A public health service is commissioned by government for the benefit of citizens. A private health service is commissioned by consumers for their own benefit.

Social services are a subcategory of public services. If there is a good reason why libraries and roads are 'public' services while education and housing are 'social', it is not immediately obvious. Conventionally, a distinction is made between public services, like roads, sewers and libraries, and social services, but the distinction is more than a little arbitrary. It is not at all clear why receiving weekly benefit should be thought of as 'welfare', when having the use of a road is not. None of the kinds of explanation which might be given sums the difference up. Public services are available for everyone; but so are some social services, typically including in Europe education and medical care in hospitals. Both public and social services are usually provided by the state. Public services are sometimes charged for; so are some social services, like public housing. Ultimately, the distinction seems to be purely conventional – it is just the way in which the services have traditionally been referred to. (At the same time, there is an important implication in the idea of a social service, which has to be recognised: it is the assumption that there is something different about the recipients of social services. Public services are for everyone; social services are often thought of, however irrationally, as being for people who have some kind of dependency. Services for older people and children are generally, then, for 'dependent' groups; services which are used by everyone are not.)

The state can provide the services directly, by the financing and employment of different social services. (Some writers, particularly in the US, describe this as a 'welfare state'.) Governments can also provide indirectly through the purchase of services for their citizens. Direct and indirect provision amount to much the same thing, because in both cases the state can effectively determine the supply of services and what demands will be met if it so chooses. However, there are some important differences. One is ideological: where governments are convinced that direct provision is intrinsically immoral or unproductive, indirect provision allows a way round. The second is practical: the purchase of services on the private market makes it possible to use the facilities of the market, in particular its responsiveness to demand, and there have been cases (notably in the provision of private residential care for older people) where the response rate has been very rapid indeed. Conversely, a government which elects to use the private market is subject to its constraints. It will have limited control of effective supply and demand – what a government is prepared to pay for health care is usually much less than what a private citizen faced with pain, disability or the prospect of death will pay. It can influence supply both by acting as a major buyer and by imposing constraints on suppliers, but it is liable to find itself acting as a guarantor to inefficient suppliers (because most social services cannot simply be allowed to go out of business).

Often, government is the most important service provider; in most cases, it is also the provider of last resort, offering services when no one else does.[215] Despite the importance of these roles, it has to be emphasised that much of the provision of welfare – and consequently of social policy – does not stem from governments at all. There is a distortion of perspective in the English-speaking literature, because the history of social policy in Britain and the US does conventionally begin with state action. The English Poor Law was the first national provision for welfare, introduced 1598-1601, and it lasted for 350 years. The principles were exported to several other countries, including both those that were part of the British Empire and others that were not – there were direct imitations of the Poor Law in some eastern states in the US. This was not, however, the trend in many other countries. Welfare systems in many countries developed through a combination of independent, mutualist or occupational organisations. In some countries, the trades unions developed systems of support; in others, employers did. The welfare states intervened in social policy fairly late in the day, often with the intention of extending such provision to those who had been left out. For example, the French *régime général* was introduced after the Second World War to include or 'generalise' provision to about half the workforce which did not have social protection. The system of unemployment insurance is still operated by a formal partnership of employers' organisations and trades unions, rather than by the state. In health services, similarly, the benefits provided by the state are supplemented for most people in employment by the *mutualités*, independent friendly societies which offer relatively generous coverage.

There is often a complex interplay between the decisions made by governments and those made by independent providers. The state has a key role in the regulation of welfare; it establishes the rules and settings under which welfare services operate. Moran and Wood, writing about the control of medical care, categorise four main types of regulation: regulation of market entry (such as who can become a doctor and where they can set up), regulation of competitive practices (like advertising), regulation of market structures (through legal rules concerning what can be bought and sold), and regulation of remuneration and prices.[216]

In some cases, governments replace independent provision; in others, they build around it. The state can use the power of purchase; it can decide where to place its resources. There are fiscal controls, through subsidy and taxation; the state can offer financial incentives to undertake certain activities, and conversely it can tax activities which it does not want people to undertake. There are legal controls, for example registration and inspection, which can be used to limit entry to the market; and it can require some firms to offer services as a condition of operating in other fields (for example by insisting that all employers should offer maternity pay). In political terms, this is sometimes described as 'corporatism', which refers (among many other things) to a system of interest group representation and state intervention in which the state bargains with other agencies, delegating functions and co-opting them into the structure of power.[217]

Comparing policies

When policy makers or service administrators are trying to review the options for policy, a common first step is to examine what other people have done. Innovation is difficult, often expensive, and fraught with problems; if someone else has worked out how things can be done, it saves considerable time and effort. Major developments, like Bismarck's social insurance scheme or the growth of high-rise housing, were influential because once they were established in some places they offered, or seemed to offer, practical solutions to complex problems in others.

The decision to adopt or transfer policies is often made on the basis of a comparison of benefits and services in one place with those in another. Several texts in comparative social policy rely mainly on the description of the range of services provided, and a number focus on particular services (for example on social security, child protection or health care finance). Mitchell has identified five main approaches to the comparison of welfare in different countries.[218]

- *Comparing explicit policy*. The first approach is to compare welfare provision in terms of the explicit terms in which actions are taken. Flora and Heidenheimer reviewed the historical development of welfare in Europe and America. They found that welfare often develops on similar lines, and that it is possible to chart the growth of certain systems – like protection for industrial injury and social insurance – as following certain well-worn paths.[219]
- *Comparing inputs*. Inputs are the resources which go into welfare provision. Castles' comparisons of welfare in Organisation for Economic Co-operation and Development (OECD) countries depend primarily on expenditure.[220]
- *Comparing production*. The third approach is concerned with the production of welfare – the rules and structures through which services operate. Esping-Andersen defines the positions adopted by different welfare states through evidence on the organisation and delivery of specific services – for example, whether or not benefits are means tested, or whether they are given by discretion or as of right – as the basis for an overall assessment of

the characteristics of different welfare systems. For example, he analyses pensions for:

> degree of program corporatism (number of status–defined separate pension plans); the etatist bias (expenditure on civil service pensions as a percentage of GDP); the relative importance of private-sector pensions (individual and occupational pension expenditures as a percentage of total pension spending); and what might be called the social security bias (proportion of total pension spending that is neither private nor civil service).[221]

The detailed work in this can be criticised, because he lets a very limited range of indicators determine his classifications,[222] but the basic principle behind it is still important – that the way in which things are done matters in its own right, and is probably the best way of representing the effects of different principles in practice.

- *Comparing operations.* Comparisons can be made of the detailed operation of benefits and services – what they do, how they are paid for, and who runs them.
- *Comparing outcomes.* The case can be made that what matters about welfare is not what is intended, nor what the process is, but whether or not people benefit from it. Social security policy, for example, has been greatly concerned with the delivery of benefits, and in particular whether benefits are means tested or not;[223] but there have been arguments for a different kind of assessment. The idea of the income 'package' has been developed to judge whether or not social security is effective; what matters in the package is not so much how it is delivered as whether it reaches the people who need it, and whether it is adequate.[224] This is the basis of the work done by the Luxembourg Income Study in assessing and comparing social security systems in different countries.[225]

These approaches are not completely distinct, and there is no reason why they should not be tackled simultaneously, but they do represent different kinds of emphasis, and they suggest different ways of understanding policy.

Comparisons of this type can be very useful for those looking for new ideas and approaches, but there are important pitfalls. Finding appropriate data for comparisons is not easy. Leichter points to five problems:

1. Policy measures are not directly comparable.
2. Some countries falsify their data.
3. There are peculiarities in the way that data are collected in different countries.

4. Often spending is unreported or hidden. Because of the different distribution of public, private, voluntary and informal welfare in different countries, not everything is likely to be counted.
5. There is variation in the cost of goods and services, which makes it difficult to compare inputs.[226]

Some of these problems point to the difficulty of understanding services and policies without knowing something about the context in which they operate. Understanding the operation of maternity benefits, for example, requires more than a comparison of rates and conditions. The benefits need to be set in the context of a range of services, including health services, antenatal and postnatal care, and alternative benefits, before it is possible to work out what they are really worth. The role of the benefit depends on the conditions of the labour market, including the participation of women and the wages which the benefits replace. And it is difficult to understand the extent to which such benefits protect women or families without knowing the circumstances of families and the position of women.

It follows that this kind of material has to be understood in its social context. The effect of treating welfare policies in isolation from their social context can be fundamentally misleading as to their potential effects. An adequate base for comparison cannot afford to stop with the operation of services themselves, and a full understanding of welfare systems calls for much more than an understanding of processes and procedures.

ISSUE FOR DISCUSSION

Policy is sometimes represented in terms of what is not done, as well as what is. If a government does not deal with child abuse, or deals with it only in part, is it still responsible for what happens?

SIX

Principles and values

Principles and values
Key values in social policy
The functions of social policy
Ideology and social welfare
Political ideologies
Left and right

Social policy, unusually in the social sciences, is directly concerned with normative issues – that is, with values: not just with what is the case, but what ought to be. social policy is not just about describing social issues or problems; it tries to change them, and the very fact of trying – the development of services and social responses – means that even if the policy is unsuccessful, things will be different. Titmuss argued that 'The definition, for most purposes, of what is a social service should take its stand on aims; not on the administrative methods and institutional devices employed to achieve them'.[227]

One of the best-known examples of this is Wilensky and Lebeaux's distinction between residual and institutional welfare.[228] This is partly a distinction between methods, but also a distinction between approaches to welfare, and ultimately between different moral views of what welfare is for. A *residual* model of welfare is one where welfare is seen as a 'safety net'. In normal circumstances, people should not have to depend on welfare; what happens, instead, is that they live on their own or their family's resources, and the only people who need to claim welfare will be those who are unable, for whatever reason, to manage on these resources. Welfare in these circumstances is described as 'residual' because it is for those who are left out. The *institutional* model of welfare is one where need and dependency are accepted as normal in society, or 'institutionalised'. Titmuss argued that the 'states of dependency' which people experienced had to be accepted as a normal part of social life. We are all children at some stage, we are all likely to be sick, or to be old; an institutional system is one which recognises social responsibility for these needs and makes general provision accordingly. The residual model of welfare leaves social protection, in most cases, to the resources of the individual; the institutional model is based in acceptance of social responsibility for socially induced conditions of dependency.

This kind of pre-packaging of ideas has been enormously influential, and there have been many imitations. To make sense of it, however, we need to understand what kind of thing these models are. They were never simply intended as 'ideal

83

types', models to which reality can be compared. Rather, they began from a historical reality – the transition from the English Poor Law (discussed in Box 6) to the welfare state. For Titmuss, values shaped the pattern of social responses, and the pattern of responses shaped the kinds of methods and policies which different governments applied. Institutional welfare was close to his vision of an ideal society.[229] It began with ideas like rights and citizenship, and consequently sought to include everyone with a pattern of comprehensive or 'universal' services. This approach led to the National Health Service – public, universal, and free at the point of delivery. Residual welfare was based in a negative, often reluctant approach to welfare, concerned to minimise it to the greatest degree.

Understanding the component elements of these models is partly about principles and values, and partly about the strategies developed to deliver services. This chapter considers the aims, values and principles that guide policy; the following chapter looks at the approaches that are associated with them – approaches like safety nets, redistribution, collective provision and the welfare state.

Principles and values

Statements of values prescribe how things ought to be done. Values like citizenship, respect for persons or the removal of disadvantage are difficult to justify except in moral terms; whether people accept them depends on their sharing the moral sentiments. Principles are guides to action. That means that they put prescriptions, or statements about what ought to be done, in general terms. They rely on statements like 'thou shalt not kill', 'it is wrong to withdraw from the individual and to commit to the community at large what private enterprise and endeavour can accomplish',[230] or 'housing should be allocated to those in the greatest need'. 'Private markets allow people to choose' is not a principle, because it contains no prescription for action; it can be shown to be true or false. 'Women should be paid the same as men' is a principle; it can be thought to be right or wrong morally, but it cannot be shown to be true or false.

It can be difficult in practice to separate values and principles from the issues with which they are concerned. 'Gender equality', for example, is as much an issue as a principle; it consists of the principle of equality (which is itself used in many different senses) applied in the context of gender relationships. 'Gender' is not in itself a normative category at all; it is a context in which principles (generalised norms governing relationships) are applied. The 'free market' is another example; the operation of the market is a process, but the question of how that process should be judged is based on consideration of that process as the context for the application of norms.

It is often difficult to separate moral issues from their practical implications. Some guides to action are concerned with practicalities or structures: 'small is beautiful', for example, is an evaluation based partly in the belief that decentralised, diverse organisations have more to offer than big ones, but also partly in a moral view about the way society should be organised. There is a utilitarian tradition, which argues that the way to tell whether or not a policy is a good thing is to look at its consequences. A principle which states that 'welfare should concentrate on people who are poorest' sounds like a very good idea until one looks at the practical problems: the effect has usually been to offer poor people inferior, stigmatised services and to miss out many of the people who might otherwise have received services. This is reflected in a prominent tradition in social policy, associated with Fabianism but no less important from other political perspectives, which has held that it was not enough to show that something was morally superior; one also had to show that it was economically desirable. The classic example of this is Titmuss's study of blood donation, which not only claimed that it was good for people to be able to give for other people's welfare, but showed that by comparison with blood sold in the private market, blood donation led to more blood being available, with a lower risk of disease.[231]

Principles, in turn, shape administrative practice. The reason why benefit systems for poor people are likely to become so complicated is not that people are trying to avoid helping; it is that principles like equity and charity demand that people who have special needs should have those needs responded to. Compensation for disabled people is complicated for several reasons, but much of it relates to a strongly felt concern that people should be compensated according to their individual circumstances, and that some return should be made where there is a particular injustice. Health services in Britain have to ration services, with waiting lists or diluted services, precisely because they are not prepared to turn people away on the basis of ability to pay.

If the study of normative principles only yielded prescriptions consistent with practical benefits, the principles themselves would not be of much interest. But there are many problems which cannot adequately be understood either in terms of practical benefit, or ideologically. If practicalities were all that mattered, there would be very little reason to protect people with intellectual disabilities abused in residential institutions, to offer poor old people defences against hypothermia or to attempt social casework with families. Decisions about care or control in relation to young people, abortion, or the patterns of treatment of mentally ill offenders, are not simply guided by political principles or practical constraints; they are profoundly moral issues.

Social policy is deeply concerned with the value of actions and the moral nature of different forms of intervention. It is worth remembering, before plunging into the practical detail which characterises so much of the subject, that social policy is a major sphere of moral action, and that one of the main reasons for studying it at all is the hope that it might be possible to do something worthwhile with it later.

Key values in social policy

It is difficult to lay out the values which affect social policy in a comprehensive or systematic fashion. It has been a common experience for people involved in policy making that values do not necessarily come to the fore until some principle has been violated – for example, the realisation that it is not possible to move old people between residences without disrupting rights to quiet enjoyment of their home, or that medical education does not necessarily justify the removal of dead children's organs. It is impossible to anticipate every moral issue, or every possible conflict of values.

Considered broadly, the kinds of value with which social policy is concerned fall into six main categories:

1. There are values which affect the circumstances of people individually – concerning issues like the promotion of welfare, the definition of need, and the weight to be given to people's interests and choices.
2. There are principles which regulate relationships with other people. These include moral duties, mutual responsibility and solidarity, freedom and rights.
3. There are principles which consider the relationship between people and the social structure, such as issues of equality and social justice.
4. Some principles govern the relationships between the person and the state: this touches on both freedom and rights (again), the role of the state in relation to property, and the provision of welfare services.
5. There are issues which concern the state and its relationship to society, including the responsibilities of the state, the nature of law, democracy, intervention and planning.
6. Finally, there are issues which concern relationships between states, including, for example, global social policy, foreign aid and the role of international organisations.

The division between categories is not a firm one; principles which govern individual relationships also limit the role of the state in relation to the individual, and principles which are based on social categories like class and gender may still have implications for individual relationships.

The discussion of some principles – issues like freedom, rights, equality and justice – is so widespread, and so common, in discussions of social policy that it is difficult to go for long without encountering them.

Freedom. Freedom, Maccallum argues, has three elements.[232] A person must be free from restraint, to do something. Freedom is, then:

- psychological – people must be able to make a choice;
- negative – people must not be prevented; and
- positive – people must be able to act.

Individualists argue for a model of freedom where people's freedom depends on their independence. Social welfare and state intervention are seen as undermining independence, and so freedom. A social model of freedom begins from the view that freedom depends on interdependence. To be able to act, people have to have the power to choose in society. In this model, poverty negates freedom. Social welfare empowers people and enhances their freedom.[233]

Rights. Rights are rules governing relationships between people; when a person, or a group of people, have 'rights' they can alter the way that other people act towards them. Moral rights are rights which are backed by a moral claim; legal rights are backed by a legal sanction. General rights are rights which apply to everyone in a group, like 'human' rights or rights of citizenship. These have been important for social policy: Marshall argued that much of the development of the 'welfare state' in the 20th century depended on the extension of social rights in addition to the civil rights (like liberty or political participation) which had developed in the 19th century.[234] This is only part of the story, however. Particular rights are rights which apply to individuals – for example, the right to have a contract observed. Many of the 'welfare states' are based in particular rights, like rights to protection obtained through insurance or the right to an occupational pension. The scope of these rights has progressively been extended until, in many countries, they have come to cover almost all the population; the final extensions have depended on supplementary or residual benefits.

Equality. Equality refers to the removal of disadvantage. It does not mean that people are the same – equality between men and women, for example, does not mean that there are no physical differences. The methods by which equality is pursued include: [235]

- *equality of treatment*. This is treatment without bias, prejudice or special conditions applying to people. (It is not treating everyone the same – equality of treatment in health services does not mean that everyone gets a tracheotomy!);
- *equality of opportunity*. This can be the opportunity to compete (in which case it is the same as equal treatment), or the chance to compete on the same footing as others (which may require some redress before the competition starts);
- *equality of provision*. There are arguments for standardisation of delivery in a range of services, particularly health and education. 'Standardisation' implies working to common standards rather than uniformity, but the effect of applying common standards implies both a common foundation and generally applicable criteria or access to higher levels of provision;
- *basic security*. A lack of basic security is caused by 'the absence of one or more factors that enable individuals and families to assume basic responsibilities and to enjoy fundamental rights'.[236] The concept, promoted by ATD-

Fourth World, has been particularly influential in the UN. Providing basic security implies that societies need to establish basic rights, to provide or secure provision of a common foundation of resources and services, and to ensure a level of redistribution that will prevent people from becoming excluded by their disadvantages;

- *equality of outcome.* Policies which are concerned with inequalities of income or health status are generally concerned with removing disadvantage in outcomes, and tend in consequence to imply differential treatment according to circumstances.

Social justice. There are two competing but very different understandings of justice in society.

- The Platonic view is that justice is what is good and right. John Rawls' idea of justice, for example, is based on what he believes reasonable people would agree to.[237]
- The Aristotelian view of justice, by contrast, sees justice in terms of proportion: corrective justice is when punishments fit crimes, and distributive justice is when people have resources in proportion to accepted criteria, like desert or needs.

Justice begins with a presumption of equality; people should not be treated differently without a reason. There may, however, be many reasons. The criteria which have been proposed as the basis for distribution are complex: they have included need, desert, contribution to society, hereditary status, and many others.

Democracy. Democracy can refer to:

- *a system of government.* 'Representative' democracy is a system of elected government. Schumpeter argues that democracy consists mainly of a competitive struggle for the popular vote, which makes governments responsive and accountable.[238] Bobbio defines a minimal democracy as characterised by a set of rules about who is eligible to vote, the rights of political parties and free and frequent elections; and a set of rules which establishes who is authorised to rule and which procedures are to be applied.[239]
- *a system of decision making.* 'Participative' or 'direct' democracy gives decisions to the people who are affected by them. Democracy, within this broad set of understandings, is concerned with prescriptions for governance, such as accountability, participation, negotiation and discussion, the representation of interests or the legitimisation of dissent. This has been the direction of much contemporary writing.[240]
- *a society where people have rights.* 'Liberal democracy' accepts majority voting only because a majority is made by the agreement of a collection of minorities.

Welfare provision has grown hand in hand with democracy. Sen claims that there has never been a famine in a democracy; this is because political rights are essential to the maintenance of social and economic rights.[241]

It may be misleading to try to describe any of these concepts in a short space. Discussions of these principles tend to be lengthy, because most of them are multidimensional; there are always qualifications, subtleties and problems of interpretation. Many of the concepts have been described as 'essentially contested': there are competing, alternative views. One cannot assume, from a statement like 'this will affect people's freedom', that others will understand the issues in the same way as the person making it. The general rule in discussing such issues is to take nothing for granted.

The functions of social policy

It is difficult to attribute 'aims' to a service or policy: aims, intentions and purposes belong, properly speaking, not to a policy or an institution but to the people who design and operate them. The argument that policies are aimed at certain kinds of objective depends on a view of policy as the product of intentional action. But it can be difficult to know just what policy makers do intend; they might not be open about their intentions, and they can of course claim in retrospect either that effects were not intended (when they are harmful) or that they were (usually, when they are beneficial). The process of policy making is complex; intentions have to be translated into practical action; and policies might produce effects which are not intended. The 'aims' of a policy are often judged in hindsight, being explained in terms of the effects which policies produce.

A better term than 'aims' might be 'functions', which refers to what services are used for without saying anything about who is using them. This seems to be a neutral term, because it depends on a description of the use rather than the intentions of the designer; the main function of a knife may be to cut things, but knives have many other functions, including piercing things, prising things apart and so forth. Similarly, we can say that the main function of schools is to educate children, but there are many other possible functions, including keeping children under control, the preparation of pupils for the world of work, the advancement of religion, the provision of childminding or socialising children into a dominant ideology.[242] However, social scientists have come to distrust the idea of a 'function' because of its association with some particularly value-laden explanations of social conduct. It can be difficult in practice to distinguish the description which is given of different kinds of social policy and the value which is attached to that policy. Describing welfare as 'the iron fist in the velvet glove'[243] or social services as 'manifestations of society's will to survive as an organic whole'[244] is not to take a neutral stance; this kind of statement is identifying welfare in terms of a set of understandings about society.

The functions which welfare is supposed to serve can be complex, and much depends on the view of the society in which social policies are applied. We need to be wary of the general assumption that social policy is generally intended to improve people's welfare. It may have a focus which is quite different from the people it ostensibly deals with. The development of the welfare reforms in Britain at the beginning of the 20th century was concerned with 'national efficiency', because the recruits for the Boer War proved unfit.[245] The American 'War on Poverty' was arguably a response to social unrest rather than the experience of poor people.[246] The eugenic policies of the Nazi government were concerned with building a master race.[247]

As an initial guide, it might be helpful to make some simple basic distinctions. Some of the functions of welfare mainly relate to individuals: they include humanitarian action, protection of the vulnerable, and the development of individual capacity. Other functions of welfare are concerned with the whole society: they include attempts to reproduce a social structure, the imposition of social control, or the promotion of economic development.

A second dimension is that social policies may be seeking to keep things as they are – to maintain the status quo – or to change people's circumstances, for better or worse. One of the problems of saying that social policy is about 'welfare' is that it tends to imply that social policy has to be good. Policies are not only intended to benefit people; they might be intended to do people damage. Although there are some policies which seem wholly destructive – like Pol Pot's regime in Cambodia – it would be a rare policy which was not intended to do someone, somewhere, some good, albeit at the expense of other people.

Some of the possible combinations are reviewed in Table 6.1.[248] It is not an exhaustive list of possible 'functions', but it gives something of the flavour of a classification based on aims. What the terms are describing is not a simple description of effects or intentions, but a judgement based in some kind of analysis of motivations and the importance of different kinds of policy in context.

TABLE 6.1: FUNCTIONS OF WELFARE

	Individuals	Society
Maintaining the status quo	Protection	Social integration; reproduction
Improving circumstances	Meeting needs; enabling	Economic development
Remedying disadvantage	Compensation; cure	Equality; social justice
Changing behaviour	Rewards; incentives; treatment	Social control
Developing potential	Developing individual capacities	Social capital; solidarity; integration
Reducing the welfare of some	Punishment	Social division

Ideology and social welfare

Policies and strategies for welfare are not formed in isolation from their social and political context; they are generally selected according to conventional understandings and representations of issues. Ideas and values are framed within a discourse – a set of common concepts, ideas and a vocabulary. Discourses are identifiable in the terminology, concepts and cultural settings which frame and shape the understanding of policy issues.[249] Even if people disagree, the language they use tends to shape the way the issues are addressed and identified. And, because political argument is based on communication and dialogue, people are pushed into using a common political vocabulary – without it they would not, otherwise, be engaging with the arguments on the other side.

'Ideologies' are patterns of thought within the general discourse. They are interrelated sets of ideas and values, which shape the way that problems are understood and acted on. The way that people think about issues is conditioned by their circumstances. One of the most frequent expressions of this is what people call 'common sense'. People are likely to think about an issue along the lines which others have thought about. Our ideas on economics, for example, are far from straightforward; the idea that economies are self-regulating, that people respond rationally to incentives and disincentives, or that higher wages lead to unemployment are based in the economic theories of the past, and although some arguments can be made in their favour they are all very disputable. 'Practical men', Keynes once wrote, 'are usually the slaves of some defunct economist'.[250] The same sort of thing is true of views of society: the way we understand responsibilities in families, what we understand as the purposes of schooling, or the value attached to different kinds of work, typically depend on an interconnected structure of ideas and values. Ideologies affect both how people think about problems and how they can act on them.

The impact of ideology is commonly interpreted in specifically political terms. Social policy is not the first concern of many people in political debates (although it is not at all clear why it should not be); people form their political views and values from a wide range of topics and influences, including, for example, self-interest, economics, policies on defence, and even the personalities of the politicians who put the ideas forward. When people are asked for opinions on topics which they might not have previously considered – like pensions, home improvement, funerals or scientific education – they are likely to base their comments on a general set of principles, values or concepts to which they can refer. If, for example, one is against the state and for the private market, it is fairly easy to work out a position in relation to these topics – pensions should be for individuals to arrange privately, home improvements are the business of the occupiers, funerals are a private affair and what people learn is up to them. Conversely, someone who believes in collective responsibility through the state can rapidly work out a contrary position: security in old age, housing

Box 6: The legacy of the Poor Law

The English Poor Law of 1601 was the not the first system of organised welfare, but it was the first national system; it lasted in one form or another from 1598 to 1948. The watershed, however, was the development of the 'New Poor Law' – the introduction of a harsher ideological regimé intended to rein back the problems generated by industrialisation.

The movement from Poor Law to welfare state has famously been characterised in terms of the models of 'residual' and 'institutional' welfare.[251] The key elements of that distinction are usually understood as covering four dimensions:

- Residual welfare is for a limited number of people (those who are unable to cope in other ways), while institutional welfare is for the general population. The Poor Law was confined to people who were destitute – that is, in extreme need, with no other resources. Institutional welfare would cover people's needs, regardless of financial circumstances, and offer social protection to everyone.
- Residual welfare is given under sufferance, and welfare under the Poor Law was viewed as a public burden. Institutional welfare would be based on an acceptance of mutual responsibility.
- The Poor Law was punitive, relying heavily on deterrence to limit liabilities. The institutional model would accept dependency as normal.
- Paupers were deprived of their rights, while the welfare state is founded on the idea of a right to welfare and citizenship.

There are many other dimensions to the arguments; three seem to be particularly important. First, the New Poor Law was liberal, based on individualism and minimal state intervention – the principle known as 'laissez-faire'. The Old Poor Law had allowed considerable variation in the quality and nature of provision. There had been local intervention in the labour market – the reformers were particularly critical of the 'roundsman' system, which allowed employers to use paupers as cheap labour, and the 'Speenhamland' system, which subsidised wages. Ricardo's 'Iron Law of Wages' suggested that these distortions would lead to wages being paid that were below subsistence – that is, what labourers needed to survive.[252] The reformers believed that this kind of intervention depressed wages and threatened the survival of the 'independent labourer'. This was the basis of the idea of 'less eligibility', which tried to make a clear distinction between the position of the pauper and the labourer. In other words, the argument is that state intervention leads to distortion of markets; that if welfare is necessary, it should be kept separate and distinct from the workings of the economy.

Second, the arguments for the Poor Law were economistic. The advocates of the Poor Law thought they understood how the economy worked, and what motivated people's actions. 'Nature has placed mankind', Jeremy Bentham wrote, 'under the governance of two sovereign masters, pain and pleasure. It is for them alone to point out what we ought to do, as well as to determine what we shall do'.[253] Benthamites believed in moving people by rewards and punishments. These ideas persist in political and academic debates into the present day – the literature on games and rational choice, resting on the premise that people will always try to maximise their individual gains,[254] is infused with the spirit of Bentham.

Third, the Poor Law was moralistic. The economistic gloss should not disguise the influence of moral judgement, and Offer argues that 'Noetic' beliefs – based in moral judgements about the value of work and desirable conduct – were rather more important than the Benthamite ones.[255] One of the key issues which excited the concern of the Poor Law Commissioners was the desire to limit 'bastardy' – the belief that the Old Poor Law had become a spur to licentious and irresponsible behaviour. Although it was not a major element in the 1834 report, in later years there was a strong distinction between the 'deserving' and 'undeserving' poor; the Guardians were encouraged to distinguish them and directed the 'deserving' towards charity while the 'undeserving' were the province of the state.

These arguments continue to shape contemporary debates on social policy. Jeremy Bentham's stuffed and preserved body is currently displayed in University College London, where he still has voting rights. There's an ill-concealed metaphor in that.

conditions and education for national needs are a collective responsibility, while funerals, as something everyone has to go through, can be insured or provided for by the state.

Political ideologies

Political positions are commonly identified in terms of a spectrum running from 'left' to 'right'. The description is said to have been drawn originally from where different parties sat in the French national assembly, with the conservative parties sitting on the right and the socialists on the left. The terms are fairly commonplace in writing about politics, but their meaning is fairly hazy; what is thought of as 'left' and 'right' has more to do with conventions than with rational association. There is a wide range of opinion on both the 'left' and the 'right': the left includes social democrats, socialists and Marxists, while the right includes movements as different as Christian democrats, conservatives, free-market liberals and fascists. An adequate description of the range of ideological views would take a book in itself, but a rapid series of thumbnail sketches will have to do here. An overview of this kind makes it possible, at least, to get some sense of the range of views and some of the major relationships; but it should be recognised that this is also at the expense of some inaccuracy, because within each school of thought there are many further differences and distinctions which should be made.

Marxism. Marxists see society in terms of a conflict between economic classes. A dominant class (the bourgeoisie or 'capitalist' class) owns and controls the means of production; an industrial working class, the 'proletariat', is exploited by them. The Marxist analysis of welfare concentrates principally on its relationship to the exercise of power. The state can be seen either as an instrument of the ruling capitalist class,[256] or as a complex set of systems which reflects the contradictions of the society it is part of.[257] It is often argued that welfare has been developed through the strength of working-class resistance to exploitation.[258]

Marxism is not a unified doctrine; it has come to stand for a wide range of opinions within an analytical framework that is critical of 'capitalist' society. Neo-Marxists argue that the state has two main functions. The first is to improve the conditions for the accumulation of capital – that is, the chance for industries to make profits. The second is to legitimate the capitalist system, by introducing measures (like welfare policies, pensions and health services) which lead people to accept the system as it stands.[259] The requirements of accumulation and legitimation may be contradictory, and the costs of legitimation have led to a 'legitimation crisis'.[260]

Socialism. 'There is no such single thing as socialism', Vincent writes. 'There are rather socialisms ... There are multiple definitions of the concept and numerous ways of actually conceptualizing it.'[261] Socialism can be taken to include:
- a general movement for the improvement of society by collective action;
- a set of methods and approaches linked with collective action, such as cooperatives, mutual aid, planning and social welfare services;
- a set of arguments for social and economic organisation based on ownership or control by the community;
- an ideal model of society based on cooperation and equality; and
- a range of values.

Some texts confuse socialism with Marxism – which pleases both Marxists, who like to think that Marxism is central, and right-wing critics – but the connection is weak; the mainstream of socialism in Europe was based in collectivist social movements, and owes little to Marx. The key socialist values are collectivism, empowerment and egalitarianism, although some socialists would add to that issues of rights and democracy.
- Socialism is collectivist: people have to be understood in a social context, rather than as individuals. Socialism is often represented in Europe in terms of 'solidarity', which means not only standing shoulder to shoulder but the creation of systems of mutual aid.
- Socialism calls for people to be enabled to do things through collective action, a principle variously referred to in terms of 'freedom' and 'empowerment'. This principle has been central to 'guild socialism' and trades unionism.
- Socialism is egalitarian, in the sense that socialists are committed to the reduction or removal of disadvantages which arise in society. The 'Fabian' tradition, a reformist movement, attempted to achieve greater equality through spending on social services.

These principles – solidarity, empowerment and equality – are usually described in other terms. They are the 'liberty, equality and fraternity' of the French revolution, interpreted in collective and social terms.

It is difficult to encapsulate the range of socialist positions about welfare, because these values go to the heart of much of what the provision of social services is about. Socialists stand for welfare; the main differences relate to method. The state is seen by some (for example Fabians) as the principal means through which welfare can be developed; others put more emphasis on collective social movements and mutual support.

Social democratic thought. Social democracy, like socialism, is best described as a set of values rather than a developed model of society. Like socialists, social democrats believe in collective action, enabling people to act, and reducing disadvantage. The differences between social democrats and socialists are hazy, because their ideals may coincide in some aspects and not in others, but two are particularly important. First, many social democrats are individualists rather than collectivists; even if they accept arguments for mutual aid or the reduction of disadvantage, they think it important to stress the liberty of the individual, to develop individual rights (as liberals do), and often to restrict the role of the state. Second, some social democrats are not concerned to remove inequality, but only to mitigate its effects through social arrangements which protect people from the worst consequences of a market society. This probably better describes Titmuss's position than the conventional representation of him as a Fabian socialist.[262]

Liberalism. Reservations about the role of the state are at the heart of the liberalism of the 'new right'. (I am using the word 'liberal' here in the sense in which it is mainly used in Europe; in America the term 'liberal' is often used to mean 'left wing'.) The emphasis on order in traditional conservatism usually means that the state has a clear and strong role in the maintenance of that order. Liberals, by contrast, mistrust the state and argue that society is likely to regulate itself if state interference is removed. Hayek argues that all state activity, whatever its intentions, is liable to undermine the freedom of the individual; that society is too complex to be tampered with; and that the activities of the free market, which is nothing more than the sum total of activities of many individuals, constitute the best protection of the rights of each individual.[263]

Conservatism. The traditional right wing is represented, not by liberalism, but by conservatism. Conservatives believe in the importance of social order. This is reflected in a respect for tradition, an emphasis on the importance of religion, and a stress on the importance of inequality – such as inequalities of class or caste – as the basis for structured social relationships.[264] Welfare is a secondary issue, but the sorts of concerns which conservatives have are likely to impose restraints on welfare, with a particular emphasis on traditional values in work, the family, and nationhood. Welfare does raise concern where it is seen to have implications for public order – one British conservative commented, in commending the Beveridge Report, that 'if you do not give the people social reform they are going to give you revolution'.[265]

Christian Democracy. Christian democratic thought is closely related to conservatism, but it also has important distinguishing features. Like conservatives, Christian democrats place a strong emphasis on order; but order is to be achieved, not primarily through state action, but by moral restraints. These restraints have principally in Europe reflected the influence of the Catholic religion. Catholic social teaching has emphasised both the limits of the state and the responsibility of people in families and communities for each other;[266] Christian democrats tend, then, to favour limitations in the role of the state while at the same time accepting moral responsibility for social welfare, solidarity and social cohesion.[267]

The extreme right. The extreme right is associated with two related but different kinds of authoritarianism. *Reaction* is the attempt to 'turn the clock back' to some previous time; reactionary movements have been important in much of Europe, where they have been associated with resistance to liberalism, nationalist movements, and an emphasis on military strength, but they have little direct relevance to welfare. *Fascism* is a form of authoritarian collectivism which argues that the state, the nation or the race is more important than any individual. There are many commentators who argue that fascism has no real ideology.[268] This criticism was based in a political position taken post-war in an attempt to deny the romantic and emotional appeal of much in fascist thought. Fascism appealed to nationalism and racism, and to the values of work, family and country. It had a strong social agenda; in Nazi Germany, the desire to foster racial supremacy included extensive state intervention in society and the economy, with a stress on socialisation (both through schooling and youth movements) and eugenic policies.[269]

The ideologies outlined up to this point represent, more or less, a spectrum moving from 'left' to 'right'. Figure 6.1 shows the key ideological positions in terms of two dimensions: individualism and collectivism, and views on equality.

One of the problems of trying to represent politics in two dimensions is that there are other points of view which are not easily described in this way. One such approach is *feminism*, which has as its central values the empowerment of women and the removal of disadvantage. Although these are values more often associated with the left than the right, there is scope for 'liberal feminism', which interprets feminist values within a liberal framework, and 'Christian feminism', which

FIGURE 6.1: LEFT AND RIGHT

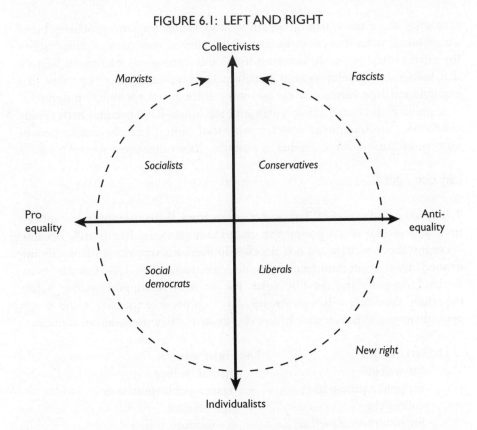

asserts the position of women within a Christian moral framework.[270] The most distinctive form of feminism is radical feminism. Radical feminism argues that gender is fundamental to all social relationships, that the relationship is one of 'patriarchy', which Mitchell describes as a 'sexual politics whereby men establish their power and maintain control.[271] Gillian Pascall criticises the welfare state on the one hand because it interferes with the private sphere, becoming an instrument of oppression, and on the other because it fails to intervene, leaving women dependent on men. She recognises the potential contradiction.[272]

The second is the *'green'* approach to politics, which is based on the rejection of the mainstream agenda and identification of alternative issues as central – conservation of the environment, the use of natural resources and the role of humans in relation to other species and the natural world. The agenda of the green movement goes far beyond the conservation of natural resources; it is also concerned with different patterns of social organisation, coupling self-reliance with the promotion of communal life and cooperative development.[273] Support for green politics stretches across the political spectrum, from committed anti-capitalists to conservatives determined to uphold the status quo. Johnston outlines four main positions that people hold about the future of the environment. 'Deep ecologists' argue for a 'natural morality', and a different kind of society based on adjustment to the environment. 'Self-reliance soft technologists' argue for anarchistic, adaptable communities. 'Environmental managers' believe that sustainable development is possible. 'Cornucopians' take the view that environmental problems can be overcome through technological progress.[274] In a political discourse where environmental issues have become increasingly prominent, the traditional concerns of social policy, like the eradication of poverty, redistribution or a belief in progress, have often taken second place.[275]

Left and right

The general distinction of 'left' and 'right' is hazy. When the terms are applied to a subject like social policy the distinction becomes hazier still, because decisions about welfare are not necessarily the basis on which ideologies are formed. Even so, in most English-speaking countries – the UK, Canada, New Zealand, Australia and the US – the 'left' is likely to support welfare, while the 'right' considers it has grown too far. It is possible to make some rough generalisations, although they have to be treated with a great deal of caution.

The **left wing** is	The **right wing** is
for welfare	against welfare
for public provision	against public provision
collectivist	individualist
for institutional welfare	for residual welfare

It is easy enough to see why these represent two alternative, consistent positions, and it is often helpful to use this kind of classification as a shorthand. Socialists who are in favour of welfare may well support public provision as a means of providing services in practice; because socialism is collectivist, there are few obstacles to recognising a collective commitment through government activity. The sense of society as a collective enterprise also supports the recognition of needs as an institutional part of social life. Conversely, the liberals of the 'new right' are individualistic, support the private market, mistrust state activity and wish to limit the role of the state to the greatest extent possible. Having said this, very few people have such a simple-minded view of the world as these positions suggest. There are some people on the right who want to distribute virtually everything through the private market, but people on the left do not believe that everything should be provided publicly; on the contrary, no one seriously argues in developed countries for public control of the distribution of food or clothing. People on the right are not necessarily residualist in every respect; many favour general support for education and culture. The 'left' and 'right' are not single, homogenised schools of thought; both are very broad coalitions of interests who agree on some issues and disagree on others. On particular issues, both the 'left' and 'right' may be divided. This is the central argument for looking at people's understandings of particular principles, like freedom, equality and social justice, as well as their general ideological approach.

The political centre. There is a 'political centre' distinct from these left-wing and right-wing positions. George and Wilding describe the centre, dismissively, as 'reluctant collectivists',[276] as if they were unable to make their minds up. But there are some consistent beliefs and approaches which can be placed somewhere between the 'left' and 'right'. The two most important are pragmatism and belief in a 'social market' economy.

Pragmatism is often seen as a 'conservative' virtue, but although Burke (one of its most eloquent exponents) is sometimes called 'the father of the British Conservative Party', he has also been acknowledged by some as a father of the Labour Party. Conservatives in Britain argued for scepticism about all doctrines, dogmas and principles. The test of whether a policy was beneficial was not whether it fitted preconceived notions, but whether it worked. The way to develop policy, then, was incrementally – trying things out, doing a little at a time, seeing what worked and what did not. This places its proponents in the political centre because they are prepared to try things regardless of the political perspective, and because the result is generally an amalgam of different approaches rather than a single, consistent pattern.

Belief in the 'social market' economy is linked with pragmatism – simply, the method of production or distribution which is best is that which happens to work – but there is also a strong theoretical basis for it. Keynes argued that although the private market had worked well in some ways, it did not work well in others. It was not, as Adam Smith and the classical economists thought, self-righting; investment, for example, was too important to be left in private hands.[277] What was needed was a judicious mix of independent action and control. The same kind of argument has been a powerful influence on welfare provision; the status quo is accepted, and the economic system can be seen as the most important factor determining welfare overall, but it is generally thought necessary to moderate its effects through the development of systems of social protection. The idea of the 'social market' has been most clearly elucidated in Germany,[278] where it stands as an alternative model to the idea of the 'welfare state'.

ISSUE FOR DISCUSSION

Why should rich people pay for the welfare of poor people?

Strategies for welfare

Welfare strategies

A strategy is a set of interrelated policies, intended to reflect a common purpose or set of aims. The emphasis in the literature on ideologies tends to suggest that there will be patterns and interrelationships between policies of different types. Because they develop from a complex, contested political environment, strategies that are followed are not necessarily coherent or internally consistent; policy makers have a range of different, sometimes conflicting objectives. The things which are done in one area of policy are not necessarily based in the same principles as in others, and in any case the things that policies can do in practice depend on a series of compromises, depending on resources, external constraints and the demands of other policies.

What happens if nothing is done?

Doing nothing is not an option that many people in social policy would want to advocate, but understanding what happens if nothing is done is important for understanding the difference that policy makes. There is considerable evidence as to what happens in these circumstances, because governments often fail to act; and perhaps surprisingly, the assumption that nothing much will happen without government intervention is far from the truth. Those who have the resources typically make their own arrangements; some give individually, and some form charitable associations. This is only a small part of the picture, however. Much more important, historically, has been the development of organised mechanisms of support, referred to in continental Europe as networks of solidarity. Some are based in occupations: for example, the pensions available to civil servants or military personnel are commonly available even in relatively poor countries. Some are mutualistic: many forms of insurance are not commercial, but non-profit-making associations where people pool risks. Some are cooperative: the building societies in the UK, for example, made funds available to their members, in the process laying the foundations for the development of major financial institutions.

One of the first options that presents itself to governments is to reinforce and encourage the general trend. As networks of solidarity become more developed and elaborate, the hope is that they will gradually fill the gaps, reducing the size of the problem that remains to be tackled otherwise. There are important limitations to this kind of development. One, perhaps obvious, problem, is that richer people are supported long before poorer people are. In less developed countries, this leads to glaring inequalities, where richer people live in gated communities with access to high-technology medicine and pensions, while poor people live in slums with no facilities. In more developed countries where governments have been relatively inactive – for example, the countries of Southern Europe, or the US – there is a patchwork quilt of provision, with notable holes in the provision that is available.

The second limitation rests in the complex, pluralistic, often muddled provision that results. Because provision is based on many different principles, there is little hope of looking for consistent policy. Some people will be protected many times over; others will be left out altogether. If a government is concerned about the impact of social services on the economy, for example, there is little reason why private and mutualistic arrangements should share that concern. Arrangements made for the benefit of contributing members are liable to be rather more conducive to those members' interests than government policies might be. (Often, they are also more expensive.) The geographical distribution of services is likely to be uneven. There will be duplication of some services, and gaps in others. The lack of coherence makes it difficult to develop a coherent, integrated policy overall or to pursue specific policy objectives to the exclusion of others.

Individual and collective approaches

One of the main principles which distinguishes different approaches to welfare depends on whether welfare is understood individualistically or collectively. The welfare of individuals is increased by examining the circumstances of each individual to see whether or not that person can be said to be better or worse off. One view of 'social welfare' is that it is the sum of the welfare of the people who make it up; in the case of public goods like parks or roads, collective action can yield more benefit for each person than the cost to each individual user. But there is also a view that societies have interests and welfare which is distinct from that of any individual member; societies also need to survive, to reproduce themselves, and to flourish.

If welfare is understood individualistically, it can be improved in many ways – for example, through growth, redistribution or improved security. If, on the other hand, it is interpreted collectively – implying solidarity in the sense of fraternity rather than mutual aid – it suggests that there are different criteria by which the welfare of a society ought to be judged. Societies can be said to have 'needs', in the sense that there are things which are necessary for a society to survive. They have to maintain order, to deal with change, and to 'reproduce' themselves for the future. The protection of children is not only of interest to the children themselves, or even to their families; societies need children if they are to exist and function in the future, which is why 'family policy' is such an important part of welfare provision in European states.[279]

The movement in the 20th century to welfare states and the development of social services can be seen as a move towards collective approaches, including not only national schemes for social provision but a range of structural responses, like economic development and public health. It is not unequivocally collective, however. Many welfare systems are based on individualised responses – personal insurance, entitlement determined through an individual work record, or subsidised commercial markets, where people continue to act as consumers. Pensions are increasingly individualised, based on individual work record, rather than being available to all as of right; some countries like Sweden and Italy extend this principle to state pensions.[280] Unemployment was seen, in the post-war period, as a structural phenomenon, and the principal responses included economic development, regional policy, job creation through public works and social protection; in recent years the response to unemployment has been individualised, with a strong emphasis on 'activation' to re-engage the unemployed person in the labour market.[281] McKeen, writing in the context of Canada, comments that 'social policy has become social casework, writ large, and structural understandings of social problems have been all but eliminated from the calculation'.[282]

The general experience of social welfare provision has been that both individual and collective responses are necessary. Systems which respond to general needs can only cover populations comprehensively if they also have the capacity to respond to exceptions; and some of the needs which are being considered, like medical care and social care, often require highly individuated responses. On the other hand, systems which rely heavily on individualised responses cannot cope with the diversity and range of problems, even in highly developed economies like the US. Once apparently individual problems, like obesity or alcoholism, become widespread, a generalised social response is needed for services to be effective.

Box 7: Social casework

Social work calls for individualised responses to problems. The idea of 'casework' rests on the view that the social worker should be able to select methods that are appropriate to the needs of the person. 'Casework' typically includes:

- problem solving (as advisor, broker or advocate);
- psychosocial therapy;
- meeting the functional tasks of the agency;
- changing behaviour; and
- crisis intervention.

The fundamental principle of casework rests on the selection of appropriate responses after identification of needs. The role of the social worker, and the methods used, depend largely on the interpretation of the problems the worker is dealing with. Where the problems are personal, the responses might include:

- psychodynamic approaches – trying to change the way that a person thinks and behaves;
- counselling, which is non-directive and encourages change from within;
- education;
- general support, often in combination with other professions (like medicine and occupational therapy); or
- contract work, where the social worker negotiates an agreement with the client to bring about changes.

Where the problems are based in relationships with others, such as family members or peer groups, the methods might still be personal, but might also include:

- family therapy – where all members are engaged jointly and individually;
- groupwork – where people are dealt with together, either because they have common relationship issues (for example women's groups) or because the group as a whole needs relations within it to be addressed;
- conciliation (as in marriage guidance) where people are brought together to resolve issues.

Problems with the social environment might call for very different approaches, including:

- advice and advocacy;
- community and neighbourhood work; and
- community education.

athough it is important to recognise that these still have a focus on the people who experience the problems, rather than the social issues themselves.

Some social workers would aim for a holistic approach, either by combining a range of methods aimed at different issues, or identifying key elements within a set of systems to bring about change strategically.[283]

Casework is intrinsically an individualistic activity. It depends heavily on the direct personal relationship between the social worker and the client, however the term 'client' is defined; it focuses on identifying the needs of the person; it generally tries, in principle, to offer a personalised response to those needs. This is sometimes problematic, because – as many social workers would argue – the source of the problems is not necessarily to be found at the level of the individual. It is not always reasonable to insist that people should adjust to the social environment; sometimes the social environment needs to adapt to them. But dealing with situations in practice, they have to do what they can – even when they know that the response is likely to be inadequate.

These approaches used to be central to social work, but their present-day role is less prominent than used to be the case; the social work profession has increasingly moved in the direction of 'care management' rather than casework. By contrast with casework, care management is characterised by planning and responsiveness to the needs of groups rather than individuals, and the specification of functional tasks.

Residualism

The core of the 'residual' model of welfare is the idea that most people can manage through their own or other people's resources; the provision of organised welfare is used residually, for those left over. Another way of representing this approach is as a 'safety net'; the net is only needed for those who fall. This was the model of the English Poor Law (see Box 6), a system which was intended only to help those who were destitute. The association of residualism with the idea of welfare as a 'public burden'[284] has been difficult to shake, and it remains generally true that residual welfare tends to be seen as stigmatising and mean.

It is possible, however, to take a different view of safety nets. Safety nets have a role in any kind of comprehensive provision, because comprehensive provision, no matter how well planned, is still vulnerable to exceptional circumstances. The French *Revenu Minimum d'Insertion* is a means-tested benefit, offering social assistance and practical support to people who are not protected by other systems. The benefit was introduced as a safety net to cover people who were left out. It is clearly, then, a residual benefit. It is presented, however, in the following terms:

> Every person who, by reason of his age, his physical or mental condition, or of the economic or employment situation, finds himself unable to work, has the right to obtain from the collectivity appropriate means of existence. The social and professional insertion of people in difficulty is a national priority. To this end, a minimum income for insertion (RMI) has been instituted, implemented in the circumstances specified by the present law. This RMI constitutes one of the elements of a general provision in the struggle against poverty, directed toward the suppression of every kind of exclusion, in

particular in the fields of education, employment, training, health and housing.[285]

Although the mechanism is residual, the intention is much broader: the benefit is part of a system intended to cover all needs institutionally.

Selectivity

A selective policy is one which selects the people who are going to receive a service – not just identifying those who ought to receive the benefits, but also those who ought not to. This is very widely and commonly confused with 'targeting'.[286] Selectivity is a form of targeting, but it is a very specific form. Targeted services do not have to be selective or exclusive, even when the target is specifically intended to be 'poor people'. Food subsidies can be targeted, for example, not because they are confined to poor people, but because they can be chosen in order to benefit poor people;[287] and soup kitchens do not need to have a test of means to ensure that only poor people use them. But selectivists argue that benefits or services which are generally distributed are wasteful; if they were confined to those in need, less money would have to be spent, and it could be spent to greater effect. The question of whether money is being saved, of course, depends greatly on the extent of the problem, and the difficulty of identifying it.

The main arguments for selectivity are arguments based in efficiency and equity. Selectivity should in principle be efficient, in the sense of reducing waste, because money does not have to be lost on paying for people who are not in need or on spillovers (that is, giving more than necessary to people with some problems). It should be equitable, because the amount that people receive will be proportionate to their circumstances. There are four main problems with this:

1. In order to be selected, individuals have to be clearly identified; there has to be some test of means or needs, and experience of such tests is that they are likely to be intrusive, complex or degrading. Townsend argues that in practice selectivity has been associated with second-class services for second-class citizens; it separates people who are poor or in need from the rest of society.[288]

2. There is the problem of defining and holding to the limits. If people receive benefits or services because they are in need, there has to be some way of distinguishing those who are entitled from those who are not. This can create inequities, because people who are just below a line might end up better off than people who are just above it, and because people whose circumstances change might find themselves unfairly advantaged or disadvantaged. This generally means that if people's circumstances improve, the services have to be withdrawn as their need decreases. This problem is usually called the 'poverty trap' in social security, because the effect is to submit poor people to very high losses if their income increases, but it happens in other

situations as well; a person who learns to cope with a disabling condition might lose benefits, or a tenant in public housing might have to leave the housing (as has happened in the US).

3. Selective benefits and services often fail to reach people who are part of the target group. People often do not claim benefits, for a number of reasons including ignorance about the services, a failure to realise that they can receive them, the complexity of the procedures to claim and a sense of shame or 'stigma'.[289]

4. There is a potential conflict between efficiency and equity. Efficiency is about reducing waste, and getting the best return for the money. In health services, the principle of 'triage' is used to direct resources to the people who are most able to benefit, not necessarily those in the worse condition. The same principle applies in other services. Keen points to what he refers to as the 'paradox' of targeting: that because people in the greatest need are probably most expensive to respond to, more needs can be dealt with, and more people can have their basic needs satisfied, if the greatest needs are passed over. This might argue for a reduction of the resources in certain cases where people's needs increase.[290] This creates a problem in equity – the pattern of distribution is not necessarily going to help those in the greatest need.

Social protection

A major main strategy for improving individual welfare cuts across issues of redistribution. It is to improve welfare, not by changing resources, but by offering security against changes in circumstances. The term 'social security' is mainly now related to financial assistance, but the general sense of the term is much wider, and it is still used in many countries to refer to provisions for health care as well as income. Most of us are likely to be in need at some point in our lives, whether it is as workers, as old people, or during sickness; it is very important to well-being not just that there is some provision, but that we know there is such provision available. Social security is important, not for what it pays, but for what it might pay in the event of need. Health care protects people who might break their legs as well as those who have done so. Although the benefits of security are not themselves material, they do have a monetary value; people in Britain, where there is a National Health Service, are receiving support which people in the US have to pay for through private insurance or a Health Maintenance Organisation.

The benefits and services which are given as social protection generally work as insurance benefits. They are there to protect people from the consequences of undesirable events, not just to respond to need. Some of the benefits offer income replacement – ensuring that people will be able to carry on with the lifestyle they had before. (This may well mean that richer people will get higher levels of support than poor people.) Others are contingent rights; people in certain circumstances, like ill-health or maternity, will be able to obtain services and to avoid extra expenditure. Social protection may include 'safety nets', but a safety net is not the same thing as social protection; means-tested benefits are there to stop people falling below a certain level, not to protect their previous position.

This principle is understood in much of Europe in terms of 'solidarity'. Social security developed, in much of Europe, from mutual aid societies or trades unions, in which members agreed to pool their risks and share responsibilities for support.[291] The idea of solidarity is seen in many countries as the basis of collective social provision; for example, the French Code of Social Security declares that:

> the organisation of social security is founded on the principle of national solidarity. It guarantees workers and their families against risks of every kind liable to reduce or suppress their ability to earn.[292]

But solidarity is not only about mutual aid; it can also be seen as a principle of 'fraternity', which takes welfare as a form of collective activity and so the responsibility of the wider society rather than of individuals.[293] Much of the history of this principle has been about the extension of solidarity to groups which were previously excluded. The central aim of French social policy has been gradually to extend the range and scope of solidaristic networks. This has led to a patchwork quilt of services, provided on many different terms but seeking to ensure that nearly everyone is included. The main approach to policy, then, has centred on two strategies: trying to identify and work within existing patterns of support,[294] and seeking to integrate or 'insert' people at the margins into the available networks.[295] In the process, a principle which initially referred primarily to insurance has come increasingly to refer to redistribution.[296]

The phrase 'nearly everyone' points to one of the central problems with the idea of solidarity. Networks of solidarity are exclusive as well as inclusive. They define the people who should not be supported as well as those who should; giving priority to some groups, like the sons and daughters of one's neighbours, works against others, like immigrants or people discharged from long-stay psychiatric care. A common arrangement in Bismarckian systems is that the people who are protected are those who are able to pay insurance contributions, while the poorest – those who are unable to contribute – are left out. The same is true in a more extreme way in many developing countries, where the middle classes may have systems of social protection, like pensions and health care, that are not available to the bulk of the population.

Universality

Universality is usually presented as the main alternative to selectivity, although – as the range of options here suggests – it is not the only alternative. The idea that services are 'universally' available suggests that everyone should have access to them, and there are many services that are not selective but not genuinely available to everyone. A targeted set of responses which is not dependent on stopping people claiming – like a needle exchange for drug addicts, or redevelopment of a poor area – is not well described as 'universal'.

Although the idea of 'universality' suggests comprehensiveness, universal benefits are often not intended for everyone. They are more likely to cover everyone within a defined category: universal basic education generally means education for children, and universal pensions are for old people. The argument for universality is the argument against selective approaches; the process of selection is inefficient, and inequitable, difficult to administer, and it fails to reach people. By contrast, universal social provision can reach everyone, on the same terms. The degree of uniformity simplifies administration; there may well be cases in which broadly based indicator targeting proves cheaper than more selective alternatives. But there are also positive reasons for universality. One is the view that everyone has basic needs, and those needs can often be supplied more simply and effectively through general provision to everyone. This is the argument for public water supplies and roads; it was extended during the 1940s to decent housing, education and health services. Second, universality has been seen as a way of establishing a different kind of society – one in which every citizen has a right to basic services, and the basic texture and pattern of social life is one in which people do not suffer unjustifiable disadvantages. This is the root of the 'institutional' model of welfare, outlined in Chapter Six.

Economic growth

One of the primary strategies for increasing welfare is to increase the amount of material goods in a society. This can be done in part by eliminating waste, but mainly it relies on a strategy of growth. This has been central to most economic policy; it is no less important for welfare which is liable to be seen as mainly a means of promoting economic development. Titmuss called this the 'handmaiden' model of welfare.[297] This approach has been influential in a number of states – notably Germany, where the 'social market' approach has tended to relegate social policy to the needs of economic policy.[298]

In developing countries, welfare has often been treated as subordinate to economic policy, because material resources have to be generated before they can be used. Growth has important advantages. The process of the development leads to the engagement of people in the formal economy, either as producers or because of their relationships with people who are producing. When people have money, it draws others into the net – traders, helpers, artisans and so on –fostering interdependence and social contact. The process is not always beneficial, but many of the material improvements in the lives of people in developing countries in the last 50 years are directly attributable to economic development.[299]

In developed countries, equally, the links between high economic production and welfare provision are strong. The countries which spend most on welfare are also usually those with the highest Gross National Products[300] – which incidentally gives the lie to the general proposition that spending on welfare provision obstructs economic development. There are two main problems with an emphasis on economic production. One is the 'green' objection: apparent increases in material resources are often gained only at the cost of other resources, both material and non-material, with the result that we stand to lose more than we gain by the pursuit of growth. The main other type of objection concerns the distribution of resources and well-being. It does not follow, because a group of people has more welfare in total, that every person in that group is better off. Societies are unequal in all sorts of ways, and some people might actually be worse off. Growth is not enough. At the same time, there is some evidence to show that richer countries are liable to be more equal than poorer countries; poorer people can share some of the benefits of better roads, communications, water supplies and nutrition, although there are still important exceptions.

These very different criticisms of economic growth are brought together in the 'anti-capitalist' movement, represented, in different ways, by the green lobby and by protests against globalisation.[301] The main case against these arguments is not necessarily 'pro-capitalist', but it is anti-poverty. Arguments against economic development – such as contemporary movements to reduce carbon emissions – demand extensive restrictions on developing countries, when the environmental problems have substantially been generated by the developed world. The proposed restrictions act to reinforce the problems and structural dependency of poorer counties. Crosland also argued that economic growth was necessary for redistribution.[302] Where there was growth, the surplus could be redistributed; in a static or shrinking economy, redistribution could only be brought about by making the middle classes suffer, and it would meet considerable political resistance. Restrictions on growth tend disproportionately to limit the actions of governments rather than private enterprise, and consequently limit social programmes for the poor.

Redistribution

Redistribution involves taking resources from some people and giving them to others. A measure is redistributive if the people who receive goods or services from a measure are not the same as the people who pay for them. If we begin from the position that this payment comes from individuals or families, all social services are, by definition, redistributive in some way.

Redistribution is conventionally classified as vertical or horizontal. Vertical redistribution may be progressive (from rich to poor) or regressive (from poor to rich); for the most part, increasing welfare involves transferring money from richer people to poorer ones. In economic terms, vertical redistribution can increase welfare in three main ways:

- Vertical redistribution increases welfare if resources are worth less to richer people than to poorer ones. Many resources have a 'diminishing marginal utility'. Utility refers to their usefulness or desirability to the people who have them. 'Marginal utility' refers to the effect of small changes in the existing distribution. Taking a small amount of money from a very rich person will hardly be noticed; to a poor person, it can be the difference between eating or not eating. The marginal utility of a pound or a dollar is much greater, then, to the poor person than it is to the rich person. 'Diminishing marginal utility' means that as resources increase, each addition becomes less important. This means that if money is taken from rich people and given to poor people, it has a smaller effect on reducing the welfare of rich people than it does on increasing the welfare of poor people.
- Keynes also argued that a wider dispersion of income and wealth can be beneficial for the economy as a whole.[303] The reason is that the wider dispersion leads to greater levels of economic activity.
- Redistribution from rich to poor is a moral imperative; the principle of charity is reinforced by most major religions. It is seen as a way of promoting social cohesion and solidarity. Sahlins suggests that the reason the principle is found throughout tribal societies is that it is necessary for the survival of a society; without redistribution, society becomes so fractured that it is not a society any more.[304]

The main 'economic' arguments which have been made against this position are:

- Rich people need incentives to produce, and by doing so increase the welfare of everyone. John Rawls suggests, in *A theory of justice*, that this would lead most reasonable people to agree to some level of inequality in a society.
- The concentration of wealth may have socially effects – de Jouvenel argues, for example, that much of our cultural heritage has been built on the previous patronage of rich people.[306]

There are also, of course, many moral arguments concerning vertical redistribution, as well as arguments based on issues of equality and social justice.

Horizontal redistribution goes from one kind of group to another – for example, from men to women, households without children to families with children, or tenants to owner-occupiers. Barr makes a general analysis of pensions. Pensions redistribute resources:

- from young to old;
- from rich to poor, in so far as the ratio of benefits to contributions is greater for people on lower incomes;
- from poor to rich, in so far as richer people live longer;
- from men to women, because women live longer and have earlier retirement.[307]

Horizontal redistribution is more complex than vertical, and the kind of arguments which are made for supporting families or women are not the same as those which relate to transfers from rich to poor. For the most part, horizontal redistribution is a way of changing patterns of behaviour in society, or encouraging behaviour (like raising children) which is seen as desirable for society overall.

Both horizontal and vertical redistribution might have quite different effects from those supposed here. Work on the welfare state in Britain suggests that much redistribution is not in fact from rich to poor or from one group to another, but rather from one part of an individual's life cycle to another.[308] The effect is referred to by Barr as 'income smoothing'.[309] People, and societies, need to save for the bad times. Sometimes this can be done privately, but in many cases – like Pharaoh's dream of the seven fat cows and the seven thin cows – the need goes beyond the capacity of individuals to provide for, and it has to be done collectively. A large part of redistribution for welfare provision is support for children, who repay when they are adults, for people who are sick, who pay when they are well, and for pensioners, who have paid while they were working.

The social services

The provision of social services represents, not one kind of strategy for improving well-being, but a whole range of different strategies. Properly speaking, the services represent different methods of addressing the issues of welfare rather than a form of welfare in themselves. The provision of welfare – that is, the establishment of social services which promote welfare in the formal sense – is only one means to achieving a general objective of promoting welfare. If that is so, why are social services thought of as such an important part of social policy overall? The answer is partly historical: the development of social services and 'welfare states' was presented, in Europe particularly in the period immediately after the Second World War, as the basic means through which social welfare could be improved for everyone. Partly, the answer is ideological; it has to do with the types of collective action and social organisation which people concerned with social policy want to promote. But much of it reflects a concern that broader economic and social strategies often fail to address important areas of concern. For most of the last two centuries, social policy has been concerned with the failures of other policies – with the people who, for whatever reasons, were left out, people who were poor, socially excluded or dispossessed.

The main social services in industrialised countries are usually taken as including social security, health services, housing, education and social work. It is difficult to give an intelligible explanation of what these terms mean without plunging into details, and learning to make sense of such details is an important part of learning about social policy. Because this book is concerned with general issues, rather than the characteristic features of the social services, I do not propose to go into these features in any detail, but a few words of introduction might be appropriate to clarify what the terms refer to.

Social security generally refers to the system of benefits for income maintenance. The term is sometimes confined to a particular pattern of benefit: in both the US and in European Union law, 'social security' largely refers to benefits for which insurance contributions have been paid. But there are many other types of benefit, including means-tested benefits – given to people whose income or wealth falls below a certain level; universal benefits, given to everyone in a particular category like children or old people; discretionary benefits, which usually depend on assessment by a caseworker; and other non-contributory benefits, like benefits for disabled people which have a test of needs but not of contribution or of means. Tax reliefs and tax credits can be difficult to distinguish from other forms of cash benefit. Social security means that people are given money to spend, rather than goods, but at times the distinctions are blurred: in the US, food stamps are limited in their use, while Medicaid is a means-tested benefit for health care.

Health services are something of a misnomer; the term usually refers to medical care and related services. It is possible to distinguish between care given by doctors and by professions ancillary to medicine, like pharmacy and dentistry, but the dominance of the medical profession is so complete that the distinction helps very little; for practical purposes, the main distinction in the kinds of services which are offered lies between care in hospitals and primary or 'ambulatory' care. There are many other ways of protecting people's health, of which the most important are protection of food, water supplies, sewerage, drainage and decent housing; and 'public health', sometimes referred to as 'environmental health', is a major service speciality in its own right. In many countries, like France, Germany and the US, medical care is primarily provided for through the mechanism of insurance; payments for insurers are used to cover people when they are sick. A handful of countries, including Britain, Italy and Sweden offer medical services without a test of contributions. More common is a two- or three-tier system where some people will pay privately or draw on funds, some will be covered by insurance contributions, and some will receive means-tested assistance.

Education is unlike most of the other services in that it is likely to be genuinely comprehensive, and not just for those in 'need'; in most countries, it is accepted that everyone should have at least a basic education. The process of education is principally identified with schooling, although in theory at least, it extends far beyond this, being concerned with intellectual and social development. The main emphasis within this is on children, although there is scope for education for all. Education has been particularly significant as an instrument of social policy, in the sense not only of policies for welfare but also, because of its importance for personal and social development, in policies intended to change the structure of society. It has been used as a vehicle for other types of social policy – health, family policy, social security and employment strategy. Education provides a convenient basis for policy for children because of its universal coverage, the acceptance of responsibility for children's welfare, and because it has been easy to justify welfare measures in educational terms.

Housing is not universally recognised as a social service, because for most people it is provided through the private market. Part of the argument for treating it in social service terms is that housing is essential to people's welfare; but the same argument could be applied to food or clothing. The reason, historically, that housing came to be treated as a social service was, in the UK, the slow realisation that the private market could not cope with the problems of public health caused by industrialisation, and elsewhere in Europe the need for reconstruction in the period after the war. As housing conditions have improved, the emphasis in social housing has shifted more towards people who are unable to secure adequate housing in the private market – homeless people, those with special needs and those in deprived areas. This also means that the concerns of social housing policy, and sometimes the methods of work, are like those of other social services.

The 'personal social services' are an odd category. The term came into use in the 1960s to describe the range of social care available outside health, education and social security to deal with people's personal needs. It includes a range of services which might or might not be included in the remit of other services: residential care, for people who have support in specialised accommodation; domiciliary care, for people who receive support or assistance in their own homes; day care, providing services for groups (like old people or people with intellectual disabilities) who can receive support or assistance on an ambulatory basis; and work in specialised settings, like courts, prisons, schools or hospitals. It is not a particularly distinct or coherent category; the services have developed piecemeal as a category of services not provided by other means. There are two main principles of operation. The first is 'social work'. Social workers offer people a range of services which depend on personal contact, including counselling, help with problem solving, emotional support, therapy, 'brokerage' – acting as an intermediary with others – and advocacy. The second is the provision of social care support and practical assistance to people who have special needs, to make it possible for them to live in their own homes or as 'normal' an environment as possible. The word 'social' in social care refers to its social organisation (as in, for example, a 'social bath'). This is also called 'community care', although (for reasons that will be explained later) it is not confined to 'the community'; it is closely linked with 'domiciliary' care or support.

On occasions the list is extended to include other services, like employment, advice services and policing, but there is no consistent usage. The kinds of activity which are described as 'social services' vary from one country to another. For example, 'social work' does not mean the same kind of activity in different countries (in France there is a range of different professions doing related but often different things); health is not necessarily thought of as a social service (although even in the US, publicly provided services at both federal and state level make up a major part of the pattern of health care); and housing is often left substantially to the private market. Conversely, there are collective activities which in other countries might be thought of as 'social services', such as employment, cultural activities or food distribution. Other services are potentially important, like those covering industrial relations or fuel, but they are more often examined from the viewpoint of particular academic disciplines, perhaps because they do not relate very directly to the other main social services. Some other services, like funeral provision or libraries, are not much studied in the field. Areas which are important for society as a whole, like cultural activities or public transport, are more likely to be considered as public services than social services. Although I do not want to consider these services in any great detail in this book, it is worth saying that much of what I have written about services and policy in general will apply equally to them.

The welfare state

In the 1940s, the idea of the 'welfare state' was used to bring together arguments on each of the areas. The Beveridge Report in the UK referred to the 'five giants' of Want, Idleness, Ignorance, Squalor and Disease.[310] Although it looks in retrospect like an idle piece of rhetoric, it caught the popular imagination at the time. The idea of the 'welfare state' – not one which Beveridge himself had used – came to encapsulate the kind of social change which Beveridge was arguing for.

Beveridge's influence was not confined to the UK. His report came in many ways to represent the future the Allies were fighting for; the report influenced both governments in exile in Britain and resistance groups in occupied territory,[311] and it is still referred to in France and Belgium as the basis for their systems of social security – however different they are from the system in the UK. To that extent, the importance of the report, and the idea of the welfare state, was symbolic. When, after the war, the British welfare state was introduced by the Labour government, the government took pains to make sure that the main legislation came into force together on the same day, 5th July 1948. It was a way of marking a new beginning.

The idea of the welfare state was not just a symbol, however. It represented an important strategy for the delivery of welfare. Beveridge knew, as every administrator of services for a century had known, that it was not possible to separate services for poverty, health, and housing. The point was made, for example, in Edwin Chadwick's report on sanitary conditions in 1842.[312] Beveridge declared that his social security system was based on some 'assumptions', without which the system could not work.[313] They included a national health service, child allowances, and full employment. Why were the assumptions there? It is tempting to dismiss them as propaganda, but they were more than that. Health care was necessarily associated with social security because, as Chadwick and later Poor Law administrators had discovered in the 19th century, ill-health was a major cause of poverty. If people were not able to obtain health care, they would have to claim poor relief. The link between unemployment and poverty was self-evident; full employment was necessary both because people would otherwise need to claim benefits and, no less important, people have to be employed to pay into the scheme and to fund it. Family allowances were necessary, in Beveridge's view, to protect the incomes of people in work, because otherwise they may have been better off out of work if they had numerous children. (There were other concerns elsewhere in Europe – in particular, fear that the birthrate would be undermined if having children became uneconomic. In France, family benefits rather than benefits for the poor were the main systems through which people who were unemployed, sick or single parents were supported.[314]) The same kind of argument could, of course, be extended to education – because both education and the welfare of children are essential for social reconstruction – and to much else besides.

The idea of the 'welfare state' was developed as a comprehensive set of systems. Much of this vision has been lost since. The separation of the elements of the welfare state into constituent parts has led more and more to separation in the language in which the services are discussed, their methods of operation and the problems they face. Poverty used to be a general, overarching theme which brought together all the services; now it is often treated as a matter for social security. The main response to ill-health is medical care; it used to be thought of as a matter of clean water, decent housing, and income. This can be seen in part as a sign of social advance. Poverty in Western and Northern Europe has become a question of income because the infrastructure of housing, health care and education seems to many people to be complete. Housing in those countries is less important for health than it was, because most housing in those countries has improved beyond recognition in the last 60 years. At the same time, the issues are interrelated; it is difficult to formulate an adequate strategy against poverty that would not cover health, housing and income maintenance, a strategy for health promotion that does not consider income, housing and the environment, or a policy for social care which ignores medical services, housing and income.

'Strategies' were referred to before as being linked by a common approach or purpose. A common purpose can mean that policies are directed towards similar ends – like the relief of poverty, the furthering of economic growth or the promotion of health in a population; or that policies in different fields are guided by similar principles, like the protection of people in a range of circumstances, the reduction of state intervention or the promotion of equality. Policies might be said to reflect a common approach when the institutions they work through, or the processes they follow, are sufficiently similar – like reliance on a private market, the use of insurance-based systems for service delivery or the establishment of decentralised local services in preference to national organisations. Both kinds of consideration are important for the understanding of 'welfare states'.

Models of welfare

Welfare strategies are often understood as package of ideas, rather than one by one. One of the most common methods of presenting packages is through the construction of 'models' of welfare. The development of modelling reflects, like so much else in the study of social policy, the influence of Richard Titmuss. Initially, Titmuss referred to the idea of 'institutional' and 'residual' welfare in terms of universal and selective social services. Later he fleshed out the concepts in terms of three main models of welfare: the residual model, the institutional-redistributive model and the industrial-achievement/performance model.[315] The distinction between residual and institutional welfare was explained earlier. The *institutional-redistributive* model of welfare is a development of the institutional model, which adds the element of 'redistribution', concerned to equalise resources between people. This is separable in theory, and some writers, like Mishra, use them as the basis for distinct models.[316] The *industrial-achievement/performance* model was least worked out in Titmuss's scheme. Some social policies could be seen as a way of supporting economic development; education, for example, can be seen as preparing children for work, health care as a way of maintaining the workforce. Probably the best example is the Bismarckian system of social insurance, which ties benefits to contributions in such a way as to reward work effort closely.[317]

'Modelling' has been of particular importance because, whatever its defects (and there are many), it has tended to set the terms of debate about policy in different countries. Titmuss's models have been a central starting point for much of the work on modelling welfare régimes. Palme's classification is used as a means of classifying different patterns of pensions provision. He identifies pensions as 'institutional', covering basic needs with a degree of

	Residual	Social protection	Institutional	Egalitarian
TABLE 7.1: FOUR MODELS OF WELFARE				
Guiding principle	Selectivity	Solidarity	Universality	Equality and social justice
Orientation	Coercive	Contractual rights	Rights of citizenship	Cooperative and inclusive
State intervention	Minimal	Supportive	Optimal	Fundamental
Responses to need	Central but restrictive	Conditional Primary	Primary	Primary
Range of services	Limited	Variable	Comprehensive	Strategic

redistribution, 'residual', covering only basic needs, 'work–merit', in which rewards are geared to occupational status, and 'citizenship', which offers basic security to everyone.[318]

Some other work seeks to characterise this kind of division in terms of political ideology. Mishra, for example, distinguishes capitalist and socialist approaches.[319] Esping-Andersen defines 'capitalist' régimes as 'liberal', 'corporatist' and 'social democratic' – moving from the least to the most committed position in relation to welfare.[320] The models here seem to move from 'right' to 'left', across a familiar political spectrum; at one end, the 'residual' or liberal view can be taken to limit the scope of welfare, while at the other the 'socialist' model guarantees welfare to all as of right. Pinker challenges that kind of divide: he examines collectivism as a model distinct from capitalism or socialism, arguing that the 'welfare states' offer a distinctly different approach to welfare.[321]

Table 7.1 shows a schematic representation of some of these models, in a presentation very loosely adapted from original ideas by Mishra.[322] The core problem with models of this kind is that they assume connections which may or may not reflect the way that ideas relate in practice. This is the same problem which occurs when commentators focus on ideology rather than principles. Titmuss suggests that there is a link between institutional welfare and egalitarian redistribution; Mishra, between collective solidarity and comprehensiveness; and Palme, between rewards in the economic market and rewards in the welfare system. The links are often tenuous. Welfare in different countries draws on several different principles and approaches simultaneously, leading to 'mixed' or 'hybrid' systems;[323] in others, there may be no guiding principles at all; and in others again, there is a principle which argues for diversity as something valuable in itself. This is referred to as 'pluralism'. The pluralist argument is that because no single system is ever likely to be perfect or ideal, a mixed system, which uses a range of different approaches, is more likely to offer a flexible and responsive range of services.

ISSUE FOR DISCUSSION

Systems based in solidarity and social protection are not necessarily available to all. Is it legitimate to cover fewer people if this means better services?

EIGHT

Welfare states

Welfare states

The idea of the 'welfare state' is an ambiguous one. In some writing, it means little more than 'welfare which is provided by the state'; in others, it stands for a developed ideal in which welfare is provided comprehensively by the state to the best possible standards.

The term 'welfare state', then, is not simply a description of the way in which welfare is organised; it is also a normative concept. The normative literature has tended to concentrate on the experience of the UK, where the 'welfare state' was introduced as a conscious attempt to set welfare provision on a new footing.[324] The 'welfare state' represented an ideal, in which everyone would be able to receive services as a right. In the UK, this was understood by contrast to the Poor Law, which had confined support to those who were destitute, sought to distinguish the position of paupers from workers and made services as unpleasant as possible (see Box 6).[325] These principles influenced thinking even in countries which did not have the English Poor Law, including the US. The welfare state was distinguished from the Poor Law by offering the protection of services to everyone, not just to the poor.

There are dangers in centring too closely on the experience of one nation. The European welfare states built on a different foundation, and the contrast before and after the Second World War was less striking than it seemed to be in the UK. The most important models were based on social insurance, which had developed from systems of mutual aid. The German approach, which was largely based on the lines set up by Bismarck, tied social insurance closely to the labour market, seeing the route to prosperity mainly in terms of participation in the economy.[326] In France, solidarity was taken as the model for further development, with the main aim of policy being to extend solidarity as far as possible.[327] Both these approaches built directly on pre-war experience. At the same time, both had to develop when European countries were engaged in the process of reconstruction, and it has become difficult to distinguish the resulting emphasis on social protection and collective solidarity from the idea of the welfare state in Europe.

Marshall refers to the idea of the welfare state as offering a right to welfare. He argued that the welfare state represented in the 20th century an extension of the rights of citizenship which had been established in the period following the French Revolution.[328] His assumption that civil rights came before social ones was not true in much of Europe. Social rights in several countries developed from of the patterns of mutual support and collective action pioneered by guilds, trades unions and friendly societies. Often this preceded the growth of civil and political rights. Differences in approach do not, however, undermine the basic principle, and reference to social rights remains one of the main tests by which welfare states might be identified.

Influences on development

The development of welfare in different countries reflects a range of influences. The dynamics of change may stem from the internal situation of a country; they might reflect, no less, external factors.

Internal influences. Catherine Jones identifies the social and economic conditions of a country as the 'raw material' on which social policy builds. Social factors include the social structure, elements of social division (like class, gender and racial inequality), and also the demographic structure – that is, the age and distribution of the population, the number of children and old people, family composition and so on. Economic development provides the resources on which welfare services are founded, and further shapes social conditions, like urbanisation and work relationships, in which welfare states operate.

Several reactions to these conditions are developed. An understanding of these responses is based partly on identifying ideologies, and partly on the political process, through which conflicting interests are mediated. There are important cultural influences; religious influences, for example, have played a considerable historical role.

'Responses' – the policies which are developed – depend crucially on constitutional development and political organisation, which provide the mechanisms through which welfare services are then developed.

Finally, Jones points to 'results'. Social policy affects the social and economic conditions which it is developed to respond to, and there is a constant interaction between its effects and the 'raw material' on which policy is based.[329]

External influences. Welfare states cannot be seen in isolation; the social and economic conditions of one country are often linked with those of another. There may be a common history or geography; countries may be linked by their experience of colonial influence. War (which Titmuss identified as a major influence on social policy[330]) is often a common influence. There may be shared cultural influences. Cultural influences can be difficult to identify directly, because they often mirror historical trends – linguistic differences, for example, reflect former patterns of influence – and it is difficult to tell which are causes and which are effects. Religious influence often developed regionally; the difference between Scandinavia, Central Europe and the periphery is reflected in the distribution of Lutheran, Catholic and Calvinist Christianity.

In an attempt to identify the relative importance of different influences, Wilensky has examined the pattern of expenditure on social security in different countries, relating this pattern to political and social influences. The number of old people is probably the greatest single influence on expenditure, but Wilensky also points to some interesting trends. First, more is spent in systems which were developed earlier; there seems to be a constant pressure to improve benefits. The second concerns the influence of politics; Wilensky finds that since politics often follow the wealth of a country, welfare spending is better explained as a product of resources than it is of ideology.[331] Castles and McKinlay argue, however, that the political situation most likely to lead to increased welfare spending is where a left-wing government is faced with an active right-wing opposition;[332] and Castles' later work suggests that there are marked differences arising through policy choices.[333] Wilensky's findings are intriguing, but they are open to other interpretations: it has been found, using the same figures, that welfare spending is directly related to how close a country is to Vienna.[334] This is not as strange a finding as it sounds at first: Vienna had claims, at the turn of the century, to be the cultural capital of Europe, and it is possible that the finding probably reflects cultural diffusion. This, in turn, reflects the historical development of welfare in Europe, including patterns of religious influence and the impact of war.

This prompts a different interpretation of the sort of classification considered in Chapter Six. The basis for such a classification is historical as well as ideological. Welfare in different countries develops through a range of influences and events. Countries which are geographically close to each other often share important links; they adopt similar policies through common historical strands, cultural diffusion (for example, shared religion and shared language), and sometimes direct imitation. The grouping of countries is not just descriptive; they have enough in common to associate particular kinds of principle or ways of operating with the different countries. There is a case for identifying welfare states, not in terms of a particular ideal type, but rather by their resemblance to other states which we think of in the same terms.[335] One of the main justifications for this approach is not simply that they bear some similarities to each other, but that there are underlying relationships which lead to them forming identifiable clusters.

	The welfare state	The social state	Scandinavian social welfare	Social protection	The southern European model
TABLE 8.1: EUROPEAN WELFARE STATES					
Origins (supposedly)	Beveridge	Bismarck	Swedish labour movement	Solidarism	Under-development
Nations supposed to hold to the ideal	UK	Germany	Norway, Finland, Sweden	France	Greece, Portugal, Spain
Basic principle	The right to welfare	Employment and economy	Equality	Solidarity	Civil society
Nature of administration	Uniform	Corporate	National and local	Social partnership	Fragmented
Types of benefit	Universal	Related to contribution	Related to occupational status	A patchwork quilt	'Rudimentary'
Treatment of the poor	Equality of status	Marginality	Participative and egalitarian	Inclusion	Exclusion

Welfare régimes

The models of welfare considered in the previous chapter are largely based in ideal types, or at least in normative understandings of welfare. Table 8.1 outlines some of the principal models currently prominent in the European Union in different terms. The most influential presentation, however, has been the work of Esping-Andersen, who structured his analysis in terms of patterns within existing data, identifying different welfare 'régimes'.[336] The primary difference between his approach and the wide range of theoretical models considered here is that the analysis and classification of welfare régimes is based on empirical evidence. The central problem is that the same evidence can be interpreted in many different ways. There have been complaints that Esping-Andersen's scheme does not adequately deal with differences between groups of countries,[337] that it ignores significant dimensions like gender,[338] and that attempts to apply it to specific aspects of welfare systems tend to founder.[339]

There are many alternative classifications which have been offered. Leibfried, for example, describes four characteristic welfare régimes in developed countries (his focus is mainly, but not exclusively, Europe). These are:

- the Scandinavian welfare states, mainly represented by Denmark, Finland, Norway and Sweden, where welfare is most highly developed;
- the 'Bismarck' countries, Austria and Germany, which in his view offer 'institutional' welfare;

- the Anglo-Saxon countries, which include the UK, the US, Australia and New Zealand, which he sees as 'residual'; and
- the 'Latin Rim', covering Greece, Italy, Portugal, Spain and perhaps France, where welfare is 'rudimentary'.[340]

These models, like the more theoretical examples considered in the previous chapter, can be useful as a shorthand description, but there is much to criticise in them. They rely on a high level of generalisation; the criteria (like 'institutional' or 'corporatist') are often vague; there are considerable variations within systems; there are different interpretations within countries about what is significant; and they tend to say little about the specifics of policy.[341] As the differences between régimes become clearer, the number and range of models needed to describe them starts to proliferate. Ditch comments: 'The devil is in the detail'.[342]

Most existing attempts to classify welfare states oversimplify, or finish with something of a jumble – which leads Mabbett and Bolderson to conclude that the systems simply cannot be classified.[343] The main justification for continuing with the discussion of 'welfare régimes' is not that it helps to describe what is being done – a much more detailed account is usually necessary for that – but that it helps us to construct explanations about social policy in different countries. The classification of systems is a way of making sense of information that can otherwise seem very disconnected and disorderly, and for that reason it has become an important part of understanding social policy.

Patterns in the development of welfare states

Convergence theory. Many industrial countries, despite their considerable differences, often seem to follow surprisingly similar paths, which suggests that the impact of ideology, culture or history is relatively limited. This trend is referred to in the literature on comparative social policy as 'convergence'. There are several reasons for convergence:

- *Common problems.* Industrialisation is a process which all developed countries have had to go through, and they face common sets of problems in consequence. At the outset, the main issues often concern the protection of workers, housing, and the urban environment; in more developed countries, nearly all now have ageing populations and falling birthrates, which means that there are more old people and progressively fewer workers replacing them. This has major implications for health and social security policies.
- *Common approaches.* People in different countries and cultures can come to share common approaches through the process of 'cultural diffusion'. In the European Union, the term 'convergence' is principally used to refer to a process of agreeing common values.[344]

- *Common methods.* The way welfare is delivered depends on the methods which are available at any point in time – a point which is sometimes referred to as 'technological determinism'. The dominance of the western model of medicine, for example, has led to very similar patterns of hospital organisation, while shared understandings about management have implied similar kinds of service response.[345]
- *Common policy.* Countries imitate each other: national insurance in the UK was influenced by national insurance in Germany, while the Beveridge Report in Britain became a blueprint not only for the UK government but for European governments in exile.

Helgøy and Homme argue that ideologies may diverge even where policy instruments are apparently similar. In the case of education, Britain, Norway and Sweden have used increasingly similar methods for regulation and accountability, but in the UK they have been used to reinforce liberal and elitist models of education, while in Norway and Sweden they have been used to emphasise equality and inclusiveness.[346]

The welfare state in crisis. An alternative analysis of common trends stresses the 'crisis' of welfare states. Pierson points to four main uses of the idea of a 'crisis':

1. *Crisis as turning point.* A crisis can be seen as a period when longstanding problems become particularly severe or aggravated.
2. *Crisis as external shock.* This can include war and problems in the international economy, like the 'oil crisis' of the 1970s.
3. *Crisis as longstanding contradiction.* This reflects the concern of Marxists with continuing pressures on the system.
4. *Crisis as any large-scale problem.*[347]

Marxists have argued that capitalism must come to an inevitable crisis. Marx had argued that capitalism was intrinsically unstable, and that it must inevitably drive the workers down into such unspeakable misery that they had to revolt. His initial predictions proved to be fairly unsuccessful – later revisions of Marx's analysis, for example by Lenin, offered alternative scenarios – but the idea that there must be such a 'crisis' remained an important element in Marxism, and reinterpretations have continued to emphasise, in different ways, the instability of the financial and industrial system. O'Connor argues that the central threat to capitalism is now a 'fiscal crisis' generated because of the expenditure required for the provision of welfare.[348] Habermas has given this argument its most authoritative form. He writes that capitalism, in order to thrive, needs both to create the conditions in which capital can be accumulated, and to legitimate its actions, through public activities like the welfare state. The cost of legitimation had grown beyond the ability of the industrial system to pay for it, creating a 'legitimation crisis'.[349]

The Marxist argument is reflected in the criticisms of the 'new right', who have also been sceptical of the ability of the industrial system to pay for welfare provision. Bacon and Eltis, for example, argued in the 1970s that expenditure on welfare and the public sector has 'crowded out' the expenditure necessary for the productive private sector to flourish.[350] But there is little reason to accept that this is true. Welfare expenditure tends to be positively, not negatively, associated with a better-developed economy; there is some reason to believe that the arguments about the 'crisis' of welfare have been at best exaggerated, and at worst misconceived.[351]

Periods of development. Although they seem to offer conflicting accounts of welfare, convergence and crisis theory are not directly contradictory; both are based on the idea that the welfare state represents, not historical accident, but rather the outcome of a set of social processes associated with industrialisation and economic development. It used to be fashionable to describe these processes in terms of periods of development. One attempt to represent such periods schematically was made by Flora and Heidenheimer.[352] They described four main stages which welfare states have undergone:

- *Experimentation* (1870s-1920s). This period was characterised by industrialisation, policy innovations which attempted to reconcile conflicting political viewpoints, and the gradual introduction of social insurance arrangements.
- *Consolidation* (1930s-1940s). A period of depression, followed by the experience of total war, led to a consensus on the need for subsequent reconstruction.
- *Expansion* (1950s-1960s). Reconstruction, sustained economic growth and full employment led to increasing expectations as well as competition for a share in increased resources.
- *Reformulation* (1970s-date). The pressures of recession and inflation led to political disaffection, a slowing down of the rate of expansion and – largely occurring since Flora and Heidenheimer's book was written – the 'backlash' associated with the political right.[353]

Carrier and Kendall advise caution about generalised models like this. Theories about the development of welfare states tend to be rather more systematic than the reality merits, and they tend to disguise considerable conflicts in the process of development. 'Periods' and 'turning points' are easily overemphasised; detailed study rarely supports the idea that there are distinct 'watersheds' or dividing lines. Development in practice tends to be piecemeal, and ideas and attitudes do not develop in clear stages.[354]

Explanations for development

The development of policy depends on factors which go beyond explicit policy or ideology, and there are several competing explanations of the development of welfare states in these terms.

Ameliorism. The first is the view that the development of the welfare state consists of a progressive improvement. This idea has been referred to by a variety of names – 'social reform', a manifestation of 'social conscience' or 'moral determinism' – but it is a very old idea, and I have used the old word for it. It begins with the view that social welfare is a response to social problems. What seems to happen is that a problem – like poverty, child abuse or poor housing – comes to public attention, and then something is done about it. In principle, if problems are gradually recognised and are responded to, things should get better over time.

This idea has been fairly comprehensively rejected in the modern literature, but before explaining why, it is important to explain why it should ever have been put forward. It contains a grain of truth. In most industrial countries, conditions in relation to children, old people, education and health care have fairly generally improved in the course of the last 100 years, and although there may be setbacks it is not very convincing to suggest otherwise. At the same time, there are compelling reasons for making reservations about the position. It assumes a fairly constant environment: if the environment deteriorates then any amelioration due to refinements in policy may not keep pace. (The main countries experiencing a deterioration in conditions are developing countries with a history of conflict or relatively uncontrolled urbanisation.) It relies strongly on a very simplistic view of the policy process, which does rather more than identifying and responding to problems (see Chapter Five). And it assumes that policies will have, overall, a beneficial effect; but the benefits of policies are often equivocal, or confined to one sector of the population at the expense of others.

Historicism. A second view, no less commonly rejected, is the idea that there are certain 'movements' or trends in history which develop through their own inexorable logic. Karl Popper dubbed this approach 'historicism'.[355] Probably the most famous example has been Marxism: Marx argued that there were certain 'laws' which would lead capitalism inevitably to its destruction. This does not have to be taken too literally – if something is 'inevitable' there is not much that can be done about it. But lesser 'laws', or predictions about society, might be seen as an example of the same kind of argument – indeed, the arguments about the 'convergence' of welfare states are fairly typical of this approach. Similar arguments have been made in the social policy of developing countries – for example, the argument that social policy is linked to modern industrial development, or that growth leads directly to a greater dispersion of resources.[356] These ideas matter, because when people believe that certain social effects can only be achieved through particular routes, it affects the policy decisions they make. The central problem with identifying historical movements is not that it cannot be done; it is that past trends are not very reliable as a means of predicting what is going to happen, and that raises questions as to whether they are really 'trends' at all.

Functionalism. In 'functionalist' theory, a response is 'functional' when it serves a particular purpose, and 'dysfunctional' when it does not. Functionalists argue that things are done in particular ways because that is the way in which they work best; welfare develops, by this argument, by a process of innovation and selection into an effective set of programmes and services. This means, among other things, that the pattern of services is likely to reflect both demands for service and constraints on them; services have to adapt in order to continue to work. There is a link between functionalism and convergence theory, because convergence often presupposes the kind of adaptation which is part of functionalist theory.

There is some overlap between functionalist and ameliorist arguments; indeed, functionalist arguments are often represented in the literature as conservative (because they approve of existing arrangements) and ameliorist (because they assume that changes are for the good). This is a misrepresentation; a functionalist can argue that patterns of activity are dysfunctional as well as functional, or that even if they serve some social purposes they can be morally unacceptable. An example can be found in the anti-fascist and anti-racist stance taken by Talcott Parsons.[357] In other words, social relationships and social policies can mutate under pressure into something which we might not like.

Conflict theory. A fourth type of explanation sees the development of welfare as the outcome of a conflict between different power blocs in society. This position is most commonly associated with Marxism, but it should be noted that there are also Marxists (like Offe[358]) who see welfare in functionalist terms. As explained earlier, Marxism is not one belief, but a whole set of different beliefs. These centre on the view that social relationships are shaped by the organisation of the capitalist economy, and that the provision of welfare necessarily reflects the structure of power. This can be taken to mean that welfare is repressive, because it works mainly in the interest of the capitalist classes;[359] that welfare is a concession which has been won by the labour movement in conflict with the capitalist class;[360] or that social welfare reflects the contradictions and power struggles which occur elsewhere in society.[361]

Institutional approaches. Social action is not always attributable to the interplay of social forces; there is also a role for agency, where people make decisions and change the world they live in. There have always been histories which explain the development of social policy as the outcome of coalitions of political interest, institutional factors and agency. There is a well-known tendency for social policy to get trapped on the tramlines, a problem called 'path dependency'; once policy has been started along a particular route, like insurance or state control, it can be difficult to stop.[362] But it is also clear that there are points at which decisions are made, where new policies are introduced, where policies change direction. The combination of institutional constraints, responding to circumstances and pressures, and agency is referred to as 'historical institutionalism'.[363]

Deconstructing development. Lastly, it is worth making a sceptical note. Theories about society and social relationships have often been countered by the argument that such relationships are not 'real' in any sense; they are artificial constructs, developed by commentators and observers. The term most often used nowadays for this kind of scepticism is 'deconstruction', a word which sums up the idea of taking apart the constructs that people have built. The welfare state is not, by this account, a 'system' or social structure; it is just a name we have put on a jumble of assorted material. There are no 'trends', no laws and no patterns except those we imagine are there. This kind of scepticism can be appealing, because it helps to raise very basic questions about the nature of what is being done in the name of welfare.

The problem with all kinds of general theory is that they cannot tell us much about the way in which policy has developed in any particular country. To that extent, deconstruction is justified. But it is difficult to sustain the argument that there are no common patterns, and that no generalisations are possible; and the position is not very useful, because it leaves no basis on which to build an understanding of what is happening. Functionalism points to the relationships between society and social policy; conflict theory points to the role of different interest blocs, and the question of whose interests policies serve. Knowing about such theories is helpful, because they point our attention towards issues which might otherwise be forgotten.

Box 8: A public burden?

One of the criticisms most frequently made of welfare states is that the effect of providing for social welfare is to hold back the development of the economy. The arguments take three main forms:

- Expenditure on welfare imposes high costs. It demands high taxation, reducing incentives to generate wealth, and high labour costs, which reduce the competitiveness of industry, limiting economic growth.
- Social protection systems lead to inflexible labour markets, reducing the mobility of labour and leading to unemployment.
- Money spent on public activity inhibits the development of the productive, private sector which is essential to economic development.

These objections were widely made through the revival of the 'new right' in the 1970s and subsequently in doctrines favoured by the US government under Reagan, the UK government under Thatcher and the policies of the International Monetary Fund and World Bank.

These arguments are all subject to question. In relation to the first, welfare in many European countries has developed through contributions rather than state taxation; the association of welfare with taxation is indirect. There is no evidence to show that high taxation limits wealth generation; high taxation is only possible in countries which have higher incomes, such as those in Scandinavia, and countries with higher incomes are generally those which are more economically successful. There is also confusion in the criticisms between taxation and expenditure. Much of the money used in welfare systems is not 'spent', but transferred – for example, expenditure on pensions is based on a transfer from the working population to the non-working population. Transfer payments are economically neutral, unless the behaviour of the recipient population is different from that of the taxpayer; there is an argument to say that poorer people are more likely to spend, and so that transfers increase economic activity.

In relation to the second, unemployment is primarily conditioned by the state of the economy and the structure of the labour market, which is why it varies markedly when social protection systems stay the same. The unemployment of the 1930s was not created by the social security system, and the full employment of the 1950s and 1960s was not prevented by it. As for the third, the idea that the private sector is productive when the public sector is not is largely based on prejudice; if expenditure on medical services is in the private sector, it does not implicitly become more 'productive' than if it occurs in the public sector.

The theoretical arguments are not conclusive in either direction. Nor is the empirical evidence. Richer countries tend to spend more on welfare than poorer countries, proportionately as well as absolutely, but they have more to spend. Most of the discussion tends to focus on a limited number of wealthy countries in the OECD. Because the numbers of countries are limited, the comparisons are vulnerable to selective interpretation, and indeed to manipulation; leaving some countries out of the statistical process can have a major effect in altering the results. If the figures exclude the former eastern bloc, it looks as if economic performance increases with welfare expenditure; leaving out the less populous countries of Northern and Central Europe can give the impression that economic performance declines with increased spending. Looked at dispassionately, there is no consistent relationship between welfare expenditure and economic performance,[364] and conversely no clear indication that the welfare state either benefits economies or imposes unsustainable levels of expenditure on developed economies.[365]

Beyond the welfare state: globalisation and social policy

The development of a global economy has implications for national welfare policies. The nation state is being 'hollowed out', with power being dispersed to localities, independent organisations and supranational bodies (like NAFTA or the European Union). Mishra argues that globalisation limits the capacity of nation states to act for social protection. Global trends have been associated with a strong neoliberal ideology, promoting inequality and representing social protection as the source of 'rigidity' in the labour market. International organisations like the World Bank and International Monetary Fund have been selling a particular brand of economic and social policy to developing countries, and the countries of Eastern Europe, focused on limited government expenditure, selective social services and private provision.[366]

This case is perhaps overstated. It is true that there has been retrenchment in many countries, and an increased focus on selective social services. At the same time, the experience of the European Union suggests an alternative perspective: the diminishing power of the nation state has to be offset against the development of other forms of regulation. Most developed countries have moved towards general coverage of the costs of hospital care and more inclusive social protection policies. There has been a greater diversification of the basis of coverage, through a combination of governmental and non-governmental provisions. Within the European Union, there have been arguments for a different base for multiple, complex solidarities, both subnational and cross-national – mutualist insurance providing the basic model.[367] It does not follow, because a measure is not based on the state, that it is not solidaristic or securely founded.

There is no consistent trend to greater inequality. For some economies, perhaps many, the effect of economic interdependence has been to promote precarious and short-term unemployment; but the same interdependence has also meant the establishment of rights of property and exchange in the market (the kind of entitlement emphasised by Sen[368]), and so of greater basic security. There is no simple formula here: there are competing, sometimes contradictory trends.

ISSUE FOR DISCUSSION

What do welfare states have in common?

Part Three
Social administration:
the organisation and delivery of welfare

NINE

The provision of welfare

The social division of welfare
The role of the public sector
The private sector
The voluntary sector
Mutual aid
The informal sector
Welfare pluralism
Welfare pluralism in practice: the planning of social care

The social division of welfare

Emphasising the political process, and the role of the state, tends to suggest that the state is central to the organisation and delivery of welfare. This is a half truth at best. The state is central to the establishment of policy, both because the state establishes a framework for the formal organisation of welfare, and because only in the state is there a locus through which conscious decisions can be taken to change or maintain the direction of welfare policy across a whole society – the ability to take such decisions being part of the definition of what a state is. But the state also has important limitations. First, there are limits to the authority of any state; the political process requires a degree of negotiation between parties, and compliance is not necessarily assured. Second, the state is not necessarily the sole, or even the main, provider of welfare services; there are many other routes through which welfare is provided.

Titmuss identified several different kinds of redistributive process, arguing that it was not possible to understand the redistributive impact of social policy without taking them fully into account. He referred to a 'social division of welfare', including three main types of welfare:

- 'social welfare', which represented the traditional 'social services' – this was the provision of welfare by the state;
- 'fiscal welfare', which was distributed through the tax system; and
- 'occupational welfare', which was distributed by industry as part of employment.[369]

Titmuss's concerns represented at the time a major extension of the traditional field of social administration, and his essay was enormously influential in broadening the definition and understanding of the subject, but the rationale behind it has never been wholly clear. If the 'social division' he described was intended to explain the channels through which redistribution might take place, it was far from complete.[370] The category of 'fiscal welfare' could be taken to include two very different types of redistribution. The first concerns subsidies, or measures which are intended to have an effect on people's behaviour. Examples are housing subsidies and tax relief on personal pensions. The second is income maintenance, which is intended to redistribute income and protect people's living standards. Occupational welfare, similarly, is not a single homogeneous category. It includes perks, which are part of a contractual relationship and not really 'welfare' at all; redistributive measures, provided by employers as a 'handmaiden' to enhance their productive functions, like sick pay or employee crèches; and private insurance, which is sometimes provided by employers, but may also be purchased by individuals. There are, besides, other avenues through which welfare is distributed. They include legal welfare, which is compensation through the legal system (particularly the courts); and, probably most important of all, the voluntary and informal sectors.

The reference to 'sectors' leads to one of the most important categories in the contemporary study of social policy, which is the distribution of welfare services through a range of social mechanisms beyond the state itself. There are four main sectors through which welfare is provided: public, private, voluntary and informal – although, as the previous discussion suggests, there is a case for considering more. The public sector consists of services provided by the state; the 'private' sector, through commercial activity; the voluntary sector, action by non-profit-making organisations (although in some countries 'private' activity is also considered to be 'voluntary'); and informal care is provided by friends, neighbours and families – or, more usually, by women in families.

The role of the public sector

The public sector is that part of the social services which is financed and managed by the state: in some of the literature this is closely identified with the idea of the 'welfare state', although this usage does not necessarily convey all the moral ideas which are associated with the term.

Public services have been important not least because there are areas of social welfare in which there is no practical alternative. The model of residual welfare sees welfare as a safety net, which is only for people who are unable to deal with the contingencies in other ways. The protection of welfare calls for at least some public services – a point acknowledged even by right-wing opponents of state welfare, like Hayek. The area of debate concerns not whether state welfare should exist, but what its scope and extent should be, and on what terms it should be delivered.

A number of arguments for the delivery of welfare by the state – like issues of social protection and control – have been considered in the course of this book. State services can be seen, simply, as the means through which state policies can be pursued. The main outstanding issue is the question of whether the public sector is the best or most appropriate medium through which these social objectives might be achieved. The arguments are strongest in three cases:

- where there are minimum universal standards to maintain, requiring either a general régime or residual provision to plug the gaps;
- where there are elements of control being exercised by the service, as in the case of protection of children in social work; and
- where there are substantial economies of scale or effort in providing material through the state, rather than through fragmented services (for example, the considerable economies achieved by national health services).

There is an argument, too, for public services to step into the breach when other sectors fail; but that may be a reason for bolstering the other sectors rather than replacing them. None of the arguments about the public sector can be considered in isolation, because necessarily they refer to the performance of the state relative to the alternatives.

The private sector

Economic liberals argue that the private market is the best way to distribute resources. It is sometimes objected to this that poor people cannot afford welfare. The reply to this is that this is a case to give poor people more money, not necessarily to provide the service publicly. The best example in practice is the distribution of food, which in most western countries works very well (although not perfectly) through the private market. If poor people cannot afford food, this is taken as a case for more social security – not for a National Food Service. Arthur Seldon argues that the price mechanism leads to choice for the consumer; a service led by the consumer rather than by the professions; more efficient services at lower costs (because this increases profitability); responsiveness to need (because their payment depends on it); and the education of people as to the implications of their choices.[371] He believes that collective provision is, conversely, inefficient and paternalistic. The issue is not that poor people might not be able to afford services. If this was the problem, then we could give them the money to decide for themselves – as we do with food and clothing; there does not have to be a publicly provided service.

There are many arguments against this position. The first set of problems relates to the social implications of depending on the private market:

- *Externalities.* These are consequences which go beyond the people involved in a transaction: education is worth something to society and to industry, not just to the person who receives it; ill-health affects more than the person who is ill, whether as part of an issue in public health or more generally in the fact that society needs healthy workers.
- *Risk.* The assessment of risk for a whole society is not the same as the assessment of risk for an individual. It may be reasonable for individuals

to take minor risks; it may be less reasonable for society as a whole. A risk of one in 1,000 is very small, but in a society with 60 million people, it would probably affect 60,000 people.

- *Social choice*. Social choices are not necessarily the same as individual choices. The problem comes out, which Galbraith describes in the US, of 'private affluence and public squalor'.[372] If individual customers had to meet the full cost of parks, there would probably be no parks. Many people in Britain resisted the introduction of sewers in the 1850s on the ground of personal cost (they were called the 'dirty party' by their opponents).[373] Parks, like roads, sewers – and possibly hospitals – are examples of 'public goods'.

- *Social priorities*. Welfare services involve more than the preferences of the people who make the decisions. Welfare services, unlike apples and pears, are not only provided for the benefit of the consumer. They may act as a 'handmaiden' to industry. They may be introduced to redistribute resources. And they may – for example in the case of probation or child abuse – be a form of social control.

The second set of problems relates to the operation of the private market itself:

- *Economies of scale and efficiency*. It may be cheaper to organise a large national service than it is to have smaller competing services. The NHS has been able to reduce the costs of health care, by closing surplus resources, and using its monopoly power to buy in materials more cheaply. The private sector can be argued to duplicate facilities unnecessarily.

- *The geographical distribution of services*. The private market does not guarantee a structure of necessary services. Services which are not profitable, because there are too few people needing them, are closed. And the services which do exist are not necessarily in the right place. Pahl gives the example of two ice-cream sellers on a beach. In a planned economy, they would be given a pitch. In the private market, however, they have free choice. This means that the first one sets up in the middle of the beach. The next one also has to set up in the middle if he is to get half the custom.[374] The effect is a tendency for competing suppliers to concentrate their efforts in one location. This works in private welfare, too – which is one reason why major hospitals were concentrated in central London before the NHS, and Harley Street became a centre for consultants.

- *Choice*. There are commodities – like health, and possibly education – which people are not well placed to choose, because they have no criteria on which to base their choice. It is in the nature of the commodity that it is difficult if not impossible for a consumer to judge the quality and value of what is being provided at the time when they need it. People actually have to buy insurance, not health care *per se*. Social care for older people is commonly obtained by relatives or professional advisers. And there are services, like social work and probation, where there may be an element of compulsion – users have no choice.

- *Coverage.* Barr points to issues of 'adverse selection' and 'moral hazard'.[375] Adverse selection occurs when insurance services exclude 'bad risks' – for example, people with multiple sclerosis, chronic schizophrenics, and older people – because the costs of providing for them are greater than the service is prepared to bear. The problem of 'moral hazard' refers to contingencies which claimants might be able to control – like pregnancy or unemployment – and which insurance companies are consequently reluctant to cover.

These arguments are not fatal to provision by the market by any means, but they limit its scope. Because the private market cannot deal with all circumstances, there will be a role for public intervention – as there has been in Europe since mediaeval times. Because public provision cannot anticipate all the conditions for which services might be needed, there will always be some commercial demand for private services. There is, Rein and van Gunsteren suggest, a 'dialectic' of sectors; there is always some pressure for the expansion of one sector or the other.[376] Almost all provision of social services occurs in mixed systems, where some provision is public, and some is private.

The voluntary sector

The voluntary sector is extremely diverse, ranging from small local societies to large, very 'professional' agencies. It covers a wide range of different types of activity, typically focused on health, social services, housing and community development, environmental, cultural and international aid agencies. Kendall and Knapp suggest that the definition of the voluntary sector can be expanded to include independent educational institutions, business and trade associations and sports clubs.[377] In the US and some European countries, the 'voluntary' sector is closely identified with non-profit associations; in some cases it may simply refer to non-governmental organisations. A 'voluntary' hospital may simply be an independent one.

Voluntary activity refers to a wide range of activities. Jones, Brown and Bradshaw classify the different types of volunteering as including direct service giving; running voluntary organisations (like the 'voluntary housing sector); participation or self-help groups; fundraising; public service (which is often unpaid); and pressure group activity.[378] To some extent, the role of the voluntary sector is simply supplementary to statutory services; in England and Wales, the National Society for the Protection of Cruelty to Children does, in large part, what would otherwise have to be done by social workers. But it can also be seen as complementary, in a number of ways: the initiation of new approaches and techniques, the development of specialised expertise and the establishment of 'partnerships' or contracts between voluntary and statutory agencies. Voluntary agencies can do things which statutory agencies could not do: for example, they can work with people (like drug addicts) who might reject any statutory service; they can criticise state services; and they can help people dealing with state services, as in welfare rights work.

Jones and others also detail some of the disadvantages of voluntary services. There are problems with staffing; the dominant ethos of charitable work in Britain tends, Gerard comments, to be 'sacrificial' rather than professional,[379] and despite substantial changes in the sector in subsequent years there is still an element of truth in that. The selection of volunteers is not always strict; things may be done judgmentally; many volunteers are unwilling to do administration. There are also problems in responsiveness to need. Services are provided not necessarily where they are needed, but where people want to give them; voluntary agencies founded to meet the needs of one period can outlast their usefulness; and agencies with a single aim can be inflexible in their use of resources. However, many of these criticisms could equally be levelled at statutory agencies.

Mutual aid

There is a particular part of the voluntary (non-profit) sector which deserves special notice, because it has quite distinctive characteristics: this is the class of services which are based on mutual aid or solidarity. There is a good case to consider this category as a sector in itself, because the organisation and behaviour of solidaristic groups is quite different from that of other non-profit organisations. Historically, mutual aid was one of the main foundations of welfare organisations, through trades unions, professional associations and friendly societies;[380] in many countries, solidaristic services of this kind have continued to be one of the main focuses through which welfare is provided.[381] The relative neglect of such arrangements in the English-speaking literature is difficult to explain – Beveridge certainly understood 'voluntary action' in these terms[382] – although David Green has argued that solidaristic approaches offer an alternative both to the state and to the commercial sector.[383]

The central principle of mutual aid has been voluntary collective effort, which is both self-interested and supportive of others. People who enter such arrangements make some kind of contribution – such as paying a subscription, offering labour, or participating in management – and receive support on a mutual basis. The most common model is probably a system of voluntary insurance, usually for income maintenance or health care, which offers social protection in return for a basic contribution. But there are many other examples, including cooperatives, self-help groups, and the trades unions themselves.

The scope of mutual aid is considerable – the mutualist arrangements for health care in Israel covered nearly 90% of the population before the government decided to break it up.[384] The main limitation is that solidarity cannot be comprehensive: some people have a limited ability to contribute, and others are likely to be excluded by the conditions of membership.

The informal sector

The 'informal sector' consists of communities, friends, neighbours and kin. The discharge of people from institutions and maintenance of individuals in the community has led to a greater emphasis on the role of carers. The experience of community care has been to stress the limitations of the state and the public sector. Bayley made the argument, in respect of people with intellectual disabilities, that most care was not being provided by the statutory services, but by informal carers. The role of the state is, realistically, to supplement, relieve or reinforce the care given by others.[385]

This approach has led to a range of criticisms. The social costs to carers need to be considered, while the economic costs are underestimated because they are not charged. Feminist writers have criticised the burden imposed on women. Pascall suggests that if a woman is present, the services will not offer support.[386] This is not strictly true; services reduce support if anyone else is present in a family, male or female.[387] But where there are both male and female present, it will in practice normally be the female who incurs the extra responsibility of care. The situation is arguably no better from the point of view of recipients. Service to dependent individuals is often unexamined; there is no guarantee that informal carers will offer the best care.

Box 9: The limits to market housing

Housing is normally treated as a market commodity which is bought and sold according to the willingness and ability of people to pay. The market is complex, however. Barlow and Duncan point to:

- *the impact of space*. Location is acutely important in the housing market; there cannot, because of it, be perfect information and full and free competition.
- *market closure*. Housing markets tend to be localised. This can mean that housing production and finance tend to be dominated by a few major players. (In some countries, this may even be true nationally.)
- *externalities*. Housing both affects the environment and is affected by it.
- *credit allocation*. The settled housing market tends to be paid for mainly by borrowing, which has to be based on predictions of future value. It is very unlike the market for food.
- *uncertainty*. Because the future is uncertain, so is the housing market.
- *market volatility*. Prices are dominated by a limited part of the market – those who are buying and selling property at any time.
- *the problem of meeting need*. If profitability is the only consideration, people will be left with needs unmet – most obviously, through homelessness.[388]

This analysis is heavily influenced by the experience of Western Europe, although it is generally extendable to most OECD countries. Arguably it misses the importance of systems of land ownership, which is limiting and sometimes exclusive; in some developing countries, where the system of landholding is not clearly established, squatting on unclaimed land, relying on building one's own shelter, may be a normal form of tenure.

Although there is a clear role for governance – regulation and intervention to reduce uncertainty and market volatility – only one of these factors points immediately and directly to a direct role for non-market provision: the problem of meeting need. Residual provision for people in need typically includes provision for homeless people, specialist residential accommodation with support for particular need groups (such as frail older people or people with mental health problems), and disaster relief. And yet provision by non-market sectors is far more extensive than this narrow focus would imply. It includes:

- publicly provided housing for communities;
- social, voluntary and not-for-profit housing to meet general needs; and
- support for particular sectors in the housing market, such as young families or large families.

The development of housing services seems to reflect a range of other considerations. These include:

- the perception of market failure – the view that the market does not provide well for people, and particularly for people on lower incomes. Wherever there is a shortage of housing, the people who end up without housing, or in the worst housing, are those with the least ability to pay.
- government intervention designed to achieve other objectives – public health, slum clearance, redevelopment, conservation and so forth. Where governments force populations to move, they take on the responsibility for replacing their accommodation. Where they prevent housing development, they arguably take on an obligation to shield people from the negative consequences.
- the sense of a moral obligation to improve the conditions of the population – a view which has influenced both democratic governments and the voluntary sector. Housing is simply too important to be left to the market alone.

Welfare pluralism

The study of different sectors makes it clear that the state does not operate in isolation; rather, it acts in conjunction with a number of non-statutory organisations. In the days before 'welfare states', charities and the voluntary sector were not necessarily as independent as they might have appeared; the state often had an active interest in regulation and support of their activities.[389] The commitment of post-war states to welfare may have given the impression that these relationships had been, or were in the process of being, supplanted; but in most industrial countries there is a complex set of relationships between the state and the other sectors of welfare, which has to be regarded as the normal pattern through which welfare is organised and distributed.[390]

This has prompted arguments about 'welfare pluralism', which is the provision of welfare services from many different sources. The idea of a 'mixed economy of welfare' emphasises the diversity of the provision of welfare in society. Table 9.1 was originally based on work by Judge and Knapp; I have developed it further from an earlier version.[391]

There are three basic, and powerful, arguments for welfare pluralism:

1. *Diversity*. The range of services offered, the kind of things which can be done, is wider with the contribution of different sectors than without them.

2. *The welfare society*. The second is a moral argument for the type of society we want to live in. Conservatives have emphasised the pluralistic nature of welfare; traditional conservatism stresses an 'organic view' of society, as a series of interconnecting relationships, and the role of family and duty. Similar sentiments are shared by those on the left: Titmuss argued that the voluntary sector also has an important social role; it allows people to be altruistic.[392] We had to become not only a 'welfare state' but a 'welfare society'.[393]

3. *The recognition of reality*. The state does not, and cannot, provide all the welfare in a society. In practice, what the state does may be relatively minor in relation to the burdens of care experienced by informal carers, and the state's task is to complement and supplement this kind of care.

TABLE 9.1: THE MIXED ECONOMY OF WELFARE

	Provision				
Finance	*Public*	*Private*	*Voluntary*	*Mutual aid*	*Informal*
Public	Social services departments	Private homes for older people	Delegated agency services	State-sponsored mutualist régimes	Foster care
Private corporate		Occupational welfare	Philanthropic foundations	Employer-sponsored workers' organisations	
Charges to to consumers	Residential care for older people	Private health care	Housing association rents	Building societies	Childminding
Mutualist (subscriptions/ contributions)	National insurance	Health Maintenance Organisations		Union pension funds	
Voluntary	Hospital friends	Purchase of services by voluntary organisations	Religious welfare organisations	Self-help groups	Family care

At the same time, some reservations should be made:

4. *Comprehensiveness.* A pluralistic welfare society might not be able to respond comprehensively to need. The extension of solidarity suffers from a basic flaw; that the definition of people to whom we hold responsibility also has the necessary effect of defining others as falling outside that area of responsibility.

5. *Equity and social justice.* Solidaristic networks are highly differentiated, and that means that they work very much more favourably for some people than they do for others. Where there is a concern with social equality – that is, the removal of disadvantages – there is the problem that those who are poorest and least able to protect themselves are also those who are least likely to be adequately supported by other social networks. The effect of trying to complement and supplement provision, rather than to redress the balance, may be to commit such people to an inferior and stigmatised form of residual provision.

Welfare pluralism in practice: the planning of social care

One of the areas in which the idea of welfare pluralism has been most influential has been in the development of social care. The implementation of social care relies strongly on the concept of the care 'package', an idea which is probably attributable to Michael Bayley.[394] Bayley argued that the statutory services could not be seen as the sole providers of services; they were not even the principal providers. They were, at best, contributors to a network of services. The provision of services became, then, not a matter of the state providing comprehensively for each individual, but the development of a range of alternative services. From this range, each individual could be offered a programme selected for that person. Bayley referred to this process as 'interweaving' state services with community support; currently the formation of the package is referred to as a 'care plan'. The principle behind establishing a diverse series of options is that it improves the robustness of planning for individual cases: a service for any individual can be selected from a range of available services.

In theory, there are some notable advantages in this kind of approach:

• It is based in a recognition of the limitations of existing services, and in particular of the services provided by the state.

• The approach makes it possible to do something. If the issue is that the services do not meet needs, then offering a range of options helps to increase the scope to meet those needs. If the level of provision is inadequate, it can be expanded.

• It makes it possible to plan services rationally and cost-effectively. Much of the literature on social care in practice has been concerned with cost-effectiveness, not (as it so often appears) in the sense of cost cutting, but in the sense of providing the level of service appropriate to the needs of each individual.

- It makes it possible to meet the needs, not only of the main categories of dependent people, but of each individual – which is a startlingly bold claim in view of the history of provision of services. Care management has been described as 'the process of tailoring services to individuals' needs'.[395] The idea of the 'care plan' depends on operation within the constraints of existing services, but the elements within each care plan of assessment, review of options, and selection of services allows (at least in theory) a high level of flexibility and responsiveness.

In practice, however, the limitations are considerable. Care plans are necessarily based on available resources, which cannot be adapted flexibly to the needs of each individual; plans are more likely to be based in a set of fixed alternatives between which choices have to be made. 'Care planning', it has been argued, 'should not be seen as matching needs with services 'off the shelf', but as an opportunity to rethink service provision for a particular individual'.[396] But the selection of the appropriate services is not made, whatever the theory, on the basis that these services best meet the needs of the individual. Plans have to be realistic, and the principal constraint on the selection of options is the type of service that has to be provided.

Take, for example, the case of a psychiatric patient who is about to be discharged from hospital after a long-term stay. The effect of being removed from social networks for an extended period is to limit resources; it is difficult in such circumstances to retain housing or employment. The patient has, like everyone else, a number of basic requirements, which will include an income, possessions, social contact and housing; a number of individual requirements, which may or may not include domestic care, engagement in leisure activities, employment prospects, medical care; and, beyond this, a number of services specific to the issues around mental illness, including as necessary monitoring, medication, certification, therapy or support. Some of these needs might be met by families, which is one reason why care plans are likely to depend on family support; but this assumes that both the family and the patient will accept such a situation indefinitely, which is often not the case. Some needs may be met by existing statutory services, but here there are well-known problems: different priorities within the services (which are designed for the general public), the lack of staff trained to deal with the circumstances (particularly in housing and social security), inadequate funding for the type of case, and problems of coordination between services. Commonly this leads to a demand for specialised services, most typically for accommodation, organised activities and psychiatric care.

The planning and provision of specialised services necessarily takes place not for an individual but a 'client group'. A service is developed to increase the range of options, or the number of places, for people with particular classes of need. One might, then, see developed as a special project a core and cluster unit for people with mental illness; a base for employment for people with intellectual disabilities; or very sheltered housing for older people. Services which are appropriate to the needs of client groups can only be flexible within limits.

An example of this kind of approach is in residential care, where accommodation is provided together with a specific programme of services and specific kinds of staff. The Wagner report made the case, appealingly, for the development of a range of services in which residential care is seen in the same light as community care, and progressively greater levels of support are given within different categories of accommodation.[397] However, because support is organised in relation to accommodation, there is an identifiable pattern of services associated with particular residential units. Some of the difficulties are practical – stemming from the pattern of buildings, organisation and staffing – but there are good organisational reasons why residential units should offer a specific pattern of services, in terms of administration, competence and control.

The planning of services is dealing, in reality, not with a 'range' of services but a set of alternative packages. This does not lend itself to a free-ranging selection of appropriate services, and it is not clear, from any existing structure of services, how packages of care can be devised. On paper, it may look as if it is possible to draw on a range of different services; the reality of welfare pluralism implies something different. The role of government in planning is to ensure a sufficient range of alternative packages, rather than services from which packages can be constructed.

ISSUE FOR DISCUSSION

What effect does the source of provision have on the character of a service? Does it matter who provides services?

The structure of public services

Public service systems
Welfare bureaucracies
Coordination
Quasi-markets
The role of people working in social service structures
Bureaucrats
Professions and semi-professions
Management
Radical alternatives
Effective organisations

Public service systems

The idea of the 'social division of welfare' was particularly important in the development of thinking about social policy, because it demonstrated that welfare policies could not be thought of only as a matter of administration. But there is a risk of leaning too far in the other direction – of ignoring issues of administration because motives and outcomes are more important. One of the common flaws of analyses of policy in terms of politics is the assumption that ideologues, reformers or governments have simply to agree what they want and they will get it. There may be times when this is true, but it is wrong as often as not. Whatever governments decide, policies cannot simply be set in motion; policies have to be translated into practice. The effect of policies may be very different from what is expected, and the administrative process plays a major role in this.

The administration of social services is complex; there is no single 'process' to identify, but many taking place at the same time. For the purposes of explanation, I am going to focus at first on some general models which try to explain how social services are structured, before looking at issues of service delivery later. This is not really enough to understand the workings of any particular service, but it should help to provide a background for the study of many of them.

The differences between different kinds of service are fundamental; it makes little sense to compare a neighbourhood advice office, a residential home and a national social security organisation. At the same time, it is important to try to develop some kind of framework within which different kinds and patterns of service can be accommodated if the roles of the services are to be understood, and it is possible to make some useful generalisations about the structure of services and their interrelationships. Services might co-exist with little relationship to each other, but this does not have to be true; and the way in which services develop means, on the contrary, that they are likely to develop on predictable lines. Where there is an existing structure of local or regional government which can be used, services might well be established within that structure; where the structure does not exist, which was the case in Victorian England, giving more responsibilities to existing services develops into some kind of structure by default.[398] It might equally happen that services are deliberately created without reference to existing structures, because this is a way of getting round their limitations: this approach was used in the US War on Poverty.[399]

'Welfare' is not a huge, amorphous administrative function – even if, from the perspective of central government, it may look that way. One of the reasons why central government posts are sometimes given umbrella titles like 'Health, Education and Welfare' (formerly used in the US), 'Health and Social Security' (the former combination in the UK) or 'Labour and Social Affairs' (Israel) is that welfare-based departments are not always considered important enough in their own right to merit the appointment of senior politicians to have responsibility for them. Within these departments, however, there is necessarily a division of labour. There are three main distinctions between different types of services: functional, client-based: and area-based:

- *Functional divisions.* The first, and most obvious, distinction between services is based on what they do – such as health, housing, social security, social work and education. This is usually referred to as a 'functional' distinction – that is, a distinction based on the division of labour between them. It works reasonably well, for the most part, but the boundaries between services are indistinct. Child guidance, for example, can be seen as education, social work or a form of health care. Supported housing for older people can be housing or personal social service. Provision for medical care can be seen as a form of social security as well as health provision. The reasons why services are blurred in this way is not simply technical; they follow from some of the issues considered earlier. If housing is justified because of its effect on public health, health care because of its importance for social protection, or social assistance as a form of personal assistance related to social work, there is no intrinsic reason why administrative boundaries should be maintained.

- *Client groups.* Services might respond only to specific groups of people – older people, children or unemployed people. A specialist service for older people might be doing much the same kind of thing as a service for younger physically disabled people; however, because they are dealing with distinct groups, there may also be some specialised knowledge, particular insights into the needs of the people, and the possible advantage of bringing together people with similar needs into social groups. The distinctions made between client groups are not necessarily functional, however; they might also depend on distinctions between people which are not directly related to the service's functions or methods of operation. The groups may have different political priority for resources, or a different history of service development. There are 'separatist' services, which deliberately duplicate the pattern of other services in order to meet the needs of a particular group who might otherwise be disadvantaged – like voluntary housing for minority ethnic groups. In the Netherlands, the traditional 'pillars' between society led to distinctions between services for Catholics, Protestants and others.[400]

One of the most useful classifications based on the distribution of roles and functions distinguishes generic from specialised work. A 'general practitioner' is a family doctor who is expected to offer continuing medical care across the full range of medical problems in the community; a 'specialist' concentrates on particular types of ailment or sets of problems, like 'anaesthetics' (a functional specialisation) or 'medicine for the elderly' (a distinction which is client-based but is also partly functional). There are similar distinctions in the role of social workers: the specialised worker relates specifically to a particular client group, whereas the generic worker tries to exercise skills which are transferable between different classes of client. Genericism has been criticised in social work on the basis that generic workers are unlikely to have all the skills and knowledge necessary for work with certain groups. In practice, genericism has often been replaced by creeping specialism, as specialists have been appointed within supposedly generic teams, and have progressively reduced the area of work within which 'generic' workers actually operate.[401]

• *Area-based divisions.* The third main division of labour within services is geographical: services are responsible for what happens within a particular area or location. In a sense, virtually all services are subject to this distinction, because nearly all services are formed at least on a national basis; equally, the basis of a service might be by region, county, district or a small community. The area covered by a service shapes its response in two main ways. One is that certain functions are possible only with a sufficient economic base; specialised functions are difficult to design at a very local level. The other is that the kind of area which is covered – urban or rural, narrow or diffused – affects decisions about whether services should be centralised or decentralised, in fixed or mobile locations.

A geographically 'centralised' service is one which is established at a level which can oversee all the geographical regions covered – which is also the level which is most remote from service recipients. Centralisation at national level, for example, occurs mainly when a national government wants to maintain the same rules and methods of procedures in each part of the structure. 'Decentralisation', by contrast, means that decisions are delegated, as far as possible, to smaller geographical units.[402] Delegation of authority to smaller areas may be necessary in circumstances where responses have to be adapted to local conditions. If the service is intended to deal directly with people or their problems, there has to be some kind of response available where the people or problems are found.

Elcock points out that decentralisation follows a number of different patterns, and that they are not confined to decentralisation for functional reasons. He distinguishes three different types:

- *Departmental decentralisation*, in which one department devolves its operations. What happens is that departments establish area offices with a full range of functions being exercised at a local level. In social work, this is represented by the 'community social worker' who has a full range of responsibility for a particular 'patch'; in housing, it is represented by the 'area housing manager' who has a comprehensive responsibility for a particular estate.

- *Corporate decentralisation*. Here the aim is to produce corporate management at a devolved level. Several departments cooperate in order to produce microcosms of a local authority in a particular location. Offices are shared by officials from a range of services – most commonly social work, housing and education. The same kind of principle is seen in health services in the primary health care centre, which can include family doctors, nurses, paramedics such as optometrists and dentists, pharmacists, health educators, physiotherapists, social workers and occupational therapists.

- *Political decentralisation*. The emphasis here is on the locality, often with the idea of 'empowering' local communities. There will be political representation, either through elected representatives like councillors or through special committees. Issues of empowerment and participation are considered further in Chapter Twelve; it should be noted, however, that political decentralisation often accompanies decentralisation for other reasons, because it is difficult otherwise to maintain political accountability for services. English local government grew out of the administration of the Poor Law, not the other way round.[403]

The arguments for decentralisation are varied, in keeping with the different patterns of delegation which these styles of organisation represent. The main argument for centralisation is the equalisation of standards and principles: Hölsch and Kraus suggest, for example, that centralised social assistance is better at redistribution than decentralised systems.[404] However, centralisation has disadvantages; it is often felt by advocates of decentralisation to be unresponsive, unaccountable and inefficient The main arguments for decentralisation are local accountability and responsiveness to local needs. Decentralisation can be criticised for tending to favour some people over others (notably local residents over outsiders), for placing the greatest responsibility on those units which have the least resources to meet their needs, and for proliferating organisational complexity. In so far as welfare provision depends on the pooling of risk, larger units are better able to deal with risks that are extraordinary, or particularly expensive. The effect of decentralised budgets can be to make local units on tight budgets unwilling to take on high costs or extended responsibilities. Decentralisation alters the character of local political debates, and there can be a tendency for financial decentralisation to reinforce views of welfare as a 'public burden'.[405]

Box 10: Who decides?

In most areas of social policy, there are conflicting arguments about who should have the authority to make decisions. The literature on democratic governance generally begins with the assumption that decisions should be made by publicly accountable authorities, while the assumption behind much of the literature favouring the private sector is that consumers should decide.

In the case of education, there are at least eight different potential locuses of authority, where decisions about educational policy might be made. They are:

1. *Central government.* Where there is a desire to ensure uniform standards – for example, admission to universal primary education and the promotion of literacy – there is an argument for locating relevant decisions at a national or regional level. The creation of universal basic education in sub-Saharan Africa has depended heavily on central government intervention – even if that intervention seemed at times to go beyond the capacity of the governments to deliver.[406] Several developed countries, including, for example, Britain and France, have more detailed and prescriptive national standards; this includes a national curriculum, which all maintained schools are expected to follow.

2. *Local government.* Local and regional authorities are seen as the democratic representatives of local interests. Localism necessarily implies variation in national standards; in India, which deals with education federally, one effect of localism has been to prevent the establishment of universal basic education, which has to rely instead on voluntary effort.[407]

3. *Interest groups.* Although the process of education in schools and colleges is normally protected from outside influence, a number of interest groups have privileged access. Religious bodies, employers and the armed forces often have special roles. Other agencies, such as the police, health and social services, may link directly with the educational system to pursue their own agendas.

4. *Schools.* Schools may be seen as bureaucratic organisations, responding to government initiatives, but they may also be self-governing units controlled by boards of governors. Schools in the independent sector may be governed in accordance with rules established by founders.

5. *Head teachers.* Schools may be treated as units of management, where the central authoritative role is held by the Head Teacher as the leader of the school.

6. *Teachers.* Within a professional model the responsibility for educational decisions, including objectives and the curriculum, is held by teachers. (Despite formal accountability to local government, this was arguably the dominant model in the UK until the 1970s.)

7. *Pupils.* Although no national system resides any extensive authority in pupils, there have been longstanding arguments for a more cooperative approach which recognises children's motivation and autonomy. Educational experiments have encouraged pupils to make their own decisions about learning and the curriculum.[408]

8. *Parents.* Consumer-based and private-market models tend to see parents, rather than children, as the principal consumers of education, making choices on behalf of their children.[409]

An educational journalist in the UK comments on the shifting balance between actors:

'When I first became an education correspondent ... we hardly bothered with what the ministers or the civil servants were thinking. That wasn't where the power lay. All the interesting stories were down in the schools – what new forms of assessment, or ways of teaching, or of curriculum were being developed in particular schools or local education authorities. Now we have ministers deciding ...'[410]

The interplay of a wide range of competing interests might seem to imply that education is a political arena. At times, it is. However, the scope for political discussion is often restricted, depending on the social and organisational context. The idea of 'historical institutionalism' referred to in Chapter Seven suggests that decisions are critically affected by agency and political context, but that once the decisions have been made, the institutional structures which have been developed can be difficult to change.[411]

Welfare bureaucracies

The idea of bureaucracy is most usually referred to the work of Weber, who outlined an 'ideal type' or rational organisation. The ideal model of bureaucracy in Weber contains a number of elements:

- People have specified tasks: 'the regular activities required for the purposes of the organisation are distributed in a fixed way as official duties'.[412] Officials have to possess a particular expertise or knowledge relevant to these functions.
- There is a hierarchy of authority, with a chain of command stretching from the top to the bottom. The progress of an official's career consists of promotion through the hierarchy.

- The system is governed by rules, which are framed in abstract terms and can then be applied to specific cases.
- The system is impersonal; outcomes are decided according to the rules, rather than personal relationships, and there is a strict separation of personal affairs from official conduct.

The presentation of an 'ideal type' can lead to the development of theories which bear little resemblance to reality; it is not really crucial that officials have to have full-time appointments, or that officials have no financial stake in the agency. Weber probably included these factors to distinguish the work of a bureaucracy from historical patterns of public service, and from other kinds of industrial organisation. But this is a valuable model from the point of view of welfare, because it points to a number of features which characterise welfare agencies. The first point concerns the functional division of labour. People in bureaucracies have particular roles, which means that to get something done one has to identify who has responsibility for the task. The structure of authority in bureaucracies is related to the functional tasks the agency performs. It is very difficult to plan for general tasks if one has no authority over the actions of those who are carrying out the tasks. This does not mean that people responsible for general planning always have authority over practitioners. In the organisation of medical care in particular, planners often have a lower status than the doctors whose actions they nominally control. It is not always the case that the people in these roles have special expertise, because bureaucracies can be organised like a production line, where the skill required to process material is minimal. This is not always a bad thing: one argument in favour of bureaucracies of this type, which most often applies in relation to social security, is that it reduces the discretion of officers. If they begin to think that they are the experts they are likely to make decisions according to their own lights. The point will be returned to shortly.

The second argument is that there is a hierarchy. Each person in a hierarchy has some kind of delegated function, for which they are responsible to someone above them. The structure of such an organisation is like a pyramid. The person at the top is able to direct people immediately below, who in turn direct their subordinates, and so on down the pyramid. Officials are directly accountable only through the hierarchy, and not personally. Consumers may be able to exercise sanctions through formal mechanisms for accountability, but they do not have a direct sanction against officials. Since the actions of government are nominally taken through a form of legitimate authority, and it is necessary for subordinates to be clearly and visibly accountable to elected authority, this approach is the one most commonly found in the executive branches of government.

The principal advantage of such a structure is that it concentrates effective control at the centre – or at least, that it appears to: appearances are very important in the establishment of legitimate structures, because control must not only be exercised but must be seen to be exercised. The main disadvantage is that control can only be exercised by fettering the discretion of people working in the lower tiers.

In practice, the structure of welfare organisations is rarely simply hierarchical. Hierarchical lines of accountability are cross-cut by interrelationships which demand negotiation, contact and collaboration. Networked organisations can have multiple leaderships, and rely on a corporate structure in which colleagues exchange expertise.[413]   Galbraith describes this pattern as the dominant model in high-tech industries, which rely on a strong division of labour between people with specialised expertise.[414] This is a better description of, for example, hospital management or university education, than a simple bureaucratic model would be.

Coordination

Describing welfare services in terms of a 'system' implies that there is some kind of interrelationship between the different parts. But there does not have to be any standard, simple relationship between them. In practice, there are different combinations, which do not have to be to be rational or cohesive; many services have 'just grown', and often there are problems of coordination and liaison between the different parts. The case of Maria Colwell is a classic example.[415] Maria was a child who died from severe neglect and abuse by her 'natural' family after she was returned to them from foster care. Many professionals knew something about the case: they included a social worker, the police, a health visitor, teacher, housing officer and educational welfare officer. But there was at the time no mechanism by which the information from different sources might be brought together, and the effect was that none of the agencies had sufficient information to justify action to save the child.

The problems which lead to lack of coordination are manifest in the structures of welfare services:

- *Functional problems.* There are functional differentiations, and distinctions between client groups, which mean that the role and function of services have been distinct. The central problem here is institutional: agencies have different aims, and different criteria by which to measure success or failure. The problem of coordinating social care is illustrative. Social security is primarily devoted to income maintenance, not to the provision of care – which means that issues like value for money or maximising effectiveness by selective purchase of resources do not arise. The primary aim of housing services is to ensure that people are adequately housed, not to improve caring relationships, so a referral which principally depended on this aspect would not necessarily receive any priority. Doctors are mainly concerned with treating sickness, and are not required or trained to make an holistic assessment of a person's needs; a lack of social contact or an unduly limiting family environment is not part of the problems doctors are meant to deal with.

- *Geographical boundaries.* Services have been organised at different geographical levels – often, for example in the division of labour between national, regional and local authorities, with different geographical boundaries. If the main services dealing with general needs work to different administrative structures, different authorities, different budgets or different boundaries, then the transfer of a person from one agency to another can have important financial implications. Moving an older person out of an acute ward, which is often essential for efficient use of medical resources, means that some other agency is going to have to pick up the tab. A person with intellectual disabilities who ceases to attend school becomes the responsibility of some other agency in the community. A psychiatric patient who is discharged from hospital will have to be supported by another agency in the community.
- *Professional problems.* The different professions involved have different methods of work, language and standards of professional practice. In housing, for example, the appropriate management of cases is usually interpreted as a rationing process giving priority to those in greatest need. In social security, the requirement is for efficient management which will enable claimants to receive their entitlements; pension agencies do not, for example, push the case of an individual whose need appears to be greater. In medicine, the emphasis falls on professional judgement to respond appropriately to the needs of each person.

Smoothing communications between agencies is a continuing problem in the administration of social services. There are many options. Hudson identifies three main approaches: authoritative strategies, incentive strategies and cooperative strategies.[416] Authoritative strategies mean that people are instructed to work together. (The creation of formal coordinating bodies is not always welcome. Marris and Rein, in one of the few studies brave enough to explain where things went wrong, describe one agency which was, perhaps unsurprisingly, rebuffed when it offered to coordinate others.[417]) Incentive strategies involve some kind of inducement for agencies to work together. Agencies can be given financial incentives or disincentives for particular types of action – either relating to individual cases, or by offering funding with a requirement for coordination before the funds can be unlocked.

In cooperative strategies, people try to work together by mutual agreement. At the level of management, working in partnership is seen as a way to achieve 'joined-up thinking' and coordinated services. Partnerships are believed to increase the capacity of partners, through:

- 'synergy' – the added value that comes when a partnership can do something that individual partners cannot do separately;

- 'transformation', because partners learn new ways of working from their engagement; or
- budget enlargement,[418] because people working together should be able to pool their resources. Often they are able to gain access to funds they cannot achieve individually.

Partnership has become a key norm of governance. Governments throughout the developing world have been encouraged by international organisations to rethink their approach to governance, working jointly with commercial and non-governmental organisations.

McDonald distinguishes between 'strategic' and 'communicative' partnerships.[419] Strategic partnerships are instrumental; they are intended to achieve particular results, such as the delivery of a service or to tackle a problem. Communicative partnerships are justified mainly in terms of the act of cooperation; they work as a forum for discussion, and a way of developing networks between organisations. Many practitioners are suspicious of 'talking shops', not without reason. It is difficult to say whether communicative partnerships actually help service delivery – but that is not what they are there to do. What should be true, in principle, is that the development of networks should help to identify mechanisms for the times when problems do arise – provided, of course, that the agencies involved, and perhaps the personnel, are reasonably stable.

At the professional level, there has been an increasing trend towards the sharing of professional tasks, such as the development of shared assessments. This is a false trail; in a professional structure, each professional is individually responsible for their decisions, and effective cooperation depends on each professional performing their own expert role, not on them doing the jobs of others.[420] One of the most effective options for dealing with individual cases has been the establishment of workers with responsibility for coordination. The resolution of the problems which lay behind the Colwell case focused in the first place on the use of the 'case conference', bringing together all the workers involved for discussion of the circumstances. This is not always successful, both because higher status workers (notably doctors) resent their time being taken up and because workers perceived as having marginal status (like teachers or advice workers) are not necessarily invited. The second main development was the nomination of a 'key worker', who would have the main responsibility for the case and to whom other workers would know to refer. This later became refined with a distinction of two roles: the nomination of a 'primary contact' who could work closely with the family, and that of a 'role coordinator' who could collate information and refer on to those who needed to know it.

Quasi-markets

An alternative approach to the coordination of services has developed through imitation of the private market. In the private market, services often duplicate each other; they compete for the custom of users, who are able to choose between different competing organisations. There is not, then, usually one organisation which might do a task, but a range of organisations. One way of bringing about this form of competition is what Gilbert and Terrell refer to as the 'purposive duplication' of services[421] – services are deliberately set up, or at least encouraged to set up, in competition with others. The same effect can be achieved by fragmenting existing services, so that independent hospitals or independent social security schemes then have to compete with each other.

The development of competition might suggest that the difficulties of coordination would be magnified; but that is not, for the most part, how a private market system works. Firms which hope to have some kind of service performed can approach a number of organisations, and where they are able to undertake the work more effectively or efficiently the firm commissions work from them. Supermarkets do not usually have their own builders to create new developments; they commission builders to develop units for them, and pay them for their services. The organisation of the social services is not quite like the organisation of a supermarket, but there are arguments for seeing some of the functions of social services in a similar way. At the simplest level, this has been the argument behind the 'privatisation' of a range of functions previously tackled in the public sector, like office cleaning, catering and building services; but the same rationale can be applied to many other kinds of work. A social services authority does not necessarily have the resources and the specialised staff to offer a régime appropriate for a young offender with severe emotional problems who also requires resocialisation and control; what has become commonplace is for one social service, or a voluntary organisation, with particular expertise to act for others, receiving payment for the service. Coordination, then, rests not on the willingness of people to cooperate, but in the functional differentiation of different organisations.

This kind of arrangement is commonly simulated in large, complex organisations through cost-centred budgeting. Every part of a firm is expected to make money; if it does not it is likely to be closed down or sold off. If a task can be performed more efficiently or cheaper by a subcontractor, it should be. The effect overall is to minimise costs and maximise output. There are, however, some reservations to make: a classic example is of a restaurant which only breaks even on its food, but makes a large profit on wine and coffee. In theory, it should stop serving food and offer drinks instead; in practice, if it did so there would be no demand for the drinks at the price offered. Similarly, it is all very well to tell a hospital that it should have a cost-centre for pharmaceutical provision, but it cannot necessarily cease to provide pharmaceuticals itself and continue to function effectively as a hospital. A more appropriate comparison for many social services is the development of corporate management. Galbraith argues that private firms have had to adapt to complex technologies by increasing the number of specialists who have to work in a multidisciplinary team.[422] The effective cost-centre becomes the team, rather than the functional speciality. The theory behind cost-centring may be valid, but it is essential to define such centres appropriately to the functions which the agency is performing.

This leads to a different mode of operation for social service hierarchies. A central authority may have oversight of policy and planning, but the responsibility for service provision can be shared between a number of autonomous organisations. A hospital which wishes to discharge patients rapidly might rely on other social services; it may employ its own staff to do so; but it also has the option of commissioning an independent organisation to undertake the work. A pensions agency may maintain its own computer staff, or it may subcontract the work to specialists. The image which emerges of welfare systems becomes less that of an ordered hierarchy than of a network of providing organisations, with a diversity of rules and methods of proceeding. Coordination of effort takes place from the top, because a planning authority is attempting to use its resources to steer the pattern of provision, and from below, in that consumers (or professionals acting on their behalf) are purchasing a range of services which are appropriate in individual cases. In other words, the social services have started to behave like a market.

Since the 1980s there have been increasing attempts to bring the activities of public sector agencies into line with the behaviour of private sector organisations. Some part of this is ideological; the 'new right' believes that the private sector is intrinsically more efficient, because of the constraints of competition, than the state. In part, it reflects some of the arguments of economists who see the implications of scarcity as inevitable, and consequently argue that public sector firms can be analysed in terms of economic theory in the same way as private sector ones. The recognition of 'welfare pluralism' has also had an impact; if the state is not a sole provider, but is one of several potential providers, then the kinds of consideration which affect the behaviour of suppliers are likely to be similar to those which affect firms in the private market, including consumer demand, the performance of competitors, and relative efficiency.

Quasi-markets are like markets, but they are not the same as markets.[423] There are important differences between social services and private enterprises. Social services organisations have other aims besides profit and loss. At the individual level, people who it is inefficient or uneconomical to treat have still to be dealt with; they cannot effectively be excluded, as they might be by private insurance. Private firms need, in the constraints of the private market, to be efficient. This means that they will produce units at the lowest unit cost. If they exceed their capacity for efficient production, unit costs start to rise and profits fall. Social services, by contrast, cannot limit production at the point where unit costs are lowest, because this will imply that some people are left without service. The private sector can hold its costs down by avoiding problematic cases. This implies, of course, that when other things are equal, private firms will be more efficient than public sector agencies. That does not mean that the private sector is better; it means that the public sector is trying to do something different.

The second main difference is that exit from the market is not an option for the public sector. Building firms frequently go out of business, sometimes with work half finished; a housing agency which is trying to provide a service for its tenants cannot permit that to happen. Nursing care for older people cannot be discontinued because an operator goes out of business. People cannot be released from prison because a private operator cannot afford to continue operations. What happens effectively is that the state, implicitly or explicitly, accepts losses on such activities when they are undertaken within the public sector, and underwrites public services activities when they are commissioned from the private sector. There is a strong case, even where activities might be done cheaper elsewhere, for maintaining them in the public sector.

The role of people working in social service structures

The organisational settings that have been discussed so far – bureaucracy, the hierarchical structure of welfare organisations, and the quasi-market – are associated with different roles for the people who work in them. These are *bureaucrats*, who perform official functions; *professionals* (and semi-professionals), who have the power to make independent decisions about responses to clients; and *managers*, who have delegated power to run sections of an organisation. These roles often overlap in practice, but considering them separately helps to understand some of the constraints which people work under.

Bureaucrats

Weber's model of bureaucracy lays great emphasis on the exercise of rules. A centralised bureaucracy should, in principle, be able to establish rules to determine the behaviour of officials in every case. The obvious problem with this kind of centralised service is that where a service is designed to deal with the public, no system of rules can possibly legislate for all circumstances. In theory, subordinates must seek authority for their actions in difficult cases. This is true even where the agency has discretion: in a rational hierarchy, giving power to the organisation does not mean that individuals at the bottom of the hierarchy have the power to make decisions. In practice, the complexity of circumstances leads to imperfect understanding of the rules,[424] leading to errors, some conservatism in the use of judgement, and decisions made without authority – in a classic study, Hall identifies the role of receptionists as crucial.[425] Bureaucrats are functionaries. They are able to exercise judgement – because someone has to decide whether a case fits the rules – but they are not allowed discretion, in the sense of a free decision in those cases where rules do not seem to apply. (The distinction between discretion and judgement is made by Davis.[426])

Weber's emphasis on the limits of personal influence reflects this concern. There is almost always some scope for such influence to be exercised, but the purpose of hierarchical organisation is to reduce this scope to the greatest degree possible. It has been argued, in the literature of public administration, that public sector workers act, like others, to maximise their status, power or income.[427] Weber's formulation outlines common constraints, but people will seek to work around these constraints; it would be naive to suppose that public bureaucrats respond solely to a conception of the 'public interest', or the interests of their agency, without reference to their personal circumstances.

Professions and semi-professions

In the provision of welfare, the position of the ideal 'bureaucrat' is untypical. The problem is that rule-based administration is not necessarily practical in all circumstances. The clearest example is probably medical care, where doctors exercise professional judgement about treatment rather than working to pre-established rules; but the same principles apply to many other workers who have to make judgements in relation to circumstances, including social workers, health visitors, counsellors, community workers, teachers, advice workers, nurses and housing managers. The position is usually discussed in terms of their 'professional' roles, as opposed to bureaucratic ones – although it is important to recognise at the outset that the exercise of such roles also takes place within a hierarchical structure.

The 'professions' refer to certain classes of occupation which give people a distinctive place in their society. In the past, the term mainly referred to doctors, lawyers and the clergy; Jones and her colleagues also identify the professions with higher educational qualifications, which are part of the process.[428] Among the many criteria that have been proposed as criteria for professional conduct are skill based on theoretical knowledge; the provision of training and occupation; tests of the competence of members; organisation; adherence to a professional code of conduct; and altruistic service.[429] These kinds of criteria have been criticised for their looseness. In the discussion of social welfare work there are few areas in which the description would not apply; since all social services can be represented as having an altruistic ethic, all governmental activities have some code of conduct, and the only thing which seems to distinguish 'professionals' from others is the process of qualification after a test of competence.

Probably the most important characteristic of the professions in practice is their use of discretion. Every application of rules, whether it is in a bureaucratic hierarchy or by an independent operator, requires some use of judgement. Discretion concerns the procedures which apply in cases where rules do not; it implies the use of autonomous judgement, where the rules do not offer guidance. Professionals reserve areas in which they can act autonomously – the 'clinical freedom' of doctors, the social work relationship, or the conduct by teachers of their classes. There are tensions here to be resolved; the need for flexibility and responsiveness has to be balanced against the agency's concerns to develop consistent practice, and professional claims are mediated through a process of constant negotiation.[430]

The 'professional' role of welfare workers requires some modification of the nature of the 'rational' hierarchy. It is difficult to say whether this is a consequence of professional claims for independence, or whether the independence of professionals reflects the functional necessity of delegating decisions to people. The test of competence required as part of professional activity can be seen as a means of protecting the profession's claim to specialised knowledge, but it can also be seen as a means of protecting their clients from incompetent handling. What is generally true is that the hierarchy has to be able to accommodate some independence of action, and that this changes the nature of the hierarchy. It is scarcely possible to delegate the power to make decisions while at the same time holding only central authority to be accountable for its actions. What happens is that authority for some decisions is maintained at the centre, with some framework of rules, while other decisions are delegated to practitioners. Professionals who have wished to maintain a greater degree of independence, like doctors and dentists, have tended to prefer 'arm's length' arrangements in which they are contracted for services rather than salaried, but from the point of view of the service agency the principle is the same; some independence has to be allowed as a precondition for work to be undertaken.

Management

The idea of 'management' in social services has been imported from literature on the private sector; this reflects the growing importance of private sector initiatives in modern welfare states. The idealised 'manager' is a specialist, not in the provision of a service, but in its organisation. Like bureaucracy, management is organised hierarchically, but the role of the manager is different from the bureaucrat:

- The work of the manager is not specialised, but generic; managers have a general responsibility for all the functions taking place below them in a hierarchy.
- The management hierarchy is governed not primarily by rules of conduct, but by performance criteria – in the private sector, by profit, and in the public sector, by measures of outcomes and performance.
- The behaviour of the manager is governed by incentives (including financial rewards) and disincentives.
- The manager motivates staff, through 'leadership'.

This is an ideal type, rather than a reflection of the way that firms are actually organised, and it has been pointed out that it really applies to only a limited number of private firms – like those involved in food distribution, rather than firms dealing with high technology.[431] The model is linked with the development of quasi-markets partly for ideological reasons, and partly because linking the role of the 'manager' with the performance of specific units or cost-centres is seen as a way of achieving the best performance from each unit.

The primary justification for this approach to management comes from a literature which is outside the area of social services, and it is difficult to know how effectively it can be applied in this context. There are some reservations. One problem concerns the nature of the work: if there are circumstances in which social services cannot work in the same way as a market, nor can their managers. There are limits, too, to how far certain tasks, like medical or social care planning, can be subject to generic management. Typically, workers in health services are simultaneously part of three structures – a professional structure, a multidisciplinary team and a service setting (like a hospital or health centre) – each of which has its own lines of communication and accountability. A second problem rests in the idea of 'leadership'. It refers, in different contexts, to the role of managers in general; to the aspects of their role relating to relationships with subordinates; to their personal attributes or traits; to the task of motivating and influencing staff; to the situation of being in charge; to methods for the achievement of tasks; or to a pattern of behaviour.[432] In social services the term is also used to mean strategic planning, the coordination of teamwork and responsibility for achieving goals. The term is, then, extraordinarily ill-defined – Wright's review of the literature shows it to be by turns authoritarian, considerate, laissez-faire, empowering, problem solving, charismatic, self-directed, instrumental or whatever else that people think it could mean. The concept has been pressed into service to justify almost any behaviour that managers might want to engage in.

Radical alternatives

Hierarchical modes of operation have been prominent in social service welfare delivery for a long time, and unsurprisingly they have engendered not only modifications but a range of counter-reactions. Gilbert and others refer to an 'activist' role, which offers an alternative approach to professional and bureaucratic organisation:

> The egalitarian/activist orientation, the polar opposite of the professional/bureaucratic model, rejects professionalism and embraces an open-system perspective of organisation. Neither the organisation nor the professionals are to be relied on: one must turn to different sources of legitimacy, wisdom and policy. These sources may be alternative institutions, such as free clinics and cooperative

schools ... or they may be the recipients of services – the people, the community, the poor.[433]

Although this is not very clearly developed as a model, it does point to something that matters. Several organisations, particularly but not exclusively in the voluntary sector, are suspicious of the role of officials in the public services and see a potential in that role for the abuse of power. 'Radical social work', for example, has developed both as a critique of the role of social workers and as a means of developing alternative patterns of practice.[434]

It is difficult to point to a common pattern of work, because there is so much variation, but at the same time, there are approaches which occur frequently in welfare services:

- The approach to decision making is collectivist, and emphasises team work. The group, not the individual worker, is responsible for decisions, and decisions are made collectively and non-hierarchically. This is fairly characteristic of feminist groups, reflected, for example, in Women's Aid, and it is also found in some social work organisations.
- The principle of non-hierarchical decision making extends beyond the workers as well as between them. There is a strong emphasis on participation by clients and advocacy on their behalf.
- Because the approach is motivated by principle, it is strongly associated with a high-minded, potentially moralistic, approach to service delivery.

The rejection of formal structures and hierarchies can circumvent some of the problems which stem from the emphasis on hierarchy and expertise – such as denying junior workers and recipients a voice in the organisation. It has the disadvantage, however, of removing protections which allow people to function in a working environment despite their differences, and group working can be difficult to sustain where the workers' beliefs lead them in different directions.

Effective organisations

There is no clear ground on which we can say that one type of organisation is better than another. Rothstein suggests that it depends on the type of tasks the agency is being asked to fulfil, and the degree of uncertainty that the agency has to deal with. Table 10.1 is based on his ideas.[435]

TABLE 10.1: CHOOSING AN APPROPRIATE ORGANISATIONAL FORM		
	Tasks	
Technique	*Uniform*	*Varied*
Standardised	Bureaucratic organisation	Semi-professional organisation
Non-standardised	Cadre (leadership-based) or management organisation	Professional organisation

This seems a plausible scheme. In practice, however, management principles have been imported wholesale into each of these categories, and clearly the advocates of such organisational approaches do not accept that there are limitations to their methods.

ISSUE FOR DISCUSSION

Are small agencies better or worse for service delivery than large ones?

ELEVEN

Service delivery

The production of welfare

The process of providing services might also be termed the 'production' of welfare. 'Production' is an umbrella term, covering many different kinds of service: social services are not necessarily involved in the same kind of activity. Some of the services which social policy is concerned with, like social security and housing, mainly involve the distribution of material goods; this means that 'production' is strongly identified with the goods provided, that is, money and housing. Others, notably social work and education, are principally provided as personal services, which require the appointment of someone who carries out the function; 'production' is mainly measured in terms of the numbers of people involved (often, in education, through class sizes). Medical services are largely personal but have a considerable material element.

Despite the differences, there are also important common elements in the process. In order for people to receive services, services have to be provided; the recipients have to gain access to them; their eligibility for receipt of services has to be determined; and the supply of services has to be matched to the requirements. This can be restated, in economic terms, as a problem of relating the supply of the services to the demand. The problem of balancing supply and demand outside the mechanism of the market is a process of 'rationing'.

Priorities

Priorities indicate some degree of precedence; something is a 'priority' when it is to be dealt with before something else. Priorities have to be settled between competing claims for resources. A 'claim' can refer to any kind of call for resources, from any source – including policy makers and administrators as well as consumers; claims differ in their strength and their content, but they have to be decided on as part of the process of allocating resources. The main determinants of a strength of a claim are support and legitimacy: support because the claim has to be negotiated in a political context, legitimacy because the claim has to be accepted within the policy-making process. The setting of priorities is a political process, then: it generally involves negotiation and arbitration between different interests.

Arguments about 'need' have to be understood mainly as a form of claim-language; conflicts between different understandings of 'need' are really conflicts between different claims, rather than disputes about the meaning of the word.[436] A claim of 'need' may be an effective part of a claim for resources, but needs are not necessarily the only, or even the main, determinants of the legitimacy of a claim: some needs are not responded to, while others which seem relatively minor may be respected. 'Needs' have to be understood in relation to the resources that are available. Gilbert Smith's studies in social work led him to comment as follows:

> 'Need', as used by welfare professionals, is not simply a single concept but rather a set of interrelated notions and assumptions about what is to be viewed as the proper object of social work activity. It is helpful to view this body of ideas in terms of a professional 'ideology' about the nature of need.[437]

In social work, emotional problems (which are intangible) are often seen as more important than material ones, and an assessment of 'risk' – the dynamics of a situation – is usually more important than presenting problems. In the allocation of social housing, by contrast, needs which are definable and measurable are treated as being more legitimate than those which are not, and actual needs are treated as being more important than potential needs. The conditions which housing officers have to work with – the limited supply of houses, the need to fill vacancies, and the problems of balancing pressures from different sources – provide the framework within which the demand for the service is expressed.[438] Priorities are not only set explicitly, because (as happens in the case of budget-setting) the administrative process can itself have an effect in determining priorities. In practice, the priorities which are established are conditioned by other administrative requirements, like the need to make sure that houses are occupied quickly, or the requirement to collect information before acting – because people cannot easily be evicted after allocation, the criteria for allocation have to be thoroughly satisfied first. The essential point is made by Rein. It is not always the case that concepts and ideals determine the way in which a service operates; it is just as likely that norms in policy are shaped by administrative structures and the conditions in which a service works.[439]

Resources

For the most part, the provision of services implies the distribution of scarce resources – scarce in the sense that needs generally exceed the capacity of services to meet them. Research into different areas of need has tended to throw up a vision of welfare as a bottomless pit, into which no amount of resources thrown could hope to satisfy every claim. It has become a cliché of some right-wing commentaries on welfare provision that the effect of providing items free to users is that there will be overconsumption.[440] This is not necessarily true; the demand for midwifery is not unlimited. Some services carry considerable non-monetary costs for the consumer: having to live in residential care is something which many of us would wish to avoid, and it is fairly easy to envisage circumstances in which the demand for residential care would fall radically. What is true is that 'needs' represent, not a fixed set of conditions which have to be met, but a range of claims; as more urgent claims are met, lesser claims may come to have greater prominence. On that basis, we can say that there will always be a shortage of finance for services, even if particular services may be overprovided relative to others.

Services have to be limited, therefore; that is, there have to be systems for their financial control. Public expenditure has proved difficult to control in practice, for a number of reasons. Public spending on any social service depends, Glennerster argues, on six main factors:

- the ideology of governments;
- the cost of various demands;
- the structure of taxation;
- the balance of power between government departments;
- the prevailing economic wisdom; and
- the state of the economy.[441]

To this we might add one of the factors which seems most influential in practice – the previous cost of services, for it is difficult to make changes immediately. Capital expenditure (on buildings and equipment) is fairly easy to change rapidly, which is why housing tends to suffer disproportionately in times of economic hardship; but revenue expenditure, of which the largest component is expenditure on labour, is difficult in practice to manage.

Public service agencies have to budget. The Chartered Institute of Management Accountants defines a budget as:

> A quantitative statement, for a defined period in time, which may include planned revenues, expenses, assets, liabilities and cash flows. A budget provides a focus for the organisation, aids the coordination of activities, and facilitates control.[442]

The main approaches to budgeting include:

- *Financial planning systems.* These predict expenditure on the basis of past expenditure plus allowances for inflation (increased costs) and growth, or minus proposed cuts. A typical approach is to say: 'everyone should plan to cut 5% of expenditure'.
- *Bidding.* Constituent agencies or cost-centres estimate their needs and bid for the allocation of funds. The figures are put together and allocations are made. This system has been used by central government to make allocations to local authorities in housing and education. The system tends to encourage overbidding, and often rewards higher spenders.
- *Planned programme budget systems (PPBS).* This was the dominant approach in UK central government for nearly 30 years, but it has fallen out of favour. PPBS works by identifying expenditure in terms of programme objectives (for example, 'services to older people', rather than 'area teams') and planning changes in funding over a number of years, using a rolling programme.
- *Zero-based budgeting.* This is a 'rational' approach, requiring planners to start from scratch and work out how to meet needs.

The difficulties of controlling expenditure in the public sector have led some critics, not unnaturally, to suggest that it may be more controllable in the private sector. It would be true that if the state has contracted for a particular service from an independent operator, it will know exactly how much that service will cost; this is not always the case when it undertakes the operation itself. It is not true, however, that the private sector has intrinsically superior systems of financial control: private firms, like the public sector, also have difficulties making assessments of its costs, and in the private sector there are many operators who make their money by reviewing the miscalculations of others as to value and buying or selling accordingly. Particular problems arise when there is a rapid, unpredictable turnover or changes in circumstance – the kinds of problem which many social services have to deal with continually.

The management of public finance differs from the private sector in several ways:

- The public sector works to fixed budgets, and the private sector often does not. In principle, if a private sector firm does better, there will be more demand for the service, and more income. The public sector, by contrast, has to work within strict limits. Doing better might mean doing the same for less; it does not mean doing more.
- The private sector is able to carry losses or profits forward from one accounting period to the next. The public sector, by contrast, has to spend exactly what has been allowed for. If it spends too much, central control is lost; if it spends too little, it risks having its budget cut for the future. Commonly this means that at the end of a financial year, money has to be spent so as not to be lost. In the context of health services, Ranade

points out that this leads to some inappropriate incentives. Services which deal with more needs increase their costs, not their income; services which perform well attract more work, but no more rewards; inferior services, conversely, have less to do without being penalised for it.[443]

- The private sector is able to balance its books in other ways than the control of expenditure; there is usually the option of supplementing income through diversifying activities. The public sector overall may be able to do something of the kind, but departments within the public sector are not.
- Public expenditure is often committed in advance, while private expenditure can usually be treated as being committed on a rolling basis. The private sector can pull the plug on its commitments in a way that, for political reasons, the public sector usually cannot (although there are exceptions: Israel has experienced 'strikes' by local authorities which have closed down local services when money ran out). This all implies a much greater limit to flexibility in the public than in the private sector.

Budgeting is not just an administrative mechanism. If budgets are set before the establishment of priorities within a service, it generally follows that financial and economic considerations are the first to be considered in the political process of establishing social policy objectives. The reason is that social priorities then have to be negotiated within the constraints of economic priorities. It may be possible to challenge economic priorities, pleading for more money in order to undertake a particular kind of objective, but it is a rare government that is prepared – like the Brazilian government in the construction of Brasilia – to damn the expense and forge ahead regardless. If money has to be found, it typically comes from borrowing, taxation or at the expense of other governmental activity. There are, of course, other possibilities – governments can, for example, run commercial enterprises to raise revenue – but they are less frequently pursued. Effectively, budgeting restricts the potential expenditure on particular service activities, and priorities have to be negotiated within the total budget. Walker comments that this has some importantly limiting effects on policy: the effect is that planning is based more on expenditure than on any assessment of need.[444]

Rationing

Rationing means that supply is balanced with demand at the point where services are delivered. Where services are scarce, some kind of rationing procedure is inevitable; come what may, someone is going to be left without a service, or the people who do receive it are going to get less. The main purpose of rationing is to limit the service received. Figure 11.1 outlines the main processes.

Rationing procedures are complex; several, like delay or deterrence, potentially have multiple effects, changing the behaviour of both providers and service users. Scrivens offers a useful framework to discuss the issues. Rationing, she

FIGURE 11.1: RATIONING PROCESSES

Potential demand

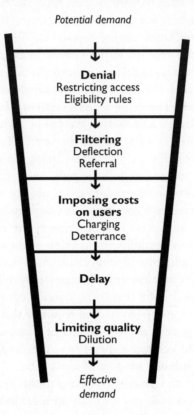

Denial
Restricting access
Eligibility rules

Filtering
Deflection
Referral

**Imposing costs
on users**
Charging
Deterrance

Delay

Limiting quality
Dilution

*Effective
demand*

suggests, can be done either by limiting the supply, or by inhibiting the demand. In this chapter, I plan to focus mainly on issues of supply; issues of demand are considered in the next chapter, along with other issues relating to users.

Within the options for limiting the supply, Scrivens identifies two main forms of restriction: restrictive or dilutant rationing. Services are restricted when people are prevented from receiving them. This can be done by denial – restricting access and eligibility rules; filtering through deflection and referral; and delay. Dilutant rationing implies some kind of reduction in the service, through accessibility, limiting the quality, or limiting the duration for which a service is given.[445]

Denial: restricting access. Simply denying access is an odd way to restrict service delivery, but there are cases where it happens: hospital wards have remained closed because there is no money to open them, public services have laid off workers when there is no money to pay for them. What is far more common is that there is some kind of selective denial – some people are let in, and others are not. In theory, this can be done randomly. A lottery can be held which will let some people in while others are barred. This is not very widely practised, but there are some examples: Elster, who has collected many remarkable illustrations of different allocation procedures, gives examples of the allocation of visas and the selection of soldiers for the draft.[446] When the Greater London Council ran its 'Homesteading' scheme, houses were allocated out of a tombola drum. But this can produce strange allocative effects, because it implies that some people will be randomly included at the expense of others. In the Netherlands, students who qualify for entry to medical education are selected by a weighted lottery, which gives more chances to those with higher grades but also allows the admission of students with lower grades.[447] This must mean that some people are excluded who might have passed, while others are included who will not.

Eligibility qualifications. Selection at the point of entry implies the use of eligibility qualifications: people who meet the qualifications are allowed in, and others are not. The criteria which are used for admission or restriction are enormously variable. It seems fairly evident that services for disabled people should be confined to people with disabilities, that child care should be for children, or that old age pensions should be designed for old people. But there are problems in definition and testing eligibility; it is much less clear that medical care should be confined to people who are sick, or that benefits intended to help poor people should be confined to those who are demonstrably poor, because either rule may exclude those for whom the service is intended.

Eligibility criteria are not simply about directing services, however; they are also important for rationing. Even if services should only be used by disabled people, there may be too many disabled people in a position to claim. It is possible to limit services to a particular level of disability: several European countries refer to '80% disability', which is 80% worth of spurious precision. It may be decided to limit coverage to particular types of disability: the rules for mobility benefits in the UK used to be limited to disabilities with an attributable organic cause, which cut out many intellectual disabilities. Alternatively, other kinds of rule may be applied: limiting services for physical disability to those under the age of 65 conveniently excludes the majority of disabled people, and this represents a considerable saving on the potential cost of a service.

Criteria are sometimes applied which have little directly to do with the subject of the service being provided. Elster again provides a wide range of examples: such issues as age, race, religion, gender, family status and sexual orientation have often been used as a criterion for acceptance or rejection.[448] Direct discrimination on the basis of gender has become much rarer – in the European Union, it violates Community law – but there are many examples. Elster points to the presumption that mothers should have custody of children in divorce, and the exemption of women from military service. Family status may be a criterion for allocation: India has penalised large families in the allocation of housing while Israel has given them priority.[449]

It is worth pointing out that the formal use of eligibility criteria is not the only way in which such criteria might be used to restrict access. If some test has to be conducted before people can be considered eligible, then one of the ways of limiting access might be to limit access to the test itself. In the days of mass clearance in England and Wales, public health officers were commonly limited in the number of houses they could declare unfit, because the classification contained a commitment to future action. In the Cleveland inquiry into the sexual abuse of children, there was a rush of referrals to the doctors as professionals realised that here were two consultants prepared to make the diagnosis. The Director of Social Services asked doctors who were diagnosing sexual abuse to slow down the rate of diagnosis, because his department was not able to investigate the circumstances rapidly enough. The doctors refused on ethical grounds; they were criticised for doing so by the inquiry.[450]

The imposition of eligibility rules seems an obvious form of rationing; if an agency has a target group, it wants to ensure that its services reach that group, and if it has to ration, it wants to restrict someone else. One example of a specialised agency with a different approach is a religious charity in Israel, Yad Sarah, which provides aids and adaptations for disabled people. They reason that if people did not think they needed specialist devices, like zimmerframes, bed pans or wheelchairs, they would not take them, and they impose no test on people who came to them for the goods. (They do, however, ask for a small deposit, to encourage people to return the goods when they no longer need them.) It is difficult to know whether this works – as they do not have any test of eligibility, they cannot check it out.

Filtering. Referral and deflection are systems for separating out people who have needs from others, without actually denying them service. General practitioners, for example, refer cases on to specialists; social work receptionists deflect cases from the social work office by sending them somewhere else, like social security. Screening people, requiring them to undergo some kind of professional assessment before they can receive specialised treatment, or advising them that another service could be more appropriate for their circumstances (for example welfare rights advice rather than social work) might be seen as a form of eligibility qualification; they are ways of shielding higher levels of service from inappropriate demand. At the same time, the services which are doing the filtering are performing a valuable function in themselves. General practitioners in medicine are monitoring people's health care and advising them. Screening offers people important reassurance as well as access to service when necessary. Giving people information, from a referral point, allows them to receive appropriate service.

Delay. Delaying the delivery of service – making people wait – is one of the most common forms of rationing, simply because it is what is going to happen if other decisions about rationing are avoided. Once a service is performing to its full capacity, there will be room for further cases only when some other activity ceases and space is created; this implies that someone will have to wait.

The simplest form of structure for waiting is a queue – where the first come is the first served. This is easily understood, and it is often upheld in housing and health services as being 'fair'. But neither housing nor health services can actually maintain a strict principle of allocation by date order. The problem is that some people have greater and more urgent needs than others. What happens is that there has to be some priority system. People who use that system can be seen as 'jumping the queue' – an accusation often levelled both at homeless people and at private patients – but the truth is that there is no 'queue'. The difference between the two circumstances is that homeless people are being taken within a priority system, according to certain rules, and private patients are being taken outside – which is why the first is fair and the second is not.

An emphasis on date order can have in itself important allocative effects. In research on the allocation of council housing, Clapham and Kintrea found that the effect of giving some priority in an allocations scheme to people according to how long they had waited was greatly to alter the prospects of rehousing for those in need. People who were in lesser need on the waiting lists were generally on higher incomes as well as in better conditions; they were more able to wait. People in worse conditions were also poorer and less able to wait. The ability to hold on was crucial to the quality of housing that people were offered; people in less need were able to refuse, while people in greater need were not. The effect was that people with more priority for waiting time got better housing, while those with more priority for need got worse housing.[451]

Dilution. The other main way of inhibiting supply is the dilution of services. This means that less is given of a service, in terms of quality or duration. Diluting the quality means that people get less – for example, time with a less qualified worker, less money, fewer checks and tests, less personal attention or a quicker termination of service.

Dilution is less common than other forms of rationing. One reason is that professionals are reluctant to do it knowingly; giving people standards which are deliberately lower runs counter to professional ethics, and if there is the alternative to exclude someone altogether in order to maintain standards for others, it tends to be preferred. There are also, it should be noted, disincentives to professionals who wish to dilute the services they offer; doctors who offer more people a cursory going-over probably have to work rather harder than those who take their time. Second, some services cannot easily be diluted. It is usually difficult to offer less by way of an operation or rehousing.

Equity and procedural fairness

The principle of 'equity' or fairness is an important issue in the delivery of scarce services. Equity means that like cases are treated alike. Where there are differences, those differences are reflected in differences of treatment; where there are none, distinctions between cases are unfair and arbitrary.

Substantive fairness. Substantive fairness is concerned with the fairness of outcomes or results. The idea of equity is linked with 'distributive justice'; people are treated 'fairly' when they receive services or resources commensurate with their circumstances.[452] There is a presumption of equality where circumstances are equivalent, and of difference where they are not. There are many different principles which might be held to guide the idea of equity: the relevant circumstances which distinguish people might be differences in their needs, but they might also be differences in their entitlements, their deserts, their previous contribution or their status.[453] Benefits for need include those which cover financial hardship or the functional problems of disability; benefits which recognise desert include war pensions; social insurance benefits (and, arguably, industrial injury benefits) are based on contribution. Health care is based on needs in so far as it responds directly to sickness; it reflects contribution to society when it is made specifically for members of the armed forces, or veterans; it reflects entitlement when it is based on insurance cover or statutory rights. Health care based on status is unusual, but apartheid in South Africa, which formerly distinguished between people on the basis of race, might be an example.

Procedural fairness is a prerequisite for substantive fairness. In order to achieve a fair result, there has to be a fair procedure. The central demand of a fair procedure is consistency – because like cases cannot otherwise be treated alike. This implies the need for impartiality, because prejudice, bias or favour towards some people will lead to inconsistent actions otherwise. It has also been argued that procedural fairness requires openness; if a procedure cannot be seen to be fair then its fairness remains open to doubt. Similarly, the opportunity to have decisions reviewed is of great importance, because otherwise unfairness cannot be corrected.

Procedural fairness is not, however, enough in itself to guarantee substantive fairness. Lotteries are fair procedures on their own terms, but they do not necessarily lead to fair results. Similarly, making people queue is widely thought of as a fair procedure, but the effect is to put those who cannot afford to wait at a disadvantage. Consistent procedures may well lead to consistent unfairness when they have failed to take into account relevant considerations, like need or urgency. For equity to be substantive, there has to be some means by which priorities can be identified and responded to.

Fair distribution. Equity is a distributive concept. It can be very difficult to work out what it means in practice, because, even when people agree about the criteria to be applied, distributions can be examined from different perspectives. Le Grand, in a discussion of redistribution and equality, points to several different measures:

- public expenditure – whether people have different amounts of money spent on them;
- final income – whether the amount of money spent has an equivalent effect on the recipients;
- use – whether people are able to use the service to an equivalent extent;
- cost – whether people suffer equivalent costs as a result of their problems;
- outcome – whether people finish in equivalent positions.[454]

There is, for example, a considerable literature examining the distribution of health care and resources, in which different assumptions about the appropriate measures leads to very different conclusions about the impact of health services.[455] This level of ambiguity makes it difficult to judge what the distributive effects of many policies really are.

Box 11: Rationing health care

The process of rationing health care is often represented as a trade-off between health and economy. Things are rarely so simple. Where health care is expensive and effective, most developed economies have found ways to make funding available. It also happens, however, that intensive treatments have diminishing returns: that as a person's health fails, there is scope for more and more invasive, possibly futile, intervention, leading to a combination of crushing expense with ineffective, and possibly counterproductive, treatment. One of the problems of market provision in health care is that the normal constraints on expenditure do not apply; people will bear almost any cost for a chance of life, when the alternative is none.

A powerful illustration comes from the case of Jaymee Bowen, 'Child B', a child who was diagnosed with cancer and refused treatment by the local health authority in Cambridge. Jaymee was given a 1% chance of responding to treatment. One has to ask whether treatment can be justified with such a low rate of survival. The health authority took the view it could not. A spokesperson for the health authority made the mistake of referring to cost, but the decision was not about money; it was about effectiveness. Treatment is painful, distressing and has unpleasant side-effects. The clinician responsible for Jaymee's care told the court deciding the case that: 'I took the view that it would not be right to subject Jaymee to all of this suffering and trauma when the prospects for success were so slight'.[456]

From the point of view of Jaymee, and her father, one chance in a hundred was better than no chance at all, and they campaigned to be allowed treatment. The court, which was bound to view things from the point of view of the individual case, took the same view. From the point of view of the health authority, however, one chance in a hundred is not a decision about one individual. It is saying that for every hundred people they treat in the same circumstances, 99 will die, with greater discomfort and pain than would otherwise be the case, and one will survive. Jaymee did receive the treatment, and she died.

The controversial nature of rationing decisions has led to the development of mechanisms intended to assess the cost-effectiveness of particular treatments. In some cases, effectiveness can be assessed without reference to costs: some drugs do not work for some conditions. But some work in some cases and not others. An example is trastumazab, which has been claimed to reduce the recurrence of breast cancer by 'approximately 50%'.[457] This claim is inflated. The numbers in the tests are not clearly stated, and they seem to be different in different tables, but nearly 1,700 women received trastuzumab for a year, and a roughly equal number did not. 127 women receiving the drug had a recurrence of their cancer, and 220 in the other group had recurring cancer – an improvement, on the face of the matter, for 42% of the treatment group, not 50%. Crudely put, 93 people, or less than one person in 18, seemed to benefit. What also needs to be mentioned is that 84 patients receiving the medication were taken off it or withdrew because of ill-effects, and that 29 people suffered symptomatic congestive heart failure. Trastuzumab seems, then, to be potentially beneficial for a few people, and potentially harmful for a few others, but if it was used routinely it would make little difference to the substantial majority.

The key problem for health services rests in the finding that some people are significantly worse off as a result of receiving the drug. When a drug is approved for use, it doesn't just go to one person; it goes to hundreds, and sometimes thousands. What risk is acceptable to improve the circumstances of some people, at the cost of danger to others? This is not a simple question of mathematics, and there is no numerical answer. The moral responsibility of decision makers is to do as much as they can to ensure that the benefits go to the people who need it, and that the dangers for others are minimised. There are more people who benefit than who suffer, which is encouraging, but not good enough. The normal procedure would be to use the results of successive tests gradually to refine the definition of the potential recipient group, so that it is used appropriately for people who stand to benefit, and avoided for those who are most at risk. That is what the procedures for testing and trial are supposed to do. However, in a recent court case in the UK, a woman took her health authority to court for refusing to prescribe the drug prior to its approval. She was convinced that not receiving the drug was tantamount to a 'death sentence', and she made several emotive appeals to the press before winning her case in court.[458] The Secretary of State for Health had already intervened to direct that she should receive the drug. The political intervention consequently stopped the process of testing undertaken to protect the public.

Managing the demand for services

The 'demand' for welfare services is not the same thing as the sum of the claims which are actually made on them. The concept of 'demand' is used by economists to refer to the amount of service which would actually be used if the service was supplied at a particular price. It is possible to distinguish 'potential demand' – demand which might arise under certain conditions – from 'effective demand', which is the demand that currently exists. People can claim services for which they do not qualify; conversely, they can have rights for services they are not prepared to use, or fail to express the needs they have.

In Chapter 11, rationing was considered in terms of restricting supply; but, as Scrivens points out, it may also be possible to ration by inhibiting demand.[459] In order to restrict demand, the supplier has to be able to change the behaviour of the people using the service. This is mainly done through increasing the cost of claiming services, relative to the benefits. Such 'costs' are not only financial; they may include limitations on access, obstacles to be overcome or stigma. Because inhibiting demand depends on the balance between costs and benefits, supply rationing plays a part in the process; but there are further restrictions which can be imposed. The most important are charging for services, limits on access, and deterrent procedures.

Charging for services is the standard way that demand is inhibited in the market; a high enough price reduces effective demand and can 'clear the market' of people waiting for service. Waiting lists are very unusual in the supply of private goods, simply because if they exist the supplier can increase prices until the waiting list disappears. This also means that those who are put off are likely to include those who cannot afford the service, and that is one of the main objections to the use of charges in social policy. If, for example, charges for home helps mean that old people do not use them, the kinds of social care and monitoring which home helps do is not going to be undertaken.

Limiting access can be done in various ways. Access can be made more difficult, for example by closing offices, or by only offering services in particular locations. This sounds a bizarre way to select clients, but it does happen in some voluntary agencies – for example, there are housing associations which 'close' their waiting lists to enquiries for part of the year. Often this is done by default: a small agency may know it cannot overextend itself, so it begins working wherever it can, and only when it gets further resources will it expand its remit. The scope for limiting access is considerable. If people have to pass several stages in order to gain access, it follows that they can be encouraged if these stages are made easier to pass, and discouraged if they are made more difficult. Lack of information, complex procedures and time limits on claiming can all have an effect on demand overall.

Deterrence is an important issue in its own right. Demand might be restricted by making a service deliberately awkward to reach, onerous to claim, unpleasant or humiliating. Specific examples of explicit deterrent policies are unusual, but there are several. Probably the most famous was the 'workhouse' of the English Poor Law, which was intended to offer a discipline 'intolerable to the indolent and disorderly'.[460] At one stage, in order to deter people from using hospital care, an instruction went out that hospital patients had to be brought through the grounds of the workhouse so that they would know just where they were.[461] Another example is the deliberate holding down of benefits for unemployed people, in the belief that otherwise the benefits will create a 'disincentive to work'. The fear is that people will find living on benefit more attractive than working; cutting benefits is a way of making them relatively unattractive. 'Workfare', developed in the US, requires claimants to do some labour as a condition of receiving benefit;[462] but some of the arguments seem more focused on increasing the burden of claiming, so as to encourage people not to claim.[463]

The difficulty here is distinguishing deterrent effects which are deliberate from those which are not. Deterrence is common at local level; officials who are faced with excessive demand for services, and who have very limited control over the supply or production of services, have few other options to manage the pressure. It is more difficult to say whether this reflects general policy. If social security offices are generally depressing and sparsely furnished, is it because there is a deliberate attempt to make them unpleasant? Or is it just that public services are generally fairly dowdy and drab unless someone makes a deliberate effort to change them? If homeless people are offered the worst public housing, is it because the housing officers are trying to put them off or is it because the officers have to find someone who is desperate enough to accept the housing they have to offer? Are medical receptionists designed to help doctors work more efficiently, or to keep out patients who would otherwise be a nuisance? One of the problems in identifying deliberate deterrence is that other deterrent effects are so prevalent: the stigmas associated with claiming psychiatric care, poverty benefits or special education are strong, and they can only be reduced by special efforts to the contrary. It is true, however, that deterrence is liable to be introduced at a local level.

Brian Smith links the arguments about restricted access with those on the structure of welfare bureaucracies. A number of organisational practices, he argues, lead to problems in access, and so to disadvantage. These include the compartmentalism that creates multiple gates for people to negotiate; the tendency of agencies to favour success, which encourages the 'creaming' of cases which are more likely to yield it; and, in systems geared to equity on the basis of individual cases, the vulnerability of those systems to negotiations which middle-class people are generally better equipped to deal with.[464] In other words, the problems of access to welfare are not solely the product of deliberate policy decisions; they also reflect structural issues in the organisation of services.

Delivering services

The allocation of services to individuals takes place only at the end of a complex set of processes. It is not enough to say that services have been provided; they have actually to be delivered. This passes through a process of implementation, which is sometimes short – because spending time being assessed by a doctor or social worker constitutes receipt of a service in itself – but can equally be long and tortuous.

An example of the process might be the delivery of services to older people being discharged from hospital. People who have been receiving treatment in an acute ward could, of course, simply be told to go away. But the situation they have come from may not be tolerable. Some may have fallen or burnt themselves because they are effectively unable to cope at home; the admission is a signal that something needs to be done. There can be domestic problems: relatives who have been caring for an older person often realise at the point where an older person has had to go into hospital that they are unable to cope any more. There can be material problems: time in hospital can lead to problems in the tenure of property and the receipt of social security benefits. New problems may have come to light. People with dementia may have succeeded in functioning in their home environment, but the point of admission to hospital can reveal the extent of mental deterioration, because they are unable to adjust to the change in their situation. And being in hospital may create problems in itself. If a person is fully recovered, then in theory discharge should not leave someone much worse off than when they entered hospital. This is not necessarily true.

From the hospital's point of view, there are further considerations. Full recovery from many procedures can take some time; but it does not necessarily call for the kind of facilities found in an acute ward, and indeed there are strong arguments for saying that acute wards are fairly bad places in which to recuperate. Older people are at risk of deterioration. The hospital can respond in part by providing rehabilitation or convalescence wards, but it is in the nature of rehabilitation that it takes time, which makes it expensive and also means that large numbers of places are required. There will still be some patients who are not likely to recover and who will require long-term residential or nursing care. While people are waiting for such care to become available, there is a risk they will 'block' acute beds. There may be some generic response which might be made to everyone in this situation, but it seems inappropriate; people might be forced to wait in hospital beds because of the state of their health, because of problems at home, because of a lack of hospital facilities or because a lack of alternative kinds of facility in the community. The situation requires, then, some kind of assessment, and some kind of allocation, or at least management, of resources in order to facilitate discharge.[465] What is happening, then, is that some judgement has to be made in order to match services to demand, and the pressure comes at least as much from the services themselves as from the needs of the client.

The outcome of this process will vary in different circumstances, and it is difficult to offer generalisations about it, but there are some points which might usefully be made. One is that the outcome is not necessarily going to be in the best interests of the client – simply because the needs of the agency are an important driving force behind the impetus for discharge. Actions taken in the interests of the client are constrained; if someone is stuck on an acute ward, and there is an insufficient range of alternatives, the agency will have to refer that person to something else both because its own priorities require it and because the patient may deteriorate if left waiting. So, where the options for referral are limited, people who are referring 'bed-blockers' on will look for whatever options are available; they may have to settle for services which are 'second best' (for example, nursing care in place of rehabilitation). Second, the problem as presented is not the problem of every part of the agency; it most specifically affects one section, the acute wards. What may happen, unless there are agreed objectives and an appropriate distribution of resources, is that that part of the service unloads its problems onto other parts. So, for example, old people might be referred to continuing care (one of the most expensive decisions which can be made) because of the absence of medium-term rehabilitation.[466]

This is illustrative of a deeper process, and one which is characteristic of many social services. Deliberate policy plays only a limited part in the determination of outcomes for services and for their recipients. The process of implementation is complex, and in this process rules have to be interpreted, practices develop, and judgements have to be made, which in themselves constitute a major part of social policy in practice. Lipsky has christened this process 'street-level' bureaucracy,[467] because many of these decisions are made at the lowest official level. Street-level bureaucrats, Lipsky argues,

> make policy in two related respects. They exercise wide discretion in
> decisions about citizens with whom they interact. Then, when taken
> in concert, their individual actions add up to agency behaviour.[468]

It might be argued that something of the kind is happening at each and every level of a bureaucracy, where discretion is called on to fill the lacunae left by the absence of policy rules. Policy makers set guidelines and constraints; officials have to work out some way to implement them.

Often, in practice, this means that officials are making judgements of the kind that otherwise have to be made in markets – the selection of options while under some form of constraint. Service ideologies – received patterns of thought and approaches to practice – are constructed under such constraints. Officials do not simply make up policies as they please; they have to develop methods of working which fit in with the circumstances of the agency. These methods become enshrined in the working patterns of officials, and are passed from one person to another. The 'common sense' which people learn in agencies consists, in large part, of the developed practice of the agency.

ISSUE FOR DISCUSSION

Is rationing by price preferable to rationing by delay, dilution or deterrence?

TWELVE

Receiving welfare

The receiving end

The picture the previous chapter conjures of the service available to welfare recipients is a depressing one. The experience of claiming welfare is not a question of having one's needs identified and met; recipients have often to overcome a series of hurdles, and when they do they are often subject to intrusive inquiries, deterrence and a low quality of service.

It is fairly easy, in studies of social policy, to lose sight of the people who are likely to receive benefits. There are good reasons for this. One is that social policy as a subject is concerned to make sense of policies and processes, and very often these make no sense at all from the point of view of the service user. Another problem is that work which is oriented towards the recipient can be seen as emphasising the negative aspects of policy, like individual dependency. I mentioned in Chapter One the argument that welfare services should be like drains – boring, safe, taken for granted and used by everyone. Ideally, there should be no more reason to discuss the individual situation of someone receiving social security or health care than there is to talk about people who use roads, take out library books or watch a public service broadcast on television. But this is not the way of the world, and the recipients of social services are not thought of in the same way as other people. They do not have very much in common, but they are all at the receiving end of the sort of process described up to this point; that of itself implies some important issues about their experience.

Claims: demand, needs and rights

In Chapter Four, I made the case that needs demand a response – a statement of need is a claim for services. The 'demand' for social services discussed in Chapter Eleven has some similarities to the concept of 'need': it refers mainly to problems which people have, which call for particular types of response. 'Need' and 'demand' are not exactly equivalent, however. Demand can exist where there is no need: a universal service, like a family allowance, may be claimed by every family even if they do not need the money, and people can have needs which are not recognised as constituting effective demand. It has been argued that the idea of 'need' is superfluous; for practical purposes, it is demand rather than need with which services are concerned.[469] The problem with this position is that the ways in which 'need' is translated into potential demand would then be concealed. There may be no 'demand' for many services for older people from people below retirement age, because they are excluded from the assessment; but the need is probably there, and where people are given the opportunity (as in schemes for early retirement) they often take it.

Bradshaw's 'taxonomy of need' is the best-known classification of needs of different types. He distinguishes four main categories of need: normative, comparative, felt and expressed.

- *Normative need* is need which is identified according to a norm; such norms are generally set by experts. Benefit levels, for example, or standards of unfitness in houses, have to be determined according to some criterion.
- *Comparative need* concerns problems which emerge by comparison with others who are not in need. One of the most common uses of this approach has been the comparison of social problems in different areas in order to determine which areas are most deprived.
- *Felt need* is need which people feel – that is, need from the perspective of the people who have it.
- *Expressed need* is the need which people say they have. People can feel need which they do not express, and they can express needs they do not feel.[470]

A 'taxonomy' is, strictly speaking, a biological classification; Bradshaw's classification does not, like taxonomies in biology, separate out distinct organisms, because a need could (as Bradshaw himself notes) fit into all four categories at once. What it is mainly concerned with is the way in which needs are actually defined, and with who defines them. Bradshaw's classification has been criticised as being limited in its practical application,[471] although Culpitt does make out a good case for its usefulness.[472] A focus on different ways of identifying need helps to suggest a range of methods through which needs can be determined, including methods of consulting users as well as experts.

'Needs' are not the only kind of claim which might be made for services. The provision of parks and libraries, and support for the arts or sport, have less to do with a concept of 'need' than the belief that welfare is positively enhanced when such things are available. The strength of a claim rests on the moral judgements that back it up, rather than its importance for welfare; people can suffer greatly from unemployment or ill-health without feeling any sense of entitlement, but they can become indignant about something they have bought, because there they are confident they have rights.

Part of the movement to 'universal' welfare systems was an attempt to give people a sense of entitlement. When people have rights, their claims are based not on need but on whether they meet the criteria for service delivery – criteria like having a child, being married, or being above a certain age. Rights, like 'need', have been described mainly in terms of the language of claims.[473] There are important differences, because there are also 'rights' (like 'parental rights') which do not seem to claim anything; but many rights do act as demands for service, for example for social security benefits, health care or education. The demand for education is defined by the number of children of school age, not by the needs of children as such. The demand for primary health care can be linked to need, but where there is a national health service it is mainly based on population estimates, because everyone requires coverage.

Claims can be based, politically, in 'moral' rights – that is, rights which are backed up by some kind of moral principle – but not every claim is enforceable. A 'positive' right is linked to some kind of sanction, such as legal redress or a system of review. This is an important difference between services which are based on need and services based on entitlement. The use of professional discretion drives out entitlement; people can be entitled positively to something only if it can be enforced, and allowing discretion means that it cannot be. Access to higher levels of health care, for example, generally depends on the assessment of a medical practitioner. What people are entitled to in the UK system is not a certain type of medical care, but medical assessment and the care which follows from it. People cannot in general obtain redress because a doctor has reasonably refused them service on medical grounds (no one is 'entitled' to an amputation), although they may do so if they are refused for other reasons, like moral judgements or economic constraints. The principle in US law has been extended to say that people can gain redress against a doctor if that doctor has made a mistake, which is not universally true elsewhere; this shifts the boundaries of the entitlement, but it does not alter the general point.

Claiming

The 'claims' referred to so far are claims in a general, 'thin' sense; they can be made by anyone, and they mainly consist of arguments or pressures for a service. 'Claims' are also used in a 'thick' sense – that is, a sense which is more specific and more developed even if it is narrower – to refer to particular applications for service. People 'claim' benefits when they fill in a form and hand it in to the appropriate office. They 'claim' medical care when they present themselves to a doctor for assessment. 'Claiming' has become an important part of the administration of services; it places the initial responsibility for receiving services on the 'claimant' or client, rather than an agency which is failing to reach people.

There are some services which do not require a 'claim' to be registered in this way. Medical care is usually initiated by the patient, but in cases where the patient is not able to do so – for example, after a road accident – it will be initiated by someone else. Social work is not always undertaken with the consent of the parties involved, let alone on their initiative, and the equivalent of the 'claim' in social work is the 'referral', where someone informs workers that their intervention might be appropriate. That 'someone' might be the client, a member of the family, someone who had come into contact with the client (like a fuel supplier or a police officer) or another professional in welfare services. By contrast, social security is almost always dependent on the registration of a claim by the prospective recipient – which is arguably unnecessary, because in a universal system it is fairly simple to make the payment of age-related benefits automatic. 'Claiming' is sometimes defended on the basis that it respects the choice of individuals: there is a view that people only have true 'rights' if they are able to choose whether to exercise them or not.[474] There are some grounds to support this in the case of medical care, where the implication otherwise would be that people would have to have compulsory medical treatment. However, the argument sometimes seems suspect: if people have money paid to them automatically they can still choose whether to use it or not.

This points to an important issue about demand. The effect of placing the burden of claiming on the recipients of welfare is that some people will not use the service. People may not use services because of a positive choice. For example, people may not want to go into residential care because they do not like the kind of lifestyle that it offers. Some medical operations are unpleasant and possibly frightening; for example, people often delay seeking help for cancer both because of pessimism about what can be done and because the treatments are generally unpleasant. However, the issues are rather more complex than the issue of 'choice' implies. There is a major problem of 'non-take-up', where people who are entitled to benefits, and for whom it is intended that they should receive the benefits, do not get them. For many years, this was described as a problem of 'stigma', because some claimants felt humiliated by claiming, but the problem is rather more complex than this suggests. Reasons for non-take-up include ignorance about benefits, the complexity and difficulty of the process, previous problems in attempting to claim, limited marginal benefits and the costs to the claimant of proceeding.[475] The financial advantage to be gained by claiming some social security benefits may be outweighed by the time, trouble and negative experience involved in claiming. Weisbrod, in a short working paper, outlined a central principle which has become one of the most important insights in this area: that the decision whether or not to claim can be understood as a balance between costs and benefits.[476]

This points to a set of issues in the way that demands are formed. The literature on 'access to welfare' is limited but important. If people are to make an effective demand for welfare, they have not only to exercise their formal entitlements but also to overcome a series of practical obstacles. In an influential paper, Kerr outlined a series of stages, which he intended to apply to social security benefits but which might equally apply to others:[477]

1. People must feel a need, or at least they must want to have what is being offered.
2. They have to find out that the service exists. Few people have heard of orthotics (which provides devices such as corrective footwear), and that means that even when they have the problems they do not necessarily know to ask about the service.
3. They have to know they are likely to receive the service; a service for 'poor people' is not certain to be taken up by people who do not think of themselves as poor.
4. They have to feel that the benefit is worth claiming. This is mainly influenced by the size of the benefit, but there are also hidden costs – such as the problem of travelling to an office or surgery, and the time that claiming is likely to take.
5. There are the beliefs and feelings of potential recipients: someone who believes that benefits are degrading is less likely to claim than another person who thinks they are an entitlement.
6. It is important that people should recognise their situation as being stable. People with debilitating illnesses are unlikely to think of themselves as 'disabled' until they know either that the condition is likely to last, or that it has lasted a long time. A newly separated mother is often unsure that her situation is going to last, and may delay claiming until her position becomes clear.

Kerr intended his model to represent a series of 'thresholds': in order to make a claim, a person has to negotiate each obstacle in turn. In practice, the divisions are rather less well defined than this might suggest: someone with negative attitudes towards a service may well know less about the service (because such a service is 'not for people like us'), while people may not get to work out whether a benefit is worth claiming until they have worked out how long their circumstances are going to last.[478] Besides, when the focus shifts to other services besides social security, there may be important differences. Filling forms is one of the banes of social security administration; it is not a major part of claiming health care in a universal system. By contrast, it is possible to deal with many social security claims remotely – by post, telephone or the internet – but health care usually relies on visits to particular locations, increasing the cost to the user of claiming health care.

Problems like this visibly affect many social services. The problem of 'non-take-up' is interpreted differently in different services. In health care, the main problem seems to be that people who are most in need are least likely to receive appropriate levels of health care. People in lower social classes have greater health needs, but they are less likely to receive services.[479] There are two main explanations for limited access. Cultural explanations locate the problem in the behaviour of people in the lower classes, who are said to be less able to explain complaints to middle-class doctors, less able to negotiate for resources and more willing to tolerate illness. Practical problems concern the difficulties of obtaining access: doctors' surgeries tend to be in more salubrious, middle-class areas, while people in lower social classes are less likely to have access to a telephone and less likely to have a car, and besides are less free to take time off work without losing pay.[480]

The costs of claiming

The benefits of claiming services are usually self-evident. Services which provide medical care, housing or education are offering a particular kind of service, and the nature of the service is the simplest explanation for why people should claim. The costs are much less obvious, because they are not necessarily material, and often they are not measurable.

The costs which might be considered are of three kinds:

- *Access*. This sort of issue has been considered in the preceding sections: it refers to problems like giving up time, travelling, consulting and overcoming obstacles.
- *Use*. In order to be recipients of different kinds of care, people often have to go without some of the things which others have. The long-term consequences of receiving psychiatric care can include unemployment and poverty, because people who enter care have to leave the labour market. People living in residential care are restricted in their freedom of movement, and their ability to live as they want in their homes; they often have limited choices about when they eat or when they go to bed.[481] At the extremes, people can be subjected to neglect, brutality and dehumanising treatment.[482]
- *Exit*. Once someone has begun receiving a service, it may be difficult to stop. This may happen simply because the benefits of the services are likely to be lost. In social security, it has been claimed that there is an 'unemployment trap', in which people might be better off receiving benefit than working for a low wage.[483] Problems also arise following changes in circumstances in other services: for example, young people leaving residential care are often particularly vulnerable to problems of unemployment and homelessness.
  In some cases, there are further costs associated with exit. Single parents looking for employment commonly have the cost of childcare to consider, if

this is not provided freely by the state. Being discharged from hospital is a difficult situation for the person who has been in an institutional environment for a long time, which combines the loss of service with all the problems of being able to establish oneself in the world outside.[484]

The precise effects of these costs are difficult to establish, because they have to be measured against the benefits. The attitudes of people who fail to claim services are often markedly different from those who do claim – which is to be expected if some have been deterred while others have not – but it is not necessarily the case that those who have claimed are not in some way affected by the costs.[485] Similarly, the existence of costs at the point of exit may delay the process, but the existence of costs of claiming, and further benefits in not doing so, may outweigh this effect. The problem with generalising about people's behaviour on the basis of incentives or disincentives – the kind of argument made by Charles Murray in *Losing ground*[486] – is that we know very little about the extent to which people will actually respond to such stimuli. This responsiveness (economists refer to it in terms of 'elasticity') might vary enormously according to circumstances, and generalisations can only be supported through empirical evidence.

Choice

The picture which all this tends to conjure of service delivery is one in which the people who receive welfare have their behaviour conditioned and determined by the services. But recipients still have to balance costs and benefits, it is usually their decision to claim, and the choices they make are an important constituent part of demand. The analysis of choice is mainly the province of economics, and in particular of welfare economics; choice is the mechanism through which utility, and so welfare, can be maximised. In the operation of social welfare services, however, the opportunity to exercise choice has often been limited.

Concerns about choice have mainly been expressed through arguments for considering the delivery of welfare in terms of a market, in which the recipients of welfare services are consumers (or even 'customers'). The central principle is that decisions are made by the person who is likely to receive the services, rather than a professional or bureaucrat on their behalf. In the operation of an economic market, consumers have the opportunity to use resources to purchase goods and services. The priorities which are determined, and so decisions about rationing, arise from the interaction of many people rather than the policy of some central authority. Part of the rationale for marketisation and the development of the 'quasi-markets' considered in Chapter Ten is that markets create opportunities for choice, and so for the maximisation of welfare for consumers according to their own lights.

This argument is a strong one; and, despite the reservations considered previously about the operation of the private market, it is very widely accepted on both right and left. When people are short of food or clothing, few people would argue for distribution by the state; the argument is much more commonly made that people need to have the money to pay for such items. Indeed, the idea that poor people might be subject to a régime in which they are unable to choose what they eat or what they wear is usually seen as a sign of repressive paternalism, rather than a liberation from the constraints of the market. Arguments for social security or income maintenance are generally arguments for the private sector – to give people the money to choose rather than giving them what they need.

By contrast, arguments are commonly made in discussions of housing, education or health which point to the inefficiencies and constraints on choice which arise in the private sector. The problem is not simply that people have unequal resources – that would be an argument for redistribution of cash instead[487] – but that the process of exercising choices leads to inequities or inappropriate distributions. Part of this is attributable to the problems of exercising choice meaningfully – people who are desperate are not in a strong bargaining position; part of it, in health care, is the problem of knowing and understanding what is being purchased; but the major part, too, is that the process of exercising choice itself leads to serious problems of disadvantage. In housing and education, the effect of choice is to produce a stratified system with profound social consequences.

The effect of permitting choice in the structure of non-market services may be to duplicate some of the inequalities of the private market. The recipients of welfare services tend to be disadvantaged, and they have fewer options from which choices can be made. In these circumstances, the opportunity to exercise choice may simply aggravate existing disadvantages. In education, parents who can afford to move into the catchment areas of the better schools are able to buy a considerable social advantage for their children. Social housing is nominally let according to some system of priorities in allocation, usually (although not always) on the basis of need.[488] But people who are offered social housing are usually given only a very limited choice – they might be allowed two or three chances – and even then their choices are likely to be limited, because they do not know what the next option will be like. They are often reluctant to accept social housing in poor areas. But some people are more able to exercise choice than others: a lot depends on whether people are able to hold on a little longer. The result is that people who are least able to exercise a choice have to take properties that others are able to refuse, and so that people who are desperate and most in need are likely to receive the worst housing.[489]

The problem with limiting choice is that it does not necessarily guarantee that disadvantages will be redressed. The real aim is not to obstruct choices and opportunities, but to ensure that those who are poorest and most disadvantaged will be able to exercise such opportunities.

Social control

The experience of many people who receive welfare is not only one of humiliation and degradation; they become subject to the control of others. Social security officers are allowed to make intrusive personal inquiries: social security is used to regulate the labour market and the behaviour of individuals.[490] Housing managers, following the model of Octavia Hill, have acted paternalistically, policing the housekeeping standards and neighbourliness of their tenants.[491] Social work can be seen as a form of 'soft policing', which ensures that the operation of families conforms with current social norms.[492]

These aspects of the provision of social service have been attacked as a form of 'social control'. There is certainly a case to answer, but the arguments on this subject are muddled.[493] The Marxist literature lumps material on social norms – for example, protection of children from abuse – together with issues about the power of a dominant class.[494] The problem has become worse with the growing influence of Foucault,[495] who combined impish vagueness with a cavalier indifference to historical evidence. Power, Foucault writes, 'is everywhere, not because it embraces everything, but because it comes from everywhere'.[496] If power is everywhere, there is nothing special or remarkable about the exercise of power; it is part of everyday life. If it comes from everywhere, complaints about the inappropriate application of power lose their force; the exercise of power cannot be avoided. This tells us little or nothing about how policy works.

People might be said to be 'controlled' by welfare services if they are being made to act in ways they would not otherwise choose. Primarily, this means that choices are denied to them, or the consequences make the options undesirable. People can be forced to go into hospital for psychiatric treatment, for example, because there is no alternative pattern of treatment available; others are forced to attend school because the penalty for not attending is severe. Conversely, people can be pushed to choose certain things because the benefits are considerable. Tax incentives for charitable donations, for example, can have a marked effect in increasing such donations; and subsidised ownership of housing can have a large effect on people's decisions about tenure. Another way of looking at this is in the terms of 'costs' and 'benefits', which were used in the discussion of rationing; and, indeed, manipulating the demand for services by deterring people or trying to stimulate interest are in themselves illustrations of 'control'.

'Control' does not always refer to direct effects; it might also be held to refer to cases where the opportunity to form different choices, rather than the costs or benefits of the options available, is limited. The 'hidden curriculum' in education has been said to impose pressure for conformity: Bowles and Gintis argue that education acts 'to teach people to be properly subordinate and render them sufficiently fragmented in consciousness to preclude their getting together to shape their own material existence'.[497]

Control of the agenda for discussion has been argued to be an important part of the exercise of power, for example in Bachrach and Baratz's study of urban policy in the US.[498] Often, this kind of issue is remote from the particular circumstances of claimants, and it belongs to a discussion of 'power' or 'hegemony' rather than control at the receiving end. But there are important issues when a person receives 'therapy' to adjust to their environment, and acceptance of the status quo is considered a positive outcome.

Control is a matter of particular concern in the distribution of welfare for three reasons. First, there is the problem of preserving the dignity of people who use services. In the parliamentary debates about the abolition of the Poor Law, Bessie Braddock MP commented that she had seen people having to parade their underwear in front of others in their attempts to get some kind of help.[499] (I've seen much the same thing myself in welfare rights work.) Anger is a common reaction, as are threats of violence. In a relatively brief career as a housing officer, I was begged, threatened and offered bribes; I once had a baby abandoned in the office. This points to a second important issue: that people who are using welfare services are often particularly vulnerable to exploitation. If workers are pressed or made offers by clients, it is because so many people are desperate; often they feel they have to do whatever they can to get a decent lifestyle. This puts a particular ethical responsibility on workers: they are in a relationship of power relative to their clients, because they control resources or services necessary to them, and it is important that the power should not be abused. Third, there are profound issues of the rights of recipients. Discretion already limits rights; being required to do what others demand of you limits them still further. Many of the worst cases of misuse of power happen in cases where the recipients have no effective redress or voice: the abuse of people in residential establishments reflects a combination of dehumanising conditions, negative attitudes and the unfettered power of workers to control their charges.

Empowerment

Countering these problems is increasingly seen as an issue of 'empowerment'. The idea of 'empowerment' means that people who are relatively powerless are able to gain more power. The term has only recently come into widespread use, and it tends to reflect its origins in social work practice. Solomon, in one of the earliest uses of the term, defines empowerment as

> a process whereby the social worker or other helping professional engages in a set of activities with the client aimed at reducing the powerlessness stemming from the experience of discrimination because the client belongs to a stigmatised collective.[500]

This has subsequently been extended to refer to 'the mechanism by which people, organisations and communities gain mastery over their lives'.[501] The nature of the change which has to be brought about, however, is very unclear. Miller comments that

> frequently, there is ambiguity about whether ... empowerment will be of individuals or communities. While both individual and collective or community empowerment are desirable, the two may not always converge.[502]

At the individual level, empowerment might be seen as a form of freedom; people are empowered when they are able to decide on issues for themselves. Arguments for 'normalisation' overlap with those of empowerment when 'normalisation' is seen as a route to autonomy. Pinderhughes thinks of power primarily in terms of social interaction, with the result that facilitating social skills and communication can be seen as a form of empowerment.[503]

At the collective level, empowerment can be taken to be a response to a lack of power; the powerlessness of stigmatised groups reflects the place of disadvantaged groups in the wider society. The movement to 'participation' in the late 1960s and early 1970s was rooted in concepts of direct democracy, and encouraged by a number of influences, including imitation of trends in the US, public interest in conservation, and the recognition of planning as a political activity. The same principles were directly extended to social housing, where they have become an accepted part of management practice. One of the arguments for participation was that it was thought to enhance the personal abilities of the participants. This made it a desirable strategy for community workers and others concerned with the position of disadvantaged groups. The other main argument was that it facilitated decision making, by providing information and permitting negotiation with service users. In other words, participation has been a means of incorporating different groups within the policy process. The established position of participatory mechanisms has made them a model for subsequent strategies concerned with empowerment.

A collectivised approach to empowerment is often realised within the structures of local communities. The strategies commonly pursued within local government and services focus on disadvantaged groups and communities. Broadly speaking, there are four main strategies defined in the literature:

- *Community social work* focuses on individuals and their social interactions in order to increase their potential within a social context.[504]
- *Neighbourhood work* consists of attempting to develop the networks and relationships in a community, by strategies of outreach and access, in order to facilitate social action.[505]
- *Community education* is concerned with developing the social skills and collective potential of disadvantaged people.

- *Community organisation* (also referred to as 'community action' and 'community development') is concerned with political mobilisation and collective action. This drew inspiration from models in the US (for example Alinsky's *Rules for radicals*[506]) which saw the roots of social problems as lying in the structure of power in society and set out in order to redress the balance.

These categories are not discrete, and several strategies can be adopted simultaneously.

The emphasis on empowerment at the collective level reflects an important ideological commitment among certain communitarian socialists. The fundamental problem is that the people who are most disadvantaged are often wholly unable to present their case individually or collectively; disruption of communication, the loss of social contact and atomisation have profoundly disempowering effects. Some psychiatric patients participate very effectively in collective organisations, but many do not; those who are homeless, in particular, may not only have lost their friends but have no residual family contact.[507]

Box 12: Empowerment and dementia

Welfare services have often suffered from the assumption that people who are dependent are unable to make decisions for themselves. Over the course of the last 30 years, there has been a growing movement to empower service users and to affirm their capacity to make decisions. The arguments for empowerment have been made for people with intellectual disabilities, people with psychiatric disorders and children. In the case of older people with dementia, however, there is still an assumption that sufferers are unable to make decisions – that the person with dementia has become, somehow, an empty shell, lacking the capacity for feeling or understanding, and that decisions have to be made by carers on their behalf.[508]

Dementia is not one disease, but a range of conditions associated with a pattern of experience. Roth defines dementia as 'a global deterioration of the individual's intellectual, emotional and conative faculties in a state of unimpaired consciousness'.[509] The deterioration of intellectual faculties implies that sufferers become progressively less able to retain new information, and so to absorb it. They become gradually cut off from their environment. The term 'conation' refers to a person's will and directed activity, and the loss of conation means that the person with dementia becomes unable to behave autonomously. The deterioration of emotional faculties shows itself in behavioural disturbance, emotional overreactions, passivity and inappropriate responses – although all of these might be a reaction to the loss of abilities otherwise experienced in dementia.

Dementia is a difficult condition – difficult for sufferers, for carers and for professionals. None of that means that a person with dementia should be assumed to be unable to express a view. Dementia is a degenerative process: people start with capacities, which they slowly lose. Many people with dementia are suffering from a progressive deterioration of mental capacity, which means that for a large part of the progression they remain aware and able to function socially despite their condition, but even those who have considerable impairment are likely to show some social reaction and awareness. People with dementia still, in general, have the ability to speak; they have often formed preferences and decisions, for their own reasons. However, the capacities of people with dementia are liable to be overlooked. People with dementia are taken to suffer a kind of 'social death', which is particularly distressing for them, and their wishes and concerns are disregarded.

Kitwood makes a strong case that people with dementia are responsive to their social environment and still show a degree of social awareness, while in other cases there may be 'rementia' or a positive regain of abilities through social interaction.[510] Researchers who have made the effort to communicate have found that communication is possible. Killick comments:

> To see the struggle for expression on people's faces, to hear the sounds tumbling over themselves in an effort to become words, phrases, sentences – this is painful. But when communication has been achieved, when the individual has leaped across the barrier to attain an utterance which embodies an insight – this is inspiring, often for both parties.[511]

The arguments for empowerment are not less strong in cases where people's ability to express their views is impaired. On the contrary, these are the circumstances where it becomes more important to ensure that people's rights are protected, and that they have a voice in what happens to them.

Rights

Allowing people rights as individuals is crucial to protection in circumstances where they are vulnerable. The use of 'rights' in this context can be understood in two main ways. One view is that the kind of rights which recipients of welfare are being given are moral rights, which give people a sense of entitlement and legitimacy. Marshall wanted the 'right to welfare' to be understood as a basic right for everyone, as part of a new understanding of citizenship.[512] The ideal of the 'welfare state' may seem remote at times from the practical problems of claimants, but it has an important persuasive role: perceived legitimacy is important in maintaining a sense of social honour, and where people feel a sense of shame or humiliation in receiving services, advice workers do refer to general principles of this kind.

The claim for 'citizenship' is a moral position, but it also has a legal meaning, as the 'right to have rights'. Welfare recipients can be denied rights in practice. The worst cases are those of people who have impaired abilities, like people with severe disabilities or dementia. The effects are devastating; they include the use of drugs to control their behaviour, admission to institutions without their consent, and even in the case of people with intellectual disabilities compulsory sterilisation. People who have limited social competence need special treatment because they are vulnerable to exploitation and abuse and because they may suffer serious harm without some kind of protection. But this is an argument, not for the reduction or limitation of their potential field of activity, but for increasing it. Harris, writing about children, represents this as a case for greater equality:

> To regard people as equals is precisely to recognise that they are not
> equally able to protect themselves, or further their own interests or are
> necessarily the same in any other sense. It is because of inequalities that
> people are in danger of arbitrary and ill usage, tyranny, exploitation
> and so on. To regard people as equals is to take a stand on how they
> are to be treated, not to make a remark about their capacities.[513]

There are several kinds of rights, and they do not apply equally to everyone. Some rights are universal, in the sense that they apply to everyone in the same position, but many are not. Some rights are contingent, which means that they apply only when certain conditions are met – examples are rights to war pensions, or widows. And many rights are particular, which means only that they apply to particular individuals. People have a general right if it applies to everyone else in similar circumstances (for example, as children, older people or people with mental illness); they have a particular right if someone has a personal obligation towards them (for example, as the result of a promise, a contract or an injurious action). On the face of the matter, particular rights look as if they ought to have only a limited role in social policy overall, but there are several countries where particular rights have become the main means through which welfare is delivered. Pensions, in much of continental Europe, are not based in the general rights of the population; they are tied closely to each person's work record, and the contributions which people make while they are working give them a contractual right to receive benefits in due course. Pensions are really 'income packages', made up of a series of particular entitlements. This kind of arrangement can never provide comprehensive coverage of a population, but it is often surprisingly effective in protecting the position of a large proportion of the population – pensioners, in France, are now being said to be better off, on average, than the working population.

Rights also have to be enforceable. Legal rights are of two main kinds: substantive and procedural. Substantive rights are rights to a good or service which is claimed. They can be enforced through procedures for the redress of grievances

– for example, internal review, or structures for appeal. Although there are many substantive rights in social services, particularly to social security benefits, they are not generally applied, for reasons which were discussed when considering the role of professionals in service delivery: wherever professional discretion is to be applied, the effect of a substantive right would be to deny the professional scope for manoeuvre. Interestingly, many of the formal rights which apply in social services are not 'claim-rights' at all, but liberties – protections against intrusion or treatment without consent.

The procedural rights include rights to information, and to rights which make the redress of grievances possible – including rights to be heard and to be represented, to be judged impartially, and to recourse to judicial procedures when other means fail. (Rights to be heard and to be judged impartially are commonly referred to as principles of 'natural justice'.[514]) Procedural rights are prerequisites for the redress of grievances; they are not enough to guarantee redress, but they are necessary.

There are often important limitations on the procedural rights available to people who receive social welfare services. First, decisions may be made solely on an individual basis; for substantive rules to be developed, there has to be some system of precedent, so that people can refer to judgements in other cases as support for their own. Second, professional or administrative discretion can drive out rights of this kind, as well as substantive rights, although it would still be true that professionals who exercise discretion are expected to do so by the standards of their profession, rather than through personal prejudice. Third, the problems which people experience are not always individual; they may be collective, like the effects of pollution, inadequacies in the education service, or a refusal to cover some contingencies for insurance. US law allows two special kinds of plea which are not necessarily permitted elsewhere – certainly not in England. These are 'class actions', in which people can sue as a group, and the 'Brandeis brief', which allows the social implications of an action to be taken into account in a legal judgment.[515] Lastly, and perhaps most important, legal redress is worth very little if people cannot gain access to it. The law in England, it has often been said, is open to everyone, like the Ritz. There has to be some mechanism which allows people to afford the legal costs, or alternatively a structure for the redress of grievances, like the use of administrative tribunals, which allows such costs to be circumvented – although it is important to note that this often means that people go unrepresented, which denies another important procedural right. For people whose social capacity or functioning is impaired, there has to be an effective route through which arguments can be made by them or on their behalf.

The gap in social protection left by the inaccessibility of legal redress has led to the development of a set of strategies usually referred to as 'welfare rights'. 'Welfare rights' refers to a range of activities in which citizens are advised and supported in their claims for social welfare services, and in particular for social security benefits. There are four main types of activity which are considered to be part of 'welfare rights':

- advice and support given to individuals who have problems with specific services;
- agencies dedicated to advocacy and specialised advice, which is intended not only to assist individuals but to challenge and test the work of agencies in the welfare field, and to establish precedents in practice;
- publicity, extending awareness of the nature of the rights;
- the political and campaigning arm of welfare rights work, which draws on information gained from practice to argue for legal and administrative changes in the treatment of recipients.

These are different approaches, but they are mutually reinforcing; campaigning work is often dependent on the authority established by a foundation of practically based knowledge and action, while casework throws up issues which require other avenues to be explored beyond the immediate scope of legal redress.

Developing user control

The development of user empowerment, Means and Smith suggest, has focused on three main strategies. These are rights, 'exit' and 'voice'.[516] The idea of 'exit', which is associated with market approaches, emphasises the importance of choice; if people are able to take their custom elsewhere, providers are to that degree accountable. The theory of the private market, from which the idea of 'exit' is drawn, also assumes competition between many providers, and responsiveness to demand through a profit motive. When these conditions are not met, there is no guarantee that services will be responsive to particular types of need, especially those considered to have low priority.

'Voice' implies that views are represented and can be put somewhere within the process. This is linked with ideas of participation, although its scope is limited; giving people a say is not the same as giving them a degree of control. Arnstein describes a 'ladder of participation' (Figure 12.1);[517] the process of listening to people is sometimes no more than a pretence. But Arnstein underestimates consultation, which is an important element in deliberative democracy. The main defence of 'voice' is that having a say is clearly better than having none, and mechanisms for voice have some value even if they cannot hope to move the balance of power. Voice is an important aspect of empowerment, and for those who are disadvantaged in their ability to exercise a voice, like people with intellectual disabilities or psychiatric patients, an advocacy movement has been developing.

FIGURE 12.1: ARNSTEIN'S LADDER OF CITIZEN PARTICIPATION

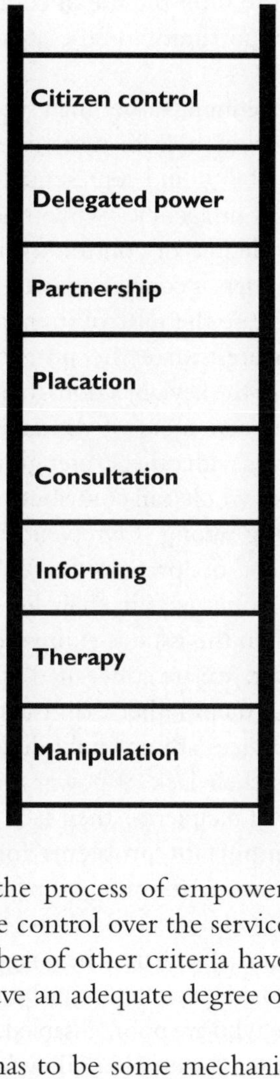

Citizen control

Delegated power

Partnership

Placation

Consultation

Informing

Therapy

Manipulation

These issues can help in the process of empowerment, but clearly none is sufficient to give users some control over the services they receive. Deakin and Wright suggest that a number of other criteria have to be examined to ensure that the users of services have an adequate degree of control. They propose six main tests:

1. *Accountability*. There has to be some mechanism through which services can be made to answer to service users for their decisions.
2. *Representation and participation*. Participation in decision making implies not only that the views of consumers are expressed, but also that their views carry some weight.
3. *Information*. People who use a service must have access to information about that service, because lack of such information denies them the opportunity for comment or control.
4. *Access*. Services have to be accessible because the effect of inaccessibility is to deny people the opportunity to use the service.
5. *Choice*. The ability to exercise choice is an important aspect of user control, because a lack of options means in itself that users are unable to control outcomes.

6. *Redress*. Obtaining redress of grievances, and even having concerns addressed, is important to limit the use of control by agencies as well as to give users the formal opportunity to raise concerns.[518]

Most of these criteria are procedural, rather than substantive, but in practice the distinction is hazy. The tests which seem most directly to be concerned with procedures, notably accountability and representation, are generally defended because they limit the actions of agencies while opening avenues for the users of services to exercise some degree of control.[519] In so far as the relationship between producers and consumers is concerned with power, the effect of limiting the producers is often to increase the relative strength of the user.

It is important not to overestimate the potential effects of this kind of procedure. Dwyer lists some of the key objections to user-based approaches. There are conflicts of interest between users of different types; users are often in competition for scarce resources with others; user groups can lose touch with their grassroots; and the process as a whole can contribute to the exclusion of marginal groups.[520] There is something wrong, Ovretveit observes in passing, with the very idea of 'user involvement' or 'participation'. 'We forget', he writes, 'that most people choose to involve services in their lives'.[521] If we begin from the perspective of the service, then the issue is expressed in terms of 'participation' or 'involvement'. If, however, we are concerned with services as being services for people, the focus shifts to them rather than the perspective of the service.

The recipients of social services are not only disadvantaged in terms of their relationship with producers; their lack of power reflects a more general social position. The stigmatisation of recipients, their lack of resources and status, and their vulnerability pose important problems for the social services. The development of formal mechanisms for protection, and substantive rights, offers a means by which the people who receive services are not solely dependent on decisions made by the producers of welfare; these rights represent one of the most important means through which recipients can be empowered. But the social disadvantages remain; people who are poor, disabled, mentally ill or unemployed cannot be expected to overcome the problems they face simply because they have more effective control over services. There are, then, limits to what it is possible to achieve in the narrow context of service delivery.

ISSUE FOR DISCUSSION

Service recipients are often in competition for scarce resources. Is it right to empower people, if it furthers the claims of some groups only at the expense of others?

Part Four
The methods and approaches of social policy

THIRTEEN

The methods and approaches of social policy

Theory and practice
Theoretical method
Description
Normative approaches
Evidence and policy
What works?
Cost-effectiveness and efficiency
The distributive impact of social policy
Evaluation and policy

Theory and practice

The 'theory of social policy' is not generally taught as an academic subject, although many social policy degrees have courses in applied political and social theory. The practical use of theory is that it helps to assess policies, and to understand the patterns of thought which lead people from general principles to policies. People who work in the field need to be aware not only what the problems are, but what elected representatives, officers and fellow workers believe about them, and what they see as legitimate action in the field of policy.

Empirical evidence is important for social policy, but it cannot establish policy or priorities itself. Empirical material has to be interpreted, problems have to be recognised as important, evidence has to be seen as pointing to some outcome, 'facts' have to be constructed in a way which relates them to possible policy responses. What happens in social policy is that theoretical insights from different disciplines can be used to give some shape to the mass of empirical material (or 'fact') which is available, and a direction about what to look for. There are often competing, contested interpretations of the same evidence. Boaz and Pawson look critically at five systematic reviews of the evidence on the same topic in social administration (that is, mentoring); they all come to different conclusions about what the evidence says.[522] Translating evidence into policy is not straightforward; interpretation and evaluation are unavoidable.

The construction that is put on evidence is difficult to recognise when problems seem 'obvious'; if children are battered by parents, people are living on the street, or there is mass unemployment, what 'construction' is being put on the material? Some reference to the history of the subject can be helpful here, because in each of these cases there has been not simply denial of these problems but a range of political views about what the problems were, what they signified and what kind of response might be appropriate. Facts are seen through particular perspectives; the received wisdom of one generation becomes the misconception of another. In a field like social policy, theory is meaningless without some reference to empirical problems; but equally, empirical issues acquire their meaning for us only because we are able to relate them to some kind of theoretical underpinning.

Theoretical method

Theory serves several purposes: they include description, analysis and normative examination.

Description

Theory helps description by providing a basis on which to categorise, or classify, phenomena. Classification is needed for the description of social phenomena; without it, it is impossible to offer any useful generalisations about cases. The use of classification is probably most obvious in attempts to compare different countries, where a distinction might be made between social democratic countries and market-oriented or liberal ones; this is really a theoretical statement, which may or may not be translated into reality.[523] But the process of classification stretches into the analysis of many more issues, often less obviously than this suggests. Classifying areas with high unemployment as 'poor' and those with low unemployment as 'not poor' depends on a whole set of assumptions, about the nature of poverty, of the relationship of unemployment to poverty, and the concentration of poverty in particular areas.

Classifications depend on the identification of common elements between cases. Not every resemblance matters; some kind of theoretical understanding is necessary to decide which resemblances are important, and in what context. Most people in the subject would accept that race and gender are important categories for social analysis; some would refer to father's occupation as an indicator of class background, although there is some dispute as to whether the approach is valid or legitimate;[524] but hardly anyone would refer, in the normal course of social policy research, to physical height or the possession of a driving licence, even if these might be relevant in some contexts. Theory is basic to the selection of the criteria for classification, although equally classification is basic to the construction of theoretical explanations. There is a trap here: finding a neat model, and a way of describing things which works, may close our minds to other classifications which are no less important. Sociologists in the 1950s were so much concerned with the explanatory power of social class that they hardly considered the social implications of gender at all. Conversely, the main risk in the current concentration on race and gender is that we neglect or forget other social divisions – like class, age, employment, and poverty – which cut across these groups, and apply as much within social groups as between them.

There are three main approaches that are used for classifying common factors: comparing reality with an ideal, identifying categories by predetermined criteria, and 'family resemblance'. A fourth approach uses contrasting factors to produce classifications:

- *Comparing reality with an ideal.* The ideal can be expressed in terms of a general concept, like 'poverty' or 'oppression'; people can then be grouped according to whether they fit the definition or not. In sociology, resemblances are mainly compared by reference to an ideal type, which is a model or template against which reality is set. The ideal type, which can be as elaborate or as artificial as the writer chooses, represents the essential elements. Titmuss's 'models' of welfare are examples.[525] The advantage of this kind of model is that it helps to get directly to the heart of an issue – the kinds of factors which make the classification important in the first place. The main disadvantage is that reality rarely squares very closely with any sort of ideal; it is not very helpful to describe the US in terms of a 'market system of welfare', any more than the old Eastern European states could usefully be described as 'communist'.

- *Identifying categories by predetermined criteria.* The criteria can be based on distinct, often dichotomous categories – services might be, for example, group-based or individualised, centralised or localised – and classification is possible across several dimensions. Several of the tables in this book present material by making distinctions of this kind. The main act of classification is done at a theoretical level, rather than empirically.

- *'Family resemblance'.* Rather than identifying what groups have in common, family resemblance tries to identify interrelated clusters of characteristics. The argument made by Wittgenstein about the structure of language, and so about most concepts, is that there is no 'essential' core to most ideas; what we have, rather, are sets of interrelated references. In a family, a mother might look like her daughter, and the daughter might look like her cousin, but it does not follow that the cousin looks like the mother, because the way that the cousin is like the daughter may be very different from the way that the mother is like the daughter. In the same way, we can say that welfare in Britain is like welfare in Denmark and welfare in Australia, but it does not follow that welfare in Denmark is like welfare in Australia. The identification of family resemblance will be influenced by theory, because the factors which are examined are likely to be chosen on that basis, but it has the advantage over the use of ideal types that it is not wholly constrained by the theory; if there are other resemblances apart from those which were first looked for, it should be possible to identify them and reassess the material from a range of data that is available.

- *Relative approaches.* Relative comparison works mainly by contrast – looking at differences rather than similarities. Deciding whether countries are 'high spending' and 'low spending' countries can really only be identified by contrasting them with what other countries do. Comparing rich with poor, men with women, or black with white is relative; the differences are important, not least because they represent the effects of very different social positions of these groups. A 'relative' definition of poverty defines poverty by comparison with others who are not poor; so, the definition of poverty as 60% of the median income of a country,[526] is relative in nature. Esping-Andersen's classification is mainly theoretical, but he also uses relative empirical data to classify countries on the tests he applies.[527]

Normative approaches

Theory helps to examine the normative elements of social policy – that is, how values are applied, and principles of action. The issues with which social policy deals are often moral issues; issues like freedom, justice or rights are part of the terms in which social policy is generally discussed.[528] The reasons why people should be involved in decisions which affect them, why states should or should not provide people with a basic income, or why one person should pay for services received by another, are not fundamentally practical or technical. The issues for discussion, raised at the end of each of this book's chapters, should help to illustrate the problems. There are no authoritative answers; most of them are, at root, moral issues.

The study of social policy is not undertaken only by a process of description and analysis. Social policy is concerned with changing the world, not just with understanding it; critical appraisal is particularly important, because of the practical relevance of policies. This has led to a distinctive concern in social policy with providing tests by which policies can be judged. Social policy relies, to a degree which is very unusual in the social sciences, on evaluation – making judgements about situations. This depends on the application of norms – expectations, standards or rules against which policies and practice can be judged. It is fair, then, to describe social policy as a 'normative' subject. The term 'normative' is ambiguous, because the norms which are applied can be moral or technical, defined socially or by 'experts'; but that ambiguity reflects a range of options which are available in practice. Many norms are 'social', in the sense that there are certain commonly shared expectations against which judgements can be made; others are imposed through the political process, by politicians, the courts, interest groups, even the media; others again reflect the priorities and concerns of practitioners or researchers.

This has implications for the kinds of method used in social policy. One of the examples most often given of this kind of standard is the 'absolute' model of poverty (so-called). Seebohm Rowntree devised a measure of poverty based on the nutritional requirements and minimum income needs for basic goods, from which he was able to construct a 'poverty line'.[529]   But there are many other examples of norms. People are sometimes considered 'homeless' if they have no roof over their head, if they have no home of their own, or if they have nowhere which is adequate to live in – three very different standards, with large differences in the numbers of people involved, and very different implications for policy. For the purposes of policy, people are 'mentally ill' when they are diagnosed as such by qualified medical practitioners. The main defence for this kind of approach is that decisions have to be made; it is usually better for the reasons to be made explicit.

Many of the expectations or standards which are used to judge social policy conceal important moral judgements. 'Poverty' and 'homelessness' are not simply descriptions of a set of conditions; they are terms which are used to considerable emotive and political effect, and the way they are defined depends strongly on what kind of response is being called for. The description of 'mental illness' in these terms is more contentious, but it is worth noting that the definition of certain kinds of behaviour in terms of 'illness' rather than 'madness' represented historically an important moral shift in attitudes towards mentally ill people.[530] The kinds of norms which are used, then, contain much more than simple descriptions against which policies might be judged; policies are commonly judged by normative principles, which makes the study of such principles an important part of the study of social policy.

Evidence and policy

Social policy is problem-oriented, and although the term is treated by some apprehension by social scientists, the analysis of social policy is often 'positivist', at least in the methods it uses. Positivism is the view that scientists are dealing with an external reality, and positivistic methods are those which attempt to identify true 'facts'.   One of the commonplaces of social research is that the best way to look at a topic is by 'triangulating' – that is, looking at an issue several ways at once. By doing so, it becomes less and less likely that the findings are the result of some quirk in the research method, and more likely that they reflect what is actually happening in society. Booth, in the early days of the study of poverty, was much impressed by the fact that Rowntree's quite different method of measuring the problem came up with very similar results – that about a third of the population was poor.[531]

I wrote earlier about 'real people' and 'practical problems'. This begs some important assumptions, and it is contentious. Positivism has been the subject of withering criticism, particularly in sociology, because it disguises the kinds of value-judgement concealed in our understanding of 'reality'.[532] Arguments about 'social reality' are now more likely to be made in terms of 'critical realism', which accepts that social structures and meanings are important parts of the way that social relationships are formed, but which claims nevertheless that what we are studying is a real set of issues.[533] Social 'reality' is complex, because much of it depends on the society of which it is part; but much social policy, if not most, begins by accepting society on its own terms, and trying to identify patterns and relationships within the constraints of that society.

Policies are evaluated mainly by scrutinising evidence in order to be able to make some judgement about them. The first thing that one needs to do in order to evaluate a policy is to establish some sort of criterion by which it can be judged. The sorts of criteria which are most often used are fairly straightforward: does this policy meet needs? does it have other benefits? is it worth what it costs? As is often the case, however, questions like these are not as simple as they appear to be. It is not always clear just what is being evaluated, or what the standards being applied are. And the criteria which are being applied are not always explicit: economic and political constraints are often taken for granted.

For the most part, evaluation begins with a view about what services are supposed to do, and how they are supposed to do it. (The issues which are raised by this will be examined further in Chapter 15, on analysing policy.) This is true of most evaluations, but it does not apply to all: sometimes the definition of aims is misleading. Policing is often assumed to be about catching criminals, but it might really be about public security; social work might be assumed to be about protecting children when in reality it is much more often about supporting families; sheltered housing was initially set up to provide support in emergencies, but the evidence that emerged was that the provision of day-to-day support was much more useful. There is also a case for 'goal free' analysis[534] to look at what policies actually do, without prior assumptions.

What works?

The central question behind many assessments of policy is whether a policy delivers what it is supposed to deliver. The simplest kind of answer is based on the outcomes of policy, but this is rarely enough to determine what works – only what does not. If outcomes are satisfactory, it is difficult to say with confidence whether the benefits are produced by the policy, or by other social conditions. For example, it is difficult to say that success in reducing crime, relieving unemployment or preserving families might be the result of what the policy has done, when these factors are heavily dependent on the external environment. By contrast, if outcomes are unsatisfactory, this is usually a good enough reason to conclude that the policy has not worked. It is possible that the judgement is mistaken, but in a world where detailed examination is costly, time-consuming and difficult, evidence that things are worse, or even no better, suggests that something else should be tried.

A focus on outcomes is sometimes referred to as a 'black box', after the work of psychologist B F Skinner.[535] Skinner argued that, to understand how people behave, it is not necessary to examine the details of process, motivations or understandings; all we need to do is to look at what the stimulus was, and to see what effect it had. In the same way, it may be possible to look at the behaviour of some organisations, like the police or schools, without being too much concerned about procedures, culture or implementation. Studies of discrimination, for example, have sometimes been concerned simply to show that there is a problem. If the outcomes show that people are disadvantaged, that is a matter of concern. There may need to be more, detailed analysis later, explaining the process by which disadvantage has come about, but in the first instance the outcome alone is enough to establish that there is a problem, and that something needs to be done about it.

It is often necessary, however, to go deeper, and to try to establish what produces an effect, for good or ill. This is typically done in two ways. Pawson and Tilley argue for 'realistic evaluation', based in the idea that services do have an effect, that the effect can and should be explained, and that there is somewhere a 'mechanism' or causal link which can explain what is going on.[536] If the explanation is correct, using the same approach in other contexts should also work. The argument for crime control by avoiding 'broken windows' is an example; if everyone is made aware that a community cares, the argument runs, they will be less likely to make problems in small or large things. However, assumptions about mechanisms can be misleading. The mechanisms are complex, and often their influence is disguised by many other contributory factors and influences. It often happens that policy makers, and policy analysts, are mistaken about the mechanisms.

The main alternative, often represented as an ideal form of evaluation, is the control trial. Control trials compare outcomes in different situations, so that differences between the environments can be distinguished from the effects of the policy. One option, the randomised control trial, works by assigning some subjects to a treatment group and others to a control group which is not treated. The approach is most commonly used in medicine for the trials of new pharmaceuticals.[537] Because some people get better just because they think they are being treated, people in control groups are commonly given 'placebos' – pretend drugs – and their progress is monitored relative to others. There are potential ethical problems with this, because the effect of withholding treatment can have very undesirable effects for the patient. This is commonly avoided by offering a different treatment, and examining the differences in outcomes.

In social policy, it is often difficult to conduct experiments with people in this way, although it is not impossible; well-known pioneering examples include experiments examining the benefits of pre-school education (Headstart in the

US[538]), or the New Jersey Income Maintenance Experiment, which sought (fairly inconclusively) to identify the effects of a basic income system on people's behaviour and in particular on work incentives.[539] Much more common in social policy is the approach in which people are compared when they are subject to different policy régimes, usually as a result of a localised project.[540]

Pawson and Tilley are critical of control trials. If they are properly designed, controls neutralise the impact of the social environment – but that, they argue, cuts out what really matters.[541] The general experience of many such trials in criminology is that initial experiments or pilots work very well, and then subsequently they fail when they are applied in other circumstances. The difference has to lie in the social conditions where they are applied – and those conditions are what control trials are designed to exclude.

This is, however, a more general problem with evaluation research. It is in the nature of research that people tend to behave differently when they are being studied, and the set-up of many experiments and pilot projects makes it difficult to be confident that results will be generalisable. It is unusual for formal evaluations of projects to be conclusive. The problems which are being dealt with are multifaceted, and even where the causal links are fairly widely accepted the results are subject to reinterpretation. For that reason, the construction of theory is central to the understanding of effects, and for the belief that some kinds of effects are produced by a policy while others are not.

Box 13: Policy without theory

In a book mainly devoted to theory, it seems appropriate to pause for a moment and to ask whether theory is always the best way to go. Critiques of social policy can be scathing about responses which seem to be addressed to 'symptoms' rather than basic causes, or which 'paper over the cracks'. That position should be treated with some scepticism. There is nothing much wrong with dealing with symptoms, which at least will have some effect, and dealing with superficial issues like discomfort and misery is no bad thing. Dealing with 'fundamental' issues, by contrast, is often wrong-headed. Box 1 and Box 3 pointed to some of the problems of relying on causal explanations. One of the principal methods of policy development is to focus, not on what ought to work, but on what does.

There are many approaches to policy which try to find solutions to problems without necessarily understanding how a problem comes about. If, for example, governments are concerned about individual behaviour, like gambling or alcoholism, they do not need to start by analysing the causes, and they may not even need a detailed understanding of the problem. An obvious first step is to limit the opportunities to gamble or to obtain alcohol. This will not stop the problem from happening, but it will generally reduce the scale of the problem. The main limitation in practice is not the lack of knowledge, but the problem of enforceability; there is a limit to what governments can do effectively, and absolute bans, like prohibition, tend to be ineffective.

An approach which is based on taking practical steps rather than general principles is called 'pragmatism'. The test of whether a policy was beneficial, Edmund Burke argues, is not whether it fitted preconceived notions, but whether it worked. The way to develop policy, then, was incremental – trying things out, doing a little at a time, seeing what worked and what did not. It was better, in Burke's view, to end up with a patchwork of things that worked rather than a grand system which didn't. 'From hence arises, not an excellence in simplicity, but one far superior, an excellence in composition.'[542]

There are, however, some vexing problems with pragmatic approaches. The first is that things that work in some places do not necessarily work in others. A common experience of pilot programmes is that approaches which seem to be promising have much less effect when they are applied more generally. Pawson and Tilley argue that unless we understand the processes and relationships, it becomes almost impossible to identify which elements of a policy are having an effect.[543]

The second problem is that dealing with a problem in part is not necessarily good enough to make a difference, and it may make things worse. It may not seem unreasonable to suppose that where a problem has several dimensions, dealing with one of them will make the problem smaller and easier to solve. However, the effects of partial remedies may be no better, and may even be worse. Economists refer to this as the 'second best' problem: second-best solutions may be worse than apparently inferior choices. When, for example, inequality in education was identified as a key social issue, the response of governments in the UK was to improve equality of access, particularly in secondary schooling and higher education. Greater equality of access should in principle have led to less inequality overall. In practice, it is not clear that it has done so; greater equality of access has made competition harder for those who are disadvantaged.[544] Where access is equalised and other issues are not, the outcomes in terms of examination results and opportunities for higher education seem to reinforce existing inequalities.

The third problem is that governments do not necessarily look in the right places. Welfare has been heavily influenced in recent years by policy in the US, a notorious welfare laggard.[545] The influence of the US is partly a result of its political and economic status, partly a result of aggressive marketing (US providers have incentives to sell their products)[546] and partly a matter of convenience, because of the accessibility of English and of published information. By contrast, countries which are brimming with interesting approaches but where the language is inaccessible (like Finland) or which are less influential (like New Zealand or the Netherlands) tend to be overlooked.

Fourth, regrettably, pragmatic approaches are slow. Measures need to be tried and tested, and that takes time.

In these circumstances, recourse to theory is inevitable. Evidence needs to be interpreted before it can be applied; policy makers need to make an informed selection; often they need to do it in a hurry. The most common procedure is neither pragmatic nor theoretical, but what Etzioni calls 'mixed scanning' – switching back and forth between pragmatic and theoretical modes in order to make informed, practical decisions.[547]

Cost-effectiveness and efficiency

Another way of referring to the question of what works is the idea of 'effectiveness'. Effectiveness has been referred to at several points in this book: it means, simply enough, that the aims of policy have been met. Saying that a policy is effective, and saying that it works, boil down to the same thing.

The issues that have to be considered, however, go beyond the question of what works. Effectiveness generally has to be balanced with the issue of resources and costs. Costs can be taken to include the resources that have to be devoted to the policy, and the costs imposed on others; economists would add 'opportunity costs', which is the cost of not doing something else. A policy is said to be 'cost-effective' when it achieves objectives at the lowest possible cost. Cost-effectiveness is one of the primary tests of public policy, and it tends to be used as a central criterion for evaluation – although it is vulnerable to the problem that, when people are vague about aims, it might be reduced to little more than an emphasis on cost reduction. There is equally a risk that the costs to the agency are all that are considered, when there are other forms of cost: it is often possible to save expenditure on social services by making clients travel to the service, but the costs to the clients (and the impact on service effectiveness) have also to be considered.

Efficiency is often confused with cost-effectiveness,[548] and it is assumed to be just as desirable, but it means something significantly different. Figure 13.1 should help to explain. It shows a production curve – the relationship between the cost per unit and the number of things produced. A policy is effective when it achieves its aims to the maximum degree, and it is cost-effective when it does so at the minimum total cost. In the graph, this point occurs at the top of the production curve, when as much as possible has been achieved. Production is efficient, by contrast, when the average cost of each unit achieved is minimised. This occurs at the bottom of the curve, when costs are lowest. This is the point that producers in a private market would be forced to, because of competition over prices.

The central difference between efficiency and cost-effectiveness is that efficiency implies a trade-off between the achievement of goals and the average cost. Commonly, agencies are able to achieve their goals – for example, medical treatment or domestic support – for many people. Reaching other people, however, can be more expensive, because their needs are greater or they are more difficult to locate. In other words, as the service increases its caseload, the cost of each additional person helped is likely to be higher, and so its average costs are also likely to increase. The point of maximum efficiency is passed when the costs of helping the next person is greater than the cost of helping the previous one. Almost invariably, this will happen before the agency has covered everyone it might otherwise cover. A concern with efficiency can, then, reduce the effectiveness of the service.

That does not mean that public service agencies are oblivious to cost. In the first place, they have to avoid waste – going above the line unnecessarily. There may also be some compromise of cost and effectiveness, but it will not be the same kind of compromise as the one made in the private sector. Figure 13.1 suggests some alternative choices. If the dotted line represents the desired balance between costs and effectiveness – a balance which has to be decided as a matter of policy – there is an argument for holding production to the point where the curve crosses that line. If there is to be some compromise between cost and effectiveness, there may be a case for getting the greatest gain over cost, which is the point where the curve is furthest from the dotted line. Both points are well up the curve.

Public services cannot usually maintain efficiency by refusing to help people at all, although it does happen.[549] More commonly, services avoid taking on liabilities by trying to pass expensive or difficult cases to other agencies. Continuing care for older people is particularly expensive, because it incorporates both residential care with extended (usually 24-hour) coverage. For any agency which is not specifically geared to providing such care, this is an inefficient option, because it greatly increases the cost of care for each resident. The only agency which would not consider it inefficient would be one specifically dedicated to the provision of such care. The effect of concentrating on 'efficiency' as a criterion, then, is to favour the setting up of agencies which are functionally differentiated. But it is debatable whether this is socially efficient, in the sense of reducing costs across the whole of welfare provision, or cost-effective; what it loses are the economies of scale which larger agencies can achieve, for example through the

FIGURE 13.1: COST-EFFECTIVENESS

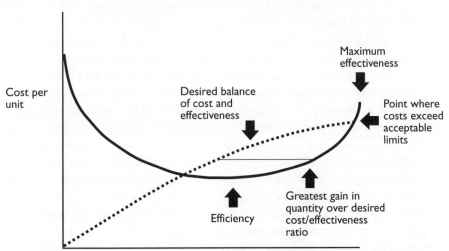

Quantity – achievement of aims

use of pooled laundry services or catering. In the context of social policy, an emphasis on 'efficiency' can be misleading; cost-effectiveness is far more relevant and appropriate to the work of social services.

The distributive impact of social policy

Social policy is not only concerned with costs. Many analyses of social policy are concerned with the question, 'who benefits?'. If benefits and services are targeted, part of the aim is that they should reach the right people. Reaching the poorest people in a population is often difficult; the combination of social exclusion, limited resources and barriers to access can lead to an 'inverse care law' where those who are most in need are also least likely to receive services.[550] In health care, the World Bank has funded a series of studies to enable services to identify how many people are receiving services, and what their relative income is.[551]

The basic concepts used in the analysis of distribution were outlined in Chapter Seven. Some of the ambiguities of the process – understanding, for example, whether distribution is horizontal or vertical, or whether it should be viewed statically or dynamically – were mentioned at that point. The questions this kind of exercise raises are far from straightforward. One problem is that the same effects can be interpreted in different ways. The effects of redistribution across the life cycle may be that apparently horizontal redistribution turns out to have unexpected vertical effects. Payments for pensions seem vertically redistributive, but if the main effect is solidaristic then their impact on redistribution between better-off and worse-off sectors of society may be limited. Conversely, payments for older children at school seem regressive, because this is often a point of peak earnings for families, but if the issue is seen across the life cycle such payments may seem relatively neutral.[552] This illustrates an important principle: the way the problem is thought about is likely to affect not only the criteria by which outcomes will be judged, but also the judgement about what the outcomes are.

The second problem is that outcomes are difficult to measure. In the case of redistribution, this is partly because it is not always clear where the benefits of particular services fall – who does benefit from social work, when it has a coercive role as well as being a system of social support? – and partly because some benefits are not based on receipt but on the possibility of receipt. Where there is a National Health Service, people are receiving a benefit – health coverage – for which people in other countries have to pay, and they would be receiving this coverage even though they do not actually use the service.

Third, in order to assess outcomes it is necessary to consider not only what the policy seems to do but what might otherwise have been true. It is difficult to judge what the benefit of health services is unless there are some indications of what would happen without them; improvements in public health have often reflected other issues (like sanitation or diet). If health services appear to have no effect on inequality, it does not necessarily mean that they have failed – it is possible that otherwise inequalities would otherwise have widened. Transport systems directly affect where people live and work, and there are implications for housing and employment opportunities which are difficult to assess directly.

These are difficult, complex issues, and this section is not trying to offer answers. The purpose, rather, is to explain the kind of task that social policy analysts are trying to deal with. The situations which are being analysed are multifaceted and confused. Often they are highly charged, emotionally and politically. There are times when the people working on these issues try to forestall debate with a detached, technocratic stance – which is a problem with the World Bank studies I have cited, because ignoring the normative elements of the analysis can be counterproductive. Conversely, there may be times when commentators become passionate and irrational.

Evaluation and policy

The kind of analysis discussed in this chapter draws heavily on a range of academic disciplines. It cannot lay claim to a distinctive view of the world, or special methods and approaches. It is defined by what it studies, not by how it goes about it. The kind of work which is described in this part of the book is not genuinely 'distinctive', in the sense of clearly setting the analysis of social policy apart from other kinds of academic study, but it is characteristic. Four features mark it out:

1. The work is *problem-oriented*. Research and evaluation are done for a purpose, quite apart from their academic interest.
2. The general approach to analysis tends to be *pragmatic*. Given that there are problems and issues, the task of social policy analysts is to find material which can effectively serve the kinds of work they intend to do. Often, as in the use of indicators, this implies a degree of compromise; such compromises are a necessary part of the approach to the subject.
3. The work is *multidisciplinary*. It is possible to confine oneself to one kind of approach, but this is not always consistent with the pragmatic concerns of work in the subject. The eclectic approach of social policy can be seen as a virtue, because the kinds of skill called for in practical fields require the kind of range and adaptability that social policy fosters.
4. The work is *political*. The analysis of policy is not simply a technical exercise, undertaken in order to choose the best methods for a range of agreed aims or goals; it is an intensely political activity in which arguments are being made for different kinds of philosophy, approach and outcomes. The relationship between policy analysts and agencies is sensitive and sometimes difficult.[553]

This brings us back to the discussion in the introduction, about the nature of social policy as a field of study. Social policy has its own knowledge base, its own literature, and a set of common approaches. Studies in social policy have a recognisable style. But the terms in which policy is interpreted are strongly affected by perceptions of the social, economic and political context in which decisions are taken; insights from all the disciplines are important as a means of understanding that context. The remit of social policy is not confined to the academic world, and it cannot afford to emphasise its academic distinctiveness at the expense of these insights.

ISSUE FOR DISCUSSION

In the care of older people, how far should effectiveness be sacrificed to efficiency?

FOURTEEN

Research for policy

The research process

Research is an essential part of the study of social policy. Understanding social conditions, and the effects which responses have on them, depends strongly on being able to draw on good information about what is happening. People who want to understand social policy in practice need to be able to interpret research material; while those who hope to develop policy need to appreciate what the effects of that policy might be, and how to find out what they really are.

The process of conducting research generally calls for a number of stages, outlined in Figure 14.1. It is necessary to select and then frame the issue or problem which is to be researched. Methods have to be chosen. Data have to be obtained. The results have to be collected, sifted through and interpreted.

It may be more accurate to say that these are tasks to be undertaken rather than stages to be gone through. Some researchers begin not with the problem they plan to study, but the data they can get or the people they have access to, and problems and issues emerge from that. Some researchers begin with a set of methods, like those used in market research, and then look for opportunities to use them. In practice, then, these tasks are often intertwined and inseparable from each other.

The selection of the research problem

Researchers select their problems in a number of ways. Academics are expected to 'do research' as part of their conditions of employment; research results and publications are important for the reputation of researchers and of institutions, and for attracting funding for further academic work. Social policy is

FIGURE 14.1: THE RESEARCH PROCESS

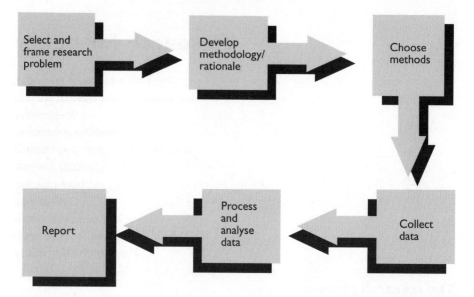

not, however, solely an 'academic' field; it is also directed to problems of interest to policy makers. Senator Proxmire, in the US, once awarded his 'Golden Bull' award for a waste of public money to a research project trying to find out why people wanted to escape from prisons. But the point of such a project is that a better understanding of who wants to escape and why helps prisons to determine what kind of security measures are necessary. Governments and service agencies may fund research because they hope it will enable a better understanding of a problem, and because it may help to identify solutions. There are obvious problems in a relationship which may require researchers to bite the hand that feeds them. This appears overtly in standard contract conditions: commissioning agencies will often insist on intellectual property, confidentiality and the right to vet any related publications or use of the material. It is not extraordinary for research contracts to state that even the existence of the research project should itself be treated as confidential (which, if taken literally, would make it very difficult to ask anyone questions as part of the research).

Governments also fund research for reasons which may have little to do with the improvement of policy. One reason might be that the government wants to be seen to be doing something, but doesn't know what to do. Another reason may be that governments want to delay action; two or three years spent finding out more facts can be helpful in taking the heat out of a situation. Third, the government may want research as a form of propaganda, to reinforce their political programme. And research may be undertaken for reasons which have nothing to do with finding out anything: the European Union has very limited powers to respond to poverty, but it is allowed to 'research' into it, and action research programmes were used throughout the 1980s and 1990s as a means of establishing the EU's right to act, or 'competence' in the area.[554]

Methodology

Research means, simply, finding out about something. There are many ways of finding things out, and there are always alternative ways of doing research in practice. One of the principal weaknesses of research in social policy is the assumption that there is a single, 'right' way to do research, such as the randomised control trial which dominates in health services, the deductive experiment which characterises psychological approaches, or the opinion poll which is used to discover what people think. There is nothing intrinsically wrong with these methods, but they are only one type of research, and whether they are appropriate depends on the circumstances where they are applied. If a policy researcher wants to find out what people think, there are alternatives to polling – for example, the range of interactive and participative methods used in the World Bank's *Voices of the poor*. If the aim is to examine people's behaviour, it can be done through observation, examination of records or anthropological approaches, as well as through experiment. However, because research can be done in so many ways, there is often a question as to whether the way that has been chosen was appropriate. Whatever the method, it needs to be justified.

Research can begin with data or with theoretical analysis. All empirical research is descriptive; material has to be gathered, selected and presented. But research also has to be interpreted; the process of selection itself requires some kind of analysis, whether or not this is explicit. Research reports often label a description of research methods as their 'methodology', but that is something of a misnomer; methodology is the study of research methods, and the methodology of a particular study consists not of a description, but a rationale for what is done and why it has been done in that way.

There are two common patterns by which research might be undertaken, which are usually referred to as 'inductive' and 'deductive' approaches. The 'inductive' approach is to begin by collecting material, and looking for patterns and relationships in the material subsequently. ('Induction' is a rather bad name for this process – the word refers to a common fallacy, based on the assumption that things which happen a lot are likely to happen again. It has been pinned on a range of research methods by people who don't think research undertaken without preconceptions is real science. A better name might be 'exploratory' research, but this is a textbook, which means that I have to use the mainstream terminology.) This is a common pattern of work in history and ethnography. The most basic historical method is to collect facts and information and to seek to assess the importance of different factors, or to interpret trends within it. Political analysis is similar to historical research; it relies, for the most part, on interpreting facts. Ethnographic research is derived mainly from social

219

anthropology. An anthropologist researches into a culture by becoming immersed in that culture, living with people, collecting information, and interpreting. This is the basis for the sociological method of 'participant observation'.[555]   Oscar Lewis's work on poverty in Mexico and Puerto Rico – work which had an enormous influence in the US, and through that on many other countries – was anthropological at the outset.[556]

The 'deductive' approach relies on the generation of propositions which can be tested. This takes two main forms:

1. *Testing hypotheses.* A hypothesis is a statement about reality which can be tested. Pawson and Tilley argue that the evaluation of policy initiatives generally rests on the identification of a 'generative mechanism' – an explanation for why something is happening the way that it is.[557]

2. *Examining models.* A model, like an ideal type, consists of a set of interrelated assumptions to which reality can be compared. I have used 'models' in the same sense as 'ideal types' for much of this book, because the models which I have been considering (like Titmuss's) have largely been theoretical ones. Models can, however, be much more precise attempts to reflect reality. The facts are then compared to the model; the model is gradually refined to improve its descriptive or predictive power. An example of a model from psychological research might be Latané and Darley's work on the unresponsive bystander. They suggest, on the basis of a series of experiments, that people are likely to help when certain conditions are satisfied.[558]   People must notice the situation; they must interpret the situation as one in which help might be needed; they must recognise that they should accept responsibility; they must decide on the form of assistance; and they must then put the help into practice. Each of these propositions can be tested independently, but together they constitute a whole series of actions.

The deductive approach does not necessarily lead to different conclusions from the inductive mode – if the research is valid, the results should converge – and the different approaches boil down to much the same thing logically, but they look different, and they are likely in practice to lead to different kinds of answer.

In practice, inductive and deductive approaches are rarely completely distinct. Inductive researchers find it difficult to avoid preconceptions which direct their work, and as they gather material they are likely to form criteria by which further selections might be made. Conversely, deductive research has to start somewhere; hypotheses have to be generated and models constructed from some kind of factual basis. The deductive approach lends itself to more rigorous testing, and for that reason it tends to be favoured in much social science research (particularly in psychology); but it is a fallacy to suppose that every problem can be translated into some proposition which can be tested – or that it should be. The problem with the deductive approach is that it puts blinkers on the researcher; by contrast, the great strength of an exploratory approach is, as Whyte comments, that we can find the answers to questions that we did not know we needed to ask.[559]

It is possible, of course, to use both types of approach simultaneously, and there are patterns of research which operate by a constant process of interpretation and refinement of ideas. This is the approach of 'grounded theory'. Grounded theory is concerned with the development of theory; it does it by looking at material and organising it. The most basic technique is to take the data and to organise it into categories, carrying on until there is no more data, or no more categories to fill.[560] These categories become the basis on which generalisations are made, and so on which theories can be generated. Action research is another example. During action research, researchers are examining processes and, at the same time, making decisions about them.[561] The basic model is one of constant experimentation; researchers try out a range of methods, see what works and what does not, and try to select likely approaches.

Operationalising the problem

Research problems have to be 'operationalised'. This means that concepts have to be translated into operational terms – terms which can be tested, measured, worked with.

Definition of terms. Defining terms is usually basic to research; if the definitions are inadequate, the whole study may be invalid. For example, a study looking at disabled people has to decide what is meant by 'disability'. An early study for the UK Department of Health and Social Security defined disability mainly in terms of the ability to move one's limbs or use one's organs, and found about 3 million people who were disabled. This excluded important areas like mental illness.[562] A 1988 OPCS study widened the 1968 definitions and found 6.2 million disabled people.[563] This was an impressive, well-conducted survey; but when the surveys were repeated in 1996, the apparent number of disabled adults had increased by over two million people in less than 10 years.[564]

Definition is not always crucial. It is difficult to define a 'dwelling' accurately, but we all know roughly what one is, and the scope for error is limited. It is important to define terms precisely in deductive research, because the definition of the problem changes the kind of information which is collected, and small changes in definition can make large differences to figures. In inductive research, definitions help to explain why a particular group is being focused on. It does not always matter if some people are included who should not be, or other people are left out; in so far as the research is collating material on factors, influences or relationships, the material which is necessary for a valid interpretation may still be there. In empowering research, finding out how people understand and use terms may be part of the exercise of the research.

Validity. The term 'validity' is used in a specialised way in empirical research studies. It refers to a particular part of the process – whether or not the 'facts' collected show what they are supposed to. 'Concept validity' is the question of whether the issue which is being tested is the same as the issue which was supposed to be tested. Some issues are relatively easily identified and tested – such as how many people over the age of 75 have a bathroom. Many concepts in social science, however, are much vaguer. Issues like altruism, embourgeoisement, or racism have not only to be defined; they also have to be identified within certain types of context. Titmuss tested altruism by people's willingness to give blood;[565] Pinker has objected that giving blood is painless and so not a good test of altruism.[566]

Reliability. Reliability is also known as 'predictive validity'. Results are said to be 'reliable' if they consistently show the same thing. In practice, the conditions under which social policy operates are constantly changing, which tends to mean that reliability is less important as a test than it is in some other fields. A study can be valid and the results may still be unreliable, because some methods – particularly interviews in depth – allow for a great deal of latitude in observation and interpretation. Results which are unreliable, however, may raise questions about whether or not research is valid. There have been three waves of surveys looking at what people think is essential to avoid poverty, conducted in 1983, 1990 and 1999. In 1983, 64% of respondents said that two meals a day were necessary for adults; in 1990, 90% said so. Sixty-three per cent of people thought that people needed to give presents once a year when the question was asked in 1983; 69% agreed in 1990; 56% agreed in 1999.[567] This may genuinely reflect a major shift in public perception, or a change in social conditions; but it may also indicate that there is something about the question which led to inconsistent responses, in which case it is difficult to tell what the true position is. Halleröd suggests that the intrinsic problem with consensual measures of poverty is that people's expectations and preferences are conditioned by what they think is realistic; because the possibilities change, so do the responses.[568]

Reliability is important for some sorts of research, but not for all. A study can be valid and the results may still be unreliable, because some methods – particularly interpretative methods – allow for a great deal of latitude in observation and interpretation. Equally, a study may be invalid and produce reliable observations, because the same facts are found repeatedly for different reasons from the ones the researcher believed.

The effect of the research process. The way that research is conducted is notoriously likely to alter the findings of the research. This might reflect researcher bias – which is possibly more common in social policy than in other social sciences, because many researchers have a strong commitment to a particular policy or approach, and because agencies commonly use 'research' as a means of arguing for extra funding. There is sometimes bias from the respondents – 'response bias' can occur when respondents are trying to be helpful and to give the researcher what they think the researcher wants. The researcher's presence alone can lead to differences in behaviour: people behave differently when they are being watched. The phenomenon is known in psychology as the 'Hawthorne effect', after a series of psychology experiments in a factory which produced unexpected responses simply because of the presence of the researchers.[569] The description of method is important, then, because it may reveal something about the process which affects interpretation of the results.

Qualitative and quantitative research

One of the most basic distinctions made between different kinds of empirical research is between 'qualitative' and 'quantitative' research. Qualitative research is primarily interpretative. The main methods include observation, interviewing in depth and examining documents. Qualitative research is commonly aimed at producing material to help explain issues, answering questions beginning with 'why?', 'who? and 'how?', as well as some questions about process – such as 'what is happening?'. Quantitative research is research which measures effects. The characteristic methods are censuses and questionnaires. Numbers are used to answer questions like 'how much?', 'to what extent?, 'what proportion?' and 'what are the differences?'. Quantitative methods can be used for tests of hypotheses, examinations of models, and predictions; numbers can also be helpful in deciding which of several factors are most important, and under what conditions certain types of things will happen. Qualitative and quantitative methods are not, of course, exclusive. Quantitative methods do require a level of interpretation to know what the numbers mean; qualitative judgements can include some element of computation. Many studies use elements of both.[570]

Because of the type of questions they address, qualitative methods are generally more appropriate for inductive approaches, quantitative methods for deductive ones. The identification is not exact, however. Qualitative methods can be used to test some hypotheses, for example about organisational behaviour, while quantitative methods can be used to sift through information – for example as in Townsend's work on poverty,[571] identifying the differences between people who are on low incomes and those who are not.

In quantitative studies – that is, studies, which rely on the use of numbers, there are two important issues to consider whenever quantitative research is being undertaken. The first is what the numbers mean. If a study aims to measure an effect, it is usually necessary to translate terms into numbers. There are a number of difficulties in doing so. First, numbers are ordinal; 2 is greater than 1, 3 is greater than 2. If one is seeking to measure something like the extent of a person's disability, the use of numbers may be misleading; is it worse to lose a hand or two feet, and how can this be assessed consistently? Second, numbers are aggregative; they can be added together, so that more things are usually considered more important. This is not always indisputable. The 1988 OPCS study on disability found overall that where someone was multiply disabled, only the three most serious disabilities really mattered for the purposes of assessment, and they disregarded lesser disabilities as a result.[572] (This has been a highly influential approach – it subsequently stretched from its original use in research to the assessment of needs for the distribution of compensation and benefits.)

The second issue is about extents. There is a general rule in computing called 'GIGO', which means, garbage in, garbage out. If the concepts and constructs do not mean what they are supposed to mean, it does not matter how sophisticated the internal mechanics of the research are. If the sample is not representative, it is not possible to make the kinds of generalisation about extent that depend on representative samples.

Graham and McDermott suggest that 'qualitative studies are routinely excluded from evidence review and policy development'.[573] That is less true than it used to be, but it is probably fair to say that there is some scepticism in policy-making circles about qualitative methods. The validity of qualitative studies is often challenged by people who think that numbers are more 'scientific' or credible. Evidence from qualitative responses is often dismissed as 'anecdotal' or 'unsystematic'. This is mainly based in a misunderstanding of the validity of quantitative research – rubbish is not turned into valuable data by having a number stuck on it. Validity in quantitative research is based in the theoretical relationship between the data and the findings. Exactly the same is true of qualitative research.

If the information from a qualitative study is correct, and correctly interpreted, it is as valid as any other data. There are various ways of trying to establish whether the information is correct, but most depend on 'triangulation' or cross-validation. Information which is cross-confirmed from different sources – the findings of other research, the testimony of other witnesses or the products of other methods – is more likely to be correct than information which is not. Typically, then, responses to qualitative questions are presented in twos or threes, in order to show that comments are not isolated.

The issue of correct interpretation is more difficult to determine; it depends on whether the interpretation is theoretically justified. The main test is whether the findings are generalisable – that is, whether there are issues and principles that can be taken out of that context and applied in others. This can only be established either by reference to theory or by looking for later cross-confirmation in subsequent studies.

Selecting methods

As this discussion suggests, there is a wide range of potential research methods. The most common in social science are probably:

- enumerations (counting things);
- observation and participant observation (observing things);
- interviews (asking things); and
- experimentation (testing things).

Zelditch suggests that different types of methods are appropriate for different types of problems. He refers only to the first three sets of methods – enumerations, participant observation and interviews; his classification is set out in Table 14.1.[574]

Zelditch's table is disputable: for example, institutions can also be examined by considering their records, and the quantitative examination of outcomes is not necessarily 'inefficient'. I referred earlier to the principle of 'triangulation'; it may be desirable to pick not one method, but several. But the essential point the table makes is that one has to choose the method according to the type of problem, and methods that are good for one purpose may be bad for another.

It would be naive to suppose, however, that research methods are selected solely because they are simply the best suited for the task at hand. Researchers choose their methods according to their competence and interests. People working within different disciplines tend to look for different sorts of empirical evidence, and to do it in different ways. Social workers, for example, are likely to use interviews in depth; economists are likely to examine monetary effects, or those which fit economic models; psychologists examine patterns of individual and group behaviour. If one is studying a topic like 'altruism' or 'poverty', the approach taken is likely to be completely different. A sociologist, economist, psychologist and anthropologist will often approach the same problem in a different way: contrast the approach taken to poverty by Peter Townsend (a sociologist)

TABLE 14.1: SELECTION OF RESEARCH METHODS

Information types	Methods		
	Enumerations	*Participant observation*	*Interviews*
Frequency distributions	Best prototype	Usually inadequate and inefficient	Usually inadequate; efficient if adequate
Incidents, histories	Inadequate	Best prototype	Adequate and efficient with precautions
Institutionalised norms and statuses	Adequate but inefficient	Adequate but inefficient; useful for unverbalised norms	Best – most efficient

with that of Oscar Lewis (an anthropologist),[575] or the views of altruism taken by Titmuss (social administration) and Latané and Darley (psychologists).[576]

Data collection

Data are gathered from many potential sources. The first, and most obvious, source is the material that other people have collated, and all research calls for some kind of review of previous work if it is to build on it and not simply to duplicate it. But empirical research is distinguished by 'primary analysis', which is the collation of new empirical material.

Some of this material exists in written form. Examples are official records, written statements, policy documents and files. As more files are maintained in an electronic format, increasingly material of this kind, including statistical data, is going to be accessible principally in that format. For the most part, however, the principal source of data in social policy is people – the people who establish the policies, administer the agencies, receive the services and have the problems and needs. The most common forms of empirical research, as a result, are concerned with human activity – principally people's behaviour, beliefs and opinions. This tends to push social policy research towards methods that are concerned with obtaining such information, such as interviewing and observation.

Sampling and censuses. Sampling addresses the issue of who is being studied. Sampling is usually necessary because very few social problems can be addressed comprehensively. A comprehensive study is referred to as a 'census'. There have been attempts at surveys of everything. In the 19th century, Charles Booth set about visiting every poor house in London;[577] surveys of rough sleepers may try to census everyone sleeping rough on a particular night, because there is no basis otherwise for a sample. (The UK government believes on the basis of street counts that local authority estimates tend to overestimate the numbers of rough sleepers;[578] an alternative view is that the street counts underestimate the total numbers, because many rough sleepers have a pattern of varied, unstable arrangements made night by night.) Inevitably, however, comprehensive surveys tend to miss people, and there is a risk that the results may be no more accurate, and even less accurate, than those from a sample. Samples are often selected, in that sense, to 'represent' a wider population. That does not mean, however, that only 'representative' samples are used. The test of whether a sample is appropriate to an issue is a theoretical one: the central question is whether or not it is possible to generalise from the results. This is a theoretical issue, not a technical one. A perfectly constructed representative sample might not support a generalisation if circumstances change; the right sort of illustrative sample might still yield information that is useful forty years on.

Probability sampling. In probability sampling, groups are selected in order to reflect the characteristics of a wider population.

- *Random samples* are selected in such a way as to avoid any artificial pattern or bias in the group. The arguments for random samples are that they avoid any unintentional systematic bias in results and that they generally produce representative samples. The arguments against are that they are massively time-consuming, and that although it is very unlikely they will not be representative, it is not impossible. One still has to be sure that the sample is taken from the right population in the first place.

- *Quota sampling.* Groups can be made representative of general populations by ensuring that certain proportions of characteristics appear in the sample. Internet surveys are supposed to work by correcting the biases that come from the uneven distribution of internet users; this is done by selecting a quota reflecting the characteristics of the general population. (Internet users may still, however, be untypical in other ways: Baker and others suggest that they are, for example, more likely to be adopters of new ideas.[579])

- *Matched samples.* People in different groups are matched one against another, so that the groups have the same characteristics in terms of age, sex, class, education or any other factor that needs to be controlled for. Results are then compared between the different groups.

- *Convenience samples.* It is often easier to find people in groups. Psychology experiments commonly use psychology students or volunteers, who are not representative of the whole population. In order to justify this for probability samples, it is necessary to argue that their common social or personal characteristics do not distort the factors being studied.

Purposive sampling. The main test in most social policy research, however, is not that the material reflects the characteristics of a population, but that it offers an insight into the issue being studied. The information has to be capable of being generalised. Many samples in policy research – arguably most – are purposive rather than numerically representative; they focus on a narrow group as a way of illustrating rather than precisely reflecting the major issues. Beyond that, researchers in social policy have become increasingly aware in recent years that there are different, often conflicting perspectives on issues, and it matters whose information is being used. Empowering research aims to give a voice to people within the policy process, and the methods which need to be adopted have to be both inclusive and enabling.

Examples of purposive samples include:

- *Illustrative cases.* Individuals or groups can be selected as illustrative cases. Illustrative cases do not have to be typical; there may be a value in selecting examples where issues are pronounced, so as to put the validity of the classification beyond dispute. A study of doctors can be used as a basis for discussion of professions, or a sample of people who have been subject to court proceedings for debt could be the basis of a study of problems with debt.

- *Extreme cases.* The same principle can be extended further; some research is based on extreme cases, selected because they are unusually revealing. It may be appropriate to look at extraordinary circumstances, like child abuse inquiries, legal cases or historical anomalies. 'Critical incident' techniques use complaints and breakdowns in procedures to identify the key issues in service delivery.[580]

- *Self-selected samples.* People have been selected on the basis that they volunteered for an activity, or even applied for a job – which indicates that they may not be like others who have not come forward.[581] The researcher has to argue that this does not distort the issue under study. In qualitative samples, it does not necessarily do so – the test is whether the observations point validly to issues and processes, not whether they are numerically representative. Similar arguments apply to 'snowball' samples, in which cases are drawn out of a network of contacts; they may be the only effective way to reach people who are otherwise hard to find.

- *Structural samples* are selected because the people have particular roles or relationships – for example in an organisational hierarchy or a political structure. A review of organisational activity would ordinarily try to obtain information from people occupying particular roles within the organisational structure.

- *Key groups.* Special groups like political representatives, police officers, social workers and claimants are all potentially valid and interesting in their own way.

- *Stakeholder research.* A stakeholder can be seen either as someone who has a role relating to the issue under study, or more generally as 'any group or individual who can affect or is affected by the achievement of the organisation's objectives'.[582] Stakeholder research usually calls on researchers not just to obtain relevant information, but to engage stakeholders in the process.[583]

Data analysis

I made the case in the previous chapter that data cannot be taken to speak for themselves; facts are not intrinsically meaningful, but acquire meanings through a process of interpretation which needs to be understood theoretically. Processing data is not very interesting in itself, but it is important to identify it as part of the research process in order to avoid the problems which arise when that process begins – as it must – to change the characteristics of the original data through selection, sifting and interpretation. A thorough account of method will usually refer to this process at some point.

Qualitative data are generally organised through a process of selection, thematic organisation and interpretation – precisely the same kind of approach which is required of those reading and writing textual material. The method is referred to as 'open coding'. Data from exploratory research are sifted, sorted and classified flexibly. The basis for classification can be drawn from theoretical principles based on knowledge of social science, or, as happens in 'grounded theory', it can be developed from a process of comparing and contrasting the material and sorting it into categories.

There are more conventions governing the organisation and presentation of quantitative data. It is not appropriate here to offer an introduction to the interpretation of this kind of material, but it is important for anyone working in this field to develop at least a nodding acquaintance with the techniques, which are necessary both for interpreting data and arguments made by others and for constructing one's own.

Descriptive statistics consist of summaries of numbers in particular categories; usually they are presented in charts or tables. Analytical statistics (the kind taught in 'statistics' courses) are used to identify associations in the data. This kind of statistical material is concerned mainly with probability, or the chance of something happening. An association is said to be 'statistically significant' if the chances of it happening are sufficiently remote to make it unlikely. Conventionally the test is set at a probability of 1 in 20; if the odds of it happening were less than this, it is thought to be 'significant'. This is usually written in the form $p<.05$; p (the probability that this will happen) is less than .05 (five chances in 100).

There are some common problems with this approach:
- *Statistical significance is not necessarily proof against chance results.* One chance in 20 is not very long odds. If we are examining complex problems – and many of the problems in social policy are complex – there is a strong possibility that there may be more than 20 associations, and if this happens it is very likely one of them will show up as 'significant'. It may be appropriate to look for a wider margin – 1 in 100 ($p<.01$), or even 1 in 1,000 ($p<.001$).
- *Associations are not proof of any relationship.* It is quite likely that we could show a rough association between deaths from coronary heart disease and mobile phone use (both are associated in industrial societies with lifestyle), but it would not mean very much. We still need a good theoretical model to explain the data. Understanding the mathematics is secondary to a critical understanding of the relationships.
- *Problems in social policy are both multifaceted and interrelated.* 'Multicollinearity' – when variables are not truly independent of each other – can lead to serious problems in statistically based research, because it is difficult to work out which factors are really important. This cannot be left to the computer to decide (although all too often it is); the importance of associations depends on the quality of the explanation which is given, not the statistical process by which they are derived.

Criticising research methods

Most research studies include a methodological analysis, in which researchers try to deal with objections. Many of these are very narrowly focused on minor issues – for example, how many times researchers visited if people were out, or how long the interviews took. These are sometimes important – if they haven't been done adequately, they may cast doubt on the findings – but they are not usually fundamental. A defective piece of research may still point to real problems, while an excellent methodology may yield results which are vulnerable to theoretical criticism, misinterpretation and political bargaining.

In order to criticise an empirical study, a number of questions need to be asked:

1. What is the study for? The purpose of a study can affect both the perceptions of the researcher and the types of method undertaken.
2. What assumptions have been made? In other words, what are the premises of the argument? How have terms been defined?
3. Is the process which has been followed appropriate to the problem?
4. Is the study valid? Is it testing what it was supposed to test?
5. Do the conclusions the researcher draws follow from the results?

Ethical issues in research

Many research projects have ethical dimensions, and consideration of the ethical issues is a standard part of research design. In general terms, the kinds of ethical consideration which are included in the published codes are of four kinds. The first elements are concerned with the *impact* of the research. They consider:

- the potential implications of research for participants;
- the potential implications of research for non-participants; and
- the uses to which research can be put.

The second set of guidelines are rules covering the *treatment of participants*. They include:

- informed consent;
- confidentiality and anonymity; and
- special consideration of vulnerable respondents.

Third, there are *disciplinary considerations*. Researchers are enjoined to:

- maintain research of high quality;
- display competence;
- act responsibly towards others in their field; and
- advance their discipline.

Fourth, there are rules concerning *research relationships*. These include:

- responsibilities of the researcher to the body commissioning the research;
- responsibilities to the host institution;
- commitments to fellow researchers; and

- integrity in dealing with participants and stakeholders.

These codes offer guidelines, not rules. None of these principles applies in every case. There are examples in the rules on consent and confidentiality. Social policy often implies work in both the private and public domains; people are entitled to privacy in some circumstances (such as details of their private lives) but not in others (in their operation of public services). Principles like 'consent' and 'confidentiality' are much less likely to be relevant in the public domain, and they cannot be taken to be universally applicable.

There are however several principles which could be argued to be central to social policy research. The first set applies in general to all forms of public service. The most fundamental principle in research ethics is 'beneficence' – the question of who benefits, and who is harmed, by the research. Each person should be respected; people should be treated as ends in themselves, rather than means; their rights should be respected to the greatest degree possible; and the work of the policy researcher should not lend itself to procedures which are offensive, degrading or detrimental to people's welfare.

The second guiding principle is public accountability. Social policy research has a critical function. Public scrutiny is essential for democracy to work, and public accountability is itself an ethical principle. In a democracy, if someone is functioning in a public role, that person is subject to public examination and criticism in that role, whether they like it or not.

Third, researchers should consider the implications of their actions, including:

- the implications for policy;
- conformity with other moral codes (such as equality, opposition to racism or respect for humanity); and
- a commitment to benefit the wider society.

Research for policy

I pointed earlier to some of the political uses of research. Social policy research does not take place in a political vacuum. The political environment affects the selection of the issues: housing policy research has been dominated in recent years by studies of privatisation and affordability, while problems of homelessness and disadvantage have been examined much less. It affects the understanding of the issues; educational outcomes, for example, are likely to be judged differently if they are considered in terms of academic success or social mobility. The evaluation of evidence, as Taylor argues, is heavily dependent on its social context, and politically contested.[584]

The applied nature of the subject means that researchers in social policy have to take into account the potential consequences of their work. Research can be a tool for changing policy – although it is important to note that the use to which work is put is not necessarily the use that researchers would wish – and those who begin with this awareness are often looking to justify a particular result. Research into poverty provides a clear example. Most commentators want to make the same basic point – that people on benefit do not receive enough to live on. But they make the point differently, defining the issues in ways which they believe will best support their political case.[585] This is an area in which knowledge is used for particular purposes, and consideration of the implications for policy is itself a crucial part of the research process.

Box 14: Scandal versus research

It is well established that research in social policy hardly ever has the impact of a scandal. Research can be ignored, dismissed or qualified out of existence. Social scientists have had plenty of practice at dismissing research themselves; there is probably no research which cannot be criticised on methodological grounds. By contrast, scandal forces the hand of politicians and decision makers; it puts them in a position when they have to respond, even if the action is ineffective or misplaced.

The distinction between research and scandal may, however, be exaggerated. Research is nothing more than finding things out, and scandal can be a remarkably effective way of finding out the details of a process. Inquiries into child abuse are generally based on a detailed examination of every aspect of the process, reviewing the experience of all major participants.[586] Equally, the shocking details of cases in mental health have played a major part in the development of policy – most clearly, in accelerating the movement of people from institutions to the community. The principle of 'critical incident techniques' in research[587] is essentially equivalent to the process that inquiries into scandals go through; focusing on the points in a process where things go wrong is an illuminating way of identifying what the process is and where its weaknesses lie.

Conversely, research may be the way in which distasteful facts are brought to public notice. Child abuse was 'discovered' in the 1940s and 1950s, which seems a bizarre statement, because neglect and cruelty had been the subject of legislation long before. However, many professionals found it hard to credit that parents could systematically abuse their children, and problems were commonly attributed to other causes, such as bone defects. The presentation of evidence about fractures in an appropriately 'scientific' format was crucial in persuading medical professionals to take the issue seriously, as was the description of the problem as a 'syndrome' in the 1960s.[588] Problems like neglect in institutions or the misuse of drugs for control of children featured in the research literature long before they became the subject of media attention.[589] Social policy research is often intended to have an impact, and much research in the field is arranged and presented to get the maximum attention. Research reports typically come nowadays with a press release, a summary of key points and text on the internet.[590]

The sociologist Gary Marx once made a spirited defence of 'muckraking' research. Muckraking is 'the searching out and public exposure of misconduct on the part of prominent individuals and the discovery of scandal and incriminating evidence'. Muckraking research, Marx suggests,

> uses the tools of social science to document unintended (or officially unacknowledged) consequences of social action, inequality, poverty, racism, exploitation, opportunism, neglect, denial of dignity, hypocrisy, inconsistency, manipulation, wasted resources and the displacement of an organization's stated goals in favor of self-perpetuation.[591]

This is research as a passionate, politically committed act.

Even if it gets attention, however, the most passionate research is not necessarily the best. Good academic research, in its very nature, tends to be equivocal; it looks at different sides of an argument and comes to a reasoned conclusion (often something dull like 'more research is needed'). The research that makes a splash is often the most sensationally presented – or scandalous. This, perhaps, is one reason why the social science that influences policy often comes over as simplistic and partial.

ISSUE FOR DISCUSSION

Is it ethical to research social problems, like homelessness or mental illness, or personal problems, like grief or distress, without the hope of doing something about them?

FIFTEEN

Analysing policy

Aims
Goals
Methods
Implementation
Outcomes
Policy analysis for practice

Social policy is an applied subject, and any adequate understanding of the subject has to be able to identify the implications of policies for practice. Much of the literature on policy analysis is concerned, like the discussion in Part Two of this book, with explaining what policy is, how it is developed and why it matters.[592] Understanding the process through which policy is made is an important part of understanding social policy overall. But the study of social policy is not simply a study of process; it is very much concerned with outcomes. The analysis of social policy has to extend beyond description; it is important to make judgements and to consider choices for action. To do this, students and practitioners working in the subject area need to be able to collate information and to evaluate policy. They need to know what effects a policy is having, whether it is being implemented appropriately and, if necessary, what to do about it. The skills and approaches which are needed to do this kind of work are still referred to as 'policy analysis', but it is a different kind of policy analysis from much of the material found in the academic literature. It is analysis *for* policy, rather than analysis *of* policy.

In principle the analysis of a policy requires at least three steps:
1. the identification of the aims of a policy;
2. the identification of its results or effects; and
3. the comparison of the effects with the aims.

There is an argument for doing rather more. The literature on public policy pertains to an elaborate model referred to as the 'rational' approach to policy making. The rational model is a lengthy list of stages that planners are supposed to go through to make informed decisions. In addition to the steps outlined here, rational policy making begins with an assessment of the initial environment. Aims have to be operationalised, or translated into achievable goals. Then there needs to be an examination of alternative means of reaching goals. The policy has to be put into practice; the rational approach argues for consideration of the process

FIGURE 15.1: THE POLICY PROCESS

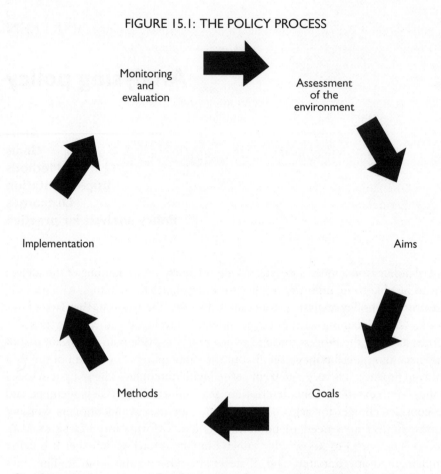

of implementation as part of understanding how a policy will work. Monitoring and evaluation of effects are equally part of a rational procedure.[593]

The approach is described differently in different places: for example, the Treasury *Green book* describes a cycle covering:

1. a *rationale* for policy;
2. identification of *objectives*;
3. *appraisal* of options;
4. implementation and *monitoring*;
5. *evaluation*, and
6. *feedback*.[594]

Although the language is slightly different, this is much the same kind of approach. It breaks policy making and practice down into stages that have to be reviewed in turn.

Rational approaches have been extensively criticised, because they do not really describe what agencies do in practice. In real life the stages are difficult to separate. Decisions depend on circumstances, negotiation, resources, compromise, pressure, discussion and many other things. The demands of rationality ask more of policy makers than may be feasible – the examination of alternative approaches and their consequences is time–consuming, expensive and often speculative.[595] But the rational model is a useful starting point for breaking down a large problem into smaller, more comprehensible issues, and it points to some important issues which otherwise might not be taken into account. In *Policy analysis for practice*, I used the rational model to provide a framework for examination.[596]

Box 15: PRSPs

Rational planning may look like an obscure academic exercise, but the process has gradually taken root in government internationally. One of the main mechanisms by which this has happened in recent years has been the Poverty Reduction Strategy Papers (PRSPs) required from governments throughout the developing world by the International Monetary Fund and the World Bank.[597] The process was announced in December 1999. At the time of writing this section in 2007, 64 developing countries had prepared PRSPs, either interim PRSPs, which identify issues and explain how the procedure will be developed, or full programmes, which are reported on annually and updated every three years. The International Monetary Fund has engaged rather more countries in related processes, and has suggested in a previous report that the numbers of countries involved will shortly go above 70.[598]

The PRSP approach requires governments to consult with social partners, to encourage participation in the development of the programme, to be explicit about their aims and intentions and to recognise what they have done or not done. The International Monetary Fund and World Bank identify the process as

> setting clear goals and targets that are linked to public actions; improving budget and monitoring systems; opening the space for discussing national priorities and policies for poverty reduction and growth; filling country-specific analytic gaps; and aligning and harmonizing donor assistance with national priorities.[599]

With the exception of the last, these are typical objectives of a rational planning process. The link with donor assistance does, however, give the clue to how the process has become so widespread; engagement with the process is essential to the receipt of international funding.

The PRSP process is not prescriptive about policies, but there are detailed guidelines about the sort of activities that governments are supposed to be involved in in order to prepare the papers. Governments are encouraged to consult, to engage social partners, to formulate plans of actions and to build capacity to assess their work. The sorts of issue which the International Monetary Fund and World Bank identify as 'good practice' include establishing a foundation of data for decision making; developing consultation and participation; building links through existing institutions; and setting realistic targets.[600]

Some reports, to be sure, fall short of those expectations. Independent organisations have been critical of some governments for their lack of consultation and engagement of civil society in the process[601] – which is a criticism, not of the principle of PRSPs, but their practice. The International Monetary Fund's approach has been uncharacteristically relaxed; the evaluation reports are long on positive encouragement, and short on negative criticism.

The gains from the process in terms of poverty reduction have been described, not unreasonably, as 'modest';[602] but it is not clear that reductions in poverty are what the policy is mainly about. What the plans actually include has to be decided at national level; it might be plans for economic growth, social policy, or political measures to incorporate different actors into the process of development. The common elements are procedural. The tests which the international organisations are applying – transparency, openness, participation, planning or the development of capacity – are issues in governance rather than poverty reduction. The PRSPs represent one of the most extraordinary exercises in international governance ever undertaken.

Aims

The identification of aims is central to the establishment of criteria by which the success or failure of a policy can be judged. Some criteria are based on principles, or generalised rules – for example, that 'social work should foster self-determination' or that 'housing should be allocated to those in the greatest need'. An alternative approach is to begin with a normative objective, or an end in sight. This may refer to a general end, like the 'abolition of poverty'; it may also refer to some model or pattern, like the 'free market'. In many cases, this amounts to the same thing as judgement by principles, but it is not always the same. There is a general problem in welfare economics of 'second-best' options: a compromise on one point may imply violation of the assumptions which made a particular option desirable.[603] It means that even if option B is less desirable than option A, a compromise between them – halfway towards A – could be worse than either. Working to a principle and aiming for a specific end can produce very different kinds of result. Principles are used to judge each stage in a process; working towards ends can be used to justify the means, even if initially people are made worse off. Lenin was reputedly fond of saying that 'you can't make an omelette without breaking eggs', but that is not a justification for breaking eggs whenever you please. Crosland, by contrast, argued that in pleading for 'equality' he was not arguing for absolute equality, but only for more equality than we had at present: equality was a principle rather than an end.[604]

Identifying the positive aims of formal agencies is probably the simplest part of the process, in the first place because such aims are often made explicit in policies, and second because by default the improvement of welfare can be taken as a basic test. Many services and agencies will explain what their broad aims are; many other aims become explicit when the critical literature is reviewed. For example, the aims of a service for older people might be to improve the welfare of older people; to preserve their independence at home for as long as possible; to offer support to frail older people and their carers; and, where it becomes necessary to consider other forms of care, to ease the transition as far as possible. These then become the tests by which the service can be judged.

At the same time, there are some important areas of uncertainty. Aims can be positive – in that there are factors which have to be achieved – or negative, in that there are things which need to be avoided. An example of a 'negative' aim is the idea that people's freedoms should be respected; policies are often counted as illegitimate if they breach this rule, and legitimate if they do not. Negative aims are more difficult to identify than positive ones, because they are unlikely to be mentioned unless the conditions are breached. So, it tends to be implicit rather than explicit that services should not cost too much; they should meet received professional standards; they should not upset their political masters; the workers should observe the rules for financial propriety; they should be able to report their results in an approved format. Time and again, services have fallen foul of a whole set of rules, often unwritten and unexplained, which mean that they are judged and found wanting.

Another source of ambiguity lies in the normative content of many aims. Criteria which might seem technical (such as whether or not a policy has particular redistributive effects, or whether it is cost-effective) may well conceal normative judgements. An example referred to earlier is the attempt to define poverty. Different tests are liable to yield very different results.

It has to be stressed, too, that the selection of relevant criteria is a political judgement. Decision making in the political arena generally rests in the negotiation of conflicting interests. The reasons why policies are adopted may not be clear. Nor is it always clear whose interests the policies serve; it does not have to be the recipients'.

Goals

Aims can be expressed in very general terms – for example, that 'this policy should offer value for money' or 'this policy should foster people's independence in their own homes'. But they can also be very specific, such as the statement that 'benefits should be calculated accurately in at least 95% of cases'. For convenience, the first class of objective is usually referred to as an 'aim' or 'objective'; the second type is a 'goal' or 'target'. The difference between the two is that the second type is 'operationalised', or translated into terms which can be acted on. Operational goals usually have some kind of general principle lurking behind them, and the usual guidance given in texts on planning is that both aims and goals need to be clarified. The process of operationalisation – translating aims into specific measures

– is crucial for policy making, but often it is obscured by a failure to recognise the distinction between the initial principles and the practical details.

Both needs and responses are commonly operationalised through the use of 'indicators', which were introduced in Chapter Three. 'Social indicators' are figures which give summary guides to social issues. 'Performance indicators' are indicators about the performance of an agency; they are used to identify what the goals of an agency should be, and to test whether or not those goals have been achieved. Figures like the 'crime rate' or the 'unemployment rate' are indicators; so are the numbers of hospital beds per 1,000 population, the numbers of children attending nursery school, or the waiting list for telephones for people with disabilities. Figures of this kind have to be constructed and developed; there are always problems about what gets taken into account and what does not. The process of turning general aims and objectives into goals requires policy makers to offer some way of finding out what effect their policies are having, and indicators are a way of doing that.

There are three important issues in the definition of indicators which relate to their use to define goals:

- *Selection*. Indicators are supposed to give a sense of more general problems, and have to be selected for that purpose. Bevan and Hood give this the rather grand name of 'synecdoche' – taking a part to stand for the whole.[605] Governments are prone, of course, to point to the indicators which serve their interests best, but even when figures are selected in good faith there are still compromises. Information is difficult to gather, and there is a tendency to select indicators which are readily available, or at least easily calculated.

- *Quantification*. Indicators are generally represented as numbers. Numbers have important properties. They are aggregative, because they can be added together or subtracted; and they are ordinal, because two is greater than one and three is greater than two. This seems almost too obvious to mention, but it is important to make those assumptions explicit, because they are not necessarily true of observations in social life. Many of the indicators from developing countries are uncertain; wherever figures point to sizeable problems, they may also mean that the capacity to collect information may be limited, and they cannot necessarily be used as a basis for relative calculations. Even where the figures are reliable, we cannot assume that social problems can be added together; does a person who has suffered a death in the family, low income and a leaking roof, necessarily have more of a problem than someone who has only had a death in the family while on a low income? The OPCS study on disability judged that where someone was multiply disabled, only the three most serious disabilities really mattered for the purposes of assessment, and they disregarded lesser disabilities as a result.[606]

- *Norms and values.* Indicators often contain – and sometimes conceal – value judgements. Unemployment is not the same problem for everyone; there is a huge difference between short-term job-changing and the experience of long-term unemployment. Crime rates against property show different trends to crimes against the person. Indicators are not simply neutral 'facts'; they have to be interpreted in their social context.

The process of operationalisation is often seen as a technical issue, but it is dangerous to leave it at that. The problem is that issues change in the process; an initial concern with unemployment, poverty or homelessness can be subtly altered into something else. Services which set out to deal with 'poverty', for example, often begin with a concern about living standards, but generally come to concentrate on low income – because low income is the best available indicator of the problems of poverty. This is liable, in turn, to lead to a redefinition of the problem. Poverty in the 19th century was primarily perceived as an urban problem; the social surveys of Booth were focused on the distribution of urban problems, but the debates on his work centred instead on the question of budgets and minimum income.[607] Rowntree built on this topic, and in doing so shifted perceptions so that the question of poverty became very much a question of income.[608] When in the 1960s and 1970s the issue of urban deprivation became a serious issue, one of the most devastating criticisms was that poverty was not geographically centralised.[609] That is undoubtedly true, but it did not follow that poor areas should not be considered in themselves a matter of concern; it shows the extent to which the understanding of 'poverty' has come to be dominated by the means we use to measure it.

Methods

A substantial part of this book has been devoted to the ways in which policy is devised and implemented, including the role of government, the institutions and agencies which are used to bring about social ends, and the constraints under which services operate. It is basic to policy making that these measures and approaches should be intended to do something, so it does not call for a great intellectual leap to realise that the means employed should be consistent with the aims and objectives. At times, however, the link between aims and methods can be tenuous. A government wants to reduce racial unrest, so it renovates housing. It may want to improve housing conditions, but decides to give people income support and call it a housing benefit. It wants to reduce juvenile crime, and provides social work to families. Or it wants to prevent obesity, and devises a programme of competitive sport.

There are several reasons for this kind of disjuncture. The first is that the declared aim may not be the genuine one. Public programmes might be funded to support interest groups, to win votes, or for governments to be seen to be doing things - not necessarily because they work. Second, policy making can be influenced by factions who have a commitment to particular approaches or ideas, and who use the opportunities created by the political environment to further their cause. Public health in Victorian England was initially a matter of engineering, rather than medicine; the process became the province of the medical profession in the 1870s. The social work services in the 1960s were developed on the basis of a policy that was supposed to be responding to youth crime. The development of policy for 'social inclusion' in Scotland was supplanted by an established lobby for urban regeneration. Third, the patterns through which policies are developed are heavily influenced by ideologies, preconceptions and assumptions about the process. There are presumed, 'common-sense' links between sport and exercise, between racial conflict and urban conditions or between teenage pregnancy and sex education, which largely disappear when the evidence is examined, but the influence of prejudice in shaping policy cannot be underestimated. And fourth, as Chapter Five emphasises, the process of policy making is an area for discussion, bargaining and compromise. It should not be surprising if the process leads to some non-sequiturs.

The rational model argues for a review of all the possible alternative measures, considering their costs, and their implications. This is not really possible – it would be hugely time-consuming and expensive. What happens, instead, is that policy makers have to review a range of plausible alternatives. The sorts of consideration which have to be made include the costs and benefits of different measures, both now and in the future. Appraising what is likely to happen, as well as what does, makes the reliability of any decision uncertain. Decisions which commit decision makers to a single course for the future are often unsafe decisions. One of the tests of good policy is 'robustness' – the ability to change tack if something goes wrong.

Implementation

Whenever policies are introduced, they have to be implemented in practice. It is rare that policies simply go into the machine at the top, and the intended effects come out at the bottom – a process of 'perfect administration'. Something happens in between; the process of implementation and service delivery changes the character of policy. In some cases, the policy becomes diluted, as compromises are necessary in practice. Governments may want to build houses, but constraints like the availability of land, negotiation of planning restrictions and the capacity of the construction industry may limit what is actually happening. Decentralised administrations have to delegate decisions to local level, creating a series of points at which policies can be delayed or forestalled.[610] In other cases, the policy changes in character – sometimes subtly, sometimes substantially. Agencies are influenced by a range of constraints, including finance, the practical problems of dealing with the public, the size of their operation and the external environment. They have to make choices about where their time, effort and resources will be devoted. Faced with the pressures of practice, community regeneration might become housing improvement; employment programmes might become personal development programmes. Agencies are influenced in these choices by professional standards, administrative conventions and 'service ideologies'. The effect of providing nursery places in schools is different from providing them in social care centres; schools tend to emphasise educational criteria, while social care centres tend to emphasise child protection. Community development is likely to be handled differently if it is the responsibility of departments dealing with housing, community education or economic development.

Much of the process of policy analysis is concerned with the activity of agencies. This can pose challenges, because many of the models used in social science are based on responses from individual subjects rather than collective ones. Institutions cannot think or feel; they do not 'act' in the way a person acts. Nevertheless, there are both behaviours and attitudes of people in organisational settings, and organisations do in practice 'act' in order to produce certain effects. Agencies can be examined by reviewing their formal policies, but that has the limitation that what agencies intend, and what they do, may be different. The practice of an agency can be reviewed by examining its records, looking at its processes, and perhaps by focusing on 'critical incidents' – the points where policy goes wrong. This can be done by recording the results of actions or by questioning service users and other stakeholders.

There are difficulties in interpreting such results. The actions of officers are not necessarily the actions of the agency – officers are individuals and may act differently. The effects of a policy or set of practices may be unintended, and even unnoticed. The results which are identified may be the result, not of the actions of the agency, but other external factors – if service users are disadvantaged, and the actions of an agency are neutral, the service users will still be disadvantaged when the policy is put into practice. Most difficult, organisations are not simply the sum of their parts. A large organisation full of well-intentioned, dedicated individuals can still act to disadvantage people through poor communication, lack of coordination, bureaucratic delays and failure to identify the consequences of a series of actions.

Many policy analyses focus almost exclusively on the process of implementation, under the name of 'audit'.[611] The governments who fund audit are not usually looking to be told that their policies are wrong, but they do want to know whether or not agencies are performing in the way they are being funded to perform. 'Process evaluation' similarly is concerned with the question of whether agencies are behaving in appropriate, or expected, ways; often this is done for newly established agencies, which have not been in place long enough to achieve clear results, in order to establish whether they are well run.

Outcomes

Although policy is intended to produce effects, the effects can sometimes be difficult to identify. There are cases where the outcomes are relatively clear, like examination results from schools, but these tend to be cursory and liable to misinterpretation – examination results say more about the initial social position of the schools than they do about the quality of the schools themselves. What tends to be considered instead is either inputs – that is, a measure of the resources used, like the amount of money spent – or outputs, the services which the resources are used to provide – for example, accommodation provided, or the number of beds. An input is what goes into a service – like the number of doctors per head of population or the cost of support for unemployed people. (Extra resources devoted to a service are easy to measure; the benefits of such resources may not be.) An output is what the service makes available, like the number of day care places, or the proportion of the population which receives education. An outcome is the result – the effect of what has been done. In some cases, the output will be the outcome – the number of houses built or the creation of a road, or the money which is redistributed through social security. In principle, however, outcomes could include other kinds of benefits, including improved health, social contact, personal development or happiness.

Policies are often assessed while they are still in progress. Some of the tests, like benchmarks or 'best value', are formed externally, or by comparison with previous schemes, and used to judge whether things are going according to plan. 'Process evaluations' are undertaken to see whether the methods of implementation conform to norms, and to indicate the impact that policies are having.

If the test is, however, whether the policy has had an impact on the wider society, it can be difficult to work out that the effects really are. A policy which is already in place cannot always conveniently be compared with some prior state; critics of rent control, for example, try to argue what the situation might have been like without it,[612] but where rent control has existed for any length of time there is no effective point for such a comparison. Where there are changes, it is not always clear that they result from the policies, rather than from some other social factor. The same problems affect comparison with other societies: there are too many possible explanations for differences.

Services are evaluated in the first place by judging whether or not the outcomes are the sort envisaged in their aims or goals. This is the test of effectiveness: a service is effective if it succeeds in achieving what it was supposed to achieve. This is not, however, the only test to be applied. There may be unexpected and undesirable effects. Faced with the problem of cholera in 19th-century London, the secretary of the Poor Law Commission, Edwin Chadwick, argued for the development of sewers. Following a strand of medical opinion at the time, Chadwick believed that cholera was caused by 'miasma' or air-borne particles, and that the important thing to do was to shift sewage away from where people lived. This is what the sewers were designed to do – and they shifted the sewage to the nearest stretch of water, the river, which unfortunately was also a major source of drinking water. People died in their thousands.[613] The policy was 'effective', in that it achieved precisely its operational objectives. In the short term, it was ineffective in terms of its general aims, which were to reduce liability to cholera; in the longer term, of course, people realised they could no longer drink the river water, and the sewage system became one of the main defences against disease.

Conversely, there may be unexpected effects which are desirable. Compulsory education has had the important side-effect of providing childminding for families; provision for homeless people has offered an escape route, however unsatisfactory, for women subject to domestic violence; sickness and invalidity benefits have helped to fill gaps in provision for unemployed people. Desirability is, of course, a matter of interpretation. Many issues in social policy are centred around a range of different interests, and measures may be desirable for some at the expense of others. Social care may improve the lifestyle of dependent people at the expense of their carers; policies for positive discrimination may favour some groups over others.

Policy analysis for practice

Although this chapter discusses the elements of policy analysis in general terms, the rationale for including those elements has a more specific purpose. Policy analysis is a set of techniques for identifying a series of interrelated issues that need to be considered to make sense of policy in practice, and the stages considered here provide a method of breaking down a complex process into a series of more manageable steps. I have used a much more detailed approach to the analysis of policy in other work,[614] but for the purposes of this introductory text, I have used a shorter, simplified process. Table 15.1 suggests a simple checklist for the analysis of policy. It is a starting point, not just for critical examination, but for the practical business of determining whether a policy does what it is supposed to do.

TABLE 15.1: POLICY ANALYSIS IN PRACTICE		
Key stage	*Indicative questions to consider ...*	*while reviewing the issues in the light of:*
Aims and goals	What is the policy supposed to do?	
	How will we be able to tell if a policy has achieved its aims?	
Methods	What are the options?	Aims and goals
	What are the constraints?	
	What resources are there?	
	Are the methods consistent with the aims?	
Implementation	Is the practice consistent with the policy?	Aims and values
		Methods
	Does the process meet the criteria and standards applicable in this field?	
Outcomes	What effects does the policy have?	Aims and values
	Has the policy achieved its aims?	Methods
		The process of implementation

ISSUE FOR DISCUSSION

Policy analysis mainly works from an acceptance of the stated aims of a policy – whatever the aims may be. Is this legitimate?

Notes

Notes to Chapter One
Introduction: the nature of social policy

1   D Donnison and others, 1965, *Social policy and administration revisited*, Allen and Unwin 1965, p 1.

2   See for example S Cairncross, E Ouano, 1990, 'Surface water drainage in urban areas', in J Hardoy, S Cairncross, D Satterthwaite (eds), *The poor die young*, London: Earthscan.

3   D Donnison, 1961, 'The teaching of social administration', *British Journal of Sociology*, 13(3), cited W Birrell, P Hillyard, A Murie, D Roche (eds), 1971, *Social administration*, Harmondsworth: Penguin, p 9.

4   R Titmuss, 1955, 'The social division of welfare', in *Essays on 'the welfare state'*, London: Allen and Unwin, 1963.

5   H Rose, 1981, 'Rereading Titmuss: the sexual division of welfare', *Journal of Social Policy*, 10(4) pp 477–502.

6   R Titmuss, 1968, *Commitment to welfare*, Allen and Unwin, pp 20–4.

7   F Lafitte (1962) 'Social policy in a free society', in W Birrell, P Hillyard, A Murie, D Roche, *Social administration*, Harmondsworth: Penguin, 1971, p 57.

8   F Williams, 1989, *Social policy: A critical introduction*, Brighton: Polity, p 13.

9   M Orton, K Rowlingson, 2007, 'A problem of riches', *Journal of Social Policy*, 36(1), p 75.

10 M Cahill, 1994, The new social policy, Oxford: Blackwell.

11 D Donnison, 1982, *The politics of poverty*, London: Heinemann.

12 D Donnison, 1985, 'Myth of a crisis', *New Society*, 18 April, 72(1164), pp 89–90.

13 C Booth, 1889, *Life and Labour of the people in London*, London: Macmillan, 1903; B Rowntree, 1901, *Poverty: A study of town life*, Bristol: The Policy Press, 2000.

14 M Bayley, 1973, *Mental handicap and community care*, London: RKP.

15 J Rowe, L Lambert, 1973, *Children who wait*, London: Association of British Adoption Agencies.

16 D Donnison, 1975, *Social policy and administration revisited*, London: George Allen and Unwin, p 13.

17 W Birrell, P Hillyard, A Murie, D Roche (eds), 1971, *Social administration*, Harmondsworth: Penguin.

18 Cited R Pinker, 1971, *Social theory and social policy*, London: Heinemann, p 4.

19 P Townsend, 1995, *The rise of international social policy*, Bristol: The Policy Press, p 7.

20 M Hill, 1996, *Social policy: A comparative analysis*, Hemel Hempstead: Prentice Hall, p xiii.

21 M Minogue, 1993, 'Theory and practice in public policy and administration', in M Hill (ed), *The policy process*, Hemel Hempstead: Harvester Wheatsheaf, p 10.

22 R Pawson, N Tilley, 1997, *Realistic evaluation*, London: Sage Publications, especially Chapter 3.

23 A Giddens, *Sociology*, Cambridge: Polity, p 22.

24 P Spicker, 2007, *The idea of poverty*, Bristol: The Policy Press.

25 H Hopkins, 1936, *Spending to save*, New York: Norton.

26 See for example D Mitchell, 1990, *Income transfers in ten welfare states*, Aldershot: Avebury.

27 J Drèze, A Sen, 1989, *Hunger and public action*, Oxford: Clarendon Press.

28 D Gordon, L Adelman, K Ashworth, J Bradshaw, R Levitas, S Middleton, C Pantazis, D Patisos, S Payne, P Townsend, J Williams, 2000, *Poverty and social exclusion in Britain*, York: Joseph Rowntree Foundation.

29 D Narayan, R Chambers, M Shah, P Petesch, 2000, *Voices of the poor*, New York: World Bank/Oxford University Press.

Notes to Chapter Two: Welfare in society

30 J Bentham, 1789, 'An introduction to the principles of morals and legislation', in M Warnock (ed), *Utilitarianism*, Glasgow: Collins, 1962, p 35.

31 P Spicker, S Leguizamon Alvarez, D Gordon (eds), 2007, *Poverty: An international glossary*, London: Zed.

32 P Townsend, 1985, 'A sociological approach to the measurement of poverty – a rejoinder to Professor Amartya Sen', *Oxford Economic Papers*, 37 p 664.

33 M Lipton, 2001, 'Poverty concepts, policies, partnership and practice', in N Middleton, P O'Keefe, R Visser (eds), *Negotiating poverty*, London: Pluto Press.

34 See for example K Ellis, H Dean (eds), 2000, *Social policy and the body*, Basingstoke: Macmillan.

35 See D Narayan, R Chambers, M Shah, P Petesch, 2000, *Voices of the poor: Crying out for change*, New York: World Bank/Oxford University Press.

36 See for example F Hayek, 1976, *Law legislation and liberty*, London: RKP.

37 M Humm (ed), 1992, *Feminisms*, Hemel Hempstead: Harvester Wheatsheaf, Chapter 7; J A Kourany, J P Sterba, R Tong (eds), 1993, *Feminist philosophies*, Hemel Hempstead: Harvester Wheatsheaf.

38 I M D Little, 1957, *A critique of welfare economics*, Oxford: Oxford University Press.

39 R Dahrendorf, 1973, *Homo sociologicus*, London: Routledge and Kegan Paul.

40 E Miller, G Gwynne, 1972, *A life apart*, London: Tavistock; P Spicker, 2000, 'Dementia and social death', *Self Agency and Society*, 2(2), pp 88-104.

41 H Qureshi, A Walker, 1989, *The caring relationship: elderly people and their families*, Basingstoke: Macmillan.

42   R Talmy, 1962, *Histoire du mouvement familial en France*, Paris: Union Nationale des Caisses d'Allocations Familiales.

43   United Nations, 1989, *Convention on the Rights of the Child*, Preamble and Article 5.

44   M Bayley, 1973, *Mental handicap and community care*, London: RKP.

45   G Hillery, 1955, 'Definitions of community: areas of agreement', *Rural Sociology*, 20, pp 111-23.

46   P Spicker, 2006, *Liberty, equality, fraternity*, Bristol: The Policy Press.

47   O Lewis, 1966, *La Vida*, London: Panther; C Valentine, 1968, *Culture and poverty*, Chicago, IL: University of Chicago Press.

48   Lin Ka, 1999, *Confucian welfare cluster*, Tampere (Sweden): University of Tampere; I Peng, 2000, 'A fresh look at the Japanese welfare state', *Social Policy and Administration*, 34(1), pp 87-114; T K Uzuhashi, 2001, 'Japan', in P Alcock, G Craig (eds), *International Social Policy*, Basingstoke: Palgrave.

49   E Kedourie, 1993, *Nationalism*, Oxford: Blackwell.

50   D Miller, 1990, *Market, state and community*, Oxford: Oxford University Press.

51   D Béland, A Lecours, 2005, 'Nationalism, public policy and institutional development', *Journal of Public Policy*, 25(2), pp 265-85.

52   M Bommes, A Geddes (eds), 2000, *Immigration and welfare*, London: Routledge.

53   P Spicker, 1996, 'Understanding particularism', in D Taylor (ed), *Critical Social Policy: A reader*, London: Sage Publications.

54   United Nations Population Division, 2006, *World migrant stock*, at http://esa.un.org/migration

55   International Organisation for Migration, 2007, *Global estimates and trends*, at www.iom.int/jahia/Jahia/pid/254

56   A Morissens, D Sainsbury, 2005, 'Migrants' social rights, ethnicity and welfare régimes', *Journal of Social Policy*, 34(4), pp 637-60.

57   R Titmuss, 1968, 'Welfare state and welfare society', in *Commitment to welfare*, London: Allen and Unwin.

58   Beveridge Report, 1942, *Social insurance and allied services*, Cmd 6404, London: HMSO, p 171.

59   P Spicker, 2006, *Liberty, equality, fraternity*, Bristol: The Policy Press.

60   K Banting, 2005, 'The multicultural welfare state', *Social Policy and Administration*, 39 (2), pp 98-115.

61   M Oakeshott, 1975, *On human conduct*, Oxford: Clarendon Press.

62   N Coote, 1989, 'Catholic social teaching', *Social Policy and Administration*, 23(2), pp 150-60.

63   See P Spicker, 2000, *The welfare state*, London: Sage Publications.

64   S Paugam, 2004, *La disqualification sociale*, Paris: Presses Universitaires de France.

65   R Lenoir, 1974, *Les exclus: Un français sur dix*, Paris: Seuil.

66   See E Carlson, 2001, *The unfit*, New York: Cold Spring Harbor Laboratory Press.

67   P Spicker, 1997, 'Exclusion', *Journal of Common Market Studies*, 35(1), pp 133-43.

68   H Ferguson, 2007, 'Abused and looked after children as "moral dirt"', *Journal of Social Policy*, 36(1), pp 123-39.

69   P Spicker, 1984, *Stigma and social welfare*, Beckenham: Croom Helm.

70   J Bentham, Papers: 1831-32, 154b, pp 602-4.

71   D Phillips, 1963, 'Rejection: a possible consequence of seeking help for mental disorders', *American Sociological Review*, 28(6), pp 963-72.

72   P Townsend, 1976, *Sociology and social policy*, Harmondsworth: Penguin, p 126.

73   R Klein, 1975, *Inflation and priorities*, Bath: Centre for Studies in social policy, p 5.

74   W Thomas, F Znaniecki, 1918, *The Polish peasant in Europe and America*, Chicago, IL: University of Chicago Press; G Sorel, 1961, *Reflections on violence*, London: RKP.

75   R Titmuss, 1968, *Commitment to welfare*, London: Allen and Unwin, p 129.

76   R Dahl, 1971, *Polyarchy*, New Haven, CT: Yale University Press.

77   E Burke, 1790, *Reflections on the revolution in France*, New York: Holt Rinehart and Winston, 1959.

78   H Spencer, 1851, *Social statics*, at http://oll.libertyfund.org/?option=com_staticxt&staticfile=show.php%3Ftitle=273

79   F Hayek, 1976, *Law liberty and legislation*, London: RKP.

80   P Spicker, 2006, *Liberty, equality, fraternity*, Bristol: The Policy Press, Chapter 3.

81   See M McIntosh, 2000, 'Feminism and social policy', and C Pateman, 2000, 'The patriarchal welfare state', both in C Pierson, F Castles (eds), *The welfare state reader*, Cambridge: Polity.

82   J Millar, C Glendinning, 1989, 'Gender and poverty', *Journal of Social Policy*, 18(3), pp 363-81.

83   R Tawney, 1913, cited M Orton, K Rowlingson, 2007, 'A problem of riches', *Journal of Social Policy*, 36(1), pp 59-77.

84   H H Gerth, C W Mills, 1948, *From Max Weber*, London: RKP.

85   J Rex, R Moore, 1967, *Race, community and conflict*, Oxford: Oxford University Press.

86   W J Wilson, 1987, *The truly disadvantaged*, Chicago, IL: Chicago University Press.

87   P Townsend, 1979, *Poverty in the United Kingdom*, Harmondsworth: Penguin.

88   R Lister, 1990, *The exclusive society*, London: Child Poverty Action Group; H Gans, cited F Gaffikin, M Morrissey, 1992, *The new unemployed*, London: Zed Books, p 84.

89   M Weber, 1967, 'The development of caste', pp 28-36 of R Bendix, S M Lipset, *Class, status and power* (2nd edition), London: Routledge and Kegan Paul, pp 31-32.

90   H Silver (ed), 1973, *Equal opportunity in education*, London: Methuen.

91   R Dworkin, 1985, *A matter of principle*, Cambridge, MA: Harvard University Press.

92   R. Linton, 1936, *The study of man*, New York: Appleton-Century.

93   P Spicker, 1984, *Stigma and social welfare*, Beckenham: Croom Helm.

94   R M Titmuss, 1968, *Commitment to welfare*, London: George Allen and Unwin, p 129.

95   P Spicker, 1988, *Principles of social welfare*, London: Routledge.

96   B Russell, 1960, *Power*, London: Unwin.

97   S Lukes, 1978, 'Power and authority', in T Bottomore, R Nisbet (eds), *A history of sociological analysis*, London: Heinemann.

98   K Millett, 1977, *Sexual politics*, London: Virago, Chapter 2; M Humm, 1989, 'Patriarchy', *The dictionary of feminist theory*, Hemel Hempstead: Harvester Wheatsheaf.

99   E Wilson, 1977, *Women and the welfare state*, London: Tavistock; H Hartman, 1992, 'Capitalism, patriarchy and job segregation by sex', in M Humm (ed), *Feminisms*, Hemel Hempstead: Harvester Wheatsheaf.

100 C Wright Mills, 1956, *The power élite*, New York: Oxford University Press; T Bottomore, 1966, *Elites and society*, Harmondsworth: Penguin; S Keller, 1963, *Beyond the ruling class*, New York: Random House; J Lee, 1963, *Social leaders and public persons*, Oxford: Oxford University Press.

101 P Dunleavy, B O'Leary, 1987, *Theories of the state*, London: Macmillan.

102 A Giddens, 1994, *Beyond left and right*, Cambridge: Polity Press.

103 A Giddens, 1994, *Beyond left and right*, Cambridge: Polity Press, pp 174, 182.

104 P Taylor Gooby, 1994, 'Postmodernism and social policy: a great leap backwards', *Journal of Social Policy*, 23(3), pp 385-404.

105 P Townsend, 1976, *Sociology and social policy*, Harmondsworth: Penguin, p 6.

106 Z Ferge, 1979, *A society in the making*, Harmondsworth: Penguin p 55.

Notes to Chapter Three: Problems and responses

107 P Townsend, 1976, *Sociology and social policy*, Harmondsworth: Penguin, p 6.

108 S E Finer, 1952, *The life and times of Edwin Chadwick*, London: Methuen, Chapter 3.

109 S Pfohl, 2003, 'The "discovery" of child abuse', in P Conrad, V Leiter (eds) *Health and health care as social problems*, Lanham, MD: Rowman Littlefield.

110 S Scott, 2001, *The politics and experience of ritual abuse*, Maidenhead: Open University Press.

111 P Berger, T Luckmann, 1967, *The social construction of reality*, New York: Anchor.

112 K Jones, 1972, *A history of the mental health services*, London: RKP.

113 Packman, 1981, *The child's generation*, Oxford: Blackwell.

114 See P Spicker, 2004, 'Developing indicators: issues in the use of quantitative data about poverty', *Policy & Politics*, 32(4), pp 431-40.

115 United Nations, 2007, *Millennium Development Goals*, www.un.org/millenniumgoals/

116 L Platt, 2007, *Poverty and ethnicity in the UK*, York: Joseph Rowntree Foundation, at www.jrf.org.uk/bookshop/eBooks/2006-ethnicity-poverty-UK.pdf

117 P Spicker, 2002, *Poverty and the welfare state*, London: Catalyst.

[118] T Lang, G Rayner, 2005, 'Obesity: a growing issue for European policy?', *Journal of European Social Policy*, 15(4), pp 301-27.

[119] See D Pick, 1989, *Faces of degeneration*, Cambridge: Cambridge University Press; E Carlson, 2001, *The unfit*, New York: Cold Spring Harbor Laboratory Press.

[120] H Boies, 1893, *Prisoners and paupers*, New York: Knickerbocker Press, p 266.

[121] C Cooley, 1902, *Human nature and the social order*, New York: Scribner, p 375.

[122] See A Estabrook, 1916, *The Jukes in 1915*, available at www.disabilitymuseum.org/lib/docs/759.htm

[123] S Christianson, 1993, 'Bad seed or bad science?', *New York Times*, 8 February.

[124] E Carlson, 2001, *The unfit*, New York: Cold Spring Harbor Laboratory Press.

[125] P Lombardo, nd, *Eugenic sterilization laws*, www.eugenicsarchive.org/html/eugenics/essay8text.html

[126] R Grunberger, 1974, *A social history of the Third Reich*, Harmondsworth: Penguin; G Rimlinger, 1987, 'Social policy under German fascism', in M Rein, G Esping-Anderson, L Rainwater (eds) *Stagnation and renewal in Social Policy*, New York: Armonk; P Weindling, 1989, *Health, race and German politics between national unification and Nazism, 1870-1945*, Cambridge: Cambridge University Press.

[127] J Trent, 1995, *Inventing the feeble mind: A history of mental retardation in the United States*, Berkeley, CA: University of California Press.

[128] R Burrows, N Pleace, D Quilgars, 1997, *Homelessness and Social Policy*, London: Routledge.

[129] R Tawney, 1930, *Equality*, London: Allen and Unwin.

[130] A Sen, 2001, *Development as freedom*, Oxford: Oxford University Press.

[131] World Bank, 2004, *Social safety nets*, at www1.worldbank.org/sp/safetynets/Targeting.asp

[132] World Bank, 1990, *World development report*, Oxford: Oxford University Press.

[133] P Spicker, 2005, 'Targeting, residual welfare and related concepts: modes of operation in public policy', *Public Administration*, 83(2), pp 345-65.

[134] Cited N Sutherland, 1976, *Breakdown*, London: Weidenfeld and Nicolson, p 225.

[135] M H Phillips, 1981, 'Favourable family impact as an objective of means support policy', in P G Brown, C Johnson, P Vernier (eds) *Income support*, Totowa, NJ: Rowman and Littlefield.

[136] J Millar, C Glendinning, 1989, 'Gender and poverty', *Journal of Social Policy*, 18(3), pp 363-81; S Payne, 1991, *Women, health and poverty*, London: Harvester Wheatsheaf; but see S Cantillon, B Nolan, 1998, 'Are married women more deprived than their husbands?', *Journal of Social Policy*, 27(2), pp 151-72.

[137] K Auletta, 1983, *The underclass*, New York: Vintage Books; C Murray, 1993, 'Underclass', in P J Baker, L Anderson, D Dorn (eds) *Social problems*, New York: Wadsworth.

[138] P Spicker, 2001, 'Poor areas and the "ecological fallacy"', *Radical Statistics*, 76, pp 38-79.

[139] R Putnam, 2000, *Bowling alone*, New York: Simon and Schuster, Chapter 19.

140   G Svendsen, J Sørensen, 2006, 'The socioeconomic power of social capital', *International Journal of Sociology and Social Policy*, 26(9/10), pp 411-29.

141   E Wilson, 1982, 'Women, community and the family', in A Walker (ed) *Community care*, Oxford: Blackwell.

142   D Rae, 1981, *Equalities*, Cambridge, MA: Harvard University Press.

143   R Goodin, J Le Grand (eds), 1987, *Not only the poor*, London: Allen and Unwin.

144   T Modood, R Berthoud, 1997, *Ethnic minorities in Britain: Diversity and disadvantage*, London: Policy Studies Institute.

145   See R Dworkin, 1985, *A matter of principle*, Cambridge, MA: Harvard University Press.

146   S Bailey, 2002, *Public sector economics*, Basingstoke: Palgrave.

147   D Weimer, A Vining, 1989, *Policy analysis* (2nd edition), Englewood Cliffs NJ: Prentice Hall.

148   R Goodin, J Le Grand (eds), 1987, *Not only the poor*, London: Allen and Unwin.

Notes to Chapter Four: Needs

149   D Winch, 1971, *Analytical welfare economics*, Harmondsworth: Penguin.

150   L Doyal, I Gough, 1991, *A theory of human need*, Basingstoke: Macmillan.

151   T Lang, G Rayner, 2005, 'Obesity: a growing issue for European policy?', *Journal of European Social Policy*, 15(4), pp 301-27.

152   L Kaplow, S Shavell, 2001, 'Any non-welfarist method of policy assessment violates the Pareto Principle', *Journal of Political Economy*, 109(2), pp 281-7.

153   A Sen, 1979, *Collective choice and social welfare*, Amsterdam: Elsevier, Chapter 6 and p 198.

154   P Spicker, 1988, *Principles of social welfare*, London: Routledge, Chapter 1.

155   J Feinberg, 1973, *Social philosophy*, Englewood Cliffs, NJ: Prentice Hall, p 111.

156   J Feinberg, 1980, *Rights, justice and the bounds of liberty*, Princeton, NJ: Princeton University Press, p 32.

157   P Spicker, S Alvarez Leguizamon, D Gordon (eds), 2007, *Poverty: An international glossary*, London: Zed.

158   L Doyal, I Gough, 1991, *A theory of human need*, Basingstoke: Macmillan.

159   See www.developmentgoals.com/Poverty.htm#percapita

160   M Kellmer Pringle, 1980, *The needs of children*, London: Hutchinson.

161   UN Millennium Project, 2005, *Investing in development: Overview*, New York: United Nations Development Programme

162   United Nations, 1989, *Convention on the Rights of the Child*, Preamble.

163   A Walker, 1980, 'The social creation of poverty and dependency in old age', *Journal of Social Policy*, 9(1), pp 49-75.

164   G Lafortune, G Balestat, 2007, *Trends in severe disability among elderly people*, OECD Health paper DELSA/HEA/WD/HWP(2007)2, Paris: OECD, available at www.oecd.org/dataoecd/13/8/38343783.pdf

165   W Rocca, C Brayne, M Breteler, M Clarke, B Cooper, J Copeland, J Dartigues, A
      Hofman, O Hagnell, T Heeren, K Engedal, C Jonker, J Lindesay, A Lobo, A Mann, P
      Molsa, K Morgan, D O'Connor, R Sulkava, D Kay, L Amaducci, A Da Silva Droux,
      1991, 'The prevalence of dementia in Europe', *International Journal of Epidemiology*,
      20(3), pp 736-48.

166   World Health Organization, 2000, *ICIDH-2*, Geneva: WHO.

167   S Edwards, 2005, *Disability: definitions, value and identity*, Abingdon: Radcliffe, p
      20.

168   U Beck, 1992, *Risk society*, London: Sage Publications.

169   P Spicker, 2001, 'Social insecurity and social protection', in R Edwards, J Glover
      (eds) *Risk and citizenship: Key issues in welfare*, London: Routledge.

170   P Spicker, 2007, 'Definitions of poverty: twelve clusters of meaning', in
      P Spicker, S Alvarez Leguizamon, D Gordon (eds) *Poverty: An international glossary*,
      London: Zed.

171   A Sen, 1981, *Poverty and famines: An essay on entitlement and deprivation*,
      Oxford: Clarendon Press.

172   D Narayan, R Chambers, M Shah, P Petesch, 2000, *Voices of the poor*, New
      York: World Bank/Oxford University Press.

173   UN Human Settlements Programme Global Urban Observatory, 2005, *Global urban
      indicators database*, at www.unhabitat.org/publication/Analysis-Final.pdf, table.

174   P Spicker, 2007, *The idea of poverty*, Bristol: The Policy Press.

175   W Bines, 1997, 'The health of single homeless people', in R Burrows, N Pleace,
      D Quilgars (eds), *Homelessness and social policy*, London: Routledge.

176   N Pleace, 1998, 'Single homelessness as social exclusion', *Social Policy and
      Administration*, 32(1), pp 46-59.

177   N Crockett, P Spicker, 1994, *Discharged: Homelessness among psychiatric patients in
      Scotland*, Edinburgh: Shelter (Scotland).

178   See P Spicker, 2007, *The idea of poverty*, Bristol: The Policy Press, ch. 13.

179   A Darling, 1999, cited *The Guardian*, 19 July, p 4.

180   See for example L Leisering, R Walker (eds), 1998, *The dynamics of modern society*,
      Bristol: The Policy Press; C Heady, 1998, 'Labour market transitions and social
      exclusion', *Journal of European Social Policy*, 7(2), pp 119-28.

181   Department for Work and Pensions, 2005, *Low income dynamics 1991-2003*,
      London: DWP, available at: www.dwp.gov.uk/asd/hbai/low_income/paper_
      M.pdf

182   G Bonoli, 2005, 'The politics of the new social policies', *Policy & Politics*, 33(3),
      pp 431-49; S Häusermann, 2007, 'Changing coalitions in social policy reforms',
      Journal of European Social Policy, 16(1), pp 5-21.

183   D Gallie, S Paugam, 2002, *Social precarity and social integration*, Luxembourg: European
      Commission.

184   S Checkland, O Checkland (eds), 1974, *The Poor Law Report of 1834*,
      Harmondsworth: Penguin.

185   J Feinberg, 1973, *Social philosophy*, Englewood Cliffs, NJ: Prentice-Hall.

186   P Spicker, D Gordon, 1997, *Planning for the needs of people with dementia*, Aldershot: Avebury.

187   P Spicker, 1993, 'Needs as claims', *Social Policy and Administration*, 27(1), pp 7-17.

Notes to Chapter Five: Public policy

188   B Hogwood, L Gunn, 1984, *Policy analysis for the real world*, Oxford: Oxford University Press.

189   P Townsend, 1976, *Sociology and social policy*, Harmondsworth: Penguin, p 6.

190   P Bachrach, M Baratz, 1970, *Power and poverty*, Oxford: Oxford University Press, p 44.

191   D Stone, 2002, *Policy paradox*, New York: Norton.

192   R Berki, 1979, 'State and society', in J Hayward, R Berki (eds) *State and society in contemporary Europe*, Oxford: Martin Robertson, p 1.

193   H L A Hart, 1961, *The concept of law*, Oxford: Oxford University Press.

194   P Spicker, 1997, 'The prospect for European laws on poverty', in A Kjonstad, J Veit-Wilson (eds) *Law, power and poverty*, Bergen: Comparative Research Programme on Poverty, pp 137-48.

195   S Benn, R Peters, 1959, *Social principles and the democratic state*, London: Allen and Unwin.

196   Law No 133, Article 2, 1963, cited in International Council on Social Welfare, 1969, *Social welfare and human rights*, New York: Columbia University Press, p 250.

197   L Cram, 1993, 'Calling the tune without paying the piper?', *Policy & Politics*, 21(2), pp 135-46.

198   J Austin, 1885, *The province of jurisprudence determined*, Cambridge: Cambridge University Press, 1995.

199   A Sen, 1981, *Poverty and famines: An essay on entitlement and deprivation*, Oxford: Clarendon Press.

200   P Spicker, 2006, 'Understanding incentives', Annexure 1 of M Steele (ed), *Report on incentive structures of social assistance grants in South Africa*, Pretoria: Republic of South Africa Department of Social Development, www.socdev.gov.za/documents/2006/incent.doc

201   P Jones, J Cullis, 2003, 'Key parameters in policy design', *Journal of Social Policy*, 32(4), pp 527-47.

202   C Murray, 1984, *Losing ground*, New York: Basic Books.

203   T Hewitt, I Smith, 1992, 'Is the world overpopulated?', in T Allen, A Thomas (eds) *Poverty and development in the 1990s*, Oxford: Oxford University Press.

204   UNICEF, 2005, *League table: Falling fertility*, www.unicef.org/pon95/leag5pa.html

205   I Allen, S Dowling, 1998 *Teenage mothers: Decisions and outcomes*, London: Policy Studies Institute; S Cater, L Coleman, 2006, *Planned teenage pregnancy*, York: Joseph Rowntree Foundation, www.jrf.org.uk/bookshop/eBooks/9781861348753.pdf

206   N Dennis, C Erdos, 1992, *Families without fatherhood*, London: IEA.

207   R Lampard, 1994, 'An examination of the relationship between marital dissolution and unemployment', in D Gallie, C Marsh, C Vogler (eds) *Social change and the experience of unemployment*, Oxford: Oxford University Press.

208   C S Fischer, M Hout, M Jankowski, S Lucas, A Swidler, K Voss, 1996, *Inequality by design*, Princeton, NJ: Princeton University Press, p 94.

209   C Murray, 1989, *The emerging British underclass*, London: Institute of Economic Affairs.

210   W J Wilson, 1987, *The truly disadvantaged*, Chicago, IL: Chicago University Press, pp 90–92.

211   P Spicker, 2002, *Poverty and the welfare state*, London: Catalyst.

212   A B Atkinson, 1995, *Incomes and the welfare state*, Cambridge: Cambridge University Press.

213   L Leisering, R Walker (eds), 1998, *The dynamics of modern society*, Bristol: The Policy Press.

214   C Murray, 1984, *Losing ground*, New York: Basic Books.

215   P Spicker, 2000, *The welfare state*, London: Sage Publications.

216   M Moran, B Wood, 1993, *States, regulation and the medical profession*, Buckingham: Open University Press.

217   M Harrison, 1984, *Corporatism and the welfare state*, Aldershot: Gower.

218   D Mitchell, 1992, 'Welfare states and welfare outcomes in the 1980s', Paper presented to the conference 'Social security 50 years after Beveridge', University of York.

219   P Flora, A Heidenheimer, 1982, *The development of welfare states in Europe and America*, New York: Transaction Books.

220   F Castles, 2004, *The future of the welfare state*, Oxford: Oxford University Press; F Castles, 2005, 'Social expenditure in the 1990s', *Policy & Politics*, 33(3), pp 411–30.

221   G Esping-Andersen, 1990, *The three worlds of welfare capitalism*, Cambridge: Polity, p 113.

222   D Mabbett, H Bolderson, 1999, 'Theories and methods in comparative social policy', in J Clasen (ed) *Comparative Social Policy: Concepts, theories and methods*, Oxford: Blackwell.

223   See for example W van Oorschot, 1995, *Realizing rights*, Aldershot: Avebury.

224   L Rainwater, M Rein, J Schwartz, 1986, *Income packaging in the welfare state*, Oxford: Oxford University Press.

225   T Smeeding, M O'Higgins, L Rainwater, 1990, *Poverty, inequality and income distribution in comparative perspective*, Hemel Hempstead: Harvester Wheatsheaf; K Nelson, 2004, 'Mechanisms of poverty alleviation', *Journal of European Social Policy*, 14(4), pp 371–90.

226   H Leichter, 1979, *A comparative approach to policy analysis*, Cambridge: Cambridge University Press.

Notes to Chapter Six: Principles and values

227   R Titmuss, 1955, 'The social division of welfare', in *Essays on 'the welfare state'*, London: Unwin, 1963, p 42.

228   H Wilensky, C Lebeaux, 1965, *Industrial society and social welfare*, New York: Free Press.

229   D Reisman, 1977, *Richard Titmuss*, London: Heinemann.

230   Pius XI, 1931, Quadragesimo Anno, Actae Apostolicae Sedis 23, p 203.

231   R M Titmuss, 1970, *The gift relationship*, Harmondsworth: Penguin.

232   G Maccallum, 1967, 'Negative and positive freedom', *Philosophical Review*, 76, pp 312-34.

233   P Spicker, 2006, *Liberty, equality, fraternity*, Bristol: The Policy Press.

234   T H Marshall, 1981, *The right to welfare*, London: Heinemann.

235   See P Spicker, 2006, *Liberty, equality, fraternity*, Bristol: The Policy Press.

236   J Wresinski, 'Wresinski Report of the Economic and Social Council of France 1987', cited in K Duffy, 1995, *Social exclusion and human dignity in Europe*, Strasbourg: Council of Europe CDPS(95) 1 Rev., p 36.

237   J Rawls, 1971, *A theory of justice*, Oxford: Oxford University Press.

238   J Schumpeter, 1967, 'Two concepts of democracy', in A Quinton (ed), *Political philosophy*, Oxford: Oxford University Press.

239   N Bobbio, 1987, *The future of democracy*, Cambridge: Polity.

240   See for example R Dahl, 1979, 'Procedural democracy', in P Laslett, J Fishkin (eds), *Philosophy, politics and society*, Oxford: Blackwell; D Beetham, 1992, *The legitimation of power*, Basingstoke: Macmillan; J Cohen, 1997, 'Deliberation and democratic legitimacy', in R Goodin, P Pettit (eds), *Contemporary political philosophy*, Oxford: Blackwell.

241   A Sen, 2001, *Development as freedom*, Oxford: Oxford University Press.

242   J Finch, 1984, *Education as social policy*, London: Longman.

243   P Halmos, 1978, *Introduction to welfare: Iron fist in velvet glove*, Milton Keynes: Open University.

244   R Titmuss, 1955, 'The social division of welfare', in *Essays on 'the welfare state'*, London: Allen and Unwin, 1963, p 39.

245   J Hay, 1983, *The origins of the liberal welfare reforms*, London: Macmillan.

246   J Higgins, 1978, *The poverty business in Europe and America*, Oxford: Blackwell, pp 34-6.

247   R Grunberger, 1974, *Social history of the Third Reich*, Harmondsworth: Penguin.

248   Adapted from P Spicker, 1993, *Poverty and social security*, London: Routledge, p 104.

249   S Schram, 1995, *Words of welfare*, Minneapolis, MN: University of Minnesota Press; G Marston, 2004, *Social policy and discourse analysis*, Aldershot: Ashgate.

250   J M Keynes, 1936, *The general theory of employment interest and money*, London: Macmillan, p 383.

251   H Wilensky, C Lebeaux, 1965, *Industrial society and social welfare*, New York: Free Press.

252   J Poynter, 1969, *Society and pauperism*, London: Routledge and Kegan Paul.

253   J Bentham, 1789, *An introduction of the principles of morals and legislation*, Oxford: Blackwell, 1960, p 125.

254   R Frank, 1994, *Microeconomics and behavior*, New York: McGraw Hill, Chapter 7.

255   J Offer, 2006, '"Virtue", "citizen character" and "social environment"', *Journal of Social Policy*, 35(2), pp 283-302.

256   R Miliband, 1969, *The state in capitalist society*, London: Weidenfeld and Nicolson.

257   N Poulantzas, 1978, *State, power, socialism*, London: NLB.

258   J Saville, 1975, 'The welfare state: an historical approach', in E Butterworth, R Holman, *Social welfare in modern Britain*, Glasgow: Fontana.

259   C Offe, 1984, *Contradictions of the welfare state*, London: Hutchinson.

260   J Habermas, 1976, *Legitimation crisis*, London: Heinemann.

261   A Vincent, 1995, *Modern political ideologies*, Oxford: Blackwell.

262   See D Reisman, 1977, *Richard Titmuss: Welfare and society*, London: Heinemann; J Welshman, 2004, 'The unknown Titmuss', *Journal of Social Policy*, 33(2), pp 225-47.

263   F Hayek, 1976, *Law legislation and liberty*, London: Routledge and Kegan Paul.

264   S Beer, 1982, *Modern British politics*, London: Faber.

265   Quintin Hogg, in *Hansard*, vol 386, col 1918.

266   N Coote, 1989, 'Catholic social teaching', *Social Policy and Administration*, 23(2), pp 150-60.

267   See for example European People's Party, 2006, *For a Europe of the citizens* (Rome Manifesto), www.epp.eu/dbimages/pdf/encondoc310306final_copy_1_copy_1.pdf

268   S Woolf (ed), 1968, *The nature of fascism*, London: Weidenfeld and Nicolson; S M Lipset, E Raab, 1978, *The politics of unreason*, Chicago, IL: University of Chicago Press.

269   R Grunberger, 1974, *A social history of the Third Reich*, Harmondsworth, Penguin; P Weindling, 1989, *Health, race and German politics between national unification and Nazism 1870-1945*, Cambridge: Cambridge University Press.

270   M Humm, 1989, *A dictionary of feminist theory*, Hemel Hempstead: Harvester Wheatsheaf.

271   J Mitchell, 1971, *Women's estate*, Harmondsworth: Penguin, p 65.

272   G Pascall, 1986, *Social policy: A feminist analysis*, London: Tavistock, p 27.

273   See J Galtung, 1992, 'The green movement: a socio-historical exploration', in A Giddens (ed) *Human societies*, Cambridge: Polity, pp 325-7.

274   R Johnston, 1989, *Environmental problems: Nature, economy and state*, London: Belhaven Press, pp 5-6.

275   But see T Fitzpatrick, 1998, 'The implications of ecological thought for social welfare', *Critical Social Policy 54* ,18(1), pp 5-26.

276 V George, P Wilding, 1985, *Ideology and social welfare*, London: Routledge and Kegan Paul.

277 J M Keynes, 1936, *The general theory of employment interest and money*, London: Macmillan.

278 G Rimlinger, 1971, *Welfare policy and industrialisation in Europe*, America and Russia, New York: Wiley.

Notes to Chapter Seven: Strategies for welfare

279 W Dumon (ed), 1989, *Family policy in EEC countries*, Luxembourg: European Communities.

280 Pensions Commission, 2005, *A new pension settlement for the 21st century*, London: The Stationery Office.

281 N Gilbert, R van Voorhuis (eds), 2001, *Activating the unemployed*, New Brunswick, NJ: Transaction; W van Oorschot, P Abrahamson, 2003, 'The Dutch and Danish miracles revisited', *Social Policy and Administration*, 37(3), pp 288-304.

282 W McKeen, 2006, 'Diminishing the concept of social policy', *Critical Social Policy*, 26(4), pp 865-87.

283 B Compton, B Galaway, B Cournoyer, 2005, *Social work processes*, Belmont, CA: Brooks/Cole.

284 R Titmuss, 1974, *Social policy – an introduction*, London: Allen and Unwin.

285 Commission Nationale d'Evaluation du Revenu Minimum d'Insertion, 1992, *RMI: Le pari de l'insertion*, Paris: La documentation française, vol 2, p 789.

286 See for example P Whiteford, 1997, 'Targeting welfare: a comment', *The Economic Record*, 73(220), pp 45-50; M Matsaganis, 2005, 'The limits of selectivity as a recipe for welfare reform: the case of Greece', *Journal of Social Policy*, 34(2), pp 235-53; D R Gwatkin, A Wagstaff, A S Yabeck (eds), 2005, *Reaching the poor with health, nutrition and population services: What works, what doesn't and why*, Washington, DC: World Bank.

287 G Cornia, F Stewart, 1995, 'Food subsidies: two errors of targeting', in F Stewart, *Adjustment and poverty*, London: Routledge.

288 P Townsend 1976, *Sociology and social policy*, Harmondsworth: Penguin, p 126.

289 P Spicker, 1984, *Stigma and social welfare*, Beckenham: Croom Helm.

290 M Keen, 1991, *Needs and targeting*, London: Institute for Fiscal Studies.

291 P Baldwin, 1990, *The politics of social solidarity*, Cambridge: Cambridge University Press.

292 Code de Sécurité Sociale, 2007, Article L111-1, sourced at: www.legislation.cnav.fr/textes/lo/css/TLR-LO_CSS_L111-1.htm

293 P Spicker, 2006, *Liberty, equality, fraternity*, Bristol: The Policy Press.

294 P Baldwin, 1990, *The politics of social solidarity*, Cambridge: Cambridge University Press.

295 R Lejeune, 1988, *Reussir l'insertion*, Paris: Syros-Alternatives; E Alfarandi, 1989, *L'Insertion*, Paris: Sirey; J Donzelot, 1991, *Face à l'exclusion*, Paris: Editions Esprit.

[296]   See P Spicker, 2000, *The welfare state*, London: Sage Publications.

[297]   R Titmuss, 1974, *Social policy – an introduction*, London: Allen and Unwin.

[298]   GV Rimlinger, 1971, *Welfare policy and industrialisation in Europe*, America and Russia, New York: Wiley.

[299]   United Nations Development Program, 1997, *Human development report*, Oxford: Oxford University Press; M Todaro, S Smith, 2006, *Economic development* (9th edition), Harlow: Pearson.

[300]   H Wilensky, 1975, *The welfare state and equality*, Berkeley, CA: UCLA.

[301]   S Tormey, 2004, *Anti-capitalism: A beginner's guide*, Oxford: Oneworld.

[302]   C A R Crosland, 1956, *The future of socialism*, London: Jonathan Cape.

[303]   J M Keynes, 1936, *The general theory of employment interest and money*, London: Macmillan.

[304]   M Sahlins, 1974, *Stone age economics*, London: Tavistock.

[305]   J Rawls, 1971, *A theory of justice*, Oxford: Oxford University Press; contrast N Daniels (ed), 1975, *Reading Rawls*, Oxford: Blackwell.

[306]   B de Jouvenel, 1951, *Ethics of redistribution*, Cambridge: Cambridge University Press.

[307]   N Barr, 2004, *The economics of the welfare state*, Oxford: Oxford University Press, pp 199-201.

[308]   J Falkingham, J Hills, C Lessof, 1993, *William Beveridge versus Robin Hood: Social security and redistribution over the life cycle*, London: LSE Suntory-Toyota Centre.

[309]   N Barr, 2004, *The economics of the welfare state*, Oxford: Oxford University Press.

[310]   Beveridge Report, 1942, *Social insurance and allied services*, Cmd 6404, London: HMSO.

[311]   J J Dupeyroux, 1966, *Evolution et tendances des systèmes de sécurité sociale des pays membres des communautés européennes et de la Grande-Bretagne*, Luxembourg: Communauté Européenne du Charbon et de L'Acier.

[312]   E Chadwick, 1842, *Report on the sanitary condition of the labouring population*, Edinburgh: Edinburgh University Press, 1965.

[313]   Beveridge Report, 1942, *Social insurance and allied services*, Cmd 6404, London: HMSO.

[314]   P Spicker, 2002, 'France', in J Dixon, R Scheurell (eds), *The state of social welfare: The twentieth century in cross-national review*, Westport, CT: Praeger.

[315]   R M Titmuss, 1974, *Social policy: An introduction*, London: Allen and Unwin.

[316]   R Mishra, 1981, *Society and social policy*, London: Macmillan.

[317]   J Clasen, R Freeman (eds), 1994, *Social policy in Germany*, Hemel Hempstead: Harvester Wheatsheaf.

[318]   J Palme, 1990, 'Models of old-age pensions', in A Ware, R Goodin (eds), *Needs and welfare*, London: Sage Publications.

[319]   R Mishra, 1981, *Society and social policy*, London: Macmillan.

[320]   G Esping-Andersen 1990, *The three worlds of welfare capitalism*, Cambridge: Polity.

[321]   R Pinker, 1979, *The idea of welfare*, London: Heinemann.

[322]   R Mishra, 1981, *Society and social policy*, London: Macmillan.

[323]   D Bannink, M Hogenboom, 2007, 'Hidden change', *Journal of European Social Policy*, 17(1), pp 19-32.

Notes to Chapter Eight: Welfare states

[324]   A Briggs, 1961, 'The welfare state in historical perspective', *European Journal of Sociology*, 2, pp 221-58.

[325]   S Checkland, O Checkland (eds), 1974, *The Poor Law report of 1834*, Harmondsworth: Penguin.

[326]   G Rimlinger, 1971, *Welfare policy and industrialisation in Europe, America and Russia*, New York: Wiley, Chapter 5.

[327]   P Spicker, 2002, 'France', in J Dixon, R Scheurell (eds), *The state of social welfare: The twentieth century in cross-national review*, Westport, CT: Praeger, pp 109-24.

[328]   T H Marshall, 1982, *The right to welfare*, London: Heinemann.

[329]   C Jones, 1986, *Patterns of social policy*, London: Tavistock.

[330]   R Titmuss, 1963, 'War and social policy', in *Essays on 'the welfare state'*, London: Allen and Unwin, Chapter 3.

[331]   H Wilensky, 1975, *The welfare state and equality*, Berkeley, CA: University of California Press.

[332]   F Castles, R McKinlay, 1979, 'Public welfare provision, Scandinavia and the sheer futility of the sociological approach to politics', *British Journal of Political Science*, 9, pp 157-71.

[333]   F Castles, 2005, 'Social expenditure in the 1990s', *Policy & Politics*, 33(3), pp 411-30.

[334]   J Barnes, T Srivenkatamarana, 1982, 'Ideology and the welfare state', *Social Service Review*, 56(2), pp 230-46.

[335]   P Spicker, 2000, *The welfare state: A general theory*, London: Sage Publications.

[336]   G Esping-Andersen, 1990, *The three worlds of welfare capitalism*, Cambridge: Polity.

[337]   W Arts, J Gelissen, 2002, 'Three worlds of welfare capitalism or more?', *Journal of European Social Policy*, 12(2), pp 137-58.

[338]   D Sainsbury, 2001, 'Gendering dimensions of welfare states', in J Fink, G Lewis, J Clarke (eds), *Rethinking European welfare*, London: Sage Publications.

[339]   See for example H Bolderson, D Mabbett, 1995, 'Mongrels or thoroughbreds: a cross-national look at social security systems', *European Journal of Political Research*, 28(1), pp 119-39; C Bambra, 2005, 'Cash versus services', *Journal of Social Policy*, 34(2), pp 195-213.

[340]   S Leibfried, 1991, *Towards a European welfare state?*, Bremen: Zentrum für Sozialpolitik.

[341]   P Spicker, 1996, 'Normative comparisons of social security systems', in L Hantrais, S Mangen (eds), *Cross-national research methods in the social sciences*, London: Pinter, pp 66-75.

[342]   J Ditch, 1999, 'Full circle: a second coming for social assistance?', in J Clasen (ed), *Comparative Social Policy: Concepts, theories and methods*, Oxford: Blackwell.

343   D Mabbett, H Bolderson, 1999, 'Theories and methods in comparative social policy', in J Clasen (ed), *Comparative social policy: Concepts, theories and methods*, Oxford: Blackwell.

344   See for example European Commission, 1991, Final Council recommendation on social protection: convergence of objectives, Luxembourg: European Commission, COM (91) 228 OJ C194.

345   S Uttley, 1988, *Technology and the welfare state*, London: Unwin Hyman.

346   I Helgøy, A Homme, 2006, 'Policy tools and institutional change', *Journal of Public Policy*, 26(2), pp 141-65.

347   C Pierson, 2006, *Beyond the welfare state?*, Brighton: Polity, p 145.

348   J O'Connor, 1973, *The fiscal crisis of the state*, New York: St Martin's Press.

349   J Habermas, 1976, *Legitimation crisis*, London: Heinemann.

350   R Bacon, W Eltis, 1978, *Britain's economic problem*, London: Macmillan.

351   C Pierson, 2006, *Beyond the welfare state?*, Brighton: Polity, Chapter 5; R Klein, 1993, 'O'Goffe's tale', in C Jones (ed), *New perspectives on the welfare state in Europe*, London: Routledge.

352   P Flora, A Heidenheimer, 1981, *The development of welfare states in Europe and America*, New Brunswick, NJ: Transaction Books.

353   H Glennerster, J Midgley (eds), 1991, *The radical right and the welfare state*, Hemel Hempstead: Harvester Wheatsheaf.

354   J Carrier, I Kendall, 1977, 'The development of welfare states', *Journal of Social Policy*, 6(3), pp 271-90.

355   K Popper, 1986, *The poverty of historicism*, London: Ark.

356   M Hardiman, J Midgley, 1982, *The social dimensions of development*, Chichester: Wiley, Chapter 2.

357   T Parsons, 1969, *Politics and social structure*, New York: Free Press.

358   C Offe, 1984, *Contradictions of the welfare state*, London: Hutchinson.

359   P Day, 1981, *Social work and social control*, London: Tavistock.

360   J Saville, 1975, 'The welfare state: an historical approach', in E Butterworth, R Holman, *Social welfare in modern Britain*, Glasgow: Fontana.

361   N Poulantzas, 1978, *State, power, socialism* (trans. P Camiller), London: New Left Books.

362   D Wilsford, 1995, 'Path dependency, or why history makes it difficult but not impossible to reform health care systems in a big way', *Journal of Public Policy*, 14(3), pp 251-83; contrast A Kay, 2005, 'A critique of the use of path dependency in policy studies', *Public Administration*, 83(3), pp 553-71.

363   D Beland, 2005, 'Ideas and social policy', *Social Policy and Administration*, 39(1), pp 1-18.

364   See A B Atkinson, 1995, 'The welfare state and economic performance', in *Incomes and the welfare state*, Cambridge: Cambridge University Press, Chapter 6.

365   C Pierson, 2006, *Beyond the welfare state?*, Brighton: Polity.

366   R Mishra, 1999, *Globalisation and the welfare state*, Cheltenham: Edward Elgar.

367   See for example Commission of the European Communities, 1994, European social policy – a way forward for the Union (White Paper), Luxembourg: European Commission, COM(94) 333 final.

368   A Sen, 2001, *Development as freedom*, Oxford: Oxford University Press.

Notes to Chapter Nine: The provision of welfare

369   R Titmuss, 1955, 'The social division of welfare', in *Essays on 'The welfare state'*, London: Allen and Unwin, 1963.

370   P Spicker, 1984, 'Titmuss's social division of welfare', in C Jones, J Stevenson (eds), *Yearbook of social policy in Britain 1983*, London: RKP.

371   A Seldon, 1977, *Charge!*, London: Temple Smith.

372   J K Galbraith, 1962, *The affluent society*, Harmondsworth: Penguin.

373   S E Finer, 1952, *The life and times of Sir Edwin Chadwick*, London: Methuen.

374   R Pahl, 1975, *Whose city?*, Harmondsworth: Penguin.

375   N Barr, 2004, *The economics of the welfare state*, Oxford: Oxford University Press.

376   M Rein, H van Gunsteren, 1984, 'The dialectic of public and private pensions', *Journal of Social Policy*, 14(2), pp 129–50.

377   J Kendall, M Knapp, 1996, *The voluntary sector in the UK*, Manchester: Manchester University Press.

378   K Jones, J Brown, J Bradshaw, 1978, *Issues in social policy*, London: RKP.

379   D Gerard, 1983, *Charities in Britain*, London: Bedford Square Press.

380   H Raynes, 1960, *Social security in Britain*, London: Pitman; J-J Dupeyroux, R Ruellan, 1998, *Droit de la sécurité sociale*, Paris: Dalloz.

381   P Baldwin, 1990, *The politics of social solidarity*, Cambridge: Cambridge University Press.

382   W Beveridge, 1948, *Voluntary action*, London: Allen and Unwin.

383   D Green, 1993, *Reinventing civil society*, London: IEA Health and Welfare Unit.

384   Y Zalmanovitch, 1997, 'Some antecedents to health care reform: Israel and the US', *Policy & Politics*, 25(3), pp 251–68.

385   M Bayley, 1973, *Mental handicap and community care*, London: RKP.

386   G Pascall, 1986, *Social policy: A feminist analysis*, London: Tavistock.

387   S Arber, N Gilbert, M Evandrou, 1988, 'Gender, household composition and receipt of domiciliary services', *Journal of Social Policy*, 17(2), pp 153–76.

388   J Barlow, S Duncan, 1994, *Success and failure in housing provision*, Oxford: Pergamon, Chapter 1.

389   J Barry, C Jones, 1991, *Medicine and charity before the welfare state*, London: Routledge.

390   P Spicker, 2000, *The welfare state*, London: Sage Publications.

391   K Judge, M Knapp, 1985, 'Efficiency in the production of welfare', in R Klein, M O'Higgins (eds), *The future of welfare*, Oxford: Blackwell; P Spicker, 1988, *Principles of social welfare*, London: Routledge.

392   R Titmuss, 1970, *The gift relationship*, Harmondsworth: Penguin.

393   W A Robson, 1976, *Welfare state and welfare society*, London: Allen and Unwin.

394   M Bayley, 1973, *Mental handicap and community care*, London: RKP.

395   Social Services Inspectorate, 1991, *Care management and assessment*, London: HMSO, p 11.

396   Social Services Inspectorate, 1991, *Care management and assessment*, London: HMSO, p 63.

397   National Institute for Social Work, 1988, *Residential care: A positive choice*, London: NISW.

Notes to Chapter Ten: The structure of public services

398   S and B Webb, 1927, *English local government: The old Poor Law*, London: Cass.

399   J Higgins, 1978, *The poverty business in Britain and America*, Oxford: Robertson.

400   M Pijl, 1993, 'The Dutch welfare state', in R Page, J Baldock (eds), *Social policy review 5*, Kent: social policy Association; but see M Vink, 2007, 'Dutch "multiculturalism" beyond the pillarisation myth', *Political Studies Review*, 5(3), pp 337-50.

401   D Challis, E Ferlie, 1988, 'The myth of generic practice: specialisation in social work', *Journal of Social Policy*, 17(1), pp 1-22.

402   B C Smith, 1985, *Decentralisation*, London: Allen and Unwin.

403   S and B Webb, 1927, *English local government: The old Poor Law*, London: Cass.

404   K Hölsch, M Kraus, 2004, 'Poverty alleviation and the degree of centralization in European schemes of social assistance', *Journal of European Social Policy*, 14(2), pp 143-64.

405   R van Berkel, 2006, 'The decentralisation of public assistance in the Netherlands', *International Journal of Sociology and Social Policy*, 26(1/2), pp 20-31.

406   R Avenstrup, 2004, *Kenya, Lesotho, Malawi and Uganda: Universal primary education and poverty reduction*, Washington DC: World Bank, http://info.worldbank.org/etools/docs/reducingpoverty/case/58/fullcase/East%20Africa%20Edu%20Full%20Case.pdf

407   See National Literacy Mission, 2007, *India, 2007*, www.nlm.nic.in/

408   A S Neill, 1968, *Summerhill*, Harmondsworth: Penguin.

409   P Brown, 1997, 'The third wave: education and the ideology of parentocracy', in A Halsey, H Lauder, P Brown, A Wells, *Education: Culture, economy and society*, Oxford: Oxford University Press.

410   P Wilby, cited in N Timmins, 1996, *The five giants*, London: Fontana, p 438.

411   D Beland, 2005, 'Ideas and social policy', *Social Policy and Administration*, 39(1), pp 1-18.

412   H H Gerth, C Wright Mills, 1948, *From Max Weber*, London: RKP.

413   A James, 1994, *Managing to care*, Harlow: Longmans, Chapter 7.

414   J K Galbraith, *The new industrial state* (revised edition), Harmondsworth: Penguin, 1972.

415   Department of Health and Social Security, 1974, *Report of the committee of inquiry into the care and supervision of Maria Colwell*, London: HMSO.

416 B Hudson, 1985, 'Collaboration in social welfare', *Policy & Politics*, 15(3), pp 175-82.

417 P Marris, M Rein, 1974, *Dilemmas of social reform*, Harmondsworth: Penguin.

418 Mackintosh, cited in M Powell, B Dowling, 2006, 'New Labour's partnerships: comparing conceptual models with existing forms', *Social Policy and Society*, 5(2), pp 305-14.

419 I McDonald, 2005, 'Theorising partnerships', *Journal of Social Policy*, 34(4), pp 579-600.

420 R Rushmer, G Pallis, 2003, 'Inter-professional working: the wisdom of integrated working and the disaster of blurred boundaries', *Public Money and Management*, 23(1), pp 59-66.

421 N Gilbert, P Terrell, 2002, *Dimensions of social welfare policy*, Boston, MA: Allyn and Bacon.

422 J K Galbraith, 1972, *The new industrial state*, Harmondsworth: Penguin.

423 J Le Grand, W Bartlett, 1993, *Quasi-markets and Social Policy*, Basingstoke: Macmillan.

424 P Spicker, 2005, 'Five types of complexity', *Benefits*, 13(1) pp 5-9; National Audit Office, 2005, *Dealing with the complexity of the benefits system*, London: Parliament, HC 592 2005-06.

425 A Hall, 1974, *The point of entry*, London: Allen and Unwin.

426 K Davis, 1966, *Discretionary justice*, Louisiana, LA: Louisiana State University.

427 M Hill, 2005, *The public policy process*, Harlow: Pearson/Longman.

428 K Jones, J Brown, J Bradshaw, 1978, *Issues in social policy*, London: RKP, p 60.

429 K Jones, J Brown, J Bradshaw, 1978, *Issues in social policy*, London: RKP, p 61.

430 J Winkler, 1981, 'The political economy of administrative discretion', in M Adler, S Asquith (eds), *Discretion and welfare*, London: Heinemann.

431 R Loveridge, K Starkey (eds), 1992, *Continuity and crisis in the NHS*, Buckingham: Open University Press.

432 P Wright, 1996, *Managerial leadership*, London: Routledge.

433 N Gilbert, P Terrell, 2002, *Dimensions of social welfare policy*, Boston, MA: Allyn and Bacon, p 150.

434 R Bailey, M Brake, 1975, *Radical social work*, London: RKP.

435 B Rothstein, 1998, *Just institutions matter*, Cambridge: Cambridge University Press, pp 90-1.

Notes to Chapter Eleven: Service delivery

436 P Spicker, 1993, 'Needs as claims', *Social Policy and Administration*, 27(1), pp 7-17.

437 G Smith, 1980, *Social need*, London: RKP, p 112.

438 P Spicker, 1987, 'Concepts of need in housing allocation', *Policy & Politics*, 15(1), pp 17-27.

439 M Rein, 1983, *From policy to practice*, London: Macmillan.

440   See for example A Culyer, K Wright, 1978, *Economic aspects of the health services*, Oxford: Martin Robertson.

441   H Glennerster, 1979, 'The determinants of public expenditure', in T Booth (ed), *Planning for welfare*, Oxford: Blackwell.

442   Cited in J Williams, A Carroll, 1998, 'Budgeting and budgetary control', in J Wilson, *Financial management for the public services*, Open University Press, p 62.

443   W Ranade, 1994, *A future for the NHS?*, London: Longmans, pp 56-7.

444   A Walker, 1984, *Social planning*, Oxford: Blackwell, Chapter 7.

445   E Scrivens, 1980, 'Towards a theory of rationing', in R Leaper (ed) *Health wealth and housing*, Oxford: Blackwell.

446   J Elster, 1992, *Local justice*, Cambridge: Cambridge University Press, pp 59, 30.

447   J Elster, 1992, *Local justice*, Cambridge: Cambridge University Press, p 110.

448   J Elster, 1992, *Local justice*, Cambridge: Cambridge University Press, pp 76ff.

449   J Elster, 1992, *Local justice*, Cambridge: Cambridge University Press, pp 78, 98-9.

450   Cm 412, 1988, *Report of the inquiry into child abuse in Cleveland 1987*, London: HMSO.

451   D Clapham, K Kintrea, 1986, 'Rationing, choice and constraint', *Journal of Social Policy*, 15(1), pp 51-68.

452   J Thomson (ed) (1953) *The ethics of Aristotle*, Harmondsworth: Penguin.

453   D Miller, 1976, *Social justice*, Oxford: Oxford University Press; P Spicker, 1988, *Principles of social welfare*, London: Routledge, Chapter 11.

454   J Le Grand, 1982, *The strategy of equality*, London: Allen and Unwin, pp 14-15.

455   See for example P Townsend, N Davidson, M Whitehead, 1988, *Inequalities in health*, Harmondsworth: Penguin; Department of Health, 1998, *Independent inquiry into inequalities in health*, London: The Stationery Office; M Bartley, 2004, Health inequality, Brighton: Polity.

456   Cited in C Ham, S Pickard, 1998, *Tragic choices in health care: The case of Child B*, London: King's Fund, pp 20-1.

457   M Piccart-Gebhart and others, 2005, 'Trastuzumab after adjuvant chemotherapy in HER2-Positive Breast Cancer', *New England Journal of Medicine*, 353, pp 1659-72.

458   D Batty, 2006, 'Woman wins Herceptin appeal', *The Guardian*, 12 April, http://society.guardian.co.uk/health/news/0,,1752310,00.html

459   E Scrivens, 1980, 'Towards a theory of rationing', in R Leaper (ed), *Health, wealth and housing*, Oxford: Blackwell.

460   S Checkland, O Checkland, 1974, *The Poor Law report of 1834*, Harmondsworth: Penguin, p 338.

461   B Abel Smith, 1964, *The hospitals 1800-1948*, London: Heinemann.

462   N Park, R van Voorhuis, 2001, 'Moving people from welfare to work in the United States', in N Gilbert, R van Voorhuis (eds), *Activating the unemployed*, New Brunswick: Transaction; E Dahl, 2003, 'Does workfare work?', *International Journal of Social Welfare*, 12(4), pp 274-88.

463   J Handler, Y Hasenfeld, 1991, *The moral construction of poverty*, New York: Sage; A Deacon, 2002, *Perspectives on welfare*, Buckingham: Open University Press..

464 B C Smith, 1988, *Bureaucracy and political power*, Hemel Hempstead: Harvester Wheatsheaf.

465 J Glasby, 2003, *Hospital discharge*, Abingdon: Radcliffe Medical Press.

466 P Spicker, J Hanslip, 1994, 'Perceived mismatches between needs and services in the health care of elderly people', *Scottish Medical Journal*, 39(6), pp 172-4.

467 M Lipsky, 1980, *Street level bureaucracy*, London: Sage Publications.

468 M Lipsky, 1980, p 13.

Notes to Chapter Twelve: Receiving welfare

469 A A Nevitt, 1977, 'Demand and need', in H Heisler (ed), *Foundations of social administration*, Basingstoke: Macmillan.

470 J Bradshaw, 1972, 'A taxonomy of social need', *New Society*, March, pp 640-3.

471 S Clayton, 1983, 'Social need revisited', *Journal of Social Policy*, 12, pp 215-34.

472 I Culpitt, 1992, *Welfare and citizenship*, London: Sage Publications.

473 M Rein, 1983, *From policy to practice*, London: Macmillan.

474 H L A Hart, 1955, 'Are there any natural rights?', *Philosophical Review*, 64, pp 175-91.

475 C Davies, J Ritchie, 1988, *Tipping the balance*, London: HMSO; P Craig, 1991, 'Costs and benefits', *Journal of Social Policy*, 20(4), pp 537-65.

476 B Weisbrod, 1970, *On the stigma effect and the demand for welfare programmes*, Madison, WI: University of Wisconsin Institute for Research on Poverty.

477 S Kerr, 1983, *Making ends meet*, London: Bedford Square Press.

478 C Davies, J Ritchie, 1988, *Tipping the balance*, London: HMSO.

479 P Townsend, N Davidson, M Whitehead, 1988, *Inequalities in health*, Harmondsworth: Penguin; Department of Health, 1998, *Independent inquiry into inequalities in health*, London: The Stationery Office.

480 M Morgan, 2003, 'Patients' help-seeking and access to health care', in M Gulliford, M Morgan (eds) *Access to health care*, London: Routledge.

481 See W Wolfensberger, 1972, *The principle of normalisation in human services*, Toronto: National Institute for Mental Retardation.

482 R Barton, 1959, *Institutional neurosis*, Bristol: Wright (3rd edition 1976); J P Martin, 1985, *Hospitals in trouble*, Oxford: Blackwell.

483 House of Commons Select Committee on Work and Pensions, 2007, *Benefits simplification*, HC 463-1, London: The Stationery Office.

484 P Bean, P Mounser, 1993, *Discharged from mental hospitals*, Basingstoke: Macmillan; P Spicker, I Anderson, R Freeman, R McGilp, 1995, 'Discharged into the community: the experience of psychiatric patients', *Social Services Research*, 1, pp 1-9.

485 P Spicker, 1984, *Stigma and social welfare*, Beckenham: Croom Helm.

486 C Murray, 1984, *Losing ground*, New York: Basic Books.

487 A Seldon, 1977, *Charge!*, London: Temple Smith.

[488]   D Mullins, H Pawson, 2005, 'The land that time forgot', *Policy & Politics*, 33(2), pp 205-330.

[489]   D Clapham, K Kintrea, 1986, 'Rationing, choice and constraint', *Journal of Social Policy*, 15(1), pp 51-68.

[490]   H Dean, 1991, *Social security and social control*, London: Routledge.

[491]   P Spicker, 1985, 'The legacy of Octavia Hill', *Housing*, 21(6), pp 39-40.

[492]   J Rodger, 1996, *Family life and social control*, Basingstoke: Macmillan.

[493]   J Higgins, 1980, 'Social control theories of social policy', *Journal of Social Policy*, 9(1), pp 1-23.

[494]   See for example P Corrigan, P Leonard, 1978, *Social work under capitalism*, London: RKP.

[495]   See for example S Watson, 2000, 'Foucault and the study of social policy', in G Lewis, S Gewirtz, J Clarke (eds), *Rethinking social policy*, London: Sage Publications.

[496]   M Foucault, 1976, *Histoire de la sexualité: La volonté de savoir*, Paris: Gallimard, pp 121-2.

[497]   S Bowles, H Gintis, 1976, *Schooling in capitalist America*, London: Routledge and Kegan Paul, pp 130-1.

[498]   P Bachrach, M Baratz, 1970, *Power and poverty*, Oxford: Oxford University Press.

[499]   Cited in O Stevenson, 1973, *Claimant or client?*, London: Allen and Unwin.

[500]   B Solomon, 1976, *Black empowerment*, New York: Columbia University Press, p 29.

[501]   Rappaport 1984, cited in L Holdsworth, 1991, *Empowerment social work with physically disabled people*, Norwich: University of East Anglia Social Work Monographs, p 3.

[502]   S Miller, 1989, 'Community development and the underclass', in M Bulmer, J Lewis, D Piachaud (eds), *The goals of social policy*, London: Unwin Hyman.

[503]   E Pinderhughes, 1983, 'Empowerment for clients and for ourselves', *Social Casework*, 64(6), pp 331-8.

[504]   National Institute of Social Work, 1982, *Social workers: Their role and tasks*, London: NISW.

[505]   P Henderson, D Thomas, 2001, *Skills in neighbourhood work*, London: Routledge.

[506]   S Alinsky, 1972, *Rules for radicals*, New York: Vintage Books.

[507]   N Crockett, P Spicker, 1994, *Discharged: Homelessness among psychiatric patients in Scotland*, Edinburgh: Shelter (Scotland).

[508]   T Kitwood, K Breden, 1992, 'Towards a theory of dementia care', *Ageing and Society*, 12(3), pp 269-87; P Spicker, 2000, 'Dementia and social death', *Self Agency and Society*, 2(2), pp 88-104.

[509]   M Roth, 1981, 'The diagnosis of dementia in late and middle life', in J Mortimer, L Schuman, *The epidemiology of dementia*, New York: Oxford University Press, p 24.

[510]   T Kitwood, K Bredin, 1992, 'Towards a theory of dementia care', *Ageing and Society*, 12(3), pp 269-87; T Kitwood, 1999, *Dementia reconsidered*, Buckingham: Open University Press.

511   J Killick, 1997, 'Confidences: the experience of writing with people with dementia', in M Marshall (ed), *State of the art in dementia care*, London: Centre for Policy on Ageing.

512   T Marshall, 1981, *The right to welfare*, London: Heinemann,

513   J Harris, 1982, 'The political status of children', in K Graham (ed) *Contemporary political philosophy*, Cambridge: Cambridge University Press.

514   See W Wade, C Forsyth, 2000, *Administrative law* (8th edition), part VI, Oxford: Oxford University Press.

515   A Prosser, 1983, *Test cases for the poor*, London: CPAG.

516   R Means, R Smith, 1994, *Community care: Policy and practice*, Basingstoke: Macmillan, Chapter 4; A Hirschman, 1970, *Exit, voice and loyalty*, Cambridge, MA: Harvard University Press.

517   S Arnstein, 1971, 'A ladder of citizen participation', *Journal of the Royal Town Planning Institute*, 57(4), pp 176-82.

518   N Deakin, A Wright (eds), 1990, *Consuming public services*, London: Routledge.

519   N Deakin, A Wright (eds), 1990, *Consuming public services*, London: Routledge; A Richardson, 1983, Participation, London: RKP; B Smith, 1988, *Bureaucracy and political power*, Brighton: Harvester Wheatsheaf.

520   P Dwyer, 2004, *Understanding social citizenship*, Bristol: The Policy Press, pp 59-60.

521   J Ovretveit, 1993, *Co-ordinating community care*, Buckingham: Open University Press, p 166.

Notes to Chapter Thirteen:
The methods and approaches of social policy

522   A Boaz, R Pawson, 2005, 'The perilous road from evidence to policy', *Journal of Social Policy*, 34(2), pp 175-94.

523   As in, for example, G Esping-Andersen, 1990, *The three worlds of welfare capitalism*, Cambridge: Polity.

524   S Edgell, 1993, *Class*, London: Routledge, pp 32-3, 98-9.

525   R M Titmuss, 1974, *Social policy: An introduction*, London: Allen and Unwin.

526   A B Atkinson, B Cantillon, E Marlier, B Nolan, 2002, *Indicators for social inclusion in the European Union*, Oxford: Oxford University Press.

527   G Esping-Andersen, 1990, *The three worlds of welfare capitalism*, Cambridge: Polity.

528   P Spicker, 1988, *Principles of social welfare*, London: Routledge.

529   B Rowntree, 1901, *Poverty: A study of town life*, Bristol: The Policy Press, 2000.

530   K Jones, 1972, *A history of the mental health services*, London: RKP.

531   Cited in B Rowntree, 1901, *Poverty: A study of town life*, Bristol: The Policy Press, 2000, p 300.

532   See A Chalmers, 1999, *What is this thing called science?*, Cambridge: Hackett.

533   See A Sayer, *Realism and social science*, London: Sage.

534   M Scriven, 1991, *Evaluation thesaurus*, London: Sage Publications.

535   B Skinner, 1971, *Beyond freedom and dignity*, London: Peregrine Books, 1988.

536   R Pawson, N Tilley, 1997, *Realistic evaluation*, London: Sage Publications, especially Chapter 3.

537   A L Cochrane, 1989, *Effectiveness and efficiency*, London: British Medical Journal/ Nuffield.

538   R Fuller, O Stevenson, 1983, *Policies programmes and disadvantage*, London: Heinemann, Chapter 8.

539   J Pechman, M Timpane, 1975, *Work incentives and income guarantees*, New York: Brookings.

540   C Weiss, J Birckmayer 2006, 'Social experimentation in public policy', in M Moran, M Rein, R Goodin (eds), *The Oxford handbook of public policy*, Oxford: OUP.

541   R Pawson, N Tilley, 1997, *Realistic evaluation*, London: Sage Publications.

542   E Burke, 1790, *Reflections on the revolution in France*, New York: Holt, Rinehart and Winston, 1959, p 209.

543   R Pawson, N Tilley, 1997, *Realistic evaluation*, London: Sage Publications.

544   J Blanden. P Gregg, S Machin, 2005, *Intergenerational mobility in Europe and America*, London: London School of Economics and Political Science, http://cep.lse.ac.uk/ about/news/IntergenerationalMobility.pdf

545   See R Goodin, B Headey, R Muffels, H-J Dirven, 2000, *The real worlds of welfare capitalism*, Cambridge: Cambridge University Press.

546   See A Pollock, 2004, NHS plc, London: Verso.

547   A Etzioni, 1977, 'Mixed scanning: a third approach to decision making', in N Gilbert, H Specht, *Planning for social welfare*, Englewood Cliffs, NJ: Prentice Hall, pp 87-97.

548   See for example P Gershon, 2004, *Releasing resources to the front line: Independent review of public sector efficiency*, London: HM Treasury.

549   T Halper, 1985, 'Life and death in a welfare state: end stage renal disease in the United Kingdom', *Milbank Memorial Fund Quarterly*, 63(1), pp 52-93.

550   G Smith, D Dorling, M Shaw (eds), 2001, *Poverty, inequality and health in Britain 1800-2000*, Bristol: The Policy Press.

551   D R Gwatkin, A Wagstaff, A S Yabeck (eds), 2005, *Reaching the poor with health, nutrition and population services: What works, what doesn't and why*, Washington, DC: World Bank.

552   J Falkingham, J Hills, C Lessof, 1993, *William Beveridge versus Robin Hood: Social security and redistribution over the life cycle*, London: LSE/Suntory-Toyota Centre for Economics and Related Disciplines.

553   A Wildavsky, 1993, *Speaking truth to power*, New Brunswick, NJ: Transaction Books; D Taylor, S Balloch (eds), 2005, *The politics of evaluation*, Bristol: The Policy Press.

Notes to Chapter 14: Research for policy

554   European Commission, 1991, *Background report: The European Poverty Programme*, Luxembourg: European Comission, ISEC/B24/91.

555   R Burgess (ed), 1982, *Field research*, London: Allen and Unwin.

556   O Lewis, 1964, *The children of Sanchez*, Harmondsworth: Penguin; O Lewis, 1966, *La Vida*, London: Panther.

557   R Pawson, N Tilley, 1997, *Realistic evaluation*, London: Sage Publications, especially Chapter 3.

558   B Latané, J Darley, 1970, *The unresponsive bystander*, Englewood Cliffs, NJ: Prentice Hall.

559   W Whyte, 1943, *Street corner society*, Chicago, IL: Chicago University Press, 1993.

560   A Bryman, R Burgess, 1994, *Analysing qualitative data*, London: Routledge, pp 4-6.

561   R Lees, 1975, *Research strategies for social welfare*, London: RKP.

562   A Harris, E Cox, C Smith, 1971, *Handicapped and impaired in Great Britain*, London: HMSO.

563   OPCS, 1988, *The prevalence of disability among adults in Britain*, London: HMSO.

564   OPCS, 1988, *The prevalence of disability among adults in Britain*, London: HMSO; E Grundy, D Ahlburg, M Ali, E Breeze, A Sloggett, 1999, Disability *in Great Britain: Results of the 1996/97 follow-up to the Family Resources Survey*, www.dwp.gov.uk/asd/asd5/94summ.asp

565   R Titmuss, 1970, *The gift relationship*, Harmondsworth: Penguin.

566   R Pinker, 1979, The idea of welfare, London: Heinemann.

567   J Mack, S Lansley, 1985, *Poor Britain*, London: Allen and Unwin; H Frayman, 1990, *Breadline Britain 1990s*, London: LWT/Domino Films; D Gordon, L Adelman, K Ashworth, J Bradshaw, R Levitas, S Middleton, C Pantazis, D Patisos, S Payne, P Townsend, J Williams, 1999, *Poverty and social exclusion in Britain*, York: Joseph Rowntree Foundation.

568   B Hallerod, 2006, 'Sour grapes', *Journal of Social Policy*, 35(3), pp 371-90.

569   R Olson, J Verley, L Santos, C Salas, 2004, 'What we teach students about the Hawthorne studies', *The Industrial-Organizational Psychologist*, 41(3), pp 23-39.

570   A Bryman, 1988, *Quantity and quality in social research*, London: Unwin Hyman.

571   P Townsend, 1979, *Poverty in the United Kingdom*, Harmondsworth: Penguin.

572   OPCS, 1988, *The prevalence of disability among adults in Britain*, London: HMSO.

573   H Graham, E McDermott, 2006, 'Qualitative research and the evidence base of policy', *Journal of Social Policy*, 35(1), p 21.

574   M Zelditch, 1979, 'Some methodological issues in field studies', in J Bynner, K M Stribley (eds), *Social research: Principles and procedures*, London: Longman.

575   P Townsend, 1979, *Poverty in the United Kingdom*, Harmondsworth: Penguin; O Lewis, 1964, *The children of Sanchez*, Harmondsworth: Penguin.

576   R Titmuss, 1970, *The gift relationship*, Harmondsworth: Penguin; B Latané, J Darley, 1970, *The unresponsive bystander*, Englewood Cliffs, NJ: Prentice Hall.

577   C Booth, 1903, *Life and labour of the people in London*, London: Macmillan; P Spicker, 1990, 'Charles Booth: the examination of poverty', *Social Policy and Administration*, 24(1), pp 21-38.

578   *Hansard*, 19th May 1999, col. 356.

579   K Baker, J Curtice, N Sparrow, 2004, *Internet poll trial, ICM*, at http://icmresearch. co.uk/white-papers/internet-poll-trial.pdf

580   J C Flanagan, 1954, 'The Critical Incident Technique', Psychological *Bulletin,* 51, pp 327-57.

581   See for example A Rogers, D Pilgrim, R Lacey, 1993, *Experiencing psychiatry*, Basingstoke: Macmillan/MIND.

582   R Freeman, cited in J Bryson, 2004, 'What to do when stakeholders matter', *Public Management Review*, 6(1), pp 21-53.

583   J Bryson, 2004, 'What to do when stakeholders matter', *Public Management Review*, 6(1), pp 21-53.

584   D Taylor, 2005, 'Governing through evidence', *Journal of Social Policy*, 34(4), pp 601-18.

585   See for example P Townsend, 1979, *Poverty in the United Kingdom*, Harmondswor th: Penguin; J Bradshaw, D Mitchell, J Morgan, 1987, 'Evaluating adequacy: the potential of budget standards', *Journal of Social Policy*, 16(2), pp 165-81; S Stitt, D Grant, 1993, *Poverty: Rowntree revisited*, Aldershot: Avebury; D Gordon, L Adelman, K Ashworth, J Bradshaw, R Levitas, S Middleton, C Pantazis, D Patisos, S Payne, P Townsend, J Williams, 2000, *Poverty and social exclusion in Britain*, York: Joseph Rowntree Foundation.

586   C Hallett, 1989, 'Child abuse inquiries and public policy', in O Stevenson (ed), *Child abuse*, Hemel Hempstead: Harvester Wheatsheaf.

587   J C Flanagan, 1954, 'The Critical Incident Technique', *Psychological Bulletin*, 51, pp 327-57.

588   S Pfohl, 2003, The 'discovery' of child abuse, in P Conrad, V Leiter (eds), *Health and health care as social problems*, Lanham, MD: Rowman Littlefield.

589   M D A Freeman, 1983, *The rights and wrongs of children*, London: Pinter.

590   Joseph Rowntree Foundation, 2007, www.jrf.org.uk/

591   G Marx, 1972, *Muckraking sociology*, New York: Transaction Books, sourced at http://web.mit.edu/gtmarx/www/ascmuck.html.

Notes to Chapter Fifteen: Analysing policy

592   See for example M Hill, 2005, *The public policy process*, Harlow: Pearson/ Longman.

593   ee for example A Faludi, 1973, *Planning theory*, Oxford: Pergamon; N Gilbert, H Specht (eds), 1977, *Planning for social welfare*, Englewood Cliffs, NJ: Prentice-Hall, part 2; S Leach, 1982, 'In defence of the rational model', in S Leach, J Stewart, *Approaches in public policy*, London: George Allen and Unwin.

594   HM Treasury, *The green book*, www.hm-treasury.gov.uk/media/785/27/Green_ Book_03.pdf, p 3.

595   A Faludi, 1973, *Planning theory*, Oxford: Pergamon.

596   P Spicker, 2006, *Policy analysis for practice: Analysing social policy*, Bristol: The Policy Press.

597   See www.imf.org/external/np/prsp/prsp.asp

598   International Monetary Fund and World Bank, 2005, *2005 review of the Poverty Reduction Strategy approach*, www.imf.org/external/np/pp/eng/2005/091905p. pdf

599   International Monetary Fund and World Bank, 2005, p 87.

600   International Monetary Fund/International Development Association, 2002, *Review of the Poverty Reduction Strategy Paper (PRSP) Approach*, www.imf.org/External/NP/ prspgen/review/2002/032602a.pdf

601   Cooperation Internationale pour le Developpment et la Solidarité/Caritas Internationalis, 2004, *PRSP: Are the IMF and World Bank delivering on promises?*, www.cidse.org/docs/200404221144166307.pdf

602   Cooperation Internationale pour le Developpment et la Solidarité/Caritas Internationalis, 2004, *PRSP: Are the IMF and World Bank delivering on promises?*, www.cidse.org/docs/200404221144166307.pdf, 3.22.

603   C Brown, P Jackson, 1978, *Public sector economics*, Oxford: Robertson, p 20.

604   C A R Crosland, 1956, *The future of socialism*, London: Jonathan Cape.

605   G Bevan, C Hood, 2006, 'What's measured is what matters', *Public Administration*, 84(3), pp 517-38.

606   OPCS, 1988, *The prevalence of disability among adults in Britain*, London: HMSO.

607   P Spicker, 1990, 'Charles Booth: the examination of poverty', *Social Policy and Administration*, 24(1), pp 21-38.

608   B Rowntree, 1901, *Poverty: A study of town life*, Bristol: The Policy Press, 2000.

609   S Holtermann, 1975, 'Areas of deprivation in Great Britain', *Social Trends*, 6, pp 43-8.

610   M Hill, P Hupe, 2003, 'The multi-layer problem in implementation research', *Public Management Review*, 5(4), pp 471-91.

611   See for example Audit Commission, 2005, *Approach to service inspections*, www. auditcommission.gov.uk/Products/NATIONAL-REPORT/78F62C1A-D68F- 4ce0-8276-631A8BAC1B47/ApproachToServiceInspections.pdf

612   P Minford, M Peel, P Ashton, 1987, *The housing morass*, London: Institute for Economic Affairs, Chapter 2.

613   S E Finer, 1952, *The life and times of Edwin Chadwick*, London: Methuen.

614   See P Spicker, 2006, *Policy analysis for practice: Analysing social policy*, Bristol: The Policy Press.

Social policy: a guide to sources

Most of the material written about social policy as a subject dates from the period after the Second World War, although there are some notable exceptions. Theoretical material does not date very rapidly, but social conditions are in constant flux, and policies change like the sands of the desert. There is, in the study of social policy, something of a fetish of the new – a tendency to disregard older material, and to assume that newer material has greater contemporary relevance. The opposite may be true: older material is often useful for its theoretical relevance or method, while even the newest material is vulnerable to changes in policy or circumstances which lead to it being dated before it appears.

A guide to sources

The internet. The World Wide Web has become an invaluable source for accessible material on social policy. The place to begin is with my own website, *An Introduction to social policy*, at http://www2.rgu.ac.uk/politics/socialpolicy/ This site gives a brief introduction to a range of topics in social policy, and links to other sites.

Because many social policy documents are ephemeral, the Web offers an excellent complement to publication – rapid and easily referenced. Government documents in particular have become widely accessible; many legal jurisdictions now place case reports on the Web. *Governments on the web*, which includes links to government sites around the world, is available at www.gksoft.com/govt/en/

Books. Textbooks are used to summarise material, and to offer a range of differing opinions. Their main use is to allow people to gain an initial overview of a field; students can absorb the material and move on, occasionally referring back for different purposes. Most students using this book will also need to get a descriptive text outlining social policy and services in their own country. The facts in such books date rapidly, however, and any information should be supplemented by drawing down facts from sites on the internet.

Academic journals. Academic journals are 'refereed', which means that articles are scrutinised by specialists before acceptance. The articles in journals are often difficult, because writers feel compelled to deck them out with academic window-dressing, and the quality is very mixed, but they are generally more up to date and much shorter than textbooks. With the advent of electronic libraries, articles in academic journals have become much easier to access in recent years. Most readers can read 10 articles in the time it takes to read one book, and they will probably have covered far more ground. The key journals in the subject are the *Journal of Social Policy*, *Social Policy and Administration* and the *Journal of European Social Policy*. There is also potentially useful information in *Critical Social Policy*, the *International Journal of Social Welfare* and *Policy & Politics*.

Collected papers. Some books are collections of articles; readers can draw from them in much the same way as from a journal. Although books in the subject are also refereed, there is rather more freedom in collected books to theorise, to speculate and to present interim conclusions. This means that the quality of collections is variable, but it has also been an important stream of ideas on social policy; much of the feminist literature in the subject, for example, has developed in this format.

Most books in social policy tend to be specialised, often putting forward a particular argument or taking a position. The contrast between views and findings from different sources becomes more striking as more ground is covered, and the wider the ground covered, the better equipped the student is to deal with the subject. Student 'readers' are, consequently, worth a special note; these are edited collections which bring together some of the principal papers on a subject. They can be invaluable both as a way of extending one's range of reading, and as a fruitful source of arguments and material.

Monographs, pamphlets and working papers. One of the undesirable side-effects of using academic referees is the delay in publication which follows. This, coupled with pressure to present material in an appropriate academic framework, means that books and journals are rarely able to carry basic research reports. Much of this kind of material appears instead in small and ephemeral publications, produced by academic institutions (for example the LSE CASE Programme), research agencies (the Policy Studies Institute), charitable foundations (the Joseph Rowntree Foundation), campaigning groups (the Child Poverty Action Group) and public sector agencies. Some of the most important papers in social policy have appeared in this kind of format. It used to be difficult to track this kind of material down, but the growth of the internet has made it much more accessible.

Newspapers and periodicals. There is always a problem with books, since however accurate the book is when published, new legislation and other developments soon make parts of it out of date. Newspapers and weeklies are helpful. Most reporting on social policy is second- or third-hand, however; most journalists are not very well informed on the subject, and newspaper reports cannot be relied on. The kinds of research monograph referred to above are key sources for many journalists.

Statistical sources. Official statistics have their problems, but they are a quick and easy way to check basic facts. There are many easily accessible international sources available. The University of Michigan has international links at www. lib.umich.edu/govdocs/forstats.html

Primary sources. In the discussion of research methods in Chapter Fourteen, I outlined a number of ways in which information might be drawn from original sources. Even for students working at a basic level, information can often be obtained directly from government, politicians and political parties; examples are consultative documents, pamphlets and manifestos. It is much harder to get to administrative decision makers, although not impossible by any means. Voluntary groups often bring together observations and comments from stakeholders and service users.

Further reading

Social policy: themes and approaches has been written for readers from around the world. The reading and source material which is referred to in this section, like most of the references in the book, have been selected because they are relevant to people in a wide range of circumstances. That means, however, that this book cannot hope to provide the kind of practical, up-to-date information that is the staple of textbooks in specific countries. The book needs to be supplemented with other material, to relate it to contemporary issues and practice in the particular context where it is being read.

The suggestions for further reading, then, are based on a special type of source material, developing the general and theoretical issues explored in this book.

Introduction. The central statements of the nature of social policy were made many years ago; the most important are in R M Titmuss, *Essays on the welfare state* (Allen and Unwin, 1976) and D V Donnison and others, *Social policy and administration revisited* (Allen and Unwin, 1975). There have been many influential restatements since, and many attempts to redefine the field; however, readers will understand that I think that many of these works have led in the wrong direction, steering social policy away from the issues that most need attention.

Part One: Social policy and society. There is an abundance of material outlining basic approaches to sociology, as well as collections of readings which offer an insight into a range of viewpoints. Most general texts on sociology will help to outline the social context, the relationship of the individual to society, and issues like class, gender and race. Rather less is available on the direct relevance of sociological concepts to social policy, which tends to be assumed.

The literature on social problems and needs is diffuse, likely to focus in detail on specific topics like poverty or disability and much more likely to be specific to the circumstances of particular countries. It is important to read widely. The *Journal of Social Policy* and *Critical Social Policy* are most relevant; another useful journal is *Social Problems*.

Part Two: Policy. The material in this part is probably best served by the theoretical literature. Michael Hill's books *The public policy process* (Pearson Longman, 2005) and *The policy process: A reader* (Prentice Hall, 1997) offer respectively an introductory text and key readings. The literature on principles and values is extensive, but it is dogged by inaccuracies and misconceptions: misrepresentations of topics like pluralism, socialism, equality and social justice are rife. My own work in this area includes *Social policy in a changing society* (written with Maurice Mullard) (Routledge, 1997) and *Liberty, equality, fraternity* (The Policy Press, 2006). The coverage of welfare strategies is mixed, but it is informed by some of the key writings in the subject, such as the work of Richard Titmuss. The most recent reader is P Alcock (ed) *Welfare and well-being* (The Policy Press, 2001). David Reisman's critical synopsis, *Richard Titmuss: Welfare and society* (Heinemann, 1977) is also helpful.

The coverage of welfare states and comparative social policy has become a small industry in its own right: Esping-Andersen's *The three worlds of welfare capitalism* (Polity, 1990) has been the most influential text, but there are many more accessible texts which offer rewarding insights. C Pierson and F Castles' (eds) *The welfare state reader* (Polity, 2006) is a useful collation of readings. The leading journals are *Social Policy and Administration* and the *Journal of European Social Policy*.

Part Three: Social administration. The literature on social administration is not well covered in social policy texts, and it is difficult to find academic discussions that take a synoptic view across many disciplines. Part of the field has been colonised by writers on public sector management: useful general guides are J Erik Lane, *The public sector* (Sage, 2000) and N Flynn, *Public sector management* (Sage, 2007). There is some coverage in books on economics: Nick Barr's textbook, *The economics of the welfare state* (Oxford University Press, 2004) has become less accessible to non-economists in later editions, but is still worth referring to. The leading journal in this area is *Policy & Politics*.

Part Four: The methods and approaches of social policy. Much of the literature on policy analysis and evaluation in practice is American: examples are M Patton and D Sawicki, *Basic methods of policy analysis and planning* (Prentice Hall, 1993), for policy analysis, or Michael Scriven's *Evaluation thesaurus* (Sage, 1991). Despite the centrality of this material, there is less directly related to social policy than might be anticipated; I wrote *Policy analysis for practice* (The Policy Press, 2006) to fill the gap. The outstanding theoretical contribution to the field in recent years, although I disagree with much of it, has to be R Pawson and N Tilley, *Realistic evaluation*

(Sage, 1997). Relevant journals include *Public Money and Management* and *Evidence & Policy.*

Texts on social research tend to be misleading; it is difficult to write a book on research without giving general advice, but in a context where methods have to be closely adapted to circumstances, general advice often turns out to be wrong. Probably the best of the recent texts is S Becker and A Bryman (eds) *Understanding research for social policy and practice* (The Policy Press, 2004); also useful is C Seale, *Social research methods: a reader* (Routledge, 2004). *Social Research Update*, at http://sru.soc.surrey.ac.uk/, offers an invaluable internet resource.

Writing about social policy:
a note for students

Using source material

Reading and collating material from various sources is one of the staple tasks for students of social policy. This is true largely because facts and materials only become meaningful if they are put in some kind of context or framework, and reading helps to provide that framework. There are occasions when practitioners are asked to resolve problems which no one else has tackled before, but this is usually rarer than they think. There is constant pressure to 'reinvent the wheel' –that is, to devise procedures and tackle problems which others have also had to work through. The starting point for tackling any problem is finding out what has already been done about it.

As a general rule, this means that people working in this field have to cover a lot of ground. Lawyers can often rely on one good, solid, authoritative textbook, which will point them directly to a relevant and authoritative source; economists can apply standard methods, learned as part of their discipline; but a student or practitioner in social policy rarely has either option. The subject demands a wide range of reading, and the central skills demanded of someone working in social policy are to be able to absorb, interpret and use information from a range of different sources.

It is fairly unusual, even in the most basic essay for social policy, to find a topic which can be directly answered with a synopsis from the textbooks or by downloading likely material from the internet. The exercise of writing is an introduction to basic research techniques and the use of original source material. Students must, however, use sources, and books are part of those sources. The purpose of using texts is:
- to show some evidence of work;
- to provide relevant material;
- to help construct an argument; and
- to put material into a context.

The material which is selected must be closely related to the problem being studied. Topics in social policy are large and complex enough to be closely related while actually having little direct relationship to each other: studies of 'community care' or 'causes of poverty' can be understood and investigated in such different terms that there is almost no point of contact between the different literatures. The difficulty this poses in social policy is that a good coverage of a problem area may still fail to address some of the important issues for policy. Equally, many of the problems which are being addressed are multifaceted. A systematic approach considers each of the different aspects in turn.

It is important to specify sources precisely, for two main reasons. The first is that a lot of the 'facts' in social policy are disputable. There is a children's game called 'Chinese Whispers', in which children whisper a message to each other in turn. What each person says can be misheard by the next, and by the time the message reaches the end of the line it bears little or no resemblance to what it was at the outset. The same happens in academic literature; the original work of Booth and Rowntree, for example, has been distorted beyond recognition, because people have cited other recent sources instead of reading the original. Students need to be alert to the drawbacks of using secondary sources; it is important not to give the 'original' source if this has not been consulted, but rather to give the actual source of the comment.

The second reason is that one of the tests of writing in this field is the demonstration of skills. For this purpose it is necessary to distinguish what has been selected by the writer and what has come from someone else; who has set the agenda for discussion; and where understandings of the material come from. The same words convey a different message about skills if they come from one place, if they come from three places, or if they come from three places and contain a reflective evaluation by the student. Plagiarism, or unattributed use of sources, is a common problem in assessed coursework: it consists of passing off the work of another person as one's own, which means not just that students copy work but also that they paraphrase it, or use the arguments, without attribution. This is a serious academic offence, and there are often heavy penalties. But it also has the effect of blurring the lines between different sources, and this means that skills cannot be demonstrated. Most plagiarism is done out of ignorance. Students who do it have often done much more work than they have made apparent, and they might well get a higher mark if only they attribute sources properly.

Writing about social policy

Students are generally asked to write both as a means to develop their skills, and in order to test their understanding. The test of understanding is that they are able to use material and put it in their own words. The main skills being assessed are:
- selection of relevant material;
- collation and ordering of material, or structuring; and
- construction of argument.

Selection demonstrates only the lowest level of understanding; argument, the highest.

Writing is commonly judged by the balance of facts and relevant material on one hand, and structure and argument on the other. These cannot strictly be separated. Facts and material are made relevant by argument, and in social science the argument cannot be strong if it is not supported by evidence or material. People writing about social policy need, then, to concentrate on both aspects.

Essays and reports

An essay is a structured discussion – a form of argument. A good argument is one that:
- is supported by evidence;
- makes points which follow one from another;
- deals with the arguments that can be raised on the other side; and
- comes to a reasoned conclusion.

Part of the purpose of studying social policy is to prepare students for work in public service, where the primary form of written presentation is a report rather than an essay. Reports differ from essays in the style of presentation. There is no 'introduction' as such, but there will be an executive summary – a precise and brief summary of what is in the following text; paragraphs are numbered, to allow for referencing and specific discussion; and instead of conclusions, there may be recommendations.

The structure of material

Planning is crucial to ordering material. It is virtually impossible to construct a coherent argument without deciding the order in which points should be made, or how to use the facts available. The standard way to plan material is from the top downwards: topics have to be classified into sub-areas, and if necessary the sub-areas should then be classified into further sub-areas. A plan develops like a tree (the analogy should be familiar to anyone who has a personal computer): the root has to be divided into two or three main branches, then each in turn has further branches which go from it. The initial plan for this book was devised by first identifying the main parts; then by sub-dividing those parts into chapters; then identifying the main areas of the chapters; and then moving on to sub-areas within these areas. Before anything was written, the plan consisted of more than 70 sub-sections, making it possible to write a first draft in sections of about 1,000 words each.

Introduction. Many people announce in the first paragraph what they are going to do, as a guide to the reader. Very few professional reports begin this way – the norm is to present an executive summary, not an introduction – and there is an argument for working to professional standards from the outset. An introduction may have advantages in explaining the shape of an argument, but problems arise in student essays and dissertations if they then do something else entirely. Introductions, abstracts and summaries are invariably best written after the rest of the material has been done.

Explaining terms. One of the most common pieces of advice given to writers is that they should 'define their terms'. This does not mean that they should give a dictionary definition (ordinary dictionaries are not very reliable for specialised terms); it means that it is important to explain what the terms mean. The language of social policy is not, for the most part, specialised and agreed; there are many disputed terms understood in different ways, such as poverty, altruism, management, equality or rationality. If a reader understands the basic terms in a different way from the writer, it is not likely that the rest of the argument will be very persuasive.

Planning how to deal with the issues. Few problems in this field are simple. For example, the question 'how can we do it?' requires consideration of both technical and political feasibility; 'what should be done?' asks not only what is possible, but also what is right.

Fortunately, there are some useful general principles which apply fairly widely in this field. Rules are made to be broken, and there are always reasons why some people writing about social policy should wish to depart from these principles, but they are helpful at the outset.

The first principle is that theory comes before practice. Theory, as explained in Chapter Thirteen, offers the framework within which practice can be discussed. If a discussion begins with practice, the problem is that there is no basis on which to select material in the discussion of practice; everything has to be put down first. If, by contrast, one begins with theory, the material can be selected and then reviewed in the terms of the theoretical discussion.

Second, context comes before specifics. The rationale for this is much the same: describing a context makes it possible to identify the principles for organising the description of specific data.

The third general principle is that problems should be discussed before responses. The reason is that if responses are to be evaluated in terms of the problems, then the responses have to be set in a framework within which those problems can be addressed.

Writing up research. For research reports, it is also helpful to note that there is a tried and tested formula which makes such material much easier to write, and (because readers have come to expect it) easier to read. The most common pattern of a research report is as follows:

Review of the *research problem*
Methodology: this really covers two topics
  Methodology (rationale for the selection of method)
  Method (what was done)
Results
Discussion.

Ordering material within sections. It is fairly essential to deal with one issue fully before going on to the next. Established writers in this field commonly use sub-headings as a guide to the subject of each section; one of the benefits is not only that it tells a reader what to expect, but also that it guides the writer. Sections should ideally begin with an explanation of what they are about, and conclude with some kind of statement which explains what they have established.

Keeping to a plan. There are two common traps which may lead to a loss of structure. One is to try to follow a chronological sequence. There are some topics which are best explained in chronological terms, but not many; what happens is that the chronology becomes a list of material in which the interconnections and relationships are simply muddied, which is of course what happens in real life.

The second trap is attempting to closely follow another person's structure and argument. An argument which has been designed for one purpose is often difficult to bend to another. Students often lack the confidence to dismantle an original argument and cannibalise the useful bits, which prompts me to offer a piece of general advice: never write an essay with a book, paper or internet article open in front of you. The text inhibits your own thinking, stopping you from linking up related facts from different sources, and so from making the best use of the material you have.

Argument

Material from different sources rarely speaks for itself; it has to be interpreted. There are important differences here in the tests which are applied to published material and to students' work. Published material is part of a political forum, and it is liable to be judged on political criteria as much as on academic merit. Students' work, by contrast, cannot legitimately be marked on its political position, because that would simply be a recipe for bias. Students have to be marked on the skills they demonstrate. But this does not mean that you must not express an opinion; on the contrary, it is rather more difficult to construct an argument if you have none. It means that you must back up what you say, and consider arguments against your position.

Arguments can be developed either by stating a case and using facts as evidence for the view, or by looking at the facts and drawing a conclusion from them. The second approach is usually (but not always) preferable. Fact and argument should not be separated into different sections, because this makes it difficult to relate them to each other.

Arguments are made much stronger by showing why the people who disagree with the position are wrong. If arguments against a position are not considered, the position remains vulnerable to those criticisms, and the case is weakened.

Lastly, it is important to be critical. Students are often far too deferential to what they read. It is important not to assume that anyone who writes a book or posts material on the internet has to make sense or to have got their facts right. You don't need, as Dr Johnson said, to be a carpenter to know that a table wobbles.

A note on style

The best writers in this field avoid a conscious 'style'. Good prose, Orwell once commented, is like glass; it does not get in the way between the reader and the sense which the writer is trying to convey. Writing is usually most clear when it is simplest and plainest, and there is a case for trying to use the clearest words and shortest sentences possible.

Conclusion

Conclusions should be drawn from the previous argument, and be consistent with it. Summaries of the main points can be helpful at this stage, but they are not essential. One of the most common vices in this field is the attempt to finish with a flourish, a problem which afflicts many established writers as well as those who write first-year student essays; the effect is to introduce new topics, and new lines of inquiry, which are uninvestigated. The time to stop writing is when everything has been said.

Glossary

Access to welfare Before people can receive welfare, either by applying or being identified as likely recipients, they have to put themselves in the position where welfare might be provided – for example learning about the service, claiming or being able to get to an office. This is the issue of 'access'.

Accountability The process through which services can be made to answer for their actions.

Administrative law Laws which regulate the administrative processes through which services are to be delivered.

Adverse selection Insurance companies refusing 'bad risks'.

Affirmative action The policy adopted in the US to correct the disadvantages of some groups relative to others by giving people from disadvantaged groups special treatment. The nearest term in the UK is ➜ 'positive discrimination'.

Ambulatory care In health care, services which people can use without requiring a stay in a hospital bed.

Ameliorism The 18th-century belief that the world is gradually improving through human effort.

Atomisation A social situation where everyone is isolated from everyone else.

Audit Initially a financial term which has come to stand for inspection, evaluation and processes of administrative accountability.

Autonomy A person's capacity for free action, which requires lack of restraint, the power to act, and the ability to choose.

Black box A technique based on reviewing effects without looking at internal processes.

Bloc A group of people who share common characteristics, for example women, minority ethnic groups or older people.

Brandeis brief In the US, a legal plea which makes it possible for evidence about the social implications of an action to be taken into account.

Budget A financial plan in quantitative form.

Bureaucracy A hierarchical organisation run through a system of rules.

Bureaucrat A person working in a hierarchical organisation who performs official functions.

Capitalism In Marxism, a system of production in which the means of production is owned by a capital-owning class in order to make profits. The term is sometimes used to indicate the general character of modern economic systems.

Care The provision of services to maintain or improve people's circumstances.

Care management/care plans In community care, the selection of a package of services for a client from a range of available options.

Casework Individuated responses made to issues in the context in which they are presented.

Christian democracy A form of conservative thought, strong in European countries, which emphasises moral restraints and responsibilities.

Citizenship A collection of rights, argued by Marshall to include basic social rights and the 'right to welfare'.

Claims A call for resources, from any source; the specific process of applying for certain benefits or services.

Class action In the US, the right of people to sue as a group.

Classes Groups in society with different economic positions, variously understood in terms of the relationship to the means of economic production; groups with different economic capacity and power; or groups with different social ➜ status.

Community A group of people linked by common characteristics or culture; a group of people linked together through social relationships; people living in defined a geographical area; people who share a set of common interests.

Community action ➜ community organisation.

Community care The provision of support and practical assistance to people who have special needs, to make it possible for them to live in their own homes or in as 'normal' an environment as possible. The term is, however, highly ambiguous.

Community development ➜ community organisation.

Community education Development of the social skills and collective potential of disadvantaged people.

Community organisation The attempt to develop political mobilisation and collective action in disadvantaged communities.

Community social work A form of social work which takes account both of individuals and of their social interactions in order to increase their potential in a social context.

Community work A collective approach to the problems of communities. ➜ neighbourhood work; community social work; community organisation; community education.

Comparative need ➜ Need determined by comparison with others who are not in need.

Comparative social policy Cross–national studies in social policy.

Conflict theory The argument that welfare is an outcome of conflict between different power blocs in society.

Conservatism A set of political beliefs emphasising social order and traditional patterns of social relationships.

Constitutional law Law which sets the framework through which policies are exercised.

Consumers. The economistic term for service users, mainly used to imply a market relationship.

Contested concepts Ideas which have different, conflicting alternative meanings, so that no agreement about them is really possible.

Control group A group of people used for comparison in order to establish the effectiveness of a measure.

Convergence In comparative social policy, the argument that different countries are coming to act similarly in the face of common pressures or circumstances; in the European Union, agreement on basic principles for action.

Corporatism The exercise of power by established corporate interests: socially, a hierarchical structure of power characterised by restricted competition between a limited number of corporate groups; economically, a system of economic organisation dominated by corporate structures; politically, a system of interest group representation in which the state negotiates with and seeks to include other agencies.

Cost-effectiveness Achieving one's aims at minimum cost.

Crisis A turning point, external shock or longstanding contradiction. The term is particularly used by Marxists to emphasise the instability they argue characterises modern industrial society.

Critical incident technique A focus on non-routine events as a means of clarifying processes and problems.

Critical social policy A view of social policy which emphasises the importance of all of structured inequality and seeks to interpret problems and policy in terms of the patterned relationships of social division.

Cultural diffusion The process through which cultures are shared and affect other cultures.

Culture Patterns of social behaviour, which may refer to language and history, common experiences, norms and values, and lifestyle.

Decentralisation The devolution of decisions to smaller geographical units.

Deconstruction The process of unpicking existing constructions of ideas by questioning or rejecting assumptions about their relationships.

Deductive approaches A pattern of research based on the generation of propositions which can then be tested.

Degeneracy A combination of genetic defects, once believed to be the root of social problems.

Demand The amount of service that might be used if the service was supplied at a particular price.

Democracy Government 'of the people, for the people, by the people'; the term is variously understood in terms of political ideals, approaches to governance or systems of government.

Dependency A state of reliance on the support of social services, which may be financial, physical or psychological.

Deterrence Reducing demand for services by making services deliberately awkward to reach, unpleasant or humiliating.

Dilution A means of reducing what is offered to clients by cutting the quality of what is offered, rather than refusing service altogether.

Direct discrimination Deliberate and overt ➜ discrimination.

Disability A set of problems and issues related to physical or mental capacity, understood in a social context; the functional restriction which results from impairment. ➜ impairment; handicap.

Discretion The scope for independent judgement that is left to officials when no rules apply.

Discrimination Adverse selection which places some people in an inferior position. ➔ direct discrimination; indirect discrimination; institutional racism.

Disincentive to work The argument that benefits, in rewarding people for not working, influence choices about work.

Domiciliary care In health and personal social services, care delivered in people's own homes.

Earnings-related Benefits which vary according to previous earnings.

Economies of scale The ability that large agencies have to make savings on purchasing or production that smaller agencies do not have.

Effective demand Current existing demand, as distinct from potential demand.

Effectiveness Achieving one's aims.

Efficiency The minimisation of waste; production of units at the minimum cost per unit.

Elasticity The extent to which a change in one factor will stimulate a response in another. The 'elasticity of demand', for example, generally refers to the extent to which demand will change as a result of a change in price.

Eligibility The criteria for whether or not people should receive a service or benefit.

Empirical Factual, based on observation or experience.

Empowerment The process through which people who are relatively powerless can gain more power.

Equality The removal of disadvantage. Note that equality does not mean sameness or uniformity.

Equity A principle of fairness: like cases should be treated alike. ➔ 'substantive' and 'procedural' fairness.

Ethnic group A group of people distinguished from the main population by differences in history and culture.

Evaluation Judgements about policy; a stage of the policy process where effectiveness is judged; or the process of appraising policy.

Exclusion People who are not part of networks of ➔ solidarity and social responsibility, because they are left out of social networks (for example, not being entitled to social protection); because they are shut out (like migrants); or because they are pushed out through ➔ stigma.

Eugenics The belief that society can be improved through the selective breeding of people.

Executive The executive branch of government is the branch which implements policy once made.

Exit Ceasing to use a service; the term is also used for the power to withdraw from the service.

Expressed need ➔ Need which people say they have.

Externalities Economic consequences which go beyond the people involved in a transaction.

Family A special kind of social unit defined in terms of a particular network of personal and social relationships and responsibilities; most usually it refers to circumstances where people who are related by birth or marriage live together.

Family resemblance A term used in the process of classification through the identification of interrelated clusters of characteristics.

Fascism A form of collective authoritarianism in which the state, the race or the nation is more important than any individual person.

Felt need ➔ Need which people feel they have.

Feminism The general class of beliefs that women should not be viewed or treated in a way inferior to men. There are many different branches, including ➔ liberal feminism, ➔ Marxist feminism and ➔ radical feminism.

Filtering A stage in rationing: a process of sifting out people who may or may not receive provision subsequently.

Financial rationing The control of expenditure.

Fiscal welfare Titmuss's term for redistribution through the tax structure.

Flat-rate Benefits paid at a single rate, by contrast with 'earnings-related' benefits, which vary according to previous earnings (and so the level of contribution made).

'Focus' of policy The kind of people or social units who the policy directly affects.

Freedom The absence of restraint and the capacity to act.

Friendly societies Mutual aid organisations developed in Britain for the protection of their members.

Functional Serving a function (in functionalism, 'useful' or serving a purpose), or pertaining to the ability to perform a function. A 'functional division of labour' is a division of labour which reflects the performance of functions, while a 'functional impairment' is an impaired ability to do something.

Functionalism A mode of analysis which argues that societies change through adaptation to changing circumstances. Adaptations are 'functional' if they support social processes and 'dysfunctional' if they do not.

Funded schemes Social security and pensions schemes which build up and pay people from a fund.

Gender roles A set of social roles, or particular expectations, which subsequently condition the activities undertaken by women and men.

Generalisation In most contexts, the process of applying particular insights more widely; in French social policy, the process of extending solidaristic networks to include as many people as possible.

Generative mechanism A cause; a set of factors and process which together produce an effect.

Genericism Generic workers work with a range of techniques with a range of different client groups.

Globalisation A process of increased communication, commerce and interconnectivity, which is seen as leading to increasingly homogenised social, cultural and economic behaviour across the world.

Green politics A set of political beliefs which rejects mainstream concerns, emphasising in their place conservation of the environment, the use of natural resources and the role of humans in relation to other species and the natural world.

Gross National Product The value of a country's total production; a country's total income.

Handicap Disadvantage in a particular role or set of social roles as a result of disability.

Hawthorne effect The effect of being observed on the behaviour of the research subject.

Health Maintenance Organisations In the US, organisations which provide medical care to members for a subscription.

Health services Services for medical care and related activities.

Hegemony The maintenance of values and norms designed to further the interests of a dominant class.

Hereditability An explanation of variance between cases in terms of heredity.

Hidden curriculum In education, the idea that part of what schools teach is a concealed means of conveying rules about social behaviour. The idea is linked with ➔ hegemony.

Hierarchy A power structure in which people are placed above and below others in some kind of rank order.

Historicism The argument that there are 'laws' of history or inexorable movements.

Homelessness Having no accommodation; having unsatisfactory or insecure accommodation.

Horizontal redistribution Redistribution between people in different social circumstances, without necessarily having regard to resources.

Household A group of people who live together, sharing resources and responsibilities.

Hypothesis A speculative proposition formed in a way which allows it subsequently to be tested.

Ideal type A theoretical model or template against which reality can be compared.

Ideology A set of interrelated beliefs and values.

Impairment A physical or mental condition implying some abnormality or loss.

Implementation The process through which policy is put into practice.

Incapacity for work The inability to continue with one's employment because of ➔ impairment or an inability to work generally because of ➔ disability

Incentive A potential gain which motivates people to change their behaviour in order to receive it.

Incidence The rate at which new problems or issues occur.

Inclusion. Bringing people into networks of social support; countering ➔ exclusion.

Income smoothing The effect intended by redistributing money from one part of a person's life cycle to another.

Indicator targeting Targeting aimed at general characteristics, such as regions, age groups, gender and so on.

Indicators Figures that are used to sum up data about social issues.

Indirect discrimination Actions which select some people with adverse effect.

Individualism A view of people which sees each person separately as being able to take action independently from other people in society. The individual is able to choose options, undertake obligations, make agreements, or try to gain redress against injustice.

Individualistic policies Policies which focus separately on each person who has needs or problems.

Inductive approach An approach to research which begins by collecting material and subsequently looks for patterns and relationships.

Industrial-achievement/performance model of welfare Titmuss's model of welfare in which welfare is seen as a complement to industrial production and economic policy.

Inequality The position where people are advantaged or disadvantaged in social terms.

Informal sector Care not provided through formal organisations, but by communities, friends, neighbours and kin.

Inputs The resources which go into welfare provision.

Insertion The French term for ➔ inclusion; used in particular to refer to the integration of people who are 'marginal' or 'excluded' into social networks.

Institutional racism The production of racial disadvantage through the policy or practice of an agency.

Institutional welfare Model of welfare in which welfare is accepted as a normal part of social life.

Integration The incorporation of people into the available social networks.

Intellectual disability A process of slow intellectual development, leading cumulatively to slow development of physical and social functioning. The term used varies widely between countries and over time.

Intensity The depth or severity of a problem.

Interest groups ➔ Pressure groups which are seeking to influence policy in ways which will benefit them directly. They are also referred to as 'representational' groups.

Interests Whatever increases people's ➔ well-being or ➔ utility.

Inter-subjectivity The process through which understanding develops in society through a series of shared perceptions and beliefs.

Judiciary The judicial branch of government adjudicates on the operation of the law. ➔ executive; legislative.

Key intervention Strategic intervention at the point in a system which will produce a range of desired effects.

Key worker A nominated worker with the main responsibility for a particular case.

Law A system of rules and procedures through which the actions of individuals and people collectively can be regulated by the state.

Leadership The role of managers in general; the aspects of their role relating to relationships with subordinates; the personal attributes of leaders; the task of motivating and influencing staff; the situation of being in charge; methods for the achievement of tasks; a pattern of behaviour; the coordination of teamwork; or the desire to invade other countries.

Learning disability A ➔ disability implying special educational needs; an ➔ intellectual disability.

Left-wing Political beliefs identified with ➔ social democracy, ➔ socialism or ➔ Marxism, which are broadly in favour of collective social provision and the reduction or mitigation of disadvantage.

Legislative The legislative branch of government which makes laws, as distinct from ➔ 'executive' and ➔ 'judicial' branches.

Legitimation crisis Neo-Marxists argue that the welfare state's attempt to legitimate capitalism is in conflict with attempts to foster the accumulation of capital, posing a crisis of legitimation.

Less eligibility The deterrent principle, in the English Poor Law, that the position of the person receiving support had to be less 'eligible' (less to be chosen) than that of the poorest independent labourer.

Liberal feminism The argument that women should have equal opportunities to men.

Liberalism A set of beliefs, related to individualism, which argue that individuals must be left free to make choices and that society is best able to regulate itself without state intervention.

Life cycle The series of changes in condition and circumstance which a person goes through in the course of his or her life – including, for example, childhood, adulthood and old age.

Macro-economic policies Policies for the whole economy.

Manager A person who runs an organisation: the ideal type of a manager is a person who is specialised in the organisation of services, and who has general responsibility for the operation of functions taking place under his or her command.

Marginal utility The change in utility which follows from a small change in circumstances from one point to another.

Marginality. A position in which people are peripheral to social networks or mechanisms of ➔ solidarity: ➔ exclusion.

Market failure Circumstances where economic markets are unable to perform as they should in economic theory because practical limitations (such as location or imperfect information) prevent mechanisms from operating effectively.

Marketisation The process of making the delivery of services more like the delivery of services in the private market, achieved either through privatisation or by turning social services into something like a market. ➔ quasi-markets.

Marxism A set of beliefs based on the idea that society is a conflict between economic classes.

Means test The process of distributing benefits or services subject to a test of income or wealth.

Mental handicap ➔ intellectual disability.

Mental illness A complex set of disturbed behaviours, perceptions and thought processes.

Methodological individualism The assumption for the purposes of analysis that society is composed of individuals, used for example as the basis of much economic theory.

Methodology The study of research methods; the rationale used for the selection of methods.

Mixed economy of welfare The description of welfare in terms of ➜ welfare pluralism.

Moral hazard The problem of insuring people who are able to control the circumstances which might produce a claim, like pregnancy or unemployment.

Multicollinearity A problem arising in statistics when variables are not truly independent of each other, so that some effects are duplicated while the influence of some important factors may be disguised.

Mutual aid The principle whereby people join with others to provide help or support for each other. Often this takes the form of mutual insurance in the event of difficulties.

Myth In social science, a belief which, true or not, affects the way that people behave.

National efficiency A term used at the turn of the century to indicate the physical capacity of people in the nation to serve their country.

Nationhood A cluster of ideas associated variously with a common history, culture or language, geographical location or membership of a political community.

Natural justice ➜ Procedural rights to be heard, and to be judged impartially.

Needs The kinds of problem which people experience; requirements for some particular kind of response; a relationship between problems and the responses available.

Neighbourhood work Development of the networks and relationships in a community in order to facilitate social action.

Non-decisions Decisions not to decide, and so to keep things as they are.

Non-take-up Failure to claim benefits and services to which one is nominally entitled.

Normal In keeping with ➜ norms.

Normalisation Enabling people to live autonomously, as others do; empowering people to act so as to participate in society.

Normative Concerned with values, expectations, standards or rules against which policies and practice can be judged.

Normative need ➜ Need identified according to a ➜ norm – probably a standard set by experts.

Norms Rules – that is, expectations coupled with sanctions (or penalties) for non-compliance; standards which are set against which actions may be judged.

Occupational welfare Welfare provided through the workplace.

Operationalisation The process through which concepts are translated into terms that can be worked with and acted on.

Participant observation A technique of social research in which the researcher seeks to become part of the process which is being studied.

Participation The process of taking part in decision making.

Paternalism The principle of doing things for people's benefit without their consent.

Path dependency. The tendency for established institutional processes to determine what policy is possible in the future.

Pathological theories Theories which see the cause of a problem in terms of the unit which has the problem.

Patriarchy A society in which men have power over women.

Person A social actor, defined in terms of social roles and relationships to others.

Personal social services The range of services available outside health, housing, education and social security which deal with people's personal needs. This includes social work, residential care and domiciliary care.

Planned Programme Budget System (PPBS) A system of financial control in which, after total expenditure has been set, areas of activity are then allocated budgets and subject to limits.

Pluralism The idea that there are many kinds of groups in society which interact in various ways; in the analysis of power, it is argued that this multiplicity of actors has the effect of diffusing power. Alternatively, a value position which argues for diversity and multiplication of the number of actors as something valuable in itself.

Politics Understood narrowly, the exercise of government; more generally, any activity in which there is some form of collective social action, or in which power is exercised.

Policy A field of activity; decisions, proposals or strategy.

Positive discrimination ➜ affirmative action. The term in the UK goes beyond equality to an argument for preferential treatment.

Positive rights Rights which are linked to some kind of effective sanction, such as a legal norm.

Positivism The view that scientists are dealing with an external reality.

Postmodernism The argument that society has moved beyond previously established patterns, becoming increasingly diverse and unpredictable.

Potential demand Demand which might arise in certain conditions, as opposed to effective demand, which is that which currently exists.

Poverty A complex term denoting material deprivation, lack of resources, disadvantage in social relationships and severe hardship. Because the term is used morally to convey conditions which are unacceptable, the definition is much disputed.

Poverty trap The position which arises with means-tested social security benefits when benefits are withdrawn as people's needs decrease.

Power The ability to direct the conduct of others who accept that direction.

Pragmatism An approach which is opposed to changes made on ideological grounds and favours finding out what works before introducing it.

Pressure groups Groups which seek to influence the political process, either to represent their own interests or to promote causes.

Prevalence A measure of how frequently a problem or issue is found.

Primary analysis Research based on original data, initial observations or experiences. ➜ secondary analysis.

Primary care In health care, services provided without requiring people to come to a hospital. The distinction is slightly arbitrary and for that reason some of the literature refers instead to ➜ 'ambulatory care'.

Principles Guides to action; in relation to welfare, the term particularly relates to normative statements about what should be done.

Priorities An order of precedence decided between competing claims.

Private sector The provision of services for profit by independent producers. Some commentators include non-profit provision by ➔ mutual aid as part of the private sector.

Probability sampling Selection of subjects for research in order to reflect the characteristics of a wider population. ➔ purposive sampling.

Procedural fairness Procedural fairness consists of rules to guarantee a fair procedure, which is a prerequisite for ➔ substantive fairness. The central rules are consistency, impartiality and openness.

Procedural rights Rights to ensure that certain rules are followed, and to make the redress of grievances possible.

Process evaluation An ➔ evaluation or ➔ audit which focuses on implementation rather than effects.

Professions Certain classes of occupation which have a particular status and claim specialised knowledge or expertise. Professionals are allowed discretion or independent judgement in their conduct on the basis of that expertise.

Progressive redistribution Transferring resources vertically from richer to poorer people. ➔ regressive redistribution.

Public goods Goods of which the benefits are not directly attributable to any particular individual or group.

Public sector Services which are financed and managed by the state.

Purposive sampling The selection of specific people as subjects for research in order to examine a particular kind of problem. ➔ probability sampling.

Qualitative research Research which is interpretative and aimed at producing material which can help to explain processes and issues.

Quantitative research Research which measures effects or enumerates.

Quasi-markets Systems set up to imitate the operation of the private market in the delivery of public services.

Race A term used variously to indicate physical differences, cultural issues and historical antecedents between different groups of people.

Racism Prejudice or discrimination against other racial groups. The term is extended by some to include the production of disadvantage, whether or not prejudice or discrimination occur. ➔ institutional racism.

Radical social work A neo-Marxist critique of the role of social workers in society, coupled with a set of arguments about alternative patterns of practice.

Rationing Allocating resources; balancing supply and demand outside the mechanism of the market.

Reaction In politics, extreme conservative or right-wing views opposed to reform and in favour of 'turning the clock back'.

Redistribution Transferring resources from some people to others.

Redress The ability of the recipient of a service to have bad practice corrected.

Regressive redistribution Transferring resources vertically from poorer to richer people. ➔ progressive redistribution.

Regulation The process by which the state establishes the rules and settings under which welfare services operate.

Relative Socially determined, as in a 'relative' view' or poverty or morality; based in examination of differences, as in 'relative deprivation'.

Reliability In social research, the likelihood that results can be reproduced or at least that they show the same thing in the same circumstances.

Residential care Care in which help and support is provided in a residential setting, for example an old people's home.

Residual welfare Model of welfare in which people receive welfare only when they are unable to cope otherwise.

Right to welfare Marshall's argument that the welfare state represented an extension of the rights of citizens gained in the 18th and 19th centuries into the social field.

Right wing Political beliefs identified with conservatism, liberalism and fascism, which are broadly against collective public provision for all.

Rights Rules, based sometimes on legal and sometimes on moral norms, which justify the provision of welfare in terms of the position of the recipient.

Risk Exposure to hazard; cumulative incidence; insecurity; unpredictable contingencies; or → vulnerability.

Sampling Selection of subjects for research.

Secondary analysis Research done on material recorded and processed by other people. →primary analysis.

Selectivity Policy which focuses resources on people in need.

Semi-professionals Workers who have to perform their activities in a hierarchical organisation but who are nevertheless permitted some of the independent judgement allowed to professionals in the conduct of their work.

Service rationing → Rationing which takes place at the point where services are delivered, as opposed to → financial rationing.

Single parents The heads of families in which there is only one parent, through divorce, death of a partner or birth outside marriage.

Social administration The study of the development, structure and practices of the social services.

Social capital The value derived from collaborative and solidaristic social action, as distinct from the actions of individuals within social structures.

Social construction The development of a pattern of relationships in society which shapes social circumstances, common understandings and the perception of issues.

Social control The process through which some people are limited by others, whether for the benefit of society or for the benefit of specific groups in society. People are controlled by social services when they are being made to act in ways which they would not otherwise choose, or when their options have been restricted.

Social definition The process through which some issues are constructed in such a way as to define the terms in which those issues are subsequently understood and discussed.

Social democracy A set of political beliefs based on the acceptance of the necessity for collective social action and social protection in a mixed economy.

Social division A social structure in which people are distinguished sharply from others in terms of certain characteristics or circumstances which then become the basis for advantage or disadvantage.

Social division of welfare Titmuss's term for the range of processes through which redistribution took place.

Social group People who share some common social contact or network; people who have common characteristics or circumstances which lead to them being treated as a group for social purposes.

Social inclusion The process of bringing people who are ➔ excluded into networks of social relationships.

Social justice A distributive principle related sometimes to desirable outcomes, or more usually to outcomes that are proportion to normative criteria, like rights, desert or needs.

Social policy The study of the social services and the welfare state; ➔ policy relating to those areas, or to society ➔ structural policy.

Social problems Issues defined in social terms as for which some kind of response is called.

Social protection Systems providing support for contingencies, like ill health, old age or unemployment, which might imply vulnerability.

Social security The system of benefits for income maintenance; in some countries the term is understood more widely to include health care, while in others it is taken more narrowly to mean social insurance.

Social services Mainly understood to include social security, housing, health, social work and education – the 'big five' – along with others which are like social services.

Social welfare The welfare of society, or the social services provided. ➔welfare.

Social work Work done by social workers, including a range of techniques to maintain or change people's circumstances or patterns of behaviour.

Socialisation The process through which people become a part of society, learning social norms, values and rules.

Socialism A set of political beliefs based in the values of collective action (or solidarity), freedom and equality.

Societal policy ➔ structural policy.

Society A network of solidaristic networks.

Soft law In the European Union, recommendations and generalised statements designed to encourage a response rather than to require action.

Solidarity Mutual responsibility; responsibilities to others in society, which are the basis for collective social action; policy built on a complex range of overlapping networks.

Spillover An aspect of inefficiency in targeting which means that more than necessary is given to some people with problems.

State The formal political institutions of a society; the means through which government power is exercised.

States of dependency Titmuss's term for conditions in which people are likely to become dependent.

Statistics The popular name for ➜ indicators; quantitative data; the mathematical analysis of quantitative data.

Status A form of social identity, identifying the way that people see themselves and how others see them.

Stigma A sense of shame, which makes people reluctant to claim benefits or services; a loss of status; an attribute or characteristic which is discrediting; a pattern of social rejection.

Strategy A group of interrelated policies, with a common approach or purpose.

Stratification Splitting something into a range of levels.

Street-level bureaucracy Lipsky's term for decisions made at the lowest administrative level, which effectively become policy because no other rules apply.

Structural dependency Dependency conditioned by economic position and relationship to society, rather than by people's intrinsic capacities.

Structural policy Policy which is intended to maintain or change the pattern of social relationships. This is sometimes referred to as 'social policy'.

Substantive fairness A fair result, judged by whatever criteria are thought applicable.

Substantive rights Rights to particular outcomes.

Targeting Focusing, directing or aiming policies at a particular category or group of people.

Technological determinism The argument that the structure of society is shaped by available technology.

Tenure In housing policy, the right by which people occupy their housing, for example owning or renting.

Triangulation In social research, the process of looking at an issue several ways at once.

Underclass A term used variously to signify the lowest social class; people who are economically non-productive and in receipt of benefits; people who are marginal to the labour market; or people who are socially undesirable.

Under-socialisation ➜ socialisation.

Unemployment Worklessness in a situation where the workless person is nevertheless considered to be part of the labour market.

Unemployment trap The situation in which people may be better off on benefits than working. ➜ less eligibility.

Universality A method of distributing welfare based on given benefits or services to everyone, or at least everyone in a broad category (such as 'children').

Utility Perceived value to people making a choice.

Validity In social research, the question of whether the results reflect what they are supposed to reflect.

Vertical redistribution Redistribution between people on different levels of income or wealth.

Voice Having some say in a service.

Voluntary sector Independent provision which is not for profit, usually on the basis of charity or mutual aid. Some commentators include private provision as 'voluntary'.

Vulnerability. The possibility that when adverse events happen, the vulnerable person might suffer harm.

Welfare Well-being; certain categories of collective provision which attempt to protect people's well-being; in the US, social security payments to the poor.

Welfare economics A branch of economics concerned with the analysis of ➜ utility; it is not closely connected with social policy.

Welfare pluralism Like ➜ pluralism, this can be taken to indicate both the situation in which services are provided from many different sources and the argument that they should be.

Welfare rights In some literature, ➜ rights to welfare; a range of activities involving advice and support in claims for social welfare services.

Welfare society A society in which people support each other through a range of solidaristic networks.

Welfare state The delivery of social services by the state; the strategy of developing interrelated services to deal with a wide range of social problems; an ideal in which services are provided comprehensively and at the best level possible.

Index

A

access to welfare 2, 48, 60, 109, 170-2, 177-8, 186-9, 199, 214, 287; *see* rationing
accountability 88, 126, 150, 151-2, 153, 154, 161, 162, 198, 199, 287
administration of services:
  role of personnel 159-64
  service delivery 165-81
  structures 147-64
adverse selection 29, 139, 287
affirmative action 31, 49, 287
aims of policy 208, 235-6, 238-9; *see* effectiveness
aims of welfare provision 89-90, 94
audit 243, 287

B

basic security 59, 87-8, 118, 132
Beveridge report 25, 64, 96, 115-16, 124, 126
biological factors 18-19, 40-1, 56
Bismarckian welfare 79, 108, 117, 121, 124
blocs 47-9, 287
the body 18-19
budgeting 151, 155, 156, 157, 167-9, 287
bureaucracy 152-4, 159-60, 164, 180

C

capitalism 30, 93-4, 100, 118, 126, 129, 287
care management and planning 9, 105, 144-6, 287
casework 104-5
causal explanations 11-12, 40-1, 42, 209, 291
child abuse and protection 27, 37, 38, 55, 81, 154, 156, 172, 191, 208, 232
children and social policy 53, 55, 196, 243; *see* child abuse; education; family policy
choice 51-2, 86, 137, 138-9, 186, 189-90, 199
citizenship 3, 23, 24, 28, 32, 84, 87, 92, 109, 118, 122, 195-6, 199, 288
claims 66, 87, 117, 165-6, 184-9, 288; *see* demand; need
class 28, 30-1, 34, 48, 50, 93-4, 129, 178, 205, 288; *see* underclass
client groups 63, 146, 148-9; *see* need groups
collectivism 19-20, 23, 43, 91-2, 93, 94-5, 96, 97, 98, 99, 102-3, 108, 112, 118, 122, 137, 163, 193-4, 197
community 17, 18, 21-2, 23, 25, 26, 42, 46

community care 10, 58, 115, 142, 144-6, 154, 245, 288; *see* care management
  as discharge from hospital 63, 141, 145, 155, 158, 179-80, 189, 232
community work 104, 193-4, 288
comparative social policy 79-81, 122-31, 288
conservativism 19, 28, 93, 95-6, 97, 99, 129, 143, 288
consumers *see* users
control trials 209-10, 288
convergence 125-6, 128, 129, 288
coordination 145-6, 154-6, 157-8
corporatism 74, 79, 80, 118, 125, 289
cost centres 157-8
cost-effectiveness 143, 144-5, 176, 212-14, 289
crime 4, 33, 38, 41, 208, 209, 240, 241, 242
crisis of welfare 94, 126-7, 289
critical realism 208; *see* causal explanations
critical social policy 28, 289
culture 22, 23, 122-3, 125, 188, 220, 289
  cultural services 50, 115

D

decentralisation 23, 84, 117, 149-51, 242, 289
degeneracy 26, 40-1, 289
demand 19, 20, 77, 139, 145-6, 166, 167, 170, 177-8, 184-5, 186-9, 198, 289; *see* rationing
dementia 20, 56-7, 179, 194-5
democracy 42, 73, 88-9, 151, 193, 198, 231, 288
dependency 27, 53, 55-7, 60, 75-7, 83, 183, 289
developing countries 18, 48, 55, 58, 60, 61, 74, 102, 108, 109-10, 128, 132, 141-2, 156, 237-8
disability 19, 26-7, 31, 53-4, 57, 62, 65, 66, 171, 187, 221-4, 240, 289
disadvantage *see* inequality
discretion 69, 71, 79, 113, 153, 154, 159-60, 180, 185, 192, 197, 289
discrimination, 23, 29, 48, 171, 192, 209, 299; *see* gender, race
distribution of income and wealth 2-3, 8, 29, 111-12; *see* poverty; redistribution
distribution of problems 39-40
distributive impact of policy 2, 50, 80, 108, 110-12, 175, 214-15
diswelfare 2-3

E

economic perspectives, 9-10, 13, 17, 19-20, 49, 51-2, 73, 91, 121
  welfare economics 52, 189, 238, 301
  see industrial achievement/performance; markets; rationing
education 26, 31, 38, 42, 55, 89, 114, 117, 126, 137, 138, 151-2, 191, 211, 243
effectiveness 44, 208-14, 216, 290
efficiency 106, 107, 137-8, 157-9, 212-14, 216, 290
elite theory 33
employment and unemployment 4, 22-3, 59, 61-3, 64, 91, 300; *see* labour markets
  employment and the economy 11, 43, 44, 103, 124, 130-1
  employment programmes 4, 42, 43
  provision for unemployment 25-6, 27, 188
empowerment 32-3, 57, 77, 94, 96, 150, 192-5, 199, 290
equality, policies for 31, 32, 42, 44, 47, 84, 87-8, 94-5, 96, 97, 109, 117, 118, 124, 126, 144, 150, 174, 196, 211, 215-16, 238, 256, 290; *see* inequality
equity 48, 106-7, 144, 174-5, 178, 290
ethnicity *see* race
eugenics 41, 90, 96, 290
European Union 25, 26, 61, 72, 113, 125, 131-2, 171, 218-19
evaluation 208-10, 236, 243-5
exclusion 23, 24, 25-8, 56, 57, 58, 105-6, 108, 112, 140, 200
exit 159, 188-9, 198, 290
externalities 137, 141, 290

F

fairness 174-5, 290; *see* equity
  procedural fairness 174, 200
family 20-1, 26, 45-6, 55-6, 116, 291
  childbirth and maternity provision 21, 56, 81, 116
  family policy 21, 45, 69, 103
  see child abuse; children; households; single parents
family resemblance 205-6, 291
fascism 96, 97
feminism 19, 28, 32-3, 46, 56, 96-7, 141; *see* gender
financial management 167-8
  cost centred budgeting 157-8;
the 'focus' of policy 42, 43-50, 63-4, 89
freedom 86-7, 94, 95, 193, 239, 290
functions of welfare 89-90, 94
functionalism 129, 130, 291

G

gender 24, 29-30, 32-3, 34-5, 84, 205, 291; *see* women
geographical distribution of services 102, 138, 149-51, 155
globalisation 110, 131-2, 291
governance 21, 72-6, 156, 237-8
green issues 97-8, 100, 109-10, 292, 130-1
growth 11, 109-10, 121, 128, 130-1

H

health care 77, 78, 107, 113, 116-17, 148, 153, 160, 172, 179-80, 185, 187-8
  demand and rationing 175-6
  inequalities in 188, 214-15
  see community care; mental illness; public health
historical perspectives 114, 122-4, 125-30, 223
  periodisation 127
  historical institutionalism 128-9, 152
homelessness 60-1, 62, 114, 141-2, 173, 178, 194, 207, 226, 233, 292
households 45-6, 292
housing 42, 47, 57, 64, 77, 106, 114, 116, 141-2, 166, 167, 171-3, 190, 300
  classes 30-1
human beings 18-20, 26, 54

I

ideal types vi, 83-4, 117-18, 124, 152-3, 162, 205, 220
ideology vi, 77, 91-100, 118, 122-3, 126, 167, 242, 292
  service ideology 166, 180-1, 243,
incapacity 62, 292
incentives 20, 46, 51, 73, 74, 75-6, 78, 90, 91, 111, 130, 155, 161, 169, 173, 178, 189, 210, 211, 292
incidence 39-40, 59, 292
indicator targeting 43, 45, 48, 109, 292
indicators 39-40, 80, 204, 215, 240-1, 292, 300
individualised responses 9, 43, 44, 103, 104, 205
individualism 17, 19-20, 25, 26, 28, 35, 43, 44, 87, 92, 95, 96-7, 98, 102-3, 292-3
industrial achievement/performance model of welfare 109, 117, 130-1, 293
inequality and disadvantage 3-4, 10, 28, 29-36, 40, 46, 48, 57, 60, 63, 102, 106, 110, 111, 132, 178, 190, 194, 198, 200, 209, 211, 243, 293; *see* equality
informal sector 47, 81, 136, 141, 143, 293
insertion 26, 105-6, 108, 293; *see* active labour market policy; social inclusion